Transliteration 1

א	Aleph	A, or any Upper CASE VOWEL
ב	Bet/ Bhet	B or BH or [V]
ג	Gimel	G or J
ד	Dalet	D
ה	Hey	H
ו	Vav	V,W,OO or OA
ז	Zayin	Z
ח	Het	[K]H or K[H]
ט	Tet	DT
י	Yod	Y
כ, ך	Kahf/Khaf	K or KH

ל		L
מ, ם	Mem	M
נ, ן	Noon	N
ס	Samekh	$ (like "S")
ע	Ayin	Bracketed UPPER CASE [VOWEL] or GH
פ, ף	Pey, Phey	P, PH or F
צ, ץ	Tsadi	TS (always read "ST" in European)
ק	Koof	Q
ר	Resh	R or WR
ש	Shin or Sin	SH or S
ת	Tahf, Thaf or Sahf	T,TH or (S)

Bet/Bhet, Kahf/Khaf, Pey/Phey, Shin/Sin, and Tahf/Thaf/Sahf are variants. Hebrew script uses diacritical marks, or "dots," to indicate whether, for example, the letter sounds like an aspirated B or a passive BH/V.

Five letters have **end forms**: ך-כ ם-מ ן-נ ף-פ ץ-צ

UPPER or lower Case:

1) Anything in lower case is not a ROOT LETTER but added to replace vowels and aid pronunciation.

2) CONSONANTS are capitalized, and are the integral part of Edenic roots.

3) VOWELS are in lower case, indicating they are merely added to help one pronounce the word.

EXCEPTIONS

1) Vav is a V or W as a consonant, but can serve as the OO or OA vowel sounds as in ROOT and BOAT. Such vowels from a Vav in Edenic word are in upper case.

2) A Yod will often render an "eeY" sound. If in the Hebrew, the "Y" is in upper case.

The Origin of Speeches

Intelligent Design in Language

The Origin of Speeches

Intelligent Design in Language
From the Language of Eden To Our Babble After Babel

ISAAC E. MOZESON

2ND EDITION, 2011

LIGHTCATCHER BOOKS

SPRINGDALE, AR

Design and electronic layout by Carol Long
Cover picture by Abel Grimmer (1570-1619)
Transliteration Key design by Mark Whitbeck and Josh Ben
Proofreading by Phil Van Riper

The Origin of Speeches

ISBN 10: 0-9792618-0-5
ISBN 13: 978-0-9792618-0-0

10 9 8 7 6 5 4 3 2 1

Printed in the United States of America

For CD's, videos, disks, foreign language lists with new discoveries contact the author at edenics.org or the publisher at *lightcatcherbooks.com*.

For information write to:
Lightcatcher Books
1204 Kissinger Ave.
Springdale, AR 72762
479-306-4459

or visit our website: lightcatcherbooks.com

I will restore to the peoples a pure language,
that they may all call upon the name of the Lord,
to serve him with one consent.

– Z E P H A N I A H   3 : 9

The stone rejected by the builders
shall become the keystone. *

– P S A L M S   1 1 8 : 2 2

* One of the possible renditions of this verse is that Biblical Hebrew, the intelligently designed foundation stone of language, and thus of thought and humanity itself, had been spurned by the builders of a flawed science known as historical linguistics – but the language of Eden shall ultimately resume its primary position.

Dedication

This book's Dedication is to my mother, Bernice Tunis who passed away 11/11/05, and to the Mother Tongue project. In my generation there have been several diligent and talented researchers, both secular scientists working on the newly viable premise of the monogenesis of language, and Edenicists whose motivation is religious. It is hoped that this book includes enough inspiring science to be of interest to both camps.

This Dedication serves as an Acknowledgement to the selfless volunteers who have helped with the immense work that made this book possible. The principals of the project's second decade are named below. The project will require further decades, and these words go out to those future people who shall keep up the enormous Edenics task of ingathering the exiled words of the world.

Our common ancestors were exiled at Eden, but mankind's Diaspora began at the Tower of Babel. Books like this can begin the process of getting us all on the same page.

Acknowledgments

Aedo, Fernando (Peru/Switzerland) – book and DVD translations into Spanish and French. Research: Amerindian, Dravidian Education, Webmaster, blogosphere, etc.

Ansley, Al L. (Lansing, MI) – audio CD narration research: sub-roots

Backon, Dr. Joshua (Jerusalem, Israel) – Hebrew, Bible media

Banai, Ehud (Israel) – singer composer of the English and Hebrew reggae song "Hebrewman," the anthem of Edenics

Beckman, Brian (Newcastle, WA) – Arabic letter variants and more

Benner, Jeff A. (Paso Robles, CA) – set up a previous website

Beeman, Dr. William (Brown University, RI) – animal names

Ben, Joshua (Birmingham, UK) – research media

Ben-Gigi, Dr. Daniel (Scottsdale, AR) – media, education, distribution

Bergman, Mats (Malmo, Sweden) – research: Swedish, Saami (Lapp)

Berkowitz, Dr. Steven (Bremerton, WA) – education (OOS began as a curriculum in his college)

Bertin, Claude (Mexico City, MX) – French Edenics slideshow, etc.

Bermeister, Kevin (Sydney, Australia) – behind the wcb games, word search and archives of *edenics.net*

Brodbeck, Anne (Pensacola, FL) – publishing, education

Bruce, Wesley (O'Connor, Australia) – Creationist science, editing

Calhoun, Cary (Suwanee, GA) – high tech expertise for Edenics resources

David, Daniel (Ra'anana, Israel) – the tech wizard of *edenics.net*

Eliassi, Kamy (Los Angeles, California) education research, Persian

Esplana, Periander (Philippines) – media, education

Feffer, Mark (Jerusalem, Israel) – promotion, education

Haggedon, Georg (Dusseldorf, Germany) – research, German

Gallin, Aryeh (Jerusalem, Israel) – media, Root & Branch Association

Garza, Adrian (Mexico/Texas) – research, Spanish audio CD education

Goldfarb, Reuven (Sefat, Israel) – audio CD narration

Ilona, Remy (Nigeria) – Igbo research

Isaacson, Leon (Jerusalem, Israel) – Spanish audio CD narration

Jackson, Rhett (Ketchikan, Alaska) – research, Inuit (Eskimo)

Kubo, Arimasa (Japan) – research, Japanese publishing

Long, James and Carol (Springdale, AR) – creation and distribution of Edenics resources, *lightcatcherbooks.com*, research, Ancient Egyptian

MacFhionnlaigh, Fearhas (Invernes, Scotland) – research, Celtic

Martin, Robert (Sderot, Israel) – education, IT. Edenics posting

Mills, Telma (Sydney, Australia) – editing, education, Edenic resource production and distribution; research, Hebrew, Hindi

Mohler, Rev. Jonathan (Keeler, TX) – research, Bantu languages

Montegu, Judy (Jerusalem, Israel) – media

Moscowitz, Lenny (Teaneck, NJ) – recording audio CDs at Core-Sound

Moguilevsky, Rabbi Simon (Buenos Aries, Argentina) – Spanish education

Nagurka, Dr. Mark (Marquette Univ.) – education, research, scientific terms

O'Donnell, Joseph A. (Allen Park, MI) – major funding, promotion, proofreading

Olk, Linda (Winston-Salem, NC) – education, media

Pau, Melody Kinneret (Toronto, Canada) – proofing, online reference. She did most of the adding of Hebrew font for the 2nd edition.

Payawal, John G. (Quezon City, the Phillipines) – technical help

Pomata, Helen (Melbourn, FL) – research, Italian

Rowe, Norman (Gold Beach, OR) – editing, education, media

Schiff, Dr. Alvin I. (Hebrew Univ./Harvard Univ.) – academic support

Shen, George (San Francisco, CA) – research, Chinese

Silverman, Philip (Atlanta, GA) – editing

Spargamino, Pastor Larry (Bethany, OK) – media, Southwest Radio Church

Strouse, Dean T. M. (Emmanuel Baptist Theological Seminary, CT) – articles, Biblical translation, academic support

Svennson, Orjan (Malmo, Sweden) – research Scandinavian and runic writings

Van den Bos, Geert (Netherlandls) – research, Dutch and sub-roots

Van Riper, Philip (Albuqurque, NM) – research, tech production, proofreading

Van Rooyen, Johann – Afrikaans research, education in S. Africa

Werling, Regina, Lioba (Germany) – vast and varied research

Whitbeck, Mark (Belleville, MI) – resource production, media

White, Craig (Australia) – education

Wright, Ann (Australia) – enabled *e-word CD Dictionary* Old Arabic

(less recent contributors of research are listed in the "*e-word CD Dictionary*")

From the Author

It was initially intended that the *E-Word CD Dictionary* be attached to this book, since the Origin of Species often refers to entries in the E-Word. The CD is available both at lightcatcherbooks.com and edenics.org with a discount for those ordering the two Edenics resources together.

Most words in our text base can be searched at edenics.net, another resource for searching words and playing the Ednics game.

Put your ear up to the shell of words. You can hear the hushed, ancient roar of our primeval past.

Conventional wisdom says that humans evolved speech over a gazillion years of grunts and gestures. By sheer luck, humans mutated a floating hyoid bone in the throat, and delicate lips, tongue etc., a miraculous hardware perfectly fitting the miraculous speech software between our ears.

If you cannot give the new evidence of our global team of Edenics researchers a fair hearing, then you risk being dismissed as an (anti-) religious fundamentalist.

It is disturbing to consider that you and your esteemed language professors and reference books are riddled with half-truths and poor guesses. Be assured that they did the best they could with what they knew at the time.

But it is a new time, and we know important new things about what appeared to be a hopeless mess of unrelated world vocabularies.

Linguists merely prove that, say, various Indian tribes were Indians. We Edenicists prove that they were human, and created, and given speech by a Creator.

Isaac Mozeson,

Sefad, Galilee January 1, 2011

Preface

Before introducing the text of *The Origin of Speeches*, here is an Op Ed piece solicited by *The Jerusalem Post*, January 2005: It presents an overview and some background information behind the Edenics thesis.

LANGUAGE: THE CHATTERING OF CHIMPS OR BABBLE FROM BABEL?

Both options seem strange. Since Darwin's *The Origin of Species* (1859) science assumes that, after millions of years of evolving mutations, some grunting apes became the gesturing Neanderthals, which led to Shakespearean sonnets. Happily, the floating, uniquely human hyoid throat bone also appeared, helping this species survive by lying, crooning, yodeling and rapping. (The world's oldest hyoid bone was unearthed near Haifa, Israel).

Secularists have always considered it mythic that some divine engineer would factory-install a language program at Eden, creating the first modern humans. And that multi-national history was then to have been neurolinguistically kick-started at the Tower of Babel, with 70 spin-offs which have since de-evolved into our 6,000 tongues.

Linguist Noam Chomsky proved that the human brain is hard-wired for language. He recently suggested that some super-intelligent alien engineered language. And recent linguists DO conclude that all Earth languages came from one universal language. But NOT that "recent West-Semitic language" called Hebrew.

The establishment Eurocentrists still support "origin unknown" for LAD (boy), even though Hebrew *yeled* and Arabic *walid* mean "boy," and the root of birthing is ל-ד *Lamed-Dalet*/L-D. The Genesis 11:1 statement on language history claims that:

kol כל

aretz ארץ

saphah שפה

echat אחת

The whole earth was of one speech.

Coincidentally, these words sound much like 1) WHOLE 2) EARTH, 3) SPEECH and 4) EACH (like "one"). The new science of Edenics now has over 23,000 such "coincidences."

Are the findings here mere chance? Wikipedia states; "The likelihood of finding a resemblance in sound and meaning in three languages is the square of its probability in two languages. In general, the probability for a single language must be raised to the (nth) power for n languages. Thus if five languages each showed a total of 8 percent sound-meaning resemblance to one another, on a chance basis one would expect (0.08) or 0.00004096 resemblances in all five languages. This is approximately 1/25,000.

Edenics works with a Proto-Semitic, "Edenic" vocabulary where each root letter has the "genes" for the wide diversity of the world's words.

Edenics doesn't use kabbalistic formulae, only bread-and-butter stuff already used to link, say, French with Italian. So, דרך *Dalet-Resh-Kahf, derekh* (way, road) is echoed in like words in over 50 other languages in the DIRECTION entry of our *E-Word CD Dictionary* and on the chart on page 14. Moreover, the ג *Gimel* of גרון *garon* (throat) can shift harder to a hard C or softer to an H. This is why EGRETS, CRANES and HERONS are all long-throated birds.

There are only a few hundred English-Edenic links as easy as רגיל *rageel* (usual) and ReGuLar. If one shifts the position of a letter instead of its sound, one knows why ReLiGion is about a spiritual path becoming a ReGuLar routine.

Instead of the divine dance of sense among sound, scholars assume that words are merely chaotic noises that we assign meaning to. But words traced back to Eden **aren't** meaningless sounds. Take mysterious animal names. In English, names like 1) GIRAFFE, 2) SKUNK, 3) GOPHER, and 4) HORSE are mere sounds. But in Biblical Hebrew, (Sephardic) 1) *Ayin-Resh*-Phey ערף *ghoref*, means neck; 2) צחן *tsokhen*, stinker, gave the Indians that delightful creature's name; 3) חפר *khopher* means digger, and 4) חרש *hoResh* is plower.

Modern Hebrew has some bone-headed new animal names. When the guardians of Modern Hebrew had to coin a word for that crustacean, the CRAB, they went to the Old High German *krebitz*. This word is thought to mean "scratching," even though crabs don't scratch. The Academy of the Hebrew Language then named the crab סרטן *sartan*, for scratching. (*Samekh-Resh-Tet* סרט is the source of SERRATED). The scholars should have noted other creatures with exoskeletons, like the *aqrab* (scorpion). From קרן *qeren* (horn) and Aramaic קרקפת *karpafta* (skull) they should have seen a KR subroot of hardness. קרן *Koof-Resh-Bhet* means battle and encroachment. So, nature's lumbering, armored tank, the CRAB, should have been called a קרבת *qarebet*.

It was an animal, a little birdie, that whispered the whole Edenic concept into my ear back in 1978. I was a doctoral literature student, a published poet, stuck with a boring linguistics requirement at New York University. The professor demonstrated the genius behind reconstructing the so-called "Indo-European root" for the generic bird word. This never-spoken laboratory reconstruction was to show how Aryans emerged from a separate troop of well-groomed apes, without any (shudder) relationship to the "inferior" races, peoples and languages.

That theoretical, generic bird word was SPER. In second grade I knew a similar generic word for bird: צפור *tsipor*. At the SPARROW entry one sees the צ-פ *Tsadi-Pey* behind bird-related words for floating, spying, being covered (as in feathers), a talon, and chirping.

In Edenics every two consonants make a sound. Sound is energy. This is a science now, no more Humanities myths. Every sound carries sense. Therefore, if we examine the simple three-letter word for flower, *Pey-Resh-Het* or פרח *perakh*, we can see that it is a combination of 1) פ-ר P-R (botanical things, as in *perot*/FRUIT) and 2) the ר ח R-K element of fragrance, seen in ריח *reyakh* (smell) or English REEK. (More of these double-roots or combined 2-letter sub-roots later.)

Here are two examples from the upcoming Japanese book. The SAMURAI, a storied warrior, was a royal guardsman. A guardian in Hebrew is a שומר *shomer*. More often, the Japanese reverses the Hebrew. KARATE is an unarmed martial art. Therefore *kara* means empty and *te* (pronounced tay) means hand. Reverse Hebrew ריק *raik* (empty) and יד *yad* (hand) to get *kara-te*.

Are we naked but gabby gibbons, or have we divinely enhanced brains (Genesis 2:7) above an ape's body? Were we engineered for speech, for literacy, perhaps even for Revealed moral instruction (G-d forbid)? Stay tuned. In our 21st Century culture wars, we will weigh in with the new science of Edenics.

Isaac Mozeson, *edenics.net* or *edenics.org*

Table of Contents

Introduction

Back in Cold War days there was a spy-comedy TV show called "Get Smart." The good agents worked for Control, the bad guys for Chaos.

A decade later in college, I realized that much of human thinking can still be divided into Control vs. Chaos.

In doctoral studies at New York University in the Seventies, I began to perceive that historical linguists were agents of Chaos. There was an impressive amount of study in the field, but the accepted theory was that words evolved by the caprice of human usage. Words were considered the meaningless sounds that we use to signify things. **Any patterns, especially between "unrelated" language groups, were mere coincidence**.

Even back then there was a minority of rebels (taken up in Chapter One) who dared to suggest that there was "monogenesis of language," that much of, perhaps all of, the planet's humans once spoke a common language. Such thinking was attacked vehemently. Sixties ideas of universal brotherhood did not jive well with the tenets of linguistics that first emerged in the heyday of German nationalism.

Someone wishing to read up on the media coverage of the monogenesis of language could look up the following:

Atlantic Monthly, "Quest for the Mother Tongue" – Robert Wright, April, 1991 p. 39
Discovery, Aug., 1990
Insight, Feb. 5, 1990
Natural History, Feb. 1989
Nature, Vol. 366, Nov. 1993
New Scientist, 16 June 1990
Newsweek, Jan 11, 1988
N.Y. Times, Nov 24, 1987. search Wilford or Shevoroshkin
Science Times/*N.Y. Times,* Mar 16, 2004 page 1, 4
The Science,s May/June 1990
Scientific American, Oct 1989 and April 1991
US News & World Report, Nov. 5, 1990 (cover story)

In the decades that followed, my independent studies of language pointed to the thesis that language is all about patterns – that sound is sense, and that **there are no coincidences.** With the internet came a small community of global researchers who would demonstrate that the entire planet learned to speak in Eden. After my teaching career was ended by a terrorism-related disability in 1997, I had the time to captain the Edenics team, and to be keeper of our growing data base.

This book will introduce much of this patterning that we uncovered, both between "unrelated" languages and within the meaningful music of vocabulary. Perhaps "recovery" is more appropriate than "discovery." The Sanhedrin allegedly required members to know something of the world's 70 original post-Babel languages (see Genesis 10 and Deuteronomy 3:8 with Genesis 46:27), so much ancient historical linguistics may have been apparently lost. Medieval grammarians probably charted all of the Semitic word-science that is touched on here. But much of this is lost or inaccessible. Until modern Indo-Aryans created modern linguistics, the world's educated people knew from Genesis 10-12 that West European languages were related to those in the Near East. And that the homeland for this language superfamily called Yaphet was in Turkey. But all this was lost, and had to be rediscovered by Sir William Jones, and those who "discovered" Indo-European. (See Prof N. Aviezer's *Fossils and Faith*.)

Perhaps by next century, the **radica**l (pun on **roots** intended) thesis of this book will be taken for granted, and this book's crude innovation will only be of historical value. Perhaps people will marvel how, back in the Early Communication Age, no one on Earth even knew why EARTH was the reverse of *terra* (Latin earth). And they'll wonder how dictionaries in the early 21st Century did not record that EARTH was ultimately from ארץ AReTZ (earth) in the language of Eden, "Edenic" (Proto-Semitic as best documented in Biblical Hebrew).

———————————————

Ah, the "B" word! So this is a fundamentalist treatise for bible believers? Not so fast. Some secular geneticists have recently concluded that the wide variety of modern humankind emerged from the gene pool of a single woman. These scientists were not afraid to refer to this hypothetical first modern woman as "Eve."

Introduction

The evidence in this study called "Edenics" similarly points towards the wide variety of human vocabulary deriving from a neurolinguistic mix-up of an original language – to be called "Edenic." The letters of Edenic words are like the genes of one proto-canine that was to diversify into a proto-wolf, proto-fox, proto-hound, etc. which were to further diversify and become our present-day menagerie of hundreds of dog breeds.

Did one antediluvian canine diversify due to Darwinian random mutation and survival of the fittest? It may not necessarily be so. The title of this book suggests an alternative to Darwin's *The Origin of Species*. Nature, or the force behind nature, is pro-diversity. Adaptation, or mutation can be pre-programmed by an intelligent designer who wanted migrating canines to survive in various environments. A better parallel to the Tower of Babel's language diversity would have some intelligent designer, after the Deluge, diversifying the ur-canine into a wolf, fox and hound, which would then go on to develop into sub-species suited to survival in new habitats. Interestingly, world words for wild dogs are from the generic Edenic כלב KeLeBH, dog – see Chapter Ten.

This thesis of planned diversity clearly recalls the scenario of Genesis 11 where the one Earth language of Eden was diversified at the Tower of Babel (in one Big Bang whose aftershocks still reverberate). The geneticists who demonstrated that we all come from one woman's gene pool ("Eve"), makes it unnecessary, and perhaps absurd or racist, to believe that any human stock accidentally mutated an advantageous skin color or shape of nose. When we take up the versatility of Edenic letters, we will se that the צ *Tsadi*'s (TS) ability to morph into an S or T, and any letter like them, is like having an Eve or an ur-canine with all the genes for future diversity.

It is suggested that The Tower of Babel story is a myth invented to explain why there are so many foreign languages. Even before you read this book there are reasons to question this easy dismissal as "myth."

Parallel legends in Chinese, Mayan and other remote and ancient lore suggest that there was some similar primeval linguistic trauma experienced by these isolated peoples. An original, universal language is widely reported as having been broken up. How did such a neuro-linguistics disturbance work to diversify language? This book begins to confront the question, but neurology may provide more answers than linguistics.

3

An abnormal aspect of this marvelous language program that we seem to have had factory-installed involves *glossolalia*, the rare but documented ability of people in altered states of consciousness to speak in languages that they have never learned.

From a *Telegraph* (UK) article of April 15, 2010 seen by Fernando Aedo:

> "The [Croatian] girl, from the southern town of Knin, had only just started studying German at school and had been reading German books and watching German TV to become better, but was by no means fluent, according to her parents.
>
> Since waking up from her 24-hour coma however, she has been unable to speak Croatian, but is able to communicate perfectly in German.
>
> Doctors at Split's KB Hospital claim that the case is so unusual, various experts have examined the girl as they try to find out what triggered the change.
>
> Hospital director Dujomir Marasovic said: 'You never know when recovering from such a trauma how the brain will react. Obviously we have some theories although at the moment we are limited in what we can say because we have to respect the privacy of the patient.'
>
> Psychiatric expert Dr. Mijo Milas added: 'In earlier times this would have been referred to as a miracle, we prefer to think that there must be a logical explanation – it's just that we haven't found it yet.'
>
> There are references to cases where people who have been seriously ill and perhaps in a coma have woken up being able to speak other languages – sometimes even the Biblical languages such as that spoken in old Babylon or Egypt."

[Upshot: the brain's ability to switch languages is far beyond current medical knowledge. The dismissal of the Tower of Babel scenario as myth reflects an incomplete awareness of neuro-linguistics.]

Another neuro-linguistic phenomenon might be behind the uniformly Edenic-speaking community suddenly speaking incomprehensible babble. A rare but officially-diagnosed disorder is called the Foreign Accent Syndrome. Victims speak with the strong accent of people in a country that they have never been to. Perhaps some form of this touched off letter-shifts, while a form of dyslexia could be behind metathesis. (More on these later.)

There is no need to consider anything recorded in the Hebrew Bible as a supernatural or miraculous event. All is natural, but the timing and placement of such events should set a logical mind to wonder.

Did some electromagnetic or other disturbance cause a unified community of humans in prehistoric Shinar (later Babel) to suddenly speak in different languages? Did the proto-Indo-European speakers, for example, then migrate north and east, with clans forming according to who spoke a similar proto-version of Sanskrit, Hellenic, Germanic or Slavonic? We may never know.

But this book outlines how that diversification appears to have happened. A study of comparative grammars is not our focus. We will deal here only with vocabulary, with words. This is about the poetic and musical sides of linguistics, the sound of sense. I stumbled upon the science of linguistics only because it was a requirement in a doctoral literature curriculum. Some of the science of linguistics, like all science, was artistic. This book, then, involves both the arts and sciences. It is about the dance of the music of meaning among the tonalities that we call letters. And that music of sound and sense begins with the earliest language… which we shall call "Edenic."

Could there have actually been a first modern human, a homo sapiens named Adam with a blown-out cranial cavity (Genesis 2:7) whose larger brain enabled him to name some animals (Genesis 2:19-20)? Let us investigate the possibility without pre-judgment. After reading the chapter on animal names, and the rest of the book, some readers may want to speculate on the wider Genesis scenario and its implications. But an agnostic should be able to read this book without pain.

The heart of the book's thesis is that all humans are in one choir, and that language is the music of meaning. It took several millennia, but now this book comes along to try and breathe life into this ancient thesis.

Prominent contemporary linguists have established that human language is hardwired into our species' unique brain. How that wiring job came to be is not a concern of science. After reading this book, one should be more inclined to accept the fact that our uniquely-speaking species has language software and hardware that were intelligently designed for each other.

Our lexicographers occasionally publish mere hunches for etymologies, but they sometimes settle for the designation "origin unknown." One such unknown origin belongs to the word LAD (boy). ילד YeLeD is a boy in Biblical Hebrew; *walid* is a boy in Arabic. *Lamed-Dalet* (LD) is the root of birthing throughout Semitic. Once some anachronistic 19th Century, racist myths about different races and languages evolving from separate simian ancestors are discarded, many such language mysteries are solved. The Old School of linguistics maintains that human vocabulary is a man-made, chaotic mess. The new discipline of Edenics attempts to demonstrate that words are worlds… beautifully arranged into solar systems and galaxies.

This book is merely the newly cleared tip of an immense iceberg. Both those who were taught that Hebrew is a late branch of West Semitic and those who were taught that Adam and Eve spoke Hebrew are predisposed to reject some aspects of Edenic theory. The academic camp must realize that the rule of simpler-means-later does not apply for the original language program – and Hebrew is the closest relative to Edenic. The religious camp must realize that a lot of water has flowed down the Tigris from Adam's Edenic to Abraham's Hebrew – so that Hebrew is merely the closest relative to Edenic. Readers from both camps are asked to scale this iceberg step-by-step, and to reserve conclusions until after they have attained the perspective of the summit.

———————————

The origin of species and of speeches …This Book does not take on all of Darwinism, but if a case can be made for intelligent design in language, then the argument for extreme atheism is surely weakened. There's something out there that wanted

humans to be able to speak and read. Perhaps there is something out there that instantly turned slow-moving mammals into oceanic creatures that could survive the Deluge. There may be better I.D. ways to explain the leg bones in porpoises, and, at any rate, I am unqualified to discuss biology.

At most, there are parallels to be suggested between the diversity of speeches and species. One must certainly assume that the spectacular variety of butterflies indicates that the species diversified and adapted on their own to different environments. It must be pondered if this was accidental Darwinian mutation and survival of the fittest, or whether the butterfly's genes were naturally programmed or intelligently designed to survive by adapting.

As for the diversity of speeches, the reader here will discover how the Edenic letters are uniquely versatile. This special alphabet, or *Aleph-Bet*, contains the "genes" for the diverse vocabularies of what are now over six thousand languages. A language is a dialect which eventually became incomprehensible to the speakers of the parent language. A simple illustration of how "new languages" were spun off from Edenic, and from its spinoffs, appears in the chart at the end of this introduction.

Is the human species more or less fit for survival with our diverse languages? How natural or accidental was this linguistic breakup? If a "Creator of speech" (Isaiah 57:19) did purposefully scramble an original language (Genesis 11), then why project towards an ultimate time when our disunited nations finally arrive back to a state of knowing a linguistic and deistic Oneness (Zephaniah 3:9)? This book addresses such difficult questions, both with speculation that readers may reject, and with data that readers may confirm.

Darwin's 1859 classic, *The Origin of Species*, offered a consistent thesis of Chaos. Since this book explores biblical modes of Control, it has to deal with several difficult problems, with some of the **whys** of religion, and not just the **hows** of science. WHY then would the Proto-Earth tongue be diversified? How could Abram the Chaldean become Abraham the Hebrew-speaker? Why is it unlikely that the traditional Torah letters evolved from hieroglyphs? How do the shapes of this *Aleph-Bet* (software) point to the engineering of the human mouth (hardware)? Such questions are addressed.

A fraction of this book involves theory. Most of it involves data that supports the hypothesis of this newest, oldest theory of language origin. This book begins to document how the Babel-babble at the Babylonian valley of Shinar-Sumer (traditionally dated 1996 from Adam) might have allowed what became English and other languages to spin-off and de-evolve from an original, universal Edenic language.

In one word, then, this book is about etymology. On the semantic surface, this merely means word history. But etymology is from the Greek *etmos*, truth. So searching and researching word history may bring about a revolution in something much larger: in truth itself.

Edenics claims that *etmos*, Greek truth, resulted from a slightly scrambled Edenic אמת EMeT, *Aleph-Mem-Tahf*, truth. An entire chapter is devoted to this phenomenon of rearranged root letters, known as metathesis in linguistics. Our current reference books and college curricula are correct to consider *etmos* a meaningless sound arbitrarily used to fill a semantic need. With only access to Hellenic "truth," it is no wonder that so many people feel that words are meaningless accidents. If ETM or EMT do not mean the same thing from sheer coincidence, then who is to say that the Greek term is not the older one? History aside, Edenics will offer the reader structural reasons why אמת EMeT is the original "truth." (See the Metathesis chapter.)

Edenics words are like chemical compounds, and readers will be amazed to discover that words (in their pristine form) are like organic chemical compounds that are loaded with unique meaning. This book cannot be mistaken for just another discussion of word origins. Readers can view much newly uncovered data in deciding for themselves between the forces of Chaos and Control, evolutionary chance or intelligent design.

Darwin's *The Origin of Species* helped science take the divine adaptability of animals and extend it to the theory of evolution. Much of Darwin's important field work took place in the Galapagos Islands. This archipelago was named for the Spanish tortoise, *galapago*. As seen in the CALIBER entry, shell words both zoological and botanical from distant lands are all variations of guttural-liquid-bilabial קלפה QLeePaH, a shell.

Only a few, easy technical terms are used in this book. The only unavoidable, newly coined terms here are **Edenic** (the language) and **Edenics** (the field of study).

This book attempts to demonstrate that **Edenic** is the original, universal Earth language spoken at Eden. It was subject to a Big Bang of diversification begun at the Tower of Babel. Traditionally, the initial trauma created seventy spinoffs. These were languages like Sanskrit, Quechua (Inca), Basque and Hellenic. More of these will be identified by more skilled Edenic researchers of the future. These proto-languages continued to split off in a process that has peaked at 6,000 "languages" (advanced dialects). Mass media may get the planet back down to seventy languages in two generations.

That singular and unique Proto-Semitic language of Edenic is most like Hebrew, but is different from Modern Hebrew. There are important roots of Edenic that are preserved in other Semitic languages. Many of these roots or words are not clearly visible in the Hebrew Bible. Citations from the Bible are used because they offer the most accessible and fully developed literary context from which to understand a word. A brief, isolated fragment from some other Semitic archeological artifact can barely compare.

Anthropologists agree that agriculture began in Israel and Jordan some ten thousand years ago. If you find a language without agricultural words, you are welcome to call it pre-Edenic. **The oldest human set of remains ever found with the hyoid bone (in the throat) for speech was unearthed in the Carmel Caves near Haifa, Israel.** The hyoid is the bone stuck in the throat of Edenics deniers. All the hard evidence points to Proto-Semitic being earliest. We are only a few decades past the time when it was taught that everything good came from dead white men from Greece and Rome. It is expected that some old school Eurocentrists will defend Atheism and Classicism from this book's brash assault.

Amid the fractious skullduggery of anthropologists digging up skulls in Africa and Asia, nobody has found an older skeleton with a hyoid bone anywhere outside of Semitic turf. The burden of proof is on scientists to prove that actual speakers, not just tool-using knuckle-walkers, might have begun civilization and literacy somewhere other than in the Middle East.

Edenics is the term coined for this new science. Internally, Edenics is concerned with the many patterned phenomena seen within Edenic that reveal language to be a hard science, much like chemistry and physics. Externally, Edenics focuses on how, with these phenomena, **the Edenic language** links together all subsequent human languages.

All words are cognates; all men are cousins. Edenics adds up to an understanding of universal brotherhood, but this is not an anthem to globalism or to a bland, new one-world order that threatens individuality. On the contrary. Nimrod of Babel, the original Saddam, wanted to be the species-wide dictator. Perhaps this is why the Genesis account focuses on a work stoppage on Nimrod's Tower of Babel, his Kremlin of centralized mind control. It was at this critical moment that multi-national human history was kick-started with the initial Big Bang of neuro-linguistic diversity that this book has begun to study.

This book is for intelligent but lay readers, not for linguists who want complex phonetic codes. To further level the playing field, there are no foreign fonts used here except for Hebrew. Everything is transliterated in familiar Latin letters, and no background in Semitics or linguistics is necessary.

Words and letters are sounds; sound is energy, so this is a book introducing a new natural science. It is not another humanities study about etymology or linguistics.

Apparently, nature, or a force behind all natural sciences, dislikes mindless uniformity and favors a diverse approach to perception. History has had to work for millennia to arrive at an Eden-like synthesis. Our Babel of discord has often been painful, but getting back to the garden may be our task. In terms of *kabbalah*, this job is gathering the sparks of shattered vessel fragments. In terms of Edenics it may be described as ingathering the world's words exiled from Eden. They are both ways of taking up the classical Jewish task of "repairing the world" – תקון עולם TiKOON [O]aLahM.

Or, TINKERING with the world… since TINKER is a metathesis (root-letter switch) of תקון TiKOON (to repair, tinker). Current dictionaries either offer "origin unknown" or provide a typically awkward etymology that reflects neither the music nor the meaning of the word TINKER.

Genesis 11's Eden-Babel scenario is often easily dismissed as a tribal myth. The evidence suggests that it is neither Hebraic nor fictitious. One must look at the wide belief in an aboriginal planetary language, and at the data analyzed here and collected in the *E-Word CD Dictionary* (available at *lightcatcherbooks.com* or *edenics.org*).

Since 7/2010 there has been a word search to supplement the Edenic postal archives and Edenic web games at *edenics.net*. In a couple of years the database should appear as a multi-volume book, *The Edenic Dictionary of the Human Language*.

This book asks you to take a second look at Genesis 11:1. Don't just look at a translation, listen to a simplified version of the original:

ויהי כל הארץ שפה אחת ודברים אחדים

(1) KoL (2) AReTS (3) SaPHaH (4) EK[H]aT (5) D[V]aR AK[H]aD.

You can now hear that the (1) WHOLE (2) EARTH had (4) one [source of EACH] (3) SPEECH and a (5) unique vocabulary – begin from דבר Da(V)aR, word, and put the first root letter, D, at the end, so that it reads VRD, like the German *vort*, and the English *word*.

This book hopes to introduce you to a former and, hopefully, future world of unity, clarity, and meaning in our thought and spoken words.

This book will demonstrate Edenic to be the axis on which languages spin – and keeps spinning new dialects. In the final chapter of this book, the world's most commonly used, thus the oldest words, are neatly fit to Edenic. After the charge of "coincidence," critics have said and may continue to say that Edenics is merely identifying words borrowed from other languages. But the Easter Islanders didn't trade with the Eskimos and Slavs. The massive data does not allow these easy dismissals. We are talking about a planet on which all spoke Edenic at the dawn of time.

We might soon be able to recognize all foreign words as cognates, and all foreign people as cousins – equally descended from our Edenic ancestors. *But viva la difference.* Edenic is no Esperanto. We can understand where others are coming from by knowing what Edenic word that culture was thinking with.

Most of the cultures/languages/peoples created at Babel have a sexist term for "woman" – even the immediate source of QUEEN, Old English *cwene*, means woman, prostitute and wife. The Edenic woman, by contrast, is simply the feminine of the word for man. There is far more than an upgraded etymology to be gained from Edenics.

In graduate linguistics we learned that unrelated languages can have as many as thirty words with similar sound and meaning by sheer coincidence. Back in 1989 when there were only 22,000 mostly English words linked to Edenic, some agents of Chaos dismissed the young project as fantasy mixed some newly discovered borrowings and pure coincidences. By 2006 the evidence was far larger, and the theory was more articulated. The "coincidence" charge can seem stronger, however, when the reader discovers that there are only **seven basically different sounds made by the human mouth**. So, with letters shifting sounds, and letters shifting local within the three-letter root consonants of Semitic, perhaps this sleight-of-hand is easy to do? Maybe the critics are right that Edenics is just some elaborate alchemy?

But this argument is flawed. World vocabulary is divided into many thousands of meanings. Any word link to Edenic must share sound AND sense. A GRILL and a GIRL have some sound correspondence, but if they are equally attractive to a young man, he needs help. It is statistically difficult to match up words in different language families that share music *and* meaning.

Do the math. If Edenics is sleight-of-hand, try tracing Navaho to Greek. Good luck.

Others will dismiss Edenics when seeing that Hebrew HaR (mountain) has nothing to do with the English word MOUNTAIN. But they should consider that HILL is only a liquid shift of *Resh*/R to the letter L. Surely a hill and a mountain are closer than a hole and a mint. And if they search the Edenics reference, they will see that the Czech mountain is *hora* and the Russian and Polish is *gora*. (Both easily forms of הר HaR, mountain, hill.)

The conveyors of Chaos also taught us that, given enough time, a monkey banging at a keyboard will accidentally write a Shakespearian sonnet.

I will settle for a haiku. The core issue here is Chaos vs. Control. The Chaos agents assume that words have no intrinsic rhyme or reason. If different words, especially from different language groups, echo with a similar ring – it is from pure coincidence.

This book posits the thesis that language is the symbiosis of sound with sense, music with meaning. If a word means GIRAFFE, this is no accident of agreed usage. In the wide world, this sound can only signify one unique creature. Very few words could be accepted as a source. 99.99% of all words would be irrelevant to giraffeness, no matter how good the sound correspondence. The dictionaries give an embarrassingly poor etymology for GIRAFFE. What does Edenic offer? *Ayin-Resh-Phey*, ערף GHoReF, means the scruff of the neck.

The reader will decide if Edenic provides superior etymologies, and a more sensible, satisfying science and world view.

Chaos or Control?

From the DIRECTION entry: All roads led from Babel. You decide if there may be something to Edenics, or if this is a bunch of lucky coincidences and unknown borrowings.

Following is a chart of selected paths taken by DeReKH: דרך (way, road, path, direction/director). Any bible concordance will confirm that דרך *Dalet-Resh-Kahf* has all the meanings below and all the "genes" for the global diversity of its Tower-of-Babel spin-offs. Here is an example of what happened to Edenic DeReKH ך ר ד – *Dalet-Resh-Khaf*.

   1) *Dalet*: D and T are "dentals" or the interchangeable tooth-made letters.
   2) *Resh*: R and L are "liquids" or the interchangeable tongue-made letters.
   3) *Khaf*: G, H, K, Q are "gutturals" or the interchangeable throat-made letters.

Language   Meaning   spelling of similar dental-liquid-guttural term דרך

Language	Meaning	
Edenic	way, manner, journey, road	De Re KH
Afrikaans	road, path	Di Re K
Ainu	through, reversal of *kari*	i R aK
Albanian	way, road	RRu Ge
American slang	street	D R aG
Arabic	highway, way	Ta Ri Q
Australian	paths	Tu Rin Gas
Australian	straight, direct	Thoo R Gool
Basque	street, road, reversal of *kali*	iL aK
Malay: Bouton	road	Da Ra
Chinese	way	Dau Lu
Czech	track, course, way	D Ra Ha
Dutch	a long journey/TREK	T R eK
Dutch	direction	Ri CHting
Finnish	course, way	To La
French	to steer, find one's way	Di Ri Ger
Gaelic	journey	Tu Rus
German	through, by way of source of THROUGH, THOROUGHFARE, THRUWAY While "through" would be DaReKH plus a prefix letter, there is Old Irish, T Re and Welch, T RWy	Du R CH
Hindi	manner	Ta Ra H
Indonesian	direction	a Ra H
Indonesian	manner, way	Tja Ra
Italian	rev. corridoio, CORRIDor	oioD iRR oC
Japanese	journey	Ryo Ko
Japanese	fashion, manner	Ryu Ko
Japanese	road	Do Ro
Japanese	street	To Ri
Korean	manner, way	Ro Khe
Korean	reversal of *kil*, road, street	Li K
Kurdish	reversal of *kolan*, street	naL oK
Latin	to direct; whence, DIRIGIBLE	Di Ri Gere
Latin	journey; whence, ITINERANT	iT eR

Nepali	way, method	T aR Kaa
Nepali	towards…a direction	T iR aa
Nepali	travel, n. and v.	yaaT R aa
Old English	reverse of *rad*, a road source of RAID, RIDE and ROAD	Da R
Old French	reverse of *rote*, way, path; source of ROTE, ROUTE, ROUTINE	eT oR
Old French	reverse of *route*, way, road; source of RUT	eT ouR
Old French	track, way, course; source of TRACE, TRACK	T R aC
Polish	course, track	To R
Polish	way	D Ro Ga
Russian	road, way	Da Ro Ga
Serbian	road	Lu Ka
Spanish	right direction, straight	De Re CHo
Swedish	way, cognate of German *weg,* English way; *Resh*/R shifts to V,W	Va G
Thai	direct, straight	Dt Ro HnG
Ukranian	to direct, or drive animals	D Ro Czyt
Ukranian	road	Do Ro Ha
Urdu	travel, trek, trip	yaT Ra
Vietnamese	path, road, street, way	Du'o' nG
Welsh	through	T Wy

This list has to be kept short. Otherwise it could run into related terms like DaRahKH, to tred, which would lead to the Greek source of TRUCK and TRUDGE, and so on…

Forms of DeReKH, like the M132 Turkish *dogru* (straight), were left out in favor of only those in perfect dental-liquid-guttural sequence. (Or the reverse.) Most European languages have a form of DIRECTOR. In Afrikaans it is *direkteur.* The Arabic director, *mudir*, has lost an end-guttural. The מדריך Ma'**DReeYCH,** guide, leader, gives the DIRECTIONS.

Note: The Albanian "way, road" is missing a dental (D,T). But it appears that they had and dropped that D. Albanian, straight is *drejt*, and a course is *drejtim.*

Other imperfect but notable entries include Italian *DiReZione* (route, trend), German *RiCHTung* (route, trend, way... source of RIGHT) and "directory" words like Albanian *Drejtori*, Manx *oRDaGH* and Malay *aRaH* (matching Indonesian *aRaH*, course). Samoan *auaLa* lacks a pronounced dental and guttural, but it means path, road, street, and way. It is but a liquid shift from the Tamil below. Italian *inDiCaRe* (to direct or IN**DIC**ATE) cannot claim the liquid (L,R) because of the suffix *-re*.

Fernando Aedo's Additions (that extend beyond the usual shifts):

Language Meaning spelling of similar dental-liquid-guttural term. The Edenic/Aramaic ꓷ/Z to ꓷ/D shift, seen at AUDIENCE, operates as a dental-to-fricative shift in some languages below.

Mayan		
Pocomchi	road, path	roq yuuq'
Quechua (Inca)	narrow street,or passage	
	Reversal of *k'ikllu*	llu kik
Dravidian *(languages of S. India)*	The unusual *Dalet*-to-S shift in Dravidian is like the *Zayin* to D dental-fricative shift seen in Edenic to Aramaic, see AUDIENCE from [O]ZeN ear	
Tamil	way, road, path, means, manner, method	a_ru
Maithili	road	sa r.a k
Sanskrit	a continuous line of road	sa ra ka
Gondi	road, walk	sa rri_
Konda	way, path	sa r-i
	plural	sa r ku
Tamil lexicon	way, road (c=ch like in change)	ca ri
Kota	road, path	a.d a.ry
	way, road, path	da_ ri
Gujarati	main,of a road	dho ri_
Sanskrit	track, line	li_ kka
Bengali	line, track, rut	li k
Tamil	way, path, public road, rule	at ar
Sinhalese	crossing, road	ta ra
Khowar (Dardic)	upper road	to_ ri

Tamil	way, road, path, right mode	ta_ ri
Telugu, Tamil	way, path	ta_ rai
Tamil	street, highway, public road	te ru
Tulu	lane, footpath	o r n:ku
Belari	way	te ru vam

More RG and RK terms related to לך LaiKH, go, עלה GHaLeH, ascend, and רגל ReeGaiL, to explore, tour, go on foot. [ALLEY] [WALK]

Another longer chart in a top entry involves the WOLF and Dog, see page 349.

Were these lucky coincidences? Is this the arbitrary manipulation of data that would really work just as well with any language? Do the 24,000 (just English) words linked to Edenic etymons (ultimate sources) compare well with the theoretical Proto-Indo-European reconstructed roots that some dictionaries now cite? Edenics reports, you decide.

One could concede that a few languages along trade routes may have borrowed a number from historical commerce. But you can look at the amazing number of similar number ONE words. Do you think they are merely historical, or does the global scope of these words say PRE-historical...when humankind all huddled together in a valley called Shinar (Sumer) ...still traumatized by the Deluge.

Then, when readers look at a score of the same guttural-liquid Number One word in reverse, ask then who would reverse a word that you are borrowing? Nobody. Unlike a mere nasalization or a single letter shift, a reversal is neurological, not historical. Kinda like what the "confounding" at the Tower of Babel was supposed to do.

Why? Was the proliferation of languages from the original human computing language some kind of punishment? No. Nimrod was history's first ruthless dictator. Mesopotamia's original Saddam Hussain. He wanted a huge Kremlin-like tower to centralize all directives from him. The new G-d would be his state. He only could control the entire Earth population because they were under a million, they all lived in Shinar, and, of course, they all spoke the same language.

Suddenly, the emperor's Kremlin skyscraper project suffered a permanent job action. The Intelligent Designer of vast species diversity did not want this global mind control. Something affected the people's brains, so that they spoke different languages. When people finally found a band of others who spoke their language, they picked up and migrated to a place where they could form their own clan, and later nation. For example, a bunch of Proto-Germanic speakers got together and headed west, trading in the Tigris and Euphrates for the Rhine and the Rhone.

Only that first breakup was a paranormal neuro-linguistic happening. Further breakups and migrations allowed splinters of that Germanic group to develop into Angle and Saxon dialects. After the invasion of French Normans, an unusually mixed, rich language began to develop on a large island north of France. This language later became known as English. For centuries English would be a cultural leader, until the advent of TV and Rap.

Chapter One

History of the Idea – A Monogenesis of Language

All Languages from a Single, Created Mother Tongue

The oldest passage in recorded history about historical linguistics is Genesis 11:1. Naturally, it is the last place that historical linguists will look for answers to the mysteries of the existence and dispersion of human language.

From the Beginning, a translation and Biblical commentary, renders Genesis 11:1 thusly [non-textual treatment in brackets]:

> [No mere chronology, the Bible completes the theme of Noah's progeny in chapter 10, and only in chapter 11 gets to the how and why they got scattered throughout the globe:]

> *At first, the whole habitable earth* [from Edenic ארץ AReTS] *had its one divinely programmed computing language –* [Edenic, Proto-Semitic, best demonstrated in Biblical Hebrew roots] *with a unique and economical vocabulary* [so, despite their numbers and racial diversity, all people were on the same page].

In the familiar KJV, Genesis 11:1 reads: "And the whole earth was of one language, and of one speech."

This book asks you to take a second look at Genesis 11:1. Don't settle for a standard translation, absorb the rendition from page 11.

If you CAN hear those echoes of Eden in the English words, it's all the more amazing that centuries of bible scholars and language scientists could not or would not hear them all this time.

The Biblical belief that a "Creator of speech" (Isaiah 57:19) still confounds speech after the Tower of Babel's Big Bang of diversity may be seen in Psalms 55:10 (55:9 in KJV): "Destroy, O Lord and **divide** their tongues."

In the Genesis account, mankind goes into Chapter Eleven (moral bankruptcy), misusing unity by nation-building totalitarianism. The punishment fit the crime, and was quite effective. Even the brutal USSR could not successfully control the Babel of its non-Russian satellites.

Until the Age of Reason, most people never doubted Genesis incidents like the Deluge or The Tower of Babel (and its ramifications of an involved Creator).

Then, 19th Century modern linguists rejected the Babel story as a typical primitive myth to explain a phenomenon (the existence of many languages). Those maverick linguists who suggested a single Proto-Earth language which broke up were harshly suppressed, and lumped together with the religious lunatics.

Finally, by the end of the 20th Century, contemporary linguists have come to accept an archeological Tower of Babel, and even the concept of a single, original global human language – as long as there is no deity first creating, then "confusing" or diversifying tongues.

For the centuries spanning these three periods, the premier evolutionists and linguists have all conceded that human language and the uniquely human capacity for language is a mystery. M.I.T.'s Noam Chomsky has famously established that the human brain was hardwired for language. Hardwired by whom? Mother Nature? Professor Chomsky had suggested some sort of superhuman engineer, something like the "intelligent designer" but less problematic to skeptics.

Many academics still posit the theory that humans developed grammars and vocabularies out of simian gestures and grunts. Some even feel that the instinct to create an insider's slang, and soon a new dialect, came from our ape ancestors. This doesn't go well with the new data showing that most humans spoke one language in the ancient Near East. It is supposed that one clan began speaking early Slavic and another early Germanic simply because they migrated away from each other.

Recent archaeologists have concluded that agriculture, the first truly human endeavor above hunting-gathering, was begun in Israel and Jordan. Besides the argument for human literacy beginning with Semitic, this finding asks us to pay careful attention to agricultural words to see if such terms have a Semitic origin. All the Edenic etymologies require research, but the SWITCH entry in the *E-Word CD Dictionary* offers an insight into pre-Bronze Age agriculture:

SWIT(CH) n.	**SHai[V]eDT**	*Shin-Bhet-Tet*
S(H)AVE-ET	שבט	**[S(H) -V-T]**

ROOTS: The oldest and best etymons available for SWITCH (stick for swatting) are Late German *zwuske* (long thin rod) and Middle Dutch *swick* (a whip). SWITCH is defined as a flexible twig, rod or stick for whipping.

שבט S(H)ai[V]eDT is a rod (*Isaiah 28:27*) or staff; a whipping rod is the implication in *Proverbs 10:13*.

שוט SHOODT, another SWT or variant of שבט *Shin-Vav-Tet* is a "whip" (*Proverbs 26:3*).

For the verb SWITCH (to transfer or change) one has to look up the earliest meaning, such as this primary definition from *Webster's New Universal Unabridged Dictionary* (1979): "to strike with or as with a switch or small twig or rod."

> **BRANCHES:** SWAT is easily related, as a verb of striking quickly – as with a SWITCH. SWATH has an obsolete meaning as a stroke (with a scythe) so that even a reaper could be a Sultan of Swat (prodigious swinger of a baseball bat). Archeologists trace the beginning of agriculture to Israel and Jordan, and the etymology of SWATH may hark back to a pre-Bronze Age time when a SWATH was swatted in a field of grain by a sturdy, sharpened rod rather than a metallic

scythe. STAFF and STAVE are more clearly sticks, rods or tree branches, but they require a 2-3 letter switch or metathesis – see SCEPTER.

For a human branch of ש-ב-ט *Shin-Bhet-Tet* – see SEPT. Words like SWAT, SWATH and STAVE favor the Edenic etymon that ends in a T, rather than the Germanic etymons ending with K.

What about the word AGRICULTURE itself? Here's the first part of the relevant entry:

AGRI(CULTURALIST)	EeKaR	Aleph-Kaph-Resh
ee-CAR	אכר	[EKR]

ROOTS: A field of AGRICULTURAL words has been harvested, processed and distilled to the Indo-European" root" *AGRO*. *Agros* (field) is Greek; *aecer* (field or ACRE) is Old English. The older German term for one who worked his ACRE was *ackermann*.

אכר EeKaR is a farmer. The plural אכרים **EeKaR**eeYM are the "*Farmers* and vinedressers" (or *husbandmen* in older translations) referred to in *II Chronicles 26:10*. Similar in Akkadian, Aramaic and Syriac. אכר EeKaiR is to farm; קרקע QaRQ[A]h is land. *Kahf-Resh-Hey*, כרה KahRaH, is to dig. Digging is at the guttural-liquid root of **AGRI**CULTURE.

The Brick and Mortar Babel – The Archaeology of Genesis 11

There are a few possible sites for the historical tower of Babel. Biblical archeologist James D. Long places the tower in present-day Turkey, nor far from Mount Ararat where mankind would have huddled together after the catastrophic Deluge. Nimrod's empire, history's first, encompassed the known world of his day. Speculation about Nimrod's tower site is therefore not to be limited to present-day Iraq. There is sufficient archeological evidence that could place a giant ziggurat, a giant, early skyscraper, in eastern Turkey. Soviet historical linguists, the ones behind the early language superfamily they called Nostratic, place the origin of language diversity and migrations precisely in this region. The ziggurats or step-pyramids of Iraq and Central America may simply be miniature tributes to a gigantic tower preserved in various ancient legends.

Even the earliest pyramid in Egypt was a step-pyramid. These terraced structures could be climbed, and the original Tower of Babel was primarily intended to be above any new flood, above any divine retribution.

Others prefer Saddam's stomping grounds.

One doesn't have to be a U.N. inspector or a geopolitical pundit to realize that Iraq (ancient Babel or Babylon) may be an appropriate site for confused language. The Bible calls the tower site Shinar, probably Sumer. Even though it is the Tower of "Babel," the Bible typically references a place name that would be better known many years later. Shinar and Babel seem to favor a Mesopotamian location, between the rivers, the Tigris and Euphrates. Both the Turkish/Ararat region and Shinar/Babel are close enough to the Black Sea, where undersea archeology has found entire submerged settlements, and the best evidence of a powerful and sudden deluge.

Cristiancourier.com has the following on its website:

> *The precise site of the ancient Tower of Babel is a matter of uncertainty, for there are remnants of several ruins in the region that are possibilities. Many writers, following Jewish and Arab traditions, locate the Tower ruins at Borsippa (the "Tongue Tower"), about 11 miles southwest of the northern portion of Babylon (formerly a suburb of the city). Others identify the site with Etemen-an-ki ("the temple of the foundation of heaven and earth"), which is located in the southern sector of the city near the right bank of the Euphrates River. One or the other of these ruins may represent the archaeological "descendant" of the original Tower of Babel.*

Unfortunately, natives have been borrowing bricks from these sites for millennia.
The Tower of Babel will have to be reconstructed brick-by-brick, word-by-word, in the study of Edenics. Cultures as diverse and far apart as the Chinese and Maya have ancient traditions about a single, global language and an instant linguistic diversification by the Creator. Scholars who shrug this off as a Semitic myth must shrug it off as a more global myth.

Evidence from Mesopotamia

In those days, the lands of Subur (and) Hamazi, Harmony-tongued (?) Sumer, the great land of the decrees of princeship, Uri, the land having all that is appropriate(?), The land Martu, resting in security, The whole universe, the people in unison (?) To Enlil in one tongue [spoke]. ...(Then) Enki, the lord of abundance, (whose) commands are trustworthy, The lord of wisdom, who understands the land, The leader of the gods, Endowed with wisdom, the lord of Eridu Changed the speech in their mouths, [brought (?)] contention into it, Into the speech of man that (until then) had been one.

"The Babel of Tongues: A Sumerian Version" by Kramer, S.N.
Journal of the American Oriental Society 88:108-11,1968

Does Genesis specifically say that Adam and Eve were created with a divine language, or that Hebrew was the language of Eden and the angels? No, but there are verbatim quotes of the Creator, the angels (even in later books like the otherwise Aramaic *Daniel* and the Hebrew *Ezekiel*), and Adam and Eve that are always and only in Hebrew. Adam only means "earthling" in Biblical Hebrew. *Kabbalah* classifies the human being as "the speaker," and it is instructive to examine the passage on the formation of Adam. If the "nostrils" are a neuro-port to the brain, we might say that a language program was "breathed" or downloaded into what would be the first Modern Man.

Check with your favorite Bible for Genesis 2:7. There, the first (modern) human has the divine spirit blown into his nostrils – (perhaps blowing out the suddenly large brain case of this strangely divine animal). In Eden, in touch with the Source of Reason and Law, Man becomes *Homo Sapiens*. Sapient means thinking, and unlike emoting, thinking requires language. Whichever way you interpret it, Adam receives the ability to think abstractly, truly something no animal can do, and something that classifies humans as being "in the image of God."

The premier Bible commentator, Rashi, (Rabbi Shlomo ben Yitschak – 1040-1105, France) writes that the language of Eden is Hebrew, echoing the 1st century Talmud

(Sanhedrin 38). Of course, they refer to Biblical Hebrew, not Modern Hebrew. It is more precise to use a term like Proto-Semitic.

Other Genesis passages quote these first *homo sapiens* (thinkers). Later on you will encounter Adam's naming of animals (Genesis 3:19), and can assess just how perceptive and apt these Edenic names in Chapter Ten.

As you read on, you can decide if Adam's name or Adam's animal names could be in any other language but an intelligently designed, universal one.

Thinking and speaking appear to be the exclusive domain of humans. Yet, the antagonist of Eden, the נחש *Nakhash*, also speaks. Some see this creature as a "Serpent," while others may prefer a more scientific label, like "Neanderthal"– a type of soulless hominid. As an animal or pre-human this *Nakhash* cannot perceive of future consequences. Either way, the *Nakhash* is not considered rational enough to be given any rules, or to get a hearing after he has broken those rules. Importantly, the *Nakhash* would only later become the limbless (all tail, all animal) snake, who abused and lost his ability to chew food (snakes merely swallow), and who has abused and lost the human ability to speak (snakes merely hiss). Just as the Bible references place names before they were named, *Nakhash* is named Serpent before this aspiring top mammal was justly demoted to the lowest of reptiles.

This drama of Eden becomes more of a struggle between a man and a cunning, erect animal, and less like a tall tale when one considers that large snakes **do** have residual limbs (used in mating). It becomes less fantastical that an intelligent designer would de-evolve the *Nakhash* for aspiring to be Eve's forbidden fruit and the top hominid.

The snake becomes all tail. Therefore, Edenic זנב *ZaNaBH,* tail (Exodus 4:4) is a fine etymon (source word) for the voodoo snake deity that named the zombie. Note the nasal shift, *Noon* to M. [ZOMBIE] The נחש *Nakhash* of Eden is relevant here as foil to *homo sapiens*, Man the thinker and speaker. Whether or not you prefer to demonize *Nakhash*, it embodies the animal, the instinctual – the opposite of what an intelligent designer of language wants, wanting us humans to overcome our inner Serpent.

As you progress in the study of Edenics, you will see why נחוש NeeKHooSH means sorcery or magic, and why terms of instinct, like GUESS and HUNCH come from נ-ח-ש *Noon-Het-Shin.*

The ח-ש *Het-Shin* sub-root is חוש [K]HOOSH, instinct. It helps to know some zoology, to be aware that snakes are blind and hunt with a unique heat sensor. This is the science behind this sophisticated neurological species. This is why the snake is susceptible to being "charmed," and why it survives by hunch and guess. Did the snake evolve by Darwinian accident? Did a brilliant Proto-Semitic caveman name the snake נחש NaK[H]aSH because he knew about heat sensors? Keep reading, and make your own decision.

No matter how well *The Origin of Speeches* makes a case for the Genesis 11 thesis, it may not be true that ALL humans think in Edenic, and that our output stage, or spoken language, is always a simple variation of the original Edenic. There is one exception that proves the rule. The exception is the language of the African Hottentots. This isolated tribe speaks in an elaborate code of clicks and whistles – not with the usual consonants (whose variants we shall soon study) nor the ordinary vowels (which even vary within neighborhoods of large cities). Are the non-speaking Hottentots truly human? Are they some sort of pre-Adamic spawn of the animal-*Nakhash* who are lacking true "souls" – (as some fear about sociopaths who have no conscience)? Such drastic theories are not necessary. Perhaps some children got lost and isolated from other speakers, and so developed a code of signals instead of the usual verbal phrases. Because the Hottentots have a human mind, their grammar and vocabulary are quite sophisticated – especially when compared to the most elaborate animal communication systems (such as that of dolphins).

Yes, there is the apocryphal story of a king who raised children without contact with speech…and those children spontaneously began to communicate in Hebrew. It's not anywhere near that simple – even if language, originally Edenic, was hardwired in the human brain. This is why Edenics requires the mastering of several simple, basic linguistic givens, and a scientific, not mystical, way to see that even Chinese, with its many dropped consonants replaced by tones, is a form of the language of Eden.

Language for *homo sapiens* is factory-installed, the language program that came with our neurological and other anatomical hardware. No mentally disturbed cat ever barked like a dog, but there is a paranormal, but not rare, phenomenon among humans where a speaker in a self-hypnotic trance can "speak in tongues." Technically called *glossolalia*, this ecstatic, unclear and repetitive speech is usually considered a speech-related neurological disturbance. Lay witnesses have claimed that the person is babbling away in an unlearned, even dead foreign language, but scientists have not verified that the brain is accessing an unknown language. More rare and less documented or understood is the phenomenon called *xenoglossia*. This *does* involve the ability to spontaneously speak a foreign language without prior exposure. **If** this is ever scientifically confirmed, it would support the Edenics scenario: where people all have a uniform, original language program, and a neurological disturbance (such as at the Tower of Babel) makes the brains of an assemblage begin to suddenly speak in variant forms of that original language. This catastrophic diversification is more complex than the scope of this book's focus on vocabulary, since it includes grammar.

The original 70 ur-languages were variants of Edenic much like a spectrum bends one light source into different colors. Just as there are many kinds of "blue," one ur-language would ultimately de-evolve into many hues or dialects. The analogy may be all the more appropriate if one reads the Genesis record with the rainbow only being manifest after prehistory's Deluge and breakup of the human community. The rainbow becomes a symbol or sign of diversity.

In any case, the dominant activity of early Genesis creation involves "separation" or diversity. Dark and light, wet and dry are separated. The Creator (equivalent to "Nature" in Hebrew numerical value) first engineered one original or "pure" language, just like the Edenic evidence indicates that there was only one proto-canine (see the Animal Names chapter). Engineered right into in the genome schematic of First Language (Edenic) and First Dog (כלב KeLeBH) was the prolific ability to adapt and diversify. This is not to be confused with random mutation and survival of the fittest – like the Darwinian Crapshoot Theory. Chinese doesn't resemble English, nor do Great Danes look like Pugs for more than accidental reasons. Adapting to different environments, being designed with the ability to evolve, makes far more sense in biology than in language. Neither randomness nor fitness diversified the ur-languages, before migrations and millennia splintered them exponentially. The data in language, as in astrophysics, points to an initial Big Bang. This first, designed diversification leads us to a catastrophic event like the tower at שנער Shinar (the lost location referenced for Bible readers as the much-later Babel).

With a fricative shift from *Shin*/SH to S and a nasal shift from *Noon*/N to M, we can discover in שנער Shinar a great city-state dug up by archeologists – Sumer. This does not make Sumerian the Mother Tongue. Sumerian was a spin-off of Edenic like everything else. But it was spoken by the one instant tribe/ur-nation who did not migrate from the city of the Tower.

This study involves the prehistory of ratiocination (the mysterious human ability to think and speak). Those engaged with the religious concept of Revelation have a clear idea why an Intelligent Designer would want humans to have literacy. The next sub-section touches on the future, instead, and a most unscientific idea. As such, it may be skipped by readers who dislike such things.

———

Biblical-oriented readers should note a verse near the end of the Hebrew Bible which appears to complement Genesis 11:1. This second Biblical passage about language predicts a revival of an Edenic or "Pure Language" which will impact our future – not just inform our distant past.

This second bookend to Genesis 11, appears to reference the pre-Babel ("pure" as original) Edenic language of Genesis 11:1. Just as the tower builders wanted to defy a heavenly authority, this verse anticipates a time when Babel is "reversed," and our multi-lingual world returns to the Eden-like sensibility of intimacy with and recognition of our Intelligent Designer.

כי אז איפך על עמים שפה ברורה

לקרא כלם בשם ה' ' לעבדו שכם אחד

צפניה ג:ט

I will restore to the peoples a pure language, that they may all call upon
the name of the Lord, to serve Him with one consent.
– Zephaniah 3:9

Here the pure, primeval Edenic speech is the subject of a pivotal prophecy describing the End Time, known to Jews as The End of Days. Knowledge of this global, unifying, uncorrupted language is envisioned to be a significant part of the worldwide Creator-consciousness of the period of peace and prosperity known as the Messianic Era. So, when does Zephaniah project that this longed-for era will come? Apparently, after the new science of Edenics spreads and takes hold. After the research begun here is made strong enough to convince everyone, of every tongue, that proof of our one Creator (who gifted our common ancestors Adam and Eve with language) is at the tip of our tongues.

———————————

Back to the chapter's history of the Mother Tongue thesis.

For millennia, the Biblical account of a Mother Tongue was not challenged by the greatest scholars and thinkers. Our first universities were first theological schools, so that the academic aversion for faith and the Bible is relatively recent.

Some interesting illustrations of this prevalent belief involve Christopher Columbus. His expedition left the rabidly anti-Jewish Inquisition Spain at the same time of the Spanish Expulsion of the world's major Jewish community. No unconverted Jew was to be given a reprieve from the public pyres of the Inquisition with a ticket on the *Nina, Pinta* or *Santa Maria.* Nonetheless, Columbus was permitted to bring a Hebrew-speaker on board the expedition. Why? When the explorers encountered exotic natives of new and distant lands it was assumed that only a Hebrew-speaker would be able to communicate with them.

The Jewish First Mate's name was Luis De Torres, and he was responsible for naming the exotic New World's large, fan-tailed pheasant. He named it a תוכי TOOKeY (exotic bird in Biblical Hebrew). Others heard it as "turkey", (perhaps assuming that the country of Turkey was somehow involved with the search for a passage to India). De Torres also named the New World cannibals כלב KeLeBH (dog in Hebrew). This was heard as "carib," and so the region of the Carib people came to be called the Caribbean.

The next chapter will involve the relatively few English words that are borrowed from actual, historical Hebrew words. The rest of the book focuses not on the words of history but on Edenic words from pre-history. The paragraphs above is only to illustrate the then catholic (worldwide) acceptance of Hebrew as the world's Mother Tongue.

For all the spread of Biblical knowledge that the conquering and colonizing early European (Catholic) powers can be "credited" for, it is only with the rise of Protestantism that awareness of the Bible's root language could be heard above the holy Roman emphasis on Latin. After all, Catholicism did not encourage Bible reading, so centuries of new Christians were barely aware of Biblical texts about language. Protestants were more aware of their theological Hebrew roots, and so were more open to links to literal, linguistic Biblical Hebrew roots. Protestant Dutch and English explorers followed the Spanish and Portuguese conquistadors.

More specifically, only when Puritan Protestantism emerges do we first find Christian scholars actively venerating Hebrew, rather than classical Greek and Latin. John Milton achieved a remarkable familiarity with the Hebrew of the Bible and of Biblical commentaries, and it informs his epics like "Paradise Lost." The Puritans of New England politicized their respect for Hebrew, considering themselves the new Adams in a new world, and the new Hebrews in a promised land. On Burial Hill in Plymouth, Massachusetts, the Pilgrim tombstones are engraved in Hebrew. Governor William Bradford's diary is in Hebrew.

The University of Kentucky website presents the following on Bradford, which may inspire many of us to take up Hebrew as a window to our primeval world or to our oldest sacred writings:

> In 1650, three years after he had ceased to chronicle the happenings at Plymouth for posterity, and at the age of sixty years, William Bradford took up the study of Hebrew. He explained why, at an advanced age, he had embarked on a new path of learning:
>
> "Though I am growne aged, yet I have a longing desire to see, with my owne eyes, something of that most ancient language, and holy tongue, in which the law and Oracles of God were written; and in which God and angels spoke to the Holy Patriarcks of old time; and what names were given to things at the Creation."
>
> It was also Bradford's way of returning to the origins of Christianity, thus of purifying his faith by seeking a more direct, unmediated experience of divinity. Rather than reading the English Biblical scriptures translated from the Latin, themselves translated from the Greek and [a surface level treatment of the] Hebrew, Bradford wanted to enter the promised landscape of the Hebrew Bible in the original.
>
> As for his desire to discover "names given to things at the Creation," read on, and when you get to animal names, parts of the body, etc. you also may agree that Edenic is the language of Creation.

The first universities in America, Harvard and Yale, had Hebrew among their course requirements and in their school mottos. The first doctoral dissertation in the New World, at Harvard's school of divinity, was about Hebrew as the Mother Tongue. A century later the Continental Congress debated whether Hebrew should become the new American language. Can you imagine if Hebrew would now be the world's *lingua franca*, as English is now?! However, regional rivals to the New England divinity-schooled delegates insisted that adopting German or French would better serve as a break from the British. Practicality won out in the end, and English was retained.

Noah Webster, America's premier lexicographer, gives many "Shemitic" (Semitic) etymologies as sources for English words in what was supposed to be the great American dictionary. For example, he cites ילד YeLeD, boy in Hebrew – (the L-D root appears throughout Semitic) – as the source of LAD. In contrast, the *Oxford English Dictionary* says "origin unknown." Webster's "Shemitic" etymologies were not disproved, but they were lustily reviled. His reference work would soon be eclipsed by the British Samuel Johnson (18th Century), and Webster's reverence for Hebrew was washed away by new

European thinking. Biblical theories were embarrassingly old-fashioned. The West had entered a new Man-centered Age of Reason. The Mother Tongue idea was now an old wives' tale of ancient superstition. So Harvard trashed the original truth in its motto, Hebrew EMeT, for the Latin motto *"veritas"* (truth). The V-R of Latin truth is from Hebrew words like BaReeY, surely, and BaRooR, evident – but we should not confuse the academic (especially humanities) enterprise for the pursuit of apolitical verity.

Benign neglect of things Biblical becomes sharpened to academic hostility, as 18th Century rationalism is stirred first by Darwinism and then by the pre-Nazi ideas of the 19th Century. Not only is industrial Man in charge of his destiny, and not some "mythical" Creator, but the human species is not the most divinely gifted creation – simply the fittest primate. All but the fittest race, the Aryans, were deemed not fit to survive.

If the 19th Century God was "dead" to secular thinkers, the concept of language being a divine gift was less than stillborn. The new German-led discipline of linguistics becomes a racial weapon in the age when the skulls of non-Aryans are measured for their racial inferiority. 19th and 20th Century Man was not about to consider the sanctity of language in the age of propaganda and advertising. When linguists think of the origin of words, they hear no more than the grunts of gorillas in the primeval mist.

───────────────

To post-Darwinian secularists, the concept of human language being intelligently designed, and not evolved from ape-men, is dangerously mythic, primitive and medieval. Even for many ministers, priests and rabbis, a literal acceptance of the Tower of Babel scenario (Genesis 11) and a belief in Hebrew as the Mother Tongue is considered overly fundamentalist.

A debate about language should be neurological, linguistic and scientific, NOT religious. If there is no Intelligent Design behind physics, there is none behind Edenic. If presented well enough, perhaps the scientist who is not moved by an overarching unity of set patterns within science can see and hear such in words. Or perhaps the humanist who has no awe for the patterns of chemistry, can begin to appreciate the science of isolated molecules of meaning in the subroots of words, and how "mutations" or letter shifts allow one Edenic word to engender a score of spin-offs.

Either Edenic is the source of all languages, or of none of them. Either the "myths" of Genesis can be understood the right way and verified, or all sacred texts are dreams of mere cultural significance. Egyptology has long denied the Biblical Exodus; now James D. Long has corrected Egyptology with his book, *The Riddle of the Exodus.* (lightcatcherbooks.com). Black Sea underwater archeology has made great strides in documenting a vast and sudden flood, but it may take decades before scientists can arrive at conclusions. Some so-called myths may become facts, and some currently taught facts may become myths. Perhaps it is time for the Genesis language thesis to be reexamined.

Readers allergic to God are allowed to take the Agnostic approach of an Intelligent Designer who does not make moral demands. It is only the Atheist position that is threatened here. A religious reader is allowed to celebrate a deepened sense of Creation, even a new respect for divinity in a new realm: language. This book articulates no follow-up ideas about the language of revelation or of a metaphorical Biblical people (the Hebrews) who spiritually impact upon all peoples. Any such conclusions are the reader's prerogative.

It would be nice if an agnostic reader finishes this book with a new sense of respect for the music and meaning of human communication. The agnostic may gain some respect for an Edenic language, even if not for some first modern humans named Adam and Eve who were placed in an Eden. At least treating Eden as a metaphor, this reader may feel more connected to other humans. All children of Adam are Edenic. All humans still think in Edenic. In this significant way all Earth peoples are Hebrews. Only a handful are Hebrews in the narrower linguistic sense. Everyone else should feel spiritual empowerment here, should feel ingathered, included by an Intelligent Designer who wanted their language and culture to exist.

No fundamentalist should feel left behind or vaguely threatened.

No fearful minister should insist that "the Bible is Greek to me." No fearful rabbi should think that Hebrew loses something when it is so easily linked to Greek or English. Fear of learning new tricks is only for old dogs. Let the tenured linguists and published lexicographers fear Edenics. Edenics involves a science-based faith, not a faith-based science – so let us put any doctrinal differences aside.

Are those who see the engineering of an Intelligent Designer or Divine Being in Edenics really the fanatics? On the contrary, serious readers of Edenics may find that believers in secular theories about the origin of ratiocination (the uniquely human ability to think and speak) are the alchemists of voodoo science, the die-hard fanatics of a soon-bygone era. It is the atheists who have taken a blind leap of faith into nihilism, and have missed the elaborate patterning that makes it obvious that language in its pristine state – Edenic, as best documented in Biblical Hebrew – has been created by the same unparalleled Engineer of anatomy, chemistry and physics.

Whether the field is geology or entomology (bugs, not words), scientists excel at WHATS, but avoid WHYS. Secular revelation's first commandment is "Evolution is the Lord thy God." The priests of godlessness can tell us that porpoises have leg-bones, and were once land creatures, but not WHY most species don't simply fail to survive as not the "fittest." WHY does the fossil record show no land mammals in the million-year process of becoming marine animals? The possibility of a Creator instantly morphing or "evolving" several species who couldn't make it to Noah's ark and allowing them to survive the Flood as sea creatures is not considered. The possible existence of a Higher Being who might care for the survival of all His creatures – even humans – is not in the equation.

> Secular science has eliminated the consideration of any divine care that may be behind Genesis, like the engineered (not accidental or mutation-related) adaptability of the created animal "kinds." For us talking bipeds, attention should be on the de-evolution of the original human programming language.

DIVIDING THE LANGUAGE

This Big Bang of language diversity was to have happened at Babel – traditionally breaking up the language of Eden into 70 ur-(original) language families. To follow the 70, see Genesis 10 where 70 ur-nations are listed. Then see Genesis 46:27, where there is a symbolic count of 70 children of Jacob enter the Diaspora, and Deuteronomy 32:8

where this symbolic number is equated to the original nations. Seventy also comes up as 70 trees at a wilderness oasis, and with 70 Tabernacles sacrifices – both times repeating the theme that the tiny Hebrews are a teaching metaphor, a unique but universal people. All these seventies echo the pre-Hebrew key event of pre-history, where our Edenic language was diversified into 70 national streams. The seventy original spin-offs have since continued to de-evolve into the 6,000 languages counted today.

When the scholars of the *American Heritage Dictionary* put out their chart of Proto-Indo-European and its derivatives they have thirteen branches coming from that theoretical, primeval ancestor language. These include Balto-Slavic, Italic (pre-Latin), Hellenic (pre-Greek), Indo-Iranian (pre-Sanskrit), and some extinct branches called Tocharian A and B. There is no written evidence that languages older than Sanskrit or Greek ever existed, so there is a possibility that Edenics can prove that Sanskrit and Greek, etc. were some of the 70 original spin-offs of Edenic at the Big Bang of Babel. When Genesis 10 lists the subfamilies of Japheth (ancestor of the Indo-Europeans) the total is fourteen (remarkably close to the AHD's thirteen subdivisions of Indo-European).

If Tocharian A and B (little known dead languages) are actually not sister languages, or if Iranian is later deemed to not be a sister language of Sanskrit, then the number of Indo-European languages goes up to fourteen, and exactly matches the listed divisions of the sons of Japheth.

It is reasonable to match up Genesis' Javan (pronounced Yavan) with the Ionians (Hellenics), and Madai with the Medes (Iranians). Gomer does sound like Cimmerian (Celtics), Tiras like (the since dead) Thracian, and Meshech might echo Moscow (Slavic). Researchers with a better grasp of ancient history will work the identities out, but it would be interesting to hear how historical linguists imagine that Genesis got so much of the picture correctly.

Genesis 10 lists 26 divisions of Shem (Semitic languages), and 30 of Ham (Hamitic languages). Current classification lumps together a Hamito-Semitic language superfamily, also called Afro-Asiatic. But the one constant of all sciences, astrophysics to linguistics, is that theories will constantly shift every several years. Perhaps Edenics will help us understand how families like Amerind (native American) or Austronesian might be better classified, and how they might be related to Near Eastern or African languages.

One factor in reclassification is Genesis topography, where no huge migrations were necessary. The single landmass (the "dry land" of verse 9) split up and provided isolated homelands for the new national-linguistic clans created at the Tower of Babel (Genesis 10:25). Continental Drift began at the Deluge, but like language diversity, it continues today. No Native Americans (now reduced to only three linguistic groups) had to hoof it over the Bering Straits, or make other Kon-Tiki odysseys of thousands of miles.

The "dryness" (Genesis 1:9) was later split up by the catastrophic bursting of "the foundations of the deep." The Deluge was no mere category 5 hurricane or regional tsunami. Genesis 10:25 refers to this breakup "in the days of Peleg," indicating that major topographic upheavals occurred in the 239 years that he lived. According to tradition, Peleg died in year 1996 after the Creation of Adam, the year of the Tower of Babel phenomenon. The suddenly-formed linguistic clans at Shinar (later Babel) only needed to cross relatively narrow waterways. But with time, the then-rapid continental drift carried them far apart.

Current historical linguistics carefully figures in migration distance, as if (switching to zoology) the African and Indian elephants evolved separately, instead of being one antediluvian herd that was separated by the newly-formed seas and continents.

Perhaps some Hamitic, melanin-blessed clans similarly found themselves separated by a vast ocean, when their ancestors had merely crossed a narrow gulf. Like the two elephant camps, one group of Cushite-like Hamites found themselves centuries later in distant India, while most of them settled what became the Horn of Africa.

Therefore, the geographical assumptions of historical linguists may need to consider alternate timelines.

In addition, linguistics classification is largely grammatical. The lexical structure, phonemes (sounds) as molecules of meaning are not known to exist. After fighting Edenics for a few decades, younger linguists will say that Edenics was "self-evident."

Joseph A. O'Donnell reports that In ***The Power of Babel:*** *A Natural History of Languages* by John McWhorter. (Perennial/ Harper Collins, 2001) the author speculates about a "language of Adam and Eve" or Proto-World:

> We will never know any words of the Proto-World. The family proto-languages that we can construct only go back several thousand years in time, whereas the first language originated ...more than 150,000 years ago.

Orthodox evolutionists could never find the language of Adam and Eve in Genesis, since they are concerned with the grunts of pre-hominid knuckle-walkers. Less rigid evolution scientists of the past had no trouble conceding that human language was a mysterious "gift." *The Origin of Speeches* does not insist that scientists accept early Genesis as Scripture or history, but it does want to make the case for Intelligent Design in language.

Scientists don't consider WHYS, but WHY might a Creator of a single human language fragment this precious gift and allow nations to talk past each other in Babel-babble? The Bible suggests that it was decided on high to kickstart multinational human history and not let Earth become the single-minded dominion of the Saddam Hussein of his time (Nimrod, the first tyrant).

The Creator behind Genesis did not want the world marching in lockstep – especially to the dictates of a human. Red China had an easier time orchestrating its millions of subjects than did the former USSR. This is largely because the Soviet Union's Babel of diversity was harder to control. Our marvelous human diversity, even religious diversity, was the divine plan. Yes, unity is good, but it is something that we humans must strive to attain after several difficult millennia. Like the exile from Eden, Babel was a Fortunate Fall. In the Creator's plan for human history, we who speak and think differently must arrive at consensus. If Zephaniah's vision is correct, the modest beginning of Edenics begun here may help a fractured planet lurch towards the spiritual and ethical unity of a glorious future. Even atheists or Buddhists with no respect for Genesis may one day acknowledge that all human words are cognates, all men are brothers, and that language was a gift from an Intelligent Designer.

DE-EVOLUTION

This will begin when we all see that human languages did get spun off from Edenic. This first language, like life itself, is too well designed to have evolved by itself. Of course Darwin's finches "evolved" diverse bills for their different environments. The genes' adaptability was part of the design, not the result of accidental mutation. We will see Edenic letters likewise adapting, mutating and shifting according to the known givens of linguistics. With language diversity, after a Big Bang at Babel, dialect making, de-evolution, took its natural course.

De-evolution is the way of nature. The religious myth of Evolution is a marvelous belief system for atheists. Apes accidentally learn to think and speak. Things get better by themselves. Do they? Sadly, science observes that there is entropy in the world. Winter follows summer; there is birth and death: a black frame around life to force us to make our lives into a work of art. Life was not intended to be an endless stroll in a garden of hedonism.

Entropy, that which drives everything to eventually break down, is certainly evident in the constant creolization or pidginization of language. The de-evolution of language, the breaking down of a parent language into dialects, is the rule. There is no evidence of languages progressing, magically coming out of Africa as apes began to lose hair and stand erect, as the "I love Lucy" anthropologists imagine. We all know how Latin broke up into French, Italian, Spanish and several other Romance dialects-turned-languages.

The elaborate tracings of our many Earth languages back to a Proto-World or Mother Tongue involved much excellent and accurate work by recent historical linguists. There is only one small error on the secular family tree of languages – involving one minor branch of West Semitic called Hebrew. The forest was obscured by the trees; the roots were mistaken for a branch.

On the surface, where academic research ended, Hebrew seems to be just another Semitic language that developed centuries later than Akkadian or Ugaritic. Professors of Hebrew are not poets nor Bible believers nor scientists. In just two more chapters you will know more about Hebrew than they ever dared to imagine. But it's more complex than just grammar-minded tree surgeons losing the ability to be forest rangers. Unlike Edenic,

Post-Biblical Hebrew DOES (on the surface) look like a later Semitic language. In grammar and vocabulary, Post-Biblical Hebrew resembles Arabic. In a few chapters, however, it will be clearly demonstrated how Arabic is a later tongue, showing all the signs of Babel-babble from its Edenic parent. Arabic is just as spun-off from Edenic as were Japanese, Quechua or Greek, but it better resembles the core vocabulary and grammar of Hebrew.

True, Edenic, the Proto-Earth language that researchers know must have existed (but despair of ever finding),is ten generations older than even Noah. It was difficult to spot Edenic within Hebrew, when Hebrew's links to non-Semitic roots were not sufficiently sought.

If one buys the conventional wisdom about the evolution of language, it is impossible to imagine that Hebrew might be the closest language to Proto-Earth. Hebrew, as the archeological record would suggest, did not appear until the Late Bronze Age. Even Genesis places Abram, who later became Abraham the founder of the Hebrew clan, ten generations **after** Noah. Even in the Tower of Babel scenario, Abram was alive and might have had his own Edenic language "confused." Abram is called a Chaldean, son of Terach the Chaldean. It would seem more logical to assume that Hebrew was a dialect that broke off from Mesopotamian roots.

ECONOMICAL LANGUAGE

Edenics theory sees it differently. A comparison of vocabulary with Sumerian, Akkadian, Ugaritic, Aramaic or Chaldean shows that these are cumbersome corruptions, and that Edenic is the pristine, more economical, thus earlier language. Such evidence will be seen later when we explore the different hallmarks of Babel-babble or language "confusion." Edenic is not merely simple, logical and natural, it IS simplicity, logic and nature. "I shall descend" is said in Edenic and Modern Hebrew in just three letters: *Aleph-Resh-Dalet*, ארד AyRaiD. (R-D means "going down" just as a **RAD**ISH or ROOT grows downwards.)

Historical linguists were not looking for any uniqueness in Hebrew, to put it mildly. Their "simpler means younger" rule for languages is true for every other language in the world. The seventy ur-languages were more complex, and the dialects that broke off from them were simplified. (Compare Sanskrit to Hindi.) Historical linguistics is most justified in classifying the simpler languages as later ones, and assuming that Hebrew appeared much later than Proto-Semitic.

To use the planet's best documented example, English is simplified and later than German – but this happened over many centuries and migration miles. At least from dictionaries, we have a passing acquaintance with Old English and Middle English. Similarly, all post-Babel language change was gradual and very human. It involves much less of the dramatic changes that we shall see in future chapters.

Such changes of root letter locations are evident in noting that Abram's Chaldean, like Basque or Quechua, was spun off from Edenic at Babel. The difference in the rate of pre-historic (Tower of Babel) versus historic language change is parallel to the sudden and drastic changes in topography and animal (intelligently designed) evolution during and after the era of the Deluge. Scientists are aware that a six-year-old recovers from a broken leg much faster than a sixty-year-old, yet carbon dating of ancient artifacts is based on contemporary rates.

Whether or not the historical linguists understandably erred in dating Hebrew as later than the language of Akkad (mentioned in Genesis), the Edenics thesis may have a problem suggesting that Abram the Chaldean spoke the unadulterated language of Adam. In the Edenics scenario the one, factory-installed language program (Edenic) for Modern Humans (Adam and Eve) was diversified with a neurological disturbance at Shinar (later Babel). As we shall note in later chapters, root letters and their sequence were not just scrambled and shifted, but different peoples, the founders of different cultures, recalled and/or used different (scrambled Edenic) terms to describe similar things. New languages were formed with new grammars, not just bent vocabulary. Each new linguistic clan, later to form a national group, thought differently.

If Abram was somehow immune to Babel-babble, then why call him a Chaldean? If he, too, was affected by Babel-babble, then how could Abram have founded a clan of Hebrew speakers? Would not his Hebrew clan speak, at most, a dialect break-off of Chaldean? Did angels or some supernatural source teach the man who would later be

Abraham the language of paradise lost? Some of the more mystical Bible commentators assume so. This book will neither duck the question nor fall back on an answer that rationalists would laugh at.

Observing the traditional timeline, it is easy to presume that Shem, son of Noah, never lost his Edenic language. Shem and his son, Ever, are thought to have taught Edenic (or *Ivrit*) to Abram. (Many believe that עברית *Ivrit* or Hebrew means the language of עבר Ever, that is, the pre-Flood, pre-Babel Edenic tongue of Adam and Noah.) The *Ivrit*-teaching theory is not Scripture but *Midrash* or lore. Tradition even notes the cave in Sefad (Northern Galilee) where this took place. Of course, the recorded longevities and the dates showing that Shem (b. 1558 of Creation – d. 2158) and Abraham (born in 1948 – d. 2123) shared 175 years of life are not usually considered when pondering a pre-Babel language or the mysterious appearance of Hebrew. Tales of the impossible re-appearance of Hebrew in the 20th Century would also set a 9th or 19th Century skeptic laughing. [All chronologies are taken from Kaplan's *The Living Torah*.]

Abram was a youngster of 48 at Babel, so his Edenic could well have been lost. Old Shem was a mature 438. Perhaps other old-timers might have retained Edenic too, but only Shem (meaning "name" or "repute") wanted to perpetuate the old, revered language with his son Ever, and with his spiritual successor, the future Abraham.

The Shem/Ever scenario allows Abram to be the founding father of the Hebrews, the *Ivri* clan (meaning "Othersiders" or the speakers of Ever's language – with Ever likely the last natural Edenic speaker).

GETTING WHYS

A literal Bible believer might unquestionably accept as fact that a divinely programmed language of Eden was divinely dispersed at Babel, at language diversity's initial Big Bang. But how do the secularists explain the history of language?

Well, scientists don't really do WHYS, like "WHY is there human language? " or "WHY are there separate languages? " They would say that The Tower of Babel is an etiological myth invented to answer the problem of language diversity; akin to the Prometheus fable to explain the existence of fire. Why do so many distant, ancient cultures have the myth of a global deluge and the myth of a single Mother Tongue that was scrambled? They're not sure, but they know they don't deal with WHYS.

The now-debunked scientists who reigned during the first two centuries of linguistics would say that separate human stocks (races, etc.) evolved from separate simian species and troops of apes. Naturally, each race had their own verbal signals evolved from millions of years of gesturing and grunting.

After the racist monkey business fell out of favor, some contemporary psychologists (see Dunbar below) posit that the conspiratorial disguising of languages with new dialects promotes select allegiances, an evolutionary trait we continue from our grooming, gossiping past as monkeys. But, like Ruhlen (see below), Dunbar also accepts the contemporary conclusion of historical linguists and geneticists that a universal, primeval Mother Tongue **did exist**. WHY, then, did that first language break up into the separate language families that subsequently de-evolved into the 6,000 dialects or tongues that we have today?

Again, WHY is the province of theology, not science.

Instead of any initial Big Bang of language diversity requiring some non-human help, it is easier to throw in several zeros and to assume that everything was human and natural, and took a few millennia.

It is certainly beyond the province of science to speculate WHY this naked ape "evolved" a unique, floating throat bone (the hyoid bone) to enable speech far more sophisticated than dolphins, or than other species that also coordinates hunting and gathering. WHY evolve audible creatures like Luciano Pavoratti or readable ones like William Shakespeare? Scientists don't like WHYS. It is most unscientific to speculate about an intended, engineered world of words, with thinking and speaking, language, literature, or even, Heaven forbid, an Intelligent Designer wanting to engage the speaking species with special writings.

Ok, then, just the HOW. The unique hyoid bone is a delicate, bone of the throat that allows human speech. How did Evolution will the hyoid bone into existence? How did random mutation allow caveman X to replace grunts and gestures with the sentence, "Let's hide in the tall grass and ambush the elk when they come to the stream to drink."

About that hyoid bone: The oldest skeletal remains EVER found ANYWHERE, with an intact hyoid bone – indicating a true human who spoke rather than the monkey-business of archaeological skullduggery – was found in the Carmel Caves near Haifa, Israel. In other words, the actual evidence indicates that, until proven otherwise, the oldest human speech was proto-Semitic. (An on-line search of this oldest speaker's skeleton –called Moshe – can be found on various websites and includes photos. The Carmel Caves are called the Kabera Caves.)

If the same remains were dug up in India, China or Africa, the so-called Indo-European roots in many dictionaries would be traced back to ancient forms of Sanskrit, Sino-Tibetan or Nilo-Saharan. You will later see many obvious examples of Indo-European roots that are mildly disguised forms of Edenic. Linguistics is about the essence of cultures and races, so it is naturally susceptible to racism. Beyond an aversion for WHYS, there is a clear antipathy for anything that points to an Intelligent Designer. The Edenics thesis would get better play if it were in *The Anglo-Saxon Chronicles*. Unfortunately, Genesis is attached to a politically incorrect book called the Bible.

As noted above, the most intelligent, educated minds of previous centuries accepted Genesis 11 as fact. After Darwinism, top scholars rejected and supplanted the Bible's take on language. Only in recent years has the weird science of the often-racist 19th Century been eclipsed by more thoughtful and objective work that envisions and has begun to document the overwhelming evidence of the existence of an ancient, global Mother Tongue. But contemporary secular linguists still assume that Proto-Earth or the world's Mother Tongue somehow evolved and de-evolved with no superhuman engineering.

Langacker (see below) expresses the old, largely dismissed view that words evolved. Words are supposed to echo sounds. But they do only for a few words like "ding" or "chickadee." The Bow-Wow theory predicts that languages would have names for dogs that sound like a bark. None do, so the Bow-Wow theory is for the dogs.

Langacker notes how dozens of unrelated languages have papa-type words for father and mama-sounding words for mother. His generation believed that these M and P sounds were the earliest made by babies, and so they evolved into terms for parents. Academics don't have many babies, or they'd know that "gaga" is the first baby sound. And there are no mother or father words like "gaga."

Of course, those tracing the roots of language would not bother searching the first language ever called the Mother Tongue in recorded history. *Aleph-Mem*, אם EM, the Edenic mother, reverses to מי MaY (from), as "from" a matrix or mother. The Edenic father, *Aleph-Bhet*, אב ABH, reverses (as in the common phenomenon of metathesis later to be explored) to בא BAh (come, as in "come from." The English preposition OF (from) reflects this. So does the Russian suffix –ov (Gorbach*OV*), a locative meaning "comes from." [MAMA] [PAPA]

Only Edenic offers the sense of sounds, the meaning of our music. But linguists don't ask WHY a sound means something – unless it's like "ding," and rings a bell.

America's most prominent linguist, M.I.T. Professor Noam Chomsky, took linguistics to a higher level than the earlier Bow Wows. No one better demonstrated that language was innate. Of late, he did allude to the possibility that some superhuman alien must have hardwired the human brain for language. But he remains obsessively opposed to the Intelligent Design concept of Edenics, or anything remotely Biblical. Noam Chomsky authored several rabidly anti-Israel books, defended the 9-11 attacks, and, in the 1990s, launched attacks against *The Word* and an Edenics newspaper column (even calling the editor).

Psychoanalysis is not needed to see that he is rejecting his father, William Chomsky, a noted Hebraist. Noam should have been the preeminent Edenicist, but a pathological disdain for things Hebrew got in the way.

SECULAR RESEARCH

The dramatic turn towards the Monogenesis of Language theory would come from godless Russia, where the Bible is irrelevant, and where scientists had no such obsessive prejudice. Cover stories of several magazines broke the electrifying news that a team of Soviet linguists working since the 1960s had concluded that much of the world's languages were linked by a common past. These magazines include:

The Sciences May-June 1990, *U.S. News & World Report* November 5, 1990, and *The Atlantic Monthly* of April, 1991. It took decades of academic battles before the old guard relinquished their Darwinian myths. They still insisted that languages must have naturally evolved, but they had to admit that there was strong evidence for Monogenesis of Language – that there once was a single human language spoken by nearly all of humanity. See the final chapter here.

The Bible and Babel was on no one's radar screen. Even professors of Hebrew all taught that Hebrew was just a branch of West Semitic. True, it had not corrupted much, but that is because it was a largely unspoken language after Jeremiah's time. The professors of Semitic saw nothing striking about the amazingly unique Hebrew vocabulary that we will study here.

This new ancestral language super-family was called Nostratic – and, yes, it even linked Indo-European languages like English with Semitic tongues like Hebrew. This flew in the face of the old racist linguistics that assumed that Aryans (now called Indo-Europeans) and Semites developed language from different monkeys –the better-groomed ones, of course, becoming the Aryan or Indo-European people. Moreover, the Soviet scientists traced the geographical homeland of this one, common, prehistoric, ancestral language to a site very close to the Mt. Ararat landing site of Noah's ark.

If only some fundamentalist Christians or Jews were behind this research, Western academia could have torn them apart. But what could be said about atheist Soviets led by a Vitaly V. Shevoroshkin?

In the years that followed, the second of this 1-2 punch against the old linguistics theories was delivered by the pseudo-scientists' greatest foes – the hard scientists. Geneticists like

L.L. Cavilli-Sforza had done much to bring the old linguistics theory in line with new archeological data. Parallel studies in genetics research with the diverse mitochondrial DNA of many human populations concluded that the entire, widely varied family of Man came from the genes of a single female ancestor. "Mitochondrial Eve" she was named in a cover story of *Newsweek* on January 11, 1988. A good follow-up article for this is in the *Discover* magazine of August, 1990. The eminently readable Stephen Jay Gould has a fine piece on this in *Natural History*, February, 1989. The article's sub-title is "The threads of our linguistic history closely match the pattern of our biological development." Gould writes about the "acrimonious rebuttal and dismissal [of] most scholars [who] balk at the very thought of direct evidence for connections among the basic "linguistic phyla."

Suffice it to say that the strident enemies of Biblical thinking have not come to the Monogenesis of Language thesis willingly, and are not likely to easily embrace the further evidence of the veracity of Genesis 11.

Scientific theories come and go, but the geneticists findings about all modern humans coming from the genes of one woman appear to persist. The following is from *The New York Times* of May 13, 2005:

> "Everyone in the world can be placed on a single family tree, in terms of their mitochondrial DNA, because everyone has inherited that piece of DNA from a single woman, the mitochondrial Eve, who lived some 200,000 years ago." – Nicholas Wade

The number of zeroes that the theorists throw at their dating problems is of little consequence. Far more important is the fact that science has now made more acceptable the Genesis scenario of a single couple as the ancestors of all Modern Humans, the thinking and speaking *homo sapiens*.

When all the archaeological dust has cleared, remember the fact (stated above), that the oldest SPEAKING humans (with the hyoid bone) were found in Israel – and that until older remains are found elsewhere it must be presumed that the earliest speakers were, at least, proto-Semitic.

Today's leading linguists, Steven Pinker and Noam Chomsky, have done much to prove than the human brain is made for language acquisition. This did not result in their understanding that language, the brain, and the mouth and throat were ingeniously and purposefully created to make Man (and only Man) a thinker and speaker. Neuro-linguistic findings logically point to the engineering work of intelligent design. An Intelligent Designer is in the details, so readers unused to more technical material are asked to proceed with patience.

Our count of over 6,000 Earth languages took a major hit from the work of Stanford Professor, Joseph H. Greenberg (who passed away in 2001). First he proved that there were only eight true African languages, not hundreds, with scores of dialects deriving from the original eight "language superfamilies." Similarly, linguists counted hundreds of American Indian languages. Greenberg proved there were only three Amerind language superfamilies. The Biblical concept of 70 original spin-offs from Edenic was looking better. We can now call then the origins of language superfamilies. Needless to say, Greenberg's work was bitterly opposed for decades, and only now is considered solid.

History went full cycle on the Mother Tongue theory. Now, most contemporary linguists can accept Monogenesis of Language, thus even envisioning a prehistorical Proto-Earth language resembling the "mythical" Tower of Babel thesis of Genesis 11. In his book, *Grooming, Gossip, and the Evolution of Language,* Robin Dunbar does not even have to add a dozen zeros to the theoretical time line. He writes:

> "Babel may not have been so very long ago. The Tower of Babel was no
> myth: it really did exist … the myth-makers of ancient Israel seem to have
> been on to something. Linguists now believe that the world's languages
> do in fact have a common origin. However, the period of this common
> language long predates the building of the Tower of Babel."

It is remarkable that an historical linguist can have such a sure grasp of prehistory, when astrophysicists, for example, adjust their dating by several zeroes a few times a year. It's not easy to convince a secular bible scholar or Semiticist that the Bible doesn't follow many current theories of human chronology. See James Long's *The Riddle of the Exodus* for a strong demonstration of historical miscalculations (and antipathy to the Biblical record). In another famous example of such folly, scholars cannot see that the Babelonian Gilgamesh Epic of the Flood was obviously a later, inferior version of the Biblical record – not the reverse. More time and data will be needed until these deep anti-Biblical prejudices can be reduced by facts. But let clear-minded people rejoice that the theory of Monogenesis of Language, a major part of the Genesis 11 scenario, has finally come into acceptance.

There is much distance to go, however, from the acceptance of a Mother Tongue thesis, to proving that an actual language is that global Mother Tongue. It may sound difficult for a Martian to believe, but many Earthlings resist the idea that the only language describing the Tower of Babel is the closest thing to that Mother Tongue of Eden: Proto-Semitic, as best documented by Biblical Hebrew, is the language which we shall call Edenic.

Besides the impact of Edenic on the world's derivative languages, the other major part of Edenics exposition involves the unique, intelligently designed architectonics of Edenic / Biblical Hebrew itself. This includes built-in sound-alike synonyms and antonyms, which a humanly evolved vocabulary would never have. *The Origin of Speeches* will both reveal Edenic internally, structurally, as a science, as well as present external, etymological and historical evidence that Edenic is mankind's Mother Tongue.

When examining individual words, word families, or specific categories (like animal names) the reader can check the *E-Word CD Dictionary* to compare an Edenic etymon (source word) with the laboratory reconstructions of Proto-Indo-European roots, or other attempts to reconstruct a Mother Tongue like Nostratic or Proto-World. The reader can discern how much clearer and more versatile (bendable to daughter languages) are the source words that are not reconstructions, but actually exist in the Bible, and are so documented by chapter and verse. This book is not meant to preach to a choir, but, with cogent evidence and data, to inspire a curious, back-row congregant to get up and sing.

THE MYTH OF THE INDO-EUROPEAN ROOT

As the lexicographers readily admit, there never was a recorded Indo-European word. Proto Indo-European (PIE) is theoretical. The dictionary reader is fed imaginative reconstructions rather than provable fact. It's the Great White Hope of linguists. The linguists take actual words from Sanskrit, Greek, Latin, Old Germanic or Icelandic, etc. Then, in the lab, the linguists fabricate a never- spoken proto root that theoretically could have de-evolved and broken up into the recorded, actual words of vaguely similar sound and sense.

Consulting the *American Heritage Dictionary of Indo-European Roots*, (ed. by Calvert Watkins, Houghton Mifflin, Boston, 1985) can be painful or puzzling. The most incongruous words are grouped together with far less discernable sound or sense than the weakest of Edenic-English links. Reading the dictionary of Indo-European (IE) roots, or noting these theoretical "roots" in *The Word* or *E-Word CD Dictionary*, can at least be humorous. Especially if one knows the Biblical Hebrew word which would have neatly tied together the forced "cognates" of a bizarre entry. The Biblical Hebrew or ancient Semitic root word (etymon) is most often only a slight deviation from their fictional "root."

Citing the IE root in most entry of the *E-Word CD Dictionary* nonetheless reflects some fine work by the historical linguists. Many of the listed cognates are logical, and help to swell the number of words that have been spun off from the Edenic etymon that the IE root may or may not be alluding to. Especially here in the introductory phase of Edenic exposition, comparing the IE root to the Edenic etymon helps the reader judge between them.

So ends a brief, bumpy history of the Bible's language thesis. It is time for humans to breathe life back into the long comatose concept that language was engineered and given to Man at Eden – then diversified at Babel. This first chapter and book is only the first musket shot fired from the Lexington-Concord bridge. It is hoped that future generations of Edenic scholarship will make *The Origin of Speeches* look primitive.

Chapter One CONCLUSION

Because this chapter involved the theory and history of the Edenic thesis, it was largely discursive. Subsequent chapters will involve actual data and more active analysis.

There is an interesting article in the Science Times section of *The New York Times* of March 16, 2005 by Nicholas Wade called *"A Biological Dig for the Roots of Language."*

Here in 2005, the year 5764 since the creation of Man, it is reported that the alleged Proto-European-Root language is around 6,000 years old. Wade's article concerns a new approach for mapping the family tree of human languages besides comparative vocabularies. The new method is archeology-based and called " linguistic paleontology."

This involves noting similar cognates for technical words that may be dated by the era they were invented. The wheel is only some 5,500 years old, so it is important to use the Sanskrit *chakras*, meaning wheel or circle, and *kuklos*, meaning wheel or circle in Greek, in reconstructing a theoretical Indo-European root like "k'ek'los" (wheel, circle).

Then, the experts figure a likely timeline for the wheel and its name, matching what is known about the early culture and the archeological record.

Should historic linguists try to reinvent the wheel, or should they, Heaven forbid, take a cue from Genesis 11? The Hebrew wheel, גלגל GaLGahL, uses the GL sub-root from *Ayin-Gimel-Vav-Lamed*, עגול GHeeGOOL, circle (I Kings 7:23). [CYCLE] The mild letter-sound shifts that turned עגול GHeeGOOL or Edenic GH-GL into Greek KKL and Sanskrit CH-KR in the neuro-linguistic Big Bang of Babel-babble, are taken up in Chapter Four.

Chapter One ACTIVITIES

1. The introduction to the *E-Word* CD) – written in 1988 – describes the prevailing linguistics attitude towards the Biblical thesis and the Monogenesis of Language concept with imagery that evoked Nazi racism? What evidence of racism is there to justify the claim that 19th Century ideology affected the new field of linguistics?

2. In the Gospels, the book of *John* opens, "In the beginning was the word." Language, thinking and speaking, appears to be central to the Christian plan of Creation. What are the two crucial Hebrew Bible passages describing the past and future of Edenic language? How similar and different are the two traditions regarding language?

3. What important clues indicate that language and neurology appear to be engineered for each other? What especially makes this evident in the ways that Edenics perceives the Babel phenomenon?

4. Why did Darwinian, evolutionary thinking, present opposition to the Monogenesis of Language thesis? How and why did linguists eventually come to accept Monogenesis of Language?

5. If contemporary linguists can now accept the concept of one original language, by what natural means do they suppose we got over 6,000 different languages or dialects today?

6. How does the Haifa, Israel discovery of a prehistoric human skeleton with an intact hyoid bone make it difficult for academia to support the possibility of: 1) a Mother Tongue that is not proto-Semitic, 2) the popular theory that modern, (speaking) humans arose in Africa, or 3) that humans beyond the Near East had civilizations of equal antiquity.

7. How were atheist Soviet researchers the allies of a Biblical thesis of language?

8. The words for Mother and Father are identical in nearly every language. What is wrong with the linguists' old reason for this, and how is a Hebrew origin more logical? (You may supplement Chapter One readings with the ABBOT and MAMA entries in the *E-Word CD Dictionary*)

9. If language diversity was as much a part of Nature's plan as was the diversity of butterfly species, then why is the recent reduction of the number of actual languages (reclassifying 1000s of languages as merely dialects of superlanguages) any support for the Genesis/Edenic language thesis?

10. How viable is the traditional number of 70 original spins-offs from the language of Eden? Genesis 10's table of nations suggests the major divisions within Semitic, Hamitic and Japhetic languages. How close is secular historical linguistics (and genetic studies) to confirming this arrangement? (The recommended articles and the superfamily theories in the last two chapters here will be helpful.)

NOTES:

When this book was just a curriculum, it asked students to read certain books. Especially here in Chapter One, those recommended readings are useful for getting a wider background of the issues. This chapter's readings, therefore, will be preserved here:

Recommended Readings:

Langacker, Ronald D. *Language and Its Structure: Some Fundamental Linguistic Concepts*. Harcourt Brace Jovanovich, NY, 1973. Harcourt Brace

Ruhlen, Merritt. *The Origin of Language: Tracing the Evolution of the Mother Tongue*. Wiley, NY, 1994.

Three recent authors who can accept a Mother Tongue, but one which developed and diversified with no intelligent design:

1) Dunbar, Robin. *Grooming, Gossip, and the Evolution of Language.*
2) Pinker, Steven. *The Language Instinct: How the Mind Creates Language.*
3) McWhorter, John H. *The Power of Babel: A Natural History of Language.*

End-of-chapter questions from the former curriculum have been replaced by optional Activities. The Activities were made more important reading for those with no desire to test their comprehension or to do their own Edenic research. Formal schools or informal classes may want these Activities to be written out by students. Answers will be provided for teachers who request them.

Chapter Two

Borrowings

The First and Easiest Challenge to Bible-Less English

For a background on the topic of language borrowings, *one may look at the suggested readings of last chapter, the Langacker book, noting chapter 7, pages 179-189. Other introductory language texts will offer much on the topic of a language borrowing or incorporating words from another language. For a website on English* borrowings, *search: Kryss Tal.*

The Edenics thesis (Genesis 11:1) states that every human word is ultimately from the language of Eden, most similar to early Biblical Hebrew.

The most urbanized cultures, like Chinese, will have words that have changed the most, and are the most challenging to trace back to Edenic. The least urbanized, like Araona in the Amazon, are easiest to trace. No borrowings penetrated the Amazon before recent decades. China, however, was on the Spice Road, so it is possible that certain words were borrowed from Semitic merchants.

Edenics is about what was engineered and implanted in the human brain in pre-history, NOT about a few dozen words that got co-opted for historical reasons. The other chapters of this book are NOT concerned with mere borrowings. Borrowings are merely human. Even the amount of words borrowed from the Hebrew Bible is a matter of contention.

The better English dictionaries will inform you if an English word is a known loan word or borrowing from Hebrew. The Oxford English Dictionary (OED) is often aware of a Hebrew borrowing, but will usually obscure it with other Semitic words or with what they consider languages of equal antiquity. Besides antipathy for non-classical source words, the famous antipathy of secular scholars for the Bible makes it almost patriotic for a dictionary to hide a Hebrew borrowing. In the last century ignorance has surpassed antipathy as the major reason why an English word that echoes a word in the Hebrew

Bible would go unrecognized. Secular lexicographers do not adequately consider that English Bible readers were exposed to much Anglicized Hebrew for many centuries. Generations of rural Americans, like Abraham Lincoln, had only one book at home with which to learn the language. That one book was The Good Book. Examples of all these points will fill this chapter.

Edenic words are transliterated in this book. This allows students to follow the sound of the Hebrew words and roots.

WHICH ENGLISH WORDS HAVE BEEN BORROWED FROM HEBREW?

Borrowings are those foreign words that one culture borrows from another. The Japanese *aisukuriimu* may seem like a funny way to spell "ice cream," but it, and all baseball or technology terms, were borrowed from the Americans. English became a significant contributor to Japanese vocabulary with the occupation after World War II. Borrowings are all about a historical meeting of two different languages and cultures. Edenic theory is about a time when all humans spoke the same language – so no foreign words could be borrowed. After Babel, Edenic is diversified and largely lost. Only a handful of peoples had much to do with Abraham's clan of Hebrews, and it would be millennia until Bible translations would spread a few mangled Hebrew words around the world.

We will soon encounter traces of prehistoric Edenic (not historic Hebrew) in distant and exotic lands. But this chapter aims to slowly introduce the new concept that Hebrew has greatly impacted English. The most modest and limited way to introduce this claim is with borrowings. We will note those limited number of acknowledged borrowings, and suggest that extensions of these are in order, and that many hundreds of English words might also be considered borrowings.

Everyone knows, and dictionaries acknowledge, that a few dozen Hebraisms were lifted right out of English Bibles. These words were merely transliterated Hebrew words, or Romanized in our familiar Latin or English letters, and not translated – words like the following:

Alphabet (yes, our very letters are acknowledged to be from the Semitic אלף-בית *Aleph-BeT* – more on this later),

Abacus (the א-ב-ג *Aleph-Bet-Gimel*, or Hebrew ABC's, are also the 1-2-3 sequence of numbers – since every letter had a numeric value. Do you think Latin *oct* (number 8) sounds like Hebrew ח K[H]eT (number 8) by coincidence?

Aloe, a non-European plant, is an example one of many Biblical flora or fauna words that most dictionaries miss or cover up. The ALOE is clearly from אהל AHahL (Numbers 24:6), but the *Oxford English Dictionary* (OED) gives the Latin and Greek, and writes that the word is "perhaps ultimately from a Dravidian language."

Amen אמן (believable truth – see the lexical truth-bending below)

Armageddon הר מגדו (Har Megiddo, the Mount Megiddo of prophecy)

Babble בבל (a confusion of tongues, so confused that dictionaries don't acknowledge Babel as a derivative)

Cherub כרוב (loving angels, as atop the Ark of the Covenant)

Bedlam בית לחם (from a hospital in Bethlehem – say Bethlehem fast in a Cockney accent)

Behemoth בהמה (BeHaiMaH is a beast in Genesis 1:25, but some dictionaries try the awkward cover-up of citing Egyptian *p-chew-mau*, a water ox)

Cider (from שיכר SHaiK[H]aR, intoxicating drink, which is even sounder as the source of Japanese *sake*)

Cinnamon (from קנמון QiNMoaN – there are a dozen lesser known spices, etc. that could go here)

Coral (from גורל GoRaL, pebble)

Eden (used for any paradise – עדן [A]iDeN means pleasure, as does Greek *hedone*, but PhDs without this book don't know that *Ayin* shifts to H, so that Eden is the source of HEDONISM)

Gauze (from cotton grown by the Philistines of Gaza – it's important to note that *Ayin-Zayin-Hey* Gaza is pronounced as עזה [A]ZaH in the Bible)

Hallelujah הללויה (praise the Lord)

Jew (from the first syllable of Judean, and before that, from יהודה YeHooDaH, Judah)

Jockey (see all the words from יעקב Ya[A]QoBh, Jacob, below)

Jot (the tiny letter י *Yod* – Y is always J to Westerners)

Jubilee (the 50-year יובל YoVaiL, when everyone is on sabbatical)

Kibbutz קבוץ (a word from Modern Israel, meaning a collective farm – though the root is Biblical)

Kosher (ritually fit or "proper" even in slang, but the Greek *katharos*, pure, is the source of CATHARSIS, which is ultimately from כשר KaSHaiR)

Leviathan לביתן (the large sea creatures of Psalms)

Manna מנה (the mysterious food for the wandering Israelites in the wilderness)

Maudlin (from Magdalene, which is from מגדל MIGDaL, tower)

Messiah (from משיח MoSHeeYaK[H], anointed), **Rabbi** (my teacher, who knows רב RaBH, much)

Sabbath שבת (the day of rest testifying to Creation)

Sapphire (Hebrew ספיר SaPeeYR – *Webster's* tries to hide this common Biblical gem behind Sanskrit *sanipraya*, dear to Saturn)

Satan שתן (a verb of impeding in the Pentateuch, but a character in Job)

Sodomy (sexual deviation named for סדום Sodom)

Seraph שרף (a fiery angel)

Torah תורה (teaching)

There are a few dozen technical terms or proper nouns that are obviously from the Bible, and are acknowledged as such. An example would be Moloch. This is not well known, but could have as many useful applications from the more popular allusions to Classical myth (like a *Herculean* task). *Webster's* defines Moloch as "a god of the ancient Phoenicians and Ammonites, to whom children were sacrificed by burning." Definition number two is "anything regarded as demanding terrible sacrifice." If the Bible were not so neglected, the borrowing Moloch could be applied to anything from taxes to the perversion of faith that has Palestinian parents pushing their children in front of Israeli fire.

Some dictionaries will include other possible borrowings, like MACABRE from מכבי Maccabee, but the general rule is that, from ignorance of the Bible, malice towards it, or both, reference books avoid crediting a word to Hebrew whenever possible. Although the Maccabees are a well-known group of fighters who have had many stage dramatizations of their bloody exploits, and even though Maccabees comprises two books in the Bible's Apocrypha, some references cite, "Greek and probably Aramaic, *maqqaba*, hammer." These "hammer" terms are from מכבת MaQeBHeT (hammer – Isaiah 44:12) and back to the MK root, מכה MaKeH, to strike (Judges 15:8). [MACCABRE] Such cover-ups of obvious Hebrew borrowings are not rare. In fact, even the first word above, ALPHABET, is often credited to Greek alone, as if those venerated illiterates didn't borrow the letters from the Phoenicians (an insignificant people, but a useful academic euphemism for Israelites). Also, once we keep in mind that ALPHABET is a borrowing from Hebrew, we must extend this to Alpha rays, a Beta software or a river Delta. At all these derivatives, and at their "Alphabet" entry itself the dictionaries won't remind you that the word has roots recorded in the Bible.

The self-congratulatory prejudice of Western academics is called Eurocentrism. Universities have recently recognized worthwhile literature by writers other than dead white men, and now much new research in many fields reveals than non-Europeans were often many centuries ahead in various sciences. Note the many science and math terms from Arabic, for example. Even the celebrated "classical" building column was a staple of Egyptian architecture when early Greeks lived in huts. The Romans are correctly accused of borrowing heavily from the "classic" Greeks. But the Ionians and Hellenics before them borrowed much from the Near East. Creative borrowing is admirable, however. Linguistic *borrowing* made English the world's richest vocabulary. So the Greeks are to be congratulated for borrowing and using the Semitic letters, numbers, and scientific principles that made Western culture possible.

According to Edenics, no human society can claim credit for our neural ratiocination, language, even alphabets and literacy. Edenics charts an engineering feat similar to whatever Intelligence created the natural world. This new humility does not detract from the centuries of chauvinism that mars the history of language study.

Where the topic is literacy, the Western guardians of culture plainly display their biases – as evident in this and the previous chapter. The watchmen atop the ivory towers of Academe do not seem pleased to be known as excellent borrowers, and have a propensity to deny any Semitic roots. Here the secularists are too reminiscent of Replacement Theology. The antipathy is much more compounded when letters and words not only seem to come from non-blondes, but from a culture associated with the nightmare of the secular worldview – the Bible.

Once a word's etymology cites a Latin or Greek form, and maybe an Arabic one as well, many dictionaries are fond of citing a Persian, and recently, a Sumerian term that is roughly equivalent. This is because Persians – and Sumerians, too (so they claim) – are Indo-Aryans. The sinking Eurocentric establishment is entitled to crown pretenders as the next Great White Hope. (For example, the Sumerian ass is *anse*, a post-Babel metathesis of Edenic אתון A$OAN, she-donkey. [ASSININE] Pre-2010 dictionaries try hard for etymologies that claimed words as Western. The crusading guardians of lexicography who try to rescue etymologies from the Semites might be seen as practicing anti-Semiticism.

For example, this what the Kryss Tal website says about CHECKMATE:

> This is a term in chess. It is from the Farsi language spoken in Iran and Afghanistan. The original phrase is **SHAH-K-MATE** (every syllable pronounced) which means "The King is Dead".

The word **SHAH** means a "king" as in the last monarch (or SHAH) of Iran. **MATE** has the same root as the English "murder" and the Spanish *matador* (killer). The word came via French (where the **SH** became a **CH**) and into English.

The etymology doesn't tell you that even Arabic *sheik* (tribal leader) is from זקן ZaQaiN, elder, tribal leader (Leviticus 24:2) and/or from שוע SHOOaGH, nobleman (Job 34:19). The end-*Noon* of זקן ZaQaiN is dropped in *sheik,* but the letters are shifted in the equivalent Algonquin Native American terms for tribal leader: *sachem* and *sagamore.* The ז *Zayin* shifts to S, the ק *Koof* to CH and G, and the נ *Noon* to M.

That covers the first half of CHECKMATE, where the SH-K means "king." The MT "dead" half of CHECKMATE is even more clearly from the Hebrew מת MaiT, dead, seen in verses like (Genesis 42:38) [CHECKMATE]

Many borrowings, even pure mere anglicizations of Hebrew words, go unrecognized. Although the Saturday day of rest is the most widespread Biblical legacy, Spanish-Portuguese *sabado*, Italian *sabato*, Rumanian *simbata*, Russian *subota* (similar in Czech, Polish and Serbo-Croatian) or Indonesian *Sabtu* are not always acknowledged to have come from שבת SHaBaT (Sabbath).

This radical idea of a 24-hour work stoppage is formalized in the Ten Statements or Commandments (Exodus 20:8), but is alluded to with the same *Shin-Bet-Tahf* שבת at Day Seven (Genesis 2:2). Then again, English dictionaries will not mention the Bible's SHaBaT when discussing obvious derivatives of SABBATH, like SABBATICAL.

In some cases, it may have been forgotten that a Biblical Hebrew word was involved. The Spanish word for religious holiday is *pascua.* The French and Italian Easter is *Paques.* In these cases, both the Catholic church and European culture are uncomfortable with the Hebrew roots of Christianity – and so they do not recognize any debt to Hebrew פסח PeSaK[H], Passover, when a **paschal** lamb was offered. In Scottish dialect, a **pasch egg** is an Easter egg.

Intelligent, independent-minded Catholics, as well as more Hebrew-Bible oriented Protestants, Freemasons, Sabbatarians, Messianics and Noahides will revel in the newly discovered Hebrew Bible roots in this book. Bahais have always believed that all languages were one. Spiritual competition is discouraged by our new science of Edenics which proves that all people are children of the same ancestors. Humans are בני אדם B'NaY ADahM – Children of Adam in Edenic.

If only the exposition of Edenics occurred centuries ago, there would be no fear and loathing of a language perceived to belong to a particular, rival tribe. This aversion to Hebrew sources and/or the ignorance of them prevents etymologists (who investigate the sources of words) from making simple, logical extensions of known Hebrew borrowings.

From the list of common borrowings above, let's consider the word AMEN. In your dictionary the word after AMEN is AMENABLE (acceptable, agreeable). אמן AhMaiN is the common Edenic refrain of belief, affirmation, and verified acceptability. This, too, is what AMENABLE infers. The dictionary, however, offers the Latin etymon *minari* (to threaten). It is all too clear who feels threatened by what. The scholars would not or could not see AMEN in AMENABLE. Will Edenics need an "Amen Corner" of supporters to knock out these incorrect cover-ups from our reference books?

(Of course, Edenics is far more than a lobbying effort to put Biblically-correct dictionaries on our shelves. It's an in-your-face, in-your-brain assault on the idea that speaking *homo sapiens* are accidents with monkey great-uncles.)

An another common Anglicization of a Biblical word involves the יובל JUBILEE. The Jubilee year (Leviticus 25: 8-17) is signaled by the blowing of the יובל YoBHaiL or – as י *Yod* is commonly Anglicized as J – יובל JoB[H]aiL (ram's horn) by the JUBILANT Israelites. Latin *jubilare* (to exult, raise a shout of joy) is clearly an echo of the Biblical practice. The ancient Romans were not observing Biblical mores, nor were they celebrating the invention of pizza. The Romans didn't have a Bible or need one to come up with a JBL word for exultation. This root was in their cerebral lexicon since the ancestors of the Italics (pre-Latin) migrated south and east of Babel, calling all the other jabbering clusters of migrants a bunch of "barbarians." [BALL]

To our reference books, pagans may JUBILATE, but Bible believers may not make the original JBL joyful sound unto the Lord. The lexicographers simply hoped that dictionary readers were as Biblically illiterate as they were. Surely the Edenic ׳ *Yod* as J was not going to fool those who have heard of יובל YOABHail, JUBILEE, at least not all of them, all the time.

In fact, there are so few "J" words in Latin that the historic ties between *judex* (English **Judge**) and Judea ought to be clear. The first judges were Judeans, and even יהודה YeHOODaH (Judah) himself was the first judge in recorded history. (Genesis 38) This episode was famous enough for Bible-reader Nathaniel Hawthorne to fashion the climactic scene of *The Scarlet Letter*, with Reverend Dimmesdale and Hester Prynne echoing Judah's condemning Tamar for having his baby out of wedlock. This is arguably the key scene in one of the greatest works of American Literature. But because the borrowed plot line involved the Bible, not some Greek myth, my graduate English professors were unfamiliar with this remarkable parallel.

The best ways to cover up Hebrew borrowings is to attribute the word to a later or another source – anything is apparently better than listing the word's ultimate biblical source.

ABBOT and ABBACY aren't listed as Hebrew borrowings, since there's the Aramaic *abbah,* father, and dictionaries don't want to go further to Hebrew אב ABH (father). Technically, usage-wise, reference books are allowed to cite only the particular language from which a word passed into English. If a word came to English from German, however, dictionaries will go on to cite Old High German roots that English speakers didn't actually use, and that do not resemble the word in question. The *American Heritage Dictionary* will even cite the theoretical laboratory invention of an Indo-European root – that was never spoken. So, at best, there is much inconsistency here.

To be consistent in **etymology** (which comes from the Greek word for truth), linguists should more often give the Hebrew root for many English borrowings attributed to other Semitic Languages. Especially in cases like the longer Aramaic *abbah* and the shorter Hebrew אב ABH. Linguists find it difficult to recognize that the shorter term is the more pristine one, since they observe later slang to be a shorter version, a simplification of the earlier one. It is true that Modern English did simplify and shorten earlier, more cumbersome forms in Middle and Old English. From the Edenic viewpoint, such simplifications are steps backward in the right direction.

As we study some aspects of historical linguistics here, we shall see that languages like Aramaic or Germanic have added cumbersome prefixes and suffixes to the economical Edenic original. Also, this was not a matter of creolization of an earlier language, but in the neurological Big Bang that diversified the original human programming language into 70 spin-offs which devolved into our current 5,000 "languages." Yes, English has gotten simpler over the centuries. That's because the older forms were from freshly corrupted Edenic, whether those older sources were native Germanic, via Greek or Latin, or from borrowings from the Syriac, Ugaritic or Aramaic. As English evolves it actually gets closer, not further, from its Edenic roots.

A chapter could easily have been devoted to English slang words, many of which actually get closer to their original Edenic sound and sense. The main DRAG is the busiest street. This is listed in the the DIRECTION entry, and becomes a cognate of a score of similar foreign words from Edenic דרך DeReKH (road, way) see page 14.

The dozens of non-standard words (most of "unknown origin") to look up in the *E-Word CD Dictionary* include: BALL UP, to COP, to CREAM, GAL, JERK, KIBOSH, NIX, NUTS, PIZAZZ, to RAG, SKIDDOO, TOKE and TOOTS.

Chinese has been spoken uninterrupted for millennia in a dense, urban locale. It has therefore evolved and shortened the most. Single syllable sounds have so many meanings that they had to be differentiated by rising and falling accents. (There are, nonetheless, a few hundred multi-syllabic words with strong links to Edenic – see the foreign language section of the *E-Word CD*.)

Hebrew itself was not a spoken language for most of history, and so it evolved or corrupted relatively little since its Edenic origin. More on language change later. Now back to the culture wars surrounding borrowings.

Various dictionary publishers express these problematic attitudes and gaps in knowledge, but *Webster's* (not at all true to Noah Webster – as per last chapter) policy is evident in its definition of JUDEA: "a part of southern Palestine under Roman rule." A land of historic impact should be defined by a brief period of foreign rule? But, such is a sneering Eurocentrism. There is no attempt to differentiate the centuries of Jerusalem sovereignty from the decades when the capital was the Roman *Judea Capitalina*. When *Webster's* has to include a Hebrew etymon, they will often indicate that the Hebrew etymon is from an "earlier" word in Egyptian, Sanskrit or Persian. (These last two, again, are Indo-Aryan).

While SATRAP is associated with Persian tyrants, *Webster's* offers, after the Old French, to cite the Old Persian phrase *khshathrapavan,* protector of the country. It doesn't have a ring to it, and I suspect the Hebrew שטר SHoDTaiR of Deuteronomy 16:18 (officer) might serve as a better ultimate source.

Instances of not citing a Hebrew etymon are especially blatant when ancient materials are involved, like: CAMPHOR, JASPER, MYRRH, NITER, SCARLET, TAMARISK, and several more. In these cases, there is a Hebraism (Anglicized Hebrew word) readily available in the KJV that English Bible readers are familiar with. But the etymologists don't read the Bible, and don't seem to want the word "Hebrew" to appear.

The scholars behind etymology demand consistency for any challenging thesis, yet they are far from consistent themselves. From Ernest David Klein, editor of *A Comprehensive Etymological Dictionary of the Hebrew Language* (Macmillan, 1987), one discovers that Greek *phukos* (seaweed, rouge, red paint) and Latin *fucus* (a rock lichen used for a red dye – an English word too) were borrowed from Hebrew פוך FOOKH. *Phey-Vav-Khaf* פוך means reddish eye makeup, the "kohl" of II Kings 9:30, and is translated *fucus* in the Schoken concordance.

Klein doesn't often offer Hebrew as the source of a foreign word. On the contrary, he feels that hundreds of Hebrew words were borrowed from Greek or Latin, with no notion that those etymons themselves may be traced to Edenic. Sure, TELEPHONE was borrowed by Modern Hebrew. But the Edenic sources of Greek *tele* and *phone* are provided in the *E-Word CD Dictionary* (and later forms, like the Edenics search function at *edenics.net*). [TELEPHONE].

When checking if other dictionaries link the classic rouge terms above to Hebrew, one is disappointed – but hardly surprised. The laboratory invention of Indo-European roots (see the *American Heritage Dictionary of Indo-European Roots*) offers *peig* (to cut, mark) as the root of DEPICT, PAINT, PICTURE, PICTURESQUE, PICTOGRAPH, PIGMENT and PIMENTO. (One may add FUCUS, PINK and PINTO.) Just as they give *peig* as the root for Latin *pingere*, to paint, we will soon study nasalization – or the adding of an N or M to a root. The ten words above are really from the Biblical Hebrew. In II Kings 9:30 Jezebel is making up her eyes with פוך POOKH. In most dictionaries, the Jezebels who spurn the Bible are covering up Hebrew etymons with cheap makeup.

Even more malicious "scholarship" is employed when Biblical Hebrew names, with established Edenic roots, are said to be borrowed BY Hebrew. A common word for the Lord's name includes the אדון ADoN root and the possessive suffix י "-I" (my). Because Phoenician has the word *adon,* meaning lord, scholars have the nerve to say that the Hebrew deity term was borrowed from the Phoenicians. Of course, they are trying to imply that the Israelite "cult" has roots in paganism, and is not based on Biblical Revelation from a Creator who is Lord. See ADONIS and the ד-נ *Dalet-Noon* root of law in entries like DEAN and MADONNA.

Also a target of Bible haters like Sigmund Freud was the name משה MoSHeH or Moses. (Siggy's Freudian slip was published as *Moses and Monotheism* in 1939.) At least here the claim that Moses' name is Egyptian, from *messu, son,* is less outrageous since he was adopted and named by Pharaoh's daughter. It does fly in the face of Exodus 2:10, however, which has Moses being named for the Hebrew act of being משך MaSHaKH, drawn out [of water]. משה MoSHeH would have other crucial occasions of drawing out, and ethical history's most important human was not named "junior." The Bible quotes and uses Egyptian names when necessary, from *Tsapnath Paneah* (Joseph's new name) to the store cities of Pithom and Ra'amses. So it's not as though some Hebrew editor had to make an Egyptian word sound Hebrew.

The Hebrew etymology of Babel is likewise given in Genesis 11:9. It is supposed to be from בלל BaLaL (confused...source of BALLED UP). But this doesn't prevent the scholars from insisting that Babel means "Gate of God," even though Assyrian words don't combine words that way – without an element for "of," and using the suffix -EL (instead of the city's local god). There aren't other Babylonian cities so named.

Of course, there are scores of English words that WERE borrowed from Arabic, Persian or Sanskrit, and a Hebrew etymon doesn't always help to understand the word as it is now used. Nonetheless, all of these borrowings are ultimately from Edenic, and often it is only the ultimate Edenic source that sheds light on the word, and opens up a world of cognates for the dictionary user seeking more than the mere pedigree of a word.

Some of the common borrowings from **Arabic** that have easy cognates in Biblical Hebrew include: admiral, albatross, alchemy, alcohol, alcove, alfalfa, algebra, alkali, amber, arsenal, assassin, average, caliber, cipher, cotton, drub, elixir, fakir, fellah, gala, garbage, garble, genie, giraffe (see below), ghoul, hashish, harem, hazard, henna, lime, lute, magazine, mask, mattress, minaret (a Moslem menora), monkey, monsoon, nadir, racket (for ball games), safari, Sahara (desert), saffron, sheikh (elder), sherbet, sheriff (noble), sofa, sultan, syrup, tamarind (the Indian date and the Hebrew meaning of Tamar's name), tariff, zenith, zero, zircon. (For the Edenic source of these words, and their surprising not-borrowed relatives, see the latest *E-Word CD*, and a planned *Edenics Dictionary of the Human Language*.)

With GIRAFFE, typical of the animal names we will encounter in a later chapter, the given Arabic etymon (source word) has no meaning – besides the term for this creature. In Hebrew, though, ערף GHoReF means scruff of neck. Exactly what Adam would name this huge walking neck.

Salaam is the Arabic "goodbye" term credited as the source for the borrowed, meaningless English term SO LONG. It was likely picked up from Arabic traders. If *salaam* means peace, it is a fine form of goodbye. Why should one care if an etymon ALSO could be Edenic? Why bother with a so-called "ultimate source" of a term? What gives one the *chutzpah* to consider Biblical Hebrew as some form of unique language from Eden? Please be patient. The full response requires this book and more. For just the SO LONG example let us say that a goodbye equivalent to the Hip-Hop "peace out" does not adequately explain why a trade or sale would end in "peace."

In Edenic the same *Shin-Lamed-Mem* of שלום SHaLOAM (peace, hello or goodbye wishes) means SHaLaiM (to pay). Only once a deal is paid up, in full (שלם SHaLaiM is full too), there is peace and completion (שלמות SHILaiMOOT) between buyer and seller. This is the same SLM root behind a "grand SLaM" (completion of action) in a game of cards or baseball.

With an explanation that is more שלם SHaLaiM (complete), you may now understand why *salaam* offers a dictionary a measure of peace, but not full closure or disclosure.

The Word book or the *E-Word CD Dictionary* doesn't bother with obvious, acknowledged borrowings that are merely Anglicized Hebrew. HALLELUJAH only gets in when discussing the ה-ל *Hey-Lamed*/HL root of praising seen in words like HAIL (to praise). In all the borrowings above, whether from Hebrew, Arabic or non-Semitic, there is an Edenic root whose many simple variations or extensions shed light on English words. Someone looking up HALLELUJAH deserves more than just "from Hebrew." It is significant to know that Nazis screaming "heil Hitler" were using a word related to הלל HaLeL (praise) and הללויה HALELUJAH.

FINDING HEBREW BORROWINGS IN PEOPLE AND PLACE NAMES

There are many Edenic words in the many borrowings based on proper nouns: place names or people names. A person might be a Nimrod (hunter, sportsman), a Solomonic (wise) judge, a (wicked) Jezebel or a (huge) Goliath. Partly reproduced below is a column on the subject of English borrowings from Hebrew, with an emphasis on names:

(The column in a Midwest newspaper chain called *The Jewish Post & Opinion* was terminated after phone threats from eminent linguist Prof. Noam Chomsky.)

EDENSPEAK: 4/7/96

Hebrew Names to English Words

Before investigating the shocking prospect of all human words being spun off from Edenic, let us begin with the more conservative thesis that scores of English words not credited to Hebrew are unacknowledged borrowings from the slightly mispronounced transliterations of Hebrew by English-speaking Bible readers.

Before demonstrating that words like Skeptic (Greek), Samurai (Japanese) and Taboo (Polynesian) are from Hebrew שקף S[H]aQaiPH (observe), שומר SHOAMeR (guardian) and תועבה TOA'[A]iBHaH (dreadful sin), let us see how reluctant our dictionaries are to acknowledge simple Hebrew name borrowings.

The most famous curse-monger in Biblical history is בלעם BiL'[A]hM (Balaam) of Numbers 22-24. This character became synonymous with cursing to millennia of Bible readers is the unacknowledged source of the word BLAME. BLAME meant to curse – as in, "I hurt my **blamed** foot!" Yet the best the dictionaries can come up with as an etymology for BLAME is Greek *blasphemein* (to profane). Profaning does not mean cursing, nor does an etymon (source word) with SPH sound anywhere near accurate. But don't blame lexicographers. They only recognize words that came from figures in Classical Greek myths. One cannot expect them to have read the Bible.

The Anglicized name Goliath comes from Hebrew גלית GoLiYo(S) of I Samuel 17:4, which the Greeks rendered *Kolios* – just as they turned the גמל GaMaL into a **c**amel. (Yes, CAMEL is an acknowledged borrowing). From the Greek version of Goliath, *Kolios*, comes COLOSSUS, COLOSSEUM and all things COLOSSAL.

Another giant oversight in our etymologies involves Og, the giant king of Bashan (Numbers 21:33). The Edenic spelling is *Ayin-Gimel*, עג which would be pronounced OG in Germany, but more like GHoaG in Greece. (Later, the reader discovers that all nations have an "Ashkenazi" and "Sephardi" accent.) The language historians suppose that a French writer (d. 1703) coined the terms for the **OG**RE and his lovely OGRESS. "-RE" is a common French suffix. Returning to the Mediterranean *Ayin* as G (as we saw in GAUZE from English Gaza and Hebrew עזה [A]ZaH above), Og's name gave us **GIG**[ANTIC], then nasalized to GIANTIC, so that the now-unrecognizable GIANT is attributed to the Greek.

Abbadon is an acknowledged Hebraism from the word אבדון ABHaDOAN meaning "place of destruction" or "lost" (Proverbs 15:11). The same ABD or *Aleph-Bet-Dalet* אבד root is behind the loss in words like OBITUARY and the (nasalized – extra N) ABANDON. Reference books attribute OBIT to Latin, as if the Romans invented the concept of loss. (Don't let the extra N, the D to T shift, or the -uary suffix bother you, this will all be discussed later.)

Just as surely as SODOMY is traced to the twin city of סדום Sodom (Genesis 19:24), GONORRHEA ought to be linked to עמורה Gomorrah. The word's spelling was influenced by the attempt to give it a Greek source. So said Joseph T. Shipley, author of etymology books and early Edenics supporter. Please remember that all non-Edenic spelling is a late and arbitrary convention – not Revelation carved in stone. The practice of spelling words according to what appears familiar is a lexicographer's exercise of "Folk Etymology." Too much of what passes for etymology in our dictionaries is more accurately termed folk etymology, as Bible-challenged lexicographers preferred etymons (source words) that reflected their Eurocentrism.

Another probably borrowed affliction is PSORIASIS. צרעת TSoRa'[A](S) the Biblical skin disease (Leviticus 14:3), is not mere "leprosy." צר TSaR, pain, indicates a SORRY SORE (words from צר TSaR, and רות TSaRoAT or TSaROA(S) can be understood as STRESS. מצרים MiTSRaYiM or Egypt infers a land of pain and stress.

If the famously salty Dead Sea area of "Sodomy and Gonorrhea" gave us another term, it would be SODIUM (the scientific word for salt). SODIUM is supposedly from Latin *soda*. Latin *soda* (foundation), just like Hebrew יסוד Ye**$OAD** (foundation) has nothing to do with sodium. Like so many of our inane etymologies, this one is bogus, but the reference writers deserve a fiction award for finding some classical word with vague sound correspondence.

Speaking of place names, a JORDAN (chamber pot) and a SCAM should come from the Biblical Jordan River and the town of Shechem (where a scam and counter-scam led to violence instead of schemed-for wealth). Perhaps the most relevant and covered up English word from a Hebrew place name has to be BABBLE. The *Oxford English Dictionary* is so troubled by a Biblical source for BABBLE (the בבל Babel of Genesis 11), that it warns readers that "no direct connection with Babel can be traced" and declares the term to be of "unknown origin." Other reference books trace BABBLE to a Dutch word for brook. Brooks do many things besides babble. We are waiting for our Bible-less reference books to do other than babble.

Names like Mo**s**es from Mo**sh**eh and **S**olomon from **Sh**lomo came about because there is no SH in Greek. This error was perpetuated because Bible Scholars were too lazy, unlearned and unmotivated (to be kind) to work from the original Hebrew instead of the Greek translation.

Many English names are from variations of the Hebrew that are not cited:

Sue or Suzy is from Susan, which is from שושנה SHoWSHaNaH (lily). The illustrious Simpson surname has been nasalized (extra M this time), but is from שמשון

SHiMSHOAN (Samson). So it is when considering other words – which are not proper nouns – one has to think Hebrew שׁ *Shin* (SH) when one hears English S. Of course, dozens of American and world place names are right from the Hebrew Bible too.

Place names are a natural place to find borrowings. Outside of a few Native American names, most place names of the U.S. Northeast recall towns that immigrants left behind (like York and Boston, England). But Americans in Rehoboth, MA or Ephrata, PA were commemorating an old new Holy Land that they had emigrated to.

Here's a modified and republished TRAVEL column :

> You don't have to travel to BETHLEHEM, Pennsylvania or to ZION, Utah to visit a place named after a Hebrew word.

> Bethlehem is בית BeiT לחם LeHeM. BeTH is a house or BOOTH, while LeHeM, normally translated "bread," sometimes means meat in Hebrew and always means meat, and especially LAMB, in Arabic.

> As for Zion, it is traceable to related terms of ציון TZioN (Mount Zion, thus all of Israel) like צנה TSeeNaH (a large shield) and צין TZeeYaiN (to make a mark or SIGN, or to be distinguished). מצוין MiTZOOYaN means standing-out, excellent. The root is about being an exemplar, or in American Colonial "Zionist" terms, "a City upon a Hill."

> Ever since we were evicted from EDEN (that Garden of HEDONism, עדן [E]yDeN, being the source of Greek *hedone*, pleasure) and then went our separate ways at BABEL, you'll find BALLED up or BABBLE-like forms of Edenic (proto-Semitic or early Biblical Hebrew) place names wherever you go on EARTH. EARTH is from ארץ AReTZ, earth, just as HEALTH is from חלוץ [K]HeeLOOTZ, vigor.

> Earth's surface is divided by continents like Asia and Europe.

ASIA is to the EAST, the land of the fiery rising sun, and so it is named for Hebrew fire, אש AiSH. מערב M'ARahBH means west, since the sun sets there in the ערב EReBH or evening. EUROPE (and much later the mythical figure of Europa) is obviously from the *Ayin-Resh-Bhet* terms for evening and west מערב but don't look for anything but anti-Semiticism in our current dictionaries.

The nation of ENGLAND was the land of the Angles, Germanic people from an ANGULAR territory. ENGLISH is not only a cognate of ANGLE, but of that angle bridging our leg and foot – the ANKLE. There's clearly something crooked about angles, ankles and Englishmen, though you won't see it until you encounter our work with nasalizations (extra N's). The vowel-guttural-liquid term that is the source of these words is Hebrew עקל [A]QeL (crooked).

We follow the English to the New World to explore AMERICA. Named for Italian navigator AMERIGO Vespucci, the earlier form of the name (Americus) is known to be a cognate of names like EMERY and AMELIA. (R and L interchange, as readers here will soon know).

All these vowel-nasal-liquid terms are traced to the Old High German root amal (work). Non-coincidentally, Hebrew עמל [A]MaL means work, just as America has meant work for generations of immigrants.

Within America are many place names provided by Native Americans. One example is IOWA (sleepy ones in Siouan), a match for איף AYeF (weary) in Edenic. The Indians of southern Florida named their river and settlement after the precious fresh, drinkable water they found: Miamus (now called MIAMI). מים MaYiM is drinkable water in Hebrew, as opposed to מרים **MaR**eeYM, the briny and bitter **MAR**INE or **MAR**ITIME water surrounding the Florida peninsula.

There are rich deposits of Hebrew to mine in South and Central America as well: BRASIL (ברזל BaRZeL, iron), PERU (פרו PiROO, be fruitful), El **SALVA**[DOR] שלוה **SHaLVaH**, the tranquility after SALVATION, and ECUADOR (the CU or QU root of E**QU**ATOR and E**QU**AL, the line or QUE), is from *Koof-Vav* or קו QaV, a line, measuring line.

Whether it's ALBANIA, ALBANY, the ALPS or LEBANON, all LBN terms are related to לבן LaBHaN (white, like the snow of these locations). All place names with CAPE in them, CAPE COD to CAPETOWN, link up to Israel's headland city, חיפה KHaYPHa (Haifa).

WHAT BORROWINGS ARE NOT

No people borrows names for what they already have, like parts of the body, topography, family member names or local animal names.

Borrowings are suspected whenever words in different languages share similar sound and sense. Otherwise they are cognates, with similar lineage, like "hole" in Swedish (*hal*), Danish (*hul*) and Norwegian (*hull*). The Hebrew hole is חלל [K]HaLaL. There are many related HL words in Hebrew and other Semitic languages. Yet no one suggests that the Hebrew is a cognate of the Scandinavian or Germanic terms. And no one suggests that either ancient Germanics or Hebrews lacked the term, and borrowed it from the other group during some time that the two groups were in contact.

What do the experts say about this lacuna or gaping hole in linguistic theory when it comes to the similarity between HOLE and חלל [K]HaLaL? They just dismiss it as a coincidence. Linguists allow up to forty coincidences of sound and meaning between unrelated languages. After all, the odds are in favor of such coincidences because the sounds made by the human mouth are limited – and readers will soon see how much that is true. This argument is based on voodoo mathematics, however, because the chances of words from two unrelated languages describing the same animal, body part, topographical term, etc. are one in tens of thousands. Unrelated languages may have 50 words like H-L, but the odds are astronomical that both would have an H-L word for an indentation or hole.

Words like these would not be borrowed. The Germans or Hebrews could not have lacked a word for "eye," so that there's a Middle English word *eyne* (eye) and a Hebrew עין [A]YiN (eye) because of cross-cultural influence. Even worse for linguists is the fact that Chinese eye is *yan*, and the Eskimo is *iye*. Later, you will see how hundreds of other words for eye fit appropriate Hebrew sources, as they all were cognates from an Edenic Mother Tongue.

This chapter on borrowings, therefore, concludes with samples of similar sounding and meaning English and Edenic words. They ought to be called cognates, but linguists would never concede that the English and Hebrew words share a common ancestry. They ought to be borrowings, then. But the words below are not Hebraisms that were transliterated, and picked up by English-speaking Bible readers. Also, these words are not the kinds of terms that a language would lack, and need to borrow. None of the words below are technical, new inventions (like RADIO, TELEVISION or DOWNLOAD) or culture-specific (like ROMANTIC, TRINITY or TORAH) that made it necessary for them to be borrowed.

This chapter on borrowings ends with far too many near-identical Hebrew-English words to ascribe to luck or to historical borrowing. To quote Dr. Joseph Shipley, author of *The Dictionary of Word Origins*, "The parallels traced seem beyond the range of coincidence, and call for a reexamination of our etymologies."

What follows is a brief list of these more-than-allowable English-Hebrew word pairs that are not considered historically related – either as cognates or borrowings. The terms are all the kinds of words that would NOT have been borrowed by a culture. Their closeness in sound and sense should force one to consider that something immense has been missed.

With updates in the *E-Word CD*, there are now around 23,000 English-from-Edenic words since the first printing of *The Word* in 1989. The few dozen words below are selected from a list of the 250 closest pairs, published and recorded separately as an audio CD and script booklet called "The Tower of Babel's Greatest Hits." With these sound-alike, mean-alike word pairs, one doesn't have to know about the various letter shifts, etc.

that come up later in this book. This selection ends the introductory, more theory-oriented part of our Edenics study, and it offers intimations of what is coming ahead.

Refer to the Transliteration Key on the first or last page of this book to see the exact spellings of the Edenic. **Almost all of these English words will have entries by that name in the *E-Word CD* for much more information.**

KEY:
1) English word,
2) from the Hebrew/Edenic,
3) meaning of the Edenic etymon,
4) Hebrew Bible citation verifying the etymon's antiquity and meaning.

Example:
(English) ADD (from the Hebrew, עוד pronounced OWED (the Hebrew word means) "in addition" (as seen in) Exodus 11:1

AGONY	יגון	yahGOAN'	great pain	Genesis 42:38
ALBINO	לבן	laVAHN'	white	Isaiah 1:18
ANCIENT	נושן	noSHAHN'	ancient	Leviticus 13:11
ANTIQUE	עתיק	ahTEAK'	very old	I Chronicles 4:22
APPETITE or CUPIDity	חפץ	haFATES' khahFATES'	desire I (The Hebrew *Het* or *Het* can be hard or soft.)	Kings 9:1
ASS, ASININE	אתון	hSOWN'	she-donkey (where an ass is made of Balaam)	Numbers 22:28
AT	עד	Uhd	up to here	Genesis 11:31

(of course, there are cognates AD infinitum.)

BABBLE	בבל	bahVEL'	ToB's location Genesis 11:9	
	בלבול	billBOOL'	means confusion.	

BALL UP	בלל	bahLULL'	mix up also	Genesis 11:9

(Are you confused yet?) Oil that is mixed up with other ingredients is Bil-LOOL'-ah.

BAR	בריח	baREEYaKH	a barricade or barrier	
				II Chronicles 14:6

BARE	באר	bahAIR'	to clear out, expose	
				Deuteronomy 26:13

BASHFUL	בוש	BOSHE	to be ashamed,	
		boo-SHAH'	embarrassment or shyness	Genesis 2:25

BAUBLE	בבה	bahVAH'	prized miniature	Zachariah 2:12

(BABY is related to the Modern Hebrew בבה, BOOB'-ah, doll)

BLEAK	בלק	bahLUCK'	empty, wasted	Isaiah 24:1

BLIST(ER)	יבלת	YaBEL'-et	wart or welt	Leviticus 22:22

BLOAT	בלט	bahLAHT'	protrude, bulge from Aramaic	

BOOR	בור	BOOR	boor, uncultivated person	Psalms 92:7

BOOT	בעט	bahAHT'	to kick or spurn	Deuteronomy 32:15

BOOTH	בית	BahYiTH'	house, interior	Genesis 35:2

(as in BETHlehem, House of Bread).

BORE [spell out]	בור	BoaR	a bore or pit	Exodus 21:33

BOTH	ב	BETH	letter and number 2 of the *Aleph-Bet*	

(seen also in the prefix BI- of bi-foculs or bi-weekly)

BROOK	בריכה	B'RAYkhah	pool	Ecclesiastes 2:6

BUCKAROO	בוקר	bowCARE'	cattleman	Amos 7:14

(bah-CAR is cattle, though you've seen the Arabic "albacore" for the meat of tuna fish).

BURN	בער	boAIR'	burn	Exodus 3:2

BY	ב	-b, letter *Bet*		

as in "by the way"   Bah Derekh, by the way of   Deuteronomy 6:17

CABLE	כבל	KEVeL	cable, strong rope	Psalms 105:18

CADDY	כד	KUD	any holder, container or KIT,	
			the water pitcher of	Genesis 24:19

CAKE	ככר	KeeKAHR'	loaf	Exodus 29: 23

Rah-KeeK of Exodus 29:2 is translated as "cake," but it probably had influence on the word CRACKER.

CALL	קול	COLE	the voice that calls out or "cries in the wilderness"	
				Isaiah 40:3

CANE	קנה	k-NEH'	stalk, stem	Genesis 41:5

(thus CANDY and hollow things like the CANOE or a CANAL)

CAR	כר	CAR	riding compartment – like the car of an elevator,	
			or as in Rachel's camel in Genesis 31:34	

CAP	כפה	keyPAH'	skullcap	

(since this only developed from a Biblical word, let's cite כובע KO'-vah, which became the modern word for hat, but was the helmet of I Samuel 17:38, this root even became the source for a head of CABBAGE.

CASE	כיס	KEESE	a pocket, or slip case	Proverbs 1:14

COAST	קץ	KAIT	end	
	קצה	KahTSAH	extremity, edge, border	Genesis 23:9

COMMON	כמו	comeO'	like	Genesis 41:39

(There are related prefixes in English, like COM-, CON- or HOMO-, but Spanish *como*, like, is a ringer.)

| CORE | עקר | EeCORE' | for essence or principal | Daniel 4:12 |
| | | | for the CORE of an apple | Leviticus 25:47 |

| COUPLE | כפל | kahFAHL' | to double | Exodus 26:9 |

CORONA, CORNER and CORNICE

| | קרן | KEHRen | a ray of light, projecting point or edge |

the correct, non-horny way to translate Exodus 34:30 and Leviticus 27:2

CORNUcopia or the uniCORN (horn of plenty or the horned horse) is from KEHR-en as a horn Deuteronomy 33:17 – (every CORNET, CORONET, CROWN etc. is from Latin *cornu*, which is from the Hebrew קרן QeReN. The CORNER and CORNICE above are extensions, while the CROWN on the Statue of Liberty shows the connection between extensions of light and majestic power.)

| COVER | כפר | kahFAR' | to cover | Exodus 26:9 |

| CRAB | עקרב | ahkRUB/KackRUB | a scorpion in | I Kings 12:11, |

but this word is the mother of all K-R hard creatures, from the COCKROACH and CRAYfish to the [S]CARAB beetle and the [S]COPRPION.

| CRACK | חרך | KharUCK | narrow opening | Songs 2:9 |

| CREAM | קרום | Kroom | crust, membrane, | |
| | | | what covers them Dry Bones in Ezekiel 37: 8 |

| CREASE, CROSS | קרס | COREuss | to bend | Isaiah 46:2 |
| | | | a hook | Exodus 26:11 |

| CREDO, CREED | חרד | KharAID | a trembling reverence | Isaiah 66:5 |

| CRY | קרא | KahRAH | loudly call out | Isaiah 58:1 is quite loud |

| CRYPT | קבר | KEVer | a grave | Genesis 23:9 |
| | | | (yes, GRAVE is from KeVeR too) | |

| CUBBY | קבה | KOOBah | compartment | Numbers 25:8 |

(a CABANA for chickens is a COOP).

CUFF   כף   CUFF   palm or CUP of the hand   Numbers 24:10

(It isn't hard to COP or CAPTURE related words, without resorting to FISTICUFFS).

CURB   כרכב   carCOVE'   ledge   Exodus 27:5

CURT   כרת   kahRATE'   to cut short   Job 33:6

(Life is CURTAILED in Numbers 13:23)

CUT among 7 related Hebrew origins, there's חצה khah-TSAH', to cut in half, at Exodus 21:35

CZAR   שר   SAR   officer   Genesis 40:22

or, if related to כתר KAISAR and CAESAR, there's KES'-er כתר crown in Esther 1:11

DAD < דוד DoaD   ידיד   YihDEED   loved one, later uncle or beloved friend

     Songs 6:3 or Deuteronomy 33:1.

DUDE and TOOTS may sound like slang, but they have roots too are in this Biblical *Dalet-Dalet* term.

DAMN   דון   DooN   to pass judgment, or to DEEM a DOOM,

     as a judge or a DEAN does Genesis 15:14 or Psalms 68:6

The name דן Dan means judgment. A דין Dah-YAN is a judge. יום הדין Yom HaDeen is judgment day.

DASH   דיש   DUHYish   to tread, thrash or trample   Deuteronomy 25:4.

True, an athlete isn't trampling in a 100-yard dash, but the sense remains that of energetic leg-work, and the sound is quite similar, given all the years and miles from Babel.

DEVOUR   ברה   VARah   to eat

     (what VORacious carniVORes do)   II Samuel 12:17

DIKE   דיק   DahYAKE   a protective siege-wall   Jeremiah 52:4

DIRECTION   דרך   DehREKH   way or path.   Genesis 16:7

He-DReeKH is to direct, while a מדריך Ma-DreeKH means a director. All roads lead to Babel. *Doroga* is a Russian highway, while *Doro* is a Japanese street, and *Tori* a Japanese street. Isn't ROAD and ROUTE simply the דר *Dalet-Resh* reversed? Yes, but here in "The Greatest Hits" we're keeping it simple, not going off the TRACK, even for TREKIES.

DIVIDED   בדד   VahDUDD   solitary, isolated as any BIT or BYTE

Lamentations 1:1

Bet-Dalet BUD also means a separated limb from a tree. How else do we get a baseball BAT?

DON   אדון   AhDOAN   a lord

his wife's a DAME or MaDONNA   Genesis 24:18

If a guy looks like a Don Juan, more than Don Corleone, he might be called a Greek god or an ADONIS.

DRIVE   דרבן   darVUN   to spur or goad to move on, like driving sheep,

Ecclesiastes 12:11

DULL   דלל   DahLUL   to dilute, to weaken or weak

like a dull pain   Isaiah 19:6 or Genesis 41:19

DUMB   דמי   DUMMY   silence   Ezekiel 27:32

There's also the soft DIM sound, or דממה DIM-ah-mah of Ezekiel 19:12

DUMMY   דומה   DOMEeh   alike; a likeness as in a store dummy.

דמות DiM(ooT) means likeness in Genesis 1:26. Why does Hebrew דם DuM mean blood? WE know from DNA and genetics that the blood carries our likeness. If you're no dummy, and are really listening to our Edenic tongue, before Babel/Babble, than you understand that all humanity has a tangible, an audible likeness from the keyboard of our Creator.

DUO or DUAL   דו   DOO   the prefix of two-ness, like di-sect or di-chotomy

or the d.i.s.- words like dissent. In Modern Hebrew דו-כנף DOO-KINAF is a biplane, with its dual canopies or wings. wd DOO is preserved in ancient Aramaic, but a Biblical Hebrew source which provides us with the T sound of number two can be heard later at the TWIN entry.

DYE   דיו   DYOWE   ink   Jeremiah 36:18

Yes, the Bible was pre-Clairol.

EARTH   ארץ   ahRETZ   land or earth   Genesis 1:1

while Eretz Yisrael means the country or Land of Israel, the ar-RETZ in Genesis 1:1 means planet Earth, the dry land or any TeRRain or Terrirory. To get Latin *terra,* earth, simply read ארץ AhReTZ backwards. If the TZ shift to TH doesn't bother you, you can hear how the Dutch earth-pig is the AARD-vark.

EDDY אד AiD the "flow" in the Garden of Eden Genesis 2:6.
Like a current, an EDDY can be air or water.

ECLIPSE חלף KhaLUFF to pass on or be over Songs 2:11
Keep in mind that the Hebrew Pay, can be a P or an F. When the Greeks borrowed this letter, they used "PH" for the softer sound. Everyone admits that letters came from the Hebrew *Aleph-Bet*, but not, God forbid, words too.

EGRET עגור AhGOOR crane or heron Jeremiah 8:7
Discount the egret's "ET" French ending. All three long-throated birds also echo the Edenic word for throat – GahROAN.

EIGHT and number 8 words like OCTogon from ח KHET, Hebrew's 8th letter and its number eight.

ELECT לקט LECKeT selecting, picking, gathering or colLECTing
Genesis 31:46

ELMHURST This place name has two elements: ELM is from אילן eelUN', a shade tree, Genesis 35:8, while HURST is from חרש hoeRESH, a thicket or small grove of trees – Ezekiel 31:3

ENSCONCE שכן shahKHAHN' to reside or dwell, like the divine presence or Shih-KHEE-Nah, does in Deuteronomy 33:12. The tabernacle is the משכן MishKAHN.

EUROPE ערב AhRAHV
or extended to מערב M'ahRAHV, meaning The West, Psalms 103:12
To people in the Near East, Europe is the land of the setting sun, of evening or EREev. What about the myth of Europa? This fable came AFTER the names existed.

EVE or EVENING העיב heyEVE to darken or become cloudy,
like the bu-AHV in I Kings 18:45 where "[quote] the sky grew black with clouds."

EVIL עול AHvel injustice, wrong, iniquity Deuteronomy 32:4

EXIT/all EX- and OUT words חוץ KHOOTS the outside Genesis 24:31

EYE עין EYein eye Exodus 21:24
To help you hear and see this one, EYE was e-i-n and e-y-n-e in earlier English.

| FIG | פוג | FuG | young fig | Songs 2:13 |

The dictionary gives Latin ficus as the source, so maybe the Romans gave Adam and Eve fig-leaves.

| FIRE | הבער | HEVer, | fire, is from Aramaic, |

while in Exodus 22:5 a Hebrew pyre is בערה BihAYrah

| FOR | בעבור | BahaVOOR | "for the sake of"/"in order that" Genesis 27:4 |

| FRUIT | פרות | FeyROAT | fruit | Genesis 1:29 |

The more common pronunciation is PEYroat, you'll hear that when you get to the PEAR.

| GALA | גילה | GE-lah | gleeful joy and regaling | Isaiah 65:18 |

| GOAT and KID | גדי | GiDeeY | kid of goat | Genesis 38:17 |

GATHER, GHETTO and GATE may be heard in גדר GADer, the noun meaning gate or "wall" in Numbers 22:24 and is also a verb, like to corral. Again, you can hear that T and D are identical, as are G and K. That's why a Japanese gate is *kado*.

| GOB (LET) | גביע | GavEEah | goblet, the large cup | Genesis 44:17 |

| GOOD | גד | GaD | fortune, success | Genesis 30:11 |

| GRADE and GRATE | גרד | GayRAID' | to scrape | Job 2:8 |

| GRAIN | גרעין | GahrEEN | kernel or seed |

which is post Biblical, but is close to the GOren, granary or "threshing floor" of Genesis 50:10, and the GarGERE, kernel or individual "berries" of Isaiah 17:6

| GRIP | אגרף | EGGrough | to clench a fist | Exodus 21:18 |

It's easy to GRasP a GRouP of cognates like GraPple, GraB and GroPe.

| GRASS | גרש | GerESH' | agricultural yield | Deuteronomy 33:14 |
| | מגרש | miGraSH | pasture | Numbers 35:3 |

| GRAZE | גרז | GorAHZ' | to cut | Psalms 31:23 |

83

GROAN   גרון   GaROAN'   throat or neck   Isaiah 58:1

Where groans come from. A person can CRANE one's neck too.

GUSH   געש   GAHush   to storm in volcanic shaking   II Samuel 22:8

It means to belch in Akkadian and vomit in Arabic, which is closer to a GUSHING GEISER.

HAIL (meaning, to express praise or approval) הלל   HaLeL'   to praise   Psalms 146:1

This is merely the first syllable of the common Hebrew borrowing HALLELUJAH.

HANG   חנק   HeNNeK   to strangle   Nahum 2: 13

HARM   חרמה   HARMah   to destroy   Deuteronomy 13:16

HAVOC   הפכה   HaFAYkhah   overturning destruction   Genesis 19:21

HAZE   הזיז   HaZEEZ   cloud   Zechariah 10:1

HE   הוא   HOO   the 2nd person pronoun, masculine, or HE

    Genesis 18:1

HEALTH   חלוץ   HeLOOTZ   vigor or strength   Isaiah 58:11

[The TZ Hebrew *TSadi* offers English a TH]

HALE   HI-ill   vigor.

HERESY   חרות   HayROOS   freedom   Ecclesiastes 10:17

HOLLOW   חלל   HaLuLL   hollow, empty space   Psalms 109:22.

In Lamentations 2:12, HaLuLL is a dead body; without a soul, we are empty or hollow.

HOOK   חכה   HaKah   fishhook   Job 40:25

As a verb, hakAYE means to wait – an occupation familiar to fisherman.

HORRID   חרד   HaRAID   to tremble or fear   Genesis 27:33.

Originally meant to shudder or be terrified. The heart is the trembling organ, so חרד khaRAID' or HaRAID' gave us CARDIO-, CARDIAC, HEART and SCARED.

HORSE חורש HoResh plougher Micah 3:12
Like most animal names, has no known source.

HOUSE חסות HahSOOS',
חסוי HeeSOOY'
הסה HaSAH' refuge, shelter or to give shelter.
There's Isaiah 30:3, Judges 9:15 or מחסה maKHAseh, a pavilion, in Isaiah 4:6

HULA חיל HeeL trembling Exodus 15:20
Miriam and the women danced a מחלה MiHoLah, the writhing Mideastern bellydance, at the Red Sea. (Of course the ancestors of the Hawaiians also spoke Edenic and migrated from Babel.) More then keeping a beat with a tambourine, this early hula dance also told a dramatic story.

IDEA ידעה YideeAH knowledge, information Genesis 31:32

IF אף UFF then, on condition Leviticus 26:24

INCITE מסית MaySEAT inciter or enticer, root seen in Deuteronomy 13:7

INSOMNIA אין שנה AIN'SHEYnah no sleep.
The negative prefix AIN, that gave us IN- and UN- is from Hebrew אין AIN, none, not (Genesis 2:5 or 30:1.) Combine this with the source of Latin somnus, sleep, which is Hebrew שנה Sheynah, sleep (Genesis 31:40.)

IOTA י YooD the smallest Hebrew letter, which is just a little JOT or IOTA. The dictionaries end at the Greek letter, not acknowledging that the Alphabet is from the אלף-בית Aleph-bet. The Greek way of turning the Hebrew י Yod into a vowel, allows us to trace EON to Hebrew יום YOM, which can mean a day or a long EON.

IRE חרה HARah angry or irate Genesis 4:6

IS יש YaiSH translated "there is" I Samuel 17:46.

IT את ET "this one" (definite accusative) Genesis 1:1

85

JET is said to come from Latin *jacere,* to throw. ידה yeeDAH' means to cast in Lamentations 3:53, and ידה YADah is to shoot in Jeremiah 50:14.

J words commonly come from a י *Yod*, like all the JACK words are from the original Jacob, יעקב YUCKov. The root of Jacob means heel, so we lift up a car with a JACK. Jacob fathered a large clan, so we have male animals like the jackrabbit.

Speaking of Hebrew names giving English words: consider JINX from יונה Jonah, who jinxed his ship, JUDGE from יהודה Judah, who judged Tamar and whose Judeans exported the first laws, and JOVE and JOVIAL from the name of the Lord associated with love and mercy.

JUBILANT   יובל   yoVEIL   the Jubilee   Leviticus 25:10

When one is full of jubilance and blows the ram's horn or יבל YaVAL – Exodus 19:13. Only JUBILEE is acknowledged as borrowed by the scholars, who aren't stupid – just prejudiced against the Bible.

KITTEN   קטן   KaTaN   small and young   Genesis 44:12

Way after Eden and Babel, the Egyptians miniaturized the big cats to our small, domestic cats. These little leopards happened to be named with a word for small. KITTEN came before CAT.

KEENING means wailing for the dead, from an old Irish custom and word קינה KEENah is just this kind of weeping and wailing for the dead in Second Samuel 1:17, and the *MikOWNin-oat* or "dirge singers" of Jeremiah 9:17 are involved in professional mourning or KEENING.

KENNEL   כן   KAIN is one of the many cages or compartments holding the animals on Noah's ark in Genesis 6:14.

KITE (the hawk, not the toy that glides like a falcon)   Edenic עיט EYE-it, better pronounced KHEYE-it, as are all words with an *Ayin*. This is the "bird of prey" of Genesis 13:11.

KNAVE   גנב   ganAV   thief   Exodus 22:1.

LAD   ילד   Y-LED   a boy   Genesis 21:8

Yal-DAH is a girl. The root is d-l L-D throughout Semitic. Even Noah Webster knew this, but the Bible-hating scholars of the 19th century rejected data like this in favor of the authoritative phrase "origin unknown"

LATE לאט l'UTT slow or sluggish Isaiah 8:6

Adam and Eve didn't have a Timex, but if someone was slow, he was late.

LAUGH – why is it spelled so funny? The given Indo-European root is *kleg* (to cry out or sound). The correct way to see why LAUGH is an LG term is to see Hebrew לעג lahUGG, to laugh at (Psalms 22:8). There's also לגלג ligLAIG, to deride or mock.

LICK – the strange spelling here too is best explained by the Hebrew:

לחך lahKHAKH to lick Numbers 22:4

LOVE - love can be emotional attachment or a hotter, physical attraction. The 1ˢᵗ Love is the לוה - LeaveAH [Genesis 29:34], as in the naming of Levi. לב LAIV, is a heart, but the extended form in Songs 4:9 is rendered "you have ravished my heart"

LUCK חלק HEYleck/KHEYleck share, portion in life Isaiah 17:14

as well as צלח tsahLUCK, prosperity, success or luck [Genesis 24:42]

MANY and MINUS are aMoNg NUMerous M-N or N-M words of aMouNts.

המון haMOAN, is that MANY or multitude in Genesis 17:4, while מין MEAN, is from, out of, or anything diMiNished from the whole or MINOR. To count MONEY in Hebrew, one is מנה MUNah or מנא minAYE one's ממון maMOAN.

The מ נ *Mem Noon* sub-root makes up a large family of **amounts**, found in many languages, just like the מד *Mem-Dalet* family gives us many measurement terms like MODEL or MID. מדה maDAH, infers measurement, size or characteristic (Exodus 26:2) like Latin *modus* or English MODEL. מד Mud, means uniform; מדר MahDAR, to measure or METE out; מדד moDADE, a measuring instrument, like a METER.

MYSTERIES נסתרות NisTaROSE' unknown things Deteronomy 29:28
ESOTERIC סתר SAYTerr secret

NO נוא NOO

Seen in the acts of annulling or saying NO to vows (Numbers 36:6 and 9), words pronounced הניא heyNEE and יניא yahNEE. He refused in Arabic is *na'a*. The common NO in Hebrew is לא lo. There is an N-L connection, but NO complex stuff. The Edenic source of YES is also not a pure affirmative, יש yaish, means to have or there is. It's the source of IS, of course (Genesis 18:24). The common Hebrew yes, כן *kane*, sounds nothing like YES, but Edenics has little to do with words in current dictionaries.

NUMB   נום   NOOM   to slumber

Like the Watcher of Israel who neither slumbers nor sleeps in Psalms 121:4.

ORGAN   ארגון   Ear-GOON   organization

From Edenic ארג ERRegg, a loom or shuttle [Judges 16:13], this evolved from the first organized organs or weaving machines. אורג oRAIG, is a weaver. If you have an ear and eye for patterns, you got the source of RUG, and many forms of WORK

OVER has 100s of spin-offs, meaning finished in time, or across in space.   עבר ahVAR means the past; עבר ahVOAR, to cross over; עבר AYver, beyond – as עבר הירדן *Ever-HaYarden* is Trans-Jordan in Genesis 50:10. מעבר m'aVAR or FORD is FOR, בעבור ba-aVOOR, crossing a river (Genesis 32:23)

PACE   פסע   pahSaH   to march, step or pace   Isaiah 27:4

PEAR   פרי   PiREE   a fruit   Genesis 1:29

As heard in the middle of aPRIcot, or the beginning of PRune. The plural of FRUIT is פרות payROTE or fayROTE. The command to be fruitful or FERtile is פרו pihROO. When you learn how fruits fall a ways from the tree, you could hear words like APPLE, PLUM or BERRY from the PR of Edenic פרי PeRRy.

PORE and PRY   פר   *Pay-Resh*   Isaiah 5:14

Terms like פיר PEER, a ditch, פער PahARE, a gap, or verbs like פעור, PahOOR, to open wide

PSORIASIS   צרעת   Tso-Ra'AS   the Biblical skin disease   Leviticus 14:3

That is not mere leprosy – צר Tsa'ar, pain, indicates a SORRY SORE, and צרות TsarROSE can be understood as STRESS – מצרים MitzRAyim or Egypt was a house of pain and stress. Not all these Greatest Hits are pleasant. Sodom and Gemorrah gave us SODOMY and GONORRHEA.

QUIET   שקט   SHEH-ket   quiet   Isaiah 7:4

is a good word for teachers to know, even if the SHH part of the source word seems to have gone quiet.

RAVEN   ערב   Oh-RAVE   raven   Genesis 8:7

This mother of all blackbirds, and source of CROW, is spelled ערב *Ayin-Resh-Bhet*. The soft, Germanic rendition of *Ayin*, or the Anglo-Saxon horofin, gave English the word RAVEN. But the harsh Mediterranean ע *Ayin* gave Latin the *CORVUS* and French the *Corbeau*. These are pronounced with the same hard C that gave us "Crow." To be ravenous or hungry is רעב – raAIVE, while a hunger of famine is רעב – rahAHV (Genesis 26:1).

REGULAR   רגיל   ra-GEEL   as usual

A regularly happening occasion is a רגל REGel, pilgrimage holiday (Numbers 22:28).

RUTH(LESS)   from the famously kind and generous heroine in the Biblical book of רות Ruth. The secular dictionary scholars haven't read or considered רות Ruth as the source. Why? They're ruthless.

SCALE is now mostly a noun, but it used to be a verb of weighing. In Edenic to weigh is שקל, SHaKAIL [Genesis:23:16]. In Israel, the monetary unit is the, שקל SHEKel.

SCOPE   שקף   sha-KAPH   to look out at   Genesis 26:8

A SCAVenger is always looking out, even if birds like the SCAUP or the שחף, shaKHUPH (a seagull) don't have TELESCOPES. A SKEPTIC will shrug off Edenics as mere "coincidence." This isn't about the SKEPTIC's logic, but psychological state. It's about his philosophical outlook, or overview, his השקפה, haSHKAPHAH. Such an emotionally blocked person will also be unable to see or hear that words like SPECtacle, SPECulate or perSPECtive are related words of vision or SCOPING out – but the SCP sequence has been modified to SPC.

Actually, SC words from Edenic שק, *Shin-Koof* words are in the minority. A SCHOOL of fish does come from אשכול, eshCOAL, a cluster (as of grapes – Genesis 40:10). Usually, however, the S leading an SC word was added on later. For example, the added S in SCULLERY prevents one from linking it to CULINARY. Both CL kitchen words are from כלי, KAYlee, vessel (Leviticus 6:21). The plural is כלים, kayLEEM. This is why a (S)CALLOP shell or a (S)CALP is from קלפה kleePAH, a shell or to shell and קלף, KLAPH, parchment or treated hide. Without knowing about this bogus S, we wouldn't know that SCALLOP and CALIBER, both shell words, are related.

It's easy to see how CUP and SCOOP should be from the same source. That fundamental SouRCe, or שרש, SHOResh, is כף, kuph. The first human CUP was the palm of the hand, as it's translated in Genesis 20:5. But the translation as "ladle" in Numbers 7:14 takes in SCOOP.

SENILE   ישן   Ya-SHAN'   old   Leviticus 26:10

SENior SENators were named to be ruling elders by way of Latin *senex*, old. If wondering about Hebrew ש SH becoming a S, remember that the Hebrew letters *Shin* and *Sin* are only a dot apart, and that Shimshon and Shoshana were rendered Samson and Susanna by English speakers.

SERPENT   שרף   SaRaPH   a burning snake - venom burns

                                                 Numbers 21:8

SET	שת	SHAT	to place	Genesis 41:35
			with the root meaning SEAT in Isaiah 20:4	

SIR, SIRE, or the Russian TZAR or CZAR are all from שר SaR officer, ruler [Jeremiah 17:25]. שרה SaRah or Sara is a princess, while כתר KeSeR (Esther 1:11 – the ת *Sahf* in an Ashkenasi or Germanic pronunciation) is the crown. Getting back to the שרף SaRaPH, this name of a type of attending angel, the Seraphim, serve the Ultimate שר SaR, and probably gave us words like "Serf" and "Servant".

SPARROW comes from the root *sper*, a word meaning generic bird. The generic word for bird named by Adam is צפור pronounced TseePORE (Deuteronomy 4:17). Is the Edenic word any more bird-worthy than what we have in dictionaries? Well, birds can either float, צפה tseePAH, in the air or remain hidden, צפון tsaPHOON, in trees, and covered צפוי tseePOOY by feathers, where they watch and SPY out, צפה tsaPHAH, for a chance to pounce with their talon, צפורן TseePoaren. Of course you can hear their whistle, צפירה tsi-pheeRAH. צפצוף tsiphTSOOPH means chirp, what the frogs, or צפרדע tsif-areDAYah, do when they take up the song at night. Morning or birdtime is צפרא TSA-rah in Aramaic. As usual – only in Edenic – like-sounding and meaning words flock together in one צבור tseeBOOR (group or congregation), and many words come home to roost and root.

SPHERES	ספירות			SePhIRoS, which means these carefully plotted astronomical spheres.

The term comes from Arabic *sifr*, but ultimately from ספר saPAIR, to count [Genesis 15: 5]. The word for a number is מספר, miSPAR. If the SPR root is about numbers, why is ספר, sayPHER, a book, and why are words like DECIPHER, SPELL, German *spiel,* and GOSPEL about letters rather than numbers? Simple. In Edenic letters ARE ALSO numbers. The 2nd letter, ב, *Bet* looks like number 2 and means much like BOTH and prefixes like BI-. As for books, remember that ספרי תורה, sifRAY toRAH, Torah scrolls are SPHERICAL.

SUPER	שפיר	ShahPEER	fine	
	שפר	SHEFer	"goodly"	Genesis 49:21

SUPERB is about excellence, not the language scholars notion of superiority.

TAURUS or TORO means ox in Latin and Spanish. These words didn't come right from Edenic, but from how the neurological Tower of Babel phenomenon that changed the sound of Aramaic letters with regularity. *Shin*/SH ש words in Hebrew became T words in Aramaic, an ancient but not the primeval language. So the Aramaic ox is a תור TOAR, instead of a שור SHOAR [Deuteronomy 33:17]. Why is only one of these from the Pure Speech of Zephania 3:9 ? Isn't this just some chauvinist bull ? No. Only the שור SHOAR is the beast created to plough with; only it makes a שורה shooRAH, a row which is, ישר yaSHAR, straight – or a SHEER SERIES. Even venerable Aramaic is comparative babble.

90

TIARA	עטרה	ahTAHRAH	crown	Songs 3:11
	עטר	ahTAR	to encircle	

The ע Ayin can be a harsh guttural sound, recalling כתר KETere or KeSere, the crown that sounds more like it fits the head of a KAISER, CZAR or CEASAR.

THEE or THOU . OK, they're old fashioned. Does the 2nd person pronoun or the "you" sound better in French or Latin *tu* ? The point is that these T-vowel words are ultimately from אתה ahTAH, you [Genesis 23:6]. The feminine is את AT. The plural, אתם ahTEM, sounds like THEM. French "we" is *nous*; in Edenic it's אנו ahNOO. English "me" is אני ahNEE. Those learning Hebrew have to deal with היא HE, meaning "she."

TIER (like a level in stadium seats) is from טור TooR, an arranged set, as the jewels in Exodus 28:17.

TOUR	תור	TOOR	to tour.

They weren't exactly TOURISTS, but many who read about the TOURING scouts sent to explore the Promised Land in Numbers 13:2 hear the obvious relationship. Related sound and sense is heard and seen with תור TORE, a turn, the TIARA term above, and דור DURE, the rim of a wheel and the source of TIRE. A round ball is like a דור DURE, or כדור K'DURE, so a ball is a כדור kaDURE.

TRIPE (garbage)	טרף	Ta-RaiPH,	a torn or ripped dead animal, now any unfit food

All non-kosher food is called "TRAIF" or טרפה TRAIPHah, the inedible meat of Exodus 22:30. We also discard the CRAW of animals and the CROP of birds, which comes from קרב KERev, animal innards [Leviticus 8:21]. Similarly, this Edenic KRB or V word gave us terms like CRAP and GARBAGE.

TOWER and TURRET are tall and vertical TR antonyms, from טירה TeeRAH, high fortifications [Numbers 31:20]. צור TSOOR, is a related rock or refuge. Cities like TROY or animals like the TURTLE find refuge here.

TEAM or TWIN	תאום	te-OAM	a twin	Genesis 25:24

OK, a TEAM should originally refer to an identical pair of work animals, but how could תאום teOAM give us TWIN? The ו *Vav* could be pronounced as a consonant, not as a vowel, so that the Hebrew תאום is like t'VOAM or t'WOAM, an identical twin of TWIN, TWAIN, or TWO.

UDDER	דד	DUD	a teat	

Yes, you can say "teat;" it's a cow's nipple   Proverbs 5:19

| URGE | ערגה | errGAH | URGENT craving | Psalms 42:2 |

VETO and VOID are negative non-starters versus positives pledges of BET, FAITH, AFFIDAVIT and WEDDING. Things seem to be getting out of hand at the end of the alphabet! Then again, a married person could see how a WEDDING is a BET taken on FAITH and certified by a FEDERAL court's AFFIDAVIT, only to face a VETO or be VOID after a breach of FIDELIITY. All the key words are Bilabial-Dentals, that is, BT, FD, FT,VD, VT or WD sounds. These similar sounding words all mean something established in trust, or, the opposite, legally nullified.

Such is the sound and sense of Edenic. Now the specifics: On the plus side: בטח BETaKH, is trust or confidence [Psalms 13:6], הבטיח heaveTEEakh, is to promise; בטחון bee-tahKHON is a guarantee or insurance; both, עבוט ahVOTE [Deuteronomy 24:10] and עבטיט avTEET [Habbakuk 2:6] are rendered as a pledge or to pledge in faith. ודאי vaDIE means certainty. Yes, VOTE is an antonym of VETO. On the negative, VETO-VOID side, בטל vahTAIL or bahTAIL is to nullify or legally vitiate [Ecclesiastes 12:3].

XENO(PHOBIA) is from Greek *xenos*, stranger. In Genesis 29:23 Leah is not hated as the שנואה sihNOOah, but she felt estranged and like the שני shayNEE, second. A real stranger or invader is the שונא soNAY [Proverbs 25:21].

| YELL | ילל | yih-LAIL | to howl | Deuteronomy 32:10 |

| YOUNG | יונק | yo-NAIK | a suckling child | Numbers 11:12 |

Babies literally YANK at the breast of their mothers, while earlier and rougher settlers called the relatively spoiled and dainty Dutch colonists YANKEES. The verb of feeding one's young is הניק heyNEEK.

ZYGOTE, the biological pair of cells at every person's origin, comes via Greek *zygon*, yoke, and ultimately from זוג ZOOG, a yoke or a pair. זוג ZeeVAIG is to join, and a husband in Arabic is a *zawg*.

Enjoy this brief encounter with Edenic cell biology.

There are many 1000s more where these came from. See the 23,000-entry CD dictionary which updated *The Word* (paper dictionary) of 1989. Future "Greatest Hits" recordings, just the top of the tip of the iceberg, will offer more near-identicals and introduce the simple ways to unscramble the affects of Babel-babble. A future volume could include slightly more challenging near-identicals, and introduce some of the simplest shifting of pronunciation and root-letter location which have kept most words disguised from their ultimate origin in Edenic. These include HiLL from הר HaR (mountain, hill R→ L), HALT from חדל *Het-Dalet-Lamed* (to cease), and ETeMology from, אמת EMeT (truth). With help from you, CDs from other languages, can be produced. A Spanish language CD and booklet are now available; an Italian version is in progress. Chinese, French, German, Italian, Japanese, Korean, Polish and Russian are among those languages with large Edenic word lists, and a CD/booklet in this series can be produced as soon as YOU would like to be a co-owner.

Chapter Two CONCLUSION

Edenics-deniers try to dismiss discovered links as merely coincidences or unknown borrowings. When a word resembles a later Hebrew word, rather than an Edenic one, and when the link is so strong that no effects of distortion at the Tower's Babel-babble is evident, it might well be a newly discovered borrowing rather than a linguistic artifact from Eden.

One good example involves the Cherokee Indians of America:

The deity name for Cherokee Indians is *Yohewah* . This is far too close to the anglicized Hebrew deity word that appears in the first part of the Yehova Witnesses. The Cherokee word does not mean a deity or creator. The word is a borrowing – rather than a word preserved from Mankind's shared past in Eden. How did American Indians get to borrow words from Hebrew-speakers in ancient Judea? See Shalom Goldman's *Hebrew and the Bible in America: The First Two Centuries* published in 1993 by University Press of New England. The second section contains an article by Cyrus Gordon, Professor Emeritus of Hebrew and Near Eastern Languages at NY University, "The Ten Lost Tribes" pp. 61-69. He discusses an 1889 Smithsonian Institution excavation at Mound 3 at Bat Creek, Loudon County, Tennessee: Cherokee country. Hebrew inscriptions were found to be Judean from about 100 C.E. Three Judean coins were also discovered. Non-coincidentally, in 1821 Chief Sequoyah is said to have invented the Cherokee writing system. The help of literate Hebrews is probable. While this episode was an historical anomaly perhaps involving a handful of seafarers, it must be admitted that some Edenic links (that are too strong) are merely newly discovered borrowings.

While a small number of borrowings may have ended up in some surprising places, the Amazon jungle is not one of them. The Araona language of the Amazon has only been recorded more recently. And Araona is one of our better documented languages with hundreds of clear traces of Edenic (Pre-Hebrew).

Chapter Two ACTIVITIES

1. Give examples in three different categories of words why a self-respecting language might borrow a word from another culture?

2. Name three proper names borrowed from Hebrew, and not mentioned above.

3. Name three place names borrowed from Hebrew, and not mentioned above.

4. All the "foreign," non-Hebrew words "borrowed" from other languages in the Hebrew Bible (not counting references to people or places) are from Edenic anyway. Search "paradise" in the *E-Word CD Dictionary*, or find your own example of this.

5. Find a Hebrew Bible name, in either a dictionary or a secular Bible studies text, where the editors claim that the name is not from Hebrew.

6. Give three examples where English words should have been traced to Hebrew by simple extensions of previously acknowledged borrowings.

7. Why is it problematic if there is a close sound and sense correspondence between English and Hebrew in word categories where there is rarely a borrowing?

8. In the TAURUS/TORO entry above, it is clear that Aramaic, not Hebrew, was the medium for the Western bull words. In what way does the Edenic source deserve to be noted, even though the TR bovine no longer sounds like the Edenic שור SHOAR ?

9.   Many animals are on the Kryss Tal or other lists of words borrowed by English. Why are the animal names above unlikely borrowings?

10. There are scores of similar sounding, similar meaning English-Edenic word pairs here in Chapter Two. Even if the dictionaries do not say the English words were borrowed, most sound like they could have been. But you notice several differences beyond an English speaker mangling a Hebrewism in his bible translation. record and describe three such examples. As you learn more, you will be able to identify how that word from Biblical Hebrew was able to pop up right there on your tongue.

Chapter Three

The Aleph-Bet as Keyboard of Creation

What the Edenic Aleph-Bet is:
The uniquely sound-based and versatile – thus universal – Keyboard of Creation
What the Edenic Aleph-Bet is NOT:
The merely evolved glyphs of previous Semitic, pictorial alphabets.

This chapter has three goals in distancing the boxy Torah *Aleph-Bet* from the evolved hieroglyphs of "Paleo-Hebrew":

1. Presenting an underground history of the Torah *Aleph-Bet*
2. Depicting the *Aleph-Bet* as a possible graphic of the human mouth forming each letter/sound.
3. Fitting this possibly suprahuman, anatomical alphabet onto a seven-sound, *do-re-mi-fa-so-la-ti* keyboard for all human music and meaning, compatible with Rashi's Law, later Grimms' Laws of interchangeable letters.

Why The Boxy Torah Letters
Did Not Evolve From Round Graphics

Obviously, the square Hebrew *Aleph-Bet* letters of the Torah Scrolls were made for carving into stone with hammer and chisel – make that rock and flint. It's pretty hard to chisel a curvy line. A new, ink-jet writing technology was later developed with a quill dripping ink on papyrus. The curvy, so-called "Paleo-Hebrew" should be dated by an unprejudiced mind to a LATER period than the square-shaped Torah print. Yes, the progression of primitive hieroglyphs to more stylized glyphs to phonetic symbols fits the evolutionary hypothesis. But Edenics consistently defies this hypothesis, and an objective mind has to consider the possibility that the boxy *Aleph-Bet* preceded the curvy hieroglyphs.

The *Baylonian Talmud* concludes that the misnamed "Babylonian or Assyrian Script" (boxy) was earlier than what was called "Hebrew Script" or (curvy) Paleo Hebrew. The name *Ktav Ashurite*/כתב אשורית is only accurate in that the original script that was taken underground by the scribes (away from the profane, assimilated masses) was preserved in Assyria, and reintroduced by Ezra the eminent scribe from Babelonia who led the Second Temple community.

The secular establishment rejects the Talmud's position as anti-evolutionary, but consider the powerful mechanical argument that chiseled (straight) letters clearly preceeded letters from flowing ink (curvy). It is the Paleo crowd that ignores evolusion and the history and mechanics of writing. Obviously the "Assyrian" font for hammer and chisel should be older than a font for the later pen and ink.

Also, the mallet is held in the right hand, the chisel in the left, when "writing." And so the original writing was from right-to-left. (Or any direction but left- to-right.) When the Mesopotamians came up with a clay think-pad and cuneiform, they still didn't write from left-to-right. Semites might still prefer right-to-left, but when the more fastidious Indo-Europeans wrote, with no literacy habits from stone-chiseling days, of course they switched to left-to-right. They could avoid sliding their hands or shirt cuffs into wet ink as they moved from left-to-right drawing the letters!

Refer to a graphic chart of alphabets on the following page. Letters like English C and Hebrew *Kaph* כ English K and Hebrew *Gimel* ג (we'll soon see how similar they are in sound too), English D and Hebrew *Tet* ט (D and T are Dentals), and English R and Hebrew *Resh* ר all reflect this mirror-opposite affect from a reverse of directions. There is much more to say about the graphics of the English alphabet and the alphabets and *Aleph-Bets* that it came from.

The Hebrew Alphabet and Three Derivatives

	th,t	sh	r	q	tz	p	o/u	s	n	m	l	c/k	i/y	t	h	z	f/v	h	d	j	b	a
1																						
2																						
3																						
4																						
5																						
6	s,t	s	r	Q	z	p	o,u	s	n	m	L	c,k	y,i	t,o	H	z	f	(E)	d,t	j,k	b	A
7		Ψ	ρ		Σ	φ	ου	ε,ο	ν	μ	λ,λ	Κ	ι		Η,η	ζ		(E)	Δ	Γ	Β	Α
8																						

Key:

1. Hebrew Phoenecian: about 8th century B.C.
2. Hebrew-Aramaic: 6th - 4th century B.C.
3. Dead Sea Scrolls: about 1st century B.C.
4. Modern Print Letters.
5. Modern Cursive Letters.
6. ENGLISH
7. GREEK
8. OLD JAPANESE

INTRODUCTION TO THE INTRODUCTION OF LITERACY

The Edenics thesis assumes that the essential infrastructure for language, like the matter of the universe itself, was intelligently designed for humans. Only in *Planet of the Apes* movies can this topic be argued with chimpanzees. Once designed for us, we humans have had a profound impact on both the environment and on language.

Did our planet develop a unique, life-sustaining atmosphere by accident? Did the unique human anatomy that allows for speech evolve due do a gazillion years of jabbering gibbons needing to upgrade communication?

The design-less theory is currently the conventional wisdom, so this book and chapter must reveal more intelligent design within words and letters to bring new evidence to the debate.

The Darwinian historical linguist would assume that developments in agriculture, urbanization and commerce spurred grunting cavemen of genius into inventing a way to visually record language, coming up with glyphs, letters, and then the detailed bills of sale that we find in ancient Semitic cuneiform.

LANGUAGE HARDWARE AND SOFTWEAR

Our greatest scientists have recently established that the human brain was hardwired for language. Besides the marvelous language softwear in our brains, we will touch on the intelligently designed anatomical speech hardware in our bodies. We discussed how the delicately floating hyoid bone in the human throat makes speech possible. Various positions of the tongue on teeth or lips, and air flow to the nose or throat control the pitch, and let us play the notes or sounds that we speakers call letters.

The analogy of letters to musical notes best fits when considering the infinite variety of music one can play from the same keyboard, and the way the same Edenic sheet music is played in seventy styles, and 6,000 varieties.

We shall soon see how the Edenic *Aleph-Bet* may depict our oral hardware, a factory-provided owner's manual guiding us how to sound out the notes of our mysterious music of meaning. In the next chapter (Letter Shifts), it will be specifically documented how these anatomically-correct Edenic letters help us to see and hear how Babel-babble works – the diversity of world vocabulary from an Edenic source.

We must first examine the strange history of this *Aleph-Bet*, and the patterns of its individual letters and sounds. If a single letter/sound is like an atomic particle, by Chapter Seven we will see how these particles or letters combine to form roots and sub-roots, molecules of meaning that echo properties we may recognize from physics and chemistry.

This is the last of the more theoretical chapters, but even here in Chapter Three there are some physical facts which may dovetail with the overarching metaphysical strategies of early Genesis. The case here for Genesis 11 and Intelligent Design is not meant to disprove science, but to improve it. Perhaps one day the Darwinists will more successfully demonstrate how mutation and survival of the fittest outfitted our species with this language softwear and hardware. Science now accepts as fact that there was one global Proto-Earth language; perhaps one day scientists will tell us why this evolved and splintered so spectacularly.

Until then, permit us to call the *Aleph-Bet* or alphabet the "Keyboard of Creation." An atheist is allowed to read the "creation" word in lower case, and to believe that anatomy and physics are also from an accidental Big Bang. (Where the ingredients of this explosion came from is another question.) A good scientist carefully reviews the new evidence first, and only later might dismiss it as Creationist cartoonery.

"Keyboard" is a musical term that does not fit the spelling-is-sacred belief of many people interested in language. There are several varieties of tone and pitch to the same "la" note, and the spelling bee-keepers will be asked to consider liquids (tongue-made sounds) *Lamed*/L and *Resh*/R as mere variations of the same note. You are asked to see and hear a place where music meets science. It is a scientific fact that sound is energy. Edenics is the confluence of sound and sense. Whether we are silently reading letters and words (notes and phrases) or speaking aloud, we are tickling the ivories of a gift called communication, a seemingly miraculous music of meaning.

ALPHABETS ARE MERELY EVOLVED PICTURE WRITING

All "normal" writing systems seem to have evolved from primitive hieroglyphs, more advanced pictographs and finally phonetic symbols (where symbols are letter-sounds not entire words). Before a symbol for the vowel and Y sound of the word "eye," there was a drawing of an eye. The Ancient Egyptians, the Maya, and the Chinese did not quite achieve a phonetic alphabet, but they did progress towards readability. This chapter will explore a different, less natural scenario for the Edenic *Aleph-Bet*. Once again, the reader should consider if Edenic is "a" language or "the" language.

Anything now in print has the usual bias that paints the Ancient Hebrews as pagan primitives whose letters evolved from centuries of other Semitic carved pictures of *Aleph* א (ox), Beth ב (house), *Gimel* ג (camel), *Dalet* ד (tent door), and so forth. These Semitic scripts are called Paleo-Hebrew. Back to the stylized "eye" drawing, the Paleo-Hebrew and Modern Hebrew script letter that sounds like eye, *Ayin* ﬠ, DOES look like an eye. This chapter exists because the print, boxy or Torah *Ayin* ﬠ DOES NOT look like an eye.

Having reproductions of various ancient alphabets will help us visualize what is being discussed here. The alphabet chart in the beginning of *The Word* and on page 97 is useful. Readers should be intrigued that the pre-Chinese, once-phonetic Japanese alphabet resembles the ancient Semitic ones. This reinforces the idea that literacy began in the Middle East, and widens the spreading of the early alphabet beyond the Greek borrowing of the Phoenician *Aleph-Bet*.

Without access to an encyclopedia, you can find the Paleo-Hebrew or ancient Semitic letters in various pocket Hebrew-English dictionaries and on several websites.

One good webpage to see is http://en.wikipedia.org/wiki/Paleo-Hebrew_alphabet

A THEORETICAL HISTORY OF THE PRIMEVAL SECRET SCRIPT: *AN ALEPH-BET BEFORE PALEO-HEBREW.*

Just as this book hopes to make it possible to consider that our once-global human language was intelligently designed (Edenic before The Tower of Babel), it might also be possible that there was once real literacy, a phonetic alphabet, that existed long before the archeological record suggests. Are Paleo-Hebrew scripts a pale attempt to reproduce a pre-existant *Aleph-Bet*? De-evolution from a previous, non-human source is consistent with the rest of Edenics theory.

Even if Adam and Eve had no need for a writing system, it is possible that with the innate gift of language came at least the ability to intuit a phonetic *Aleph-Bet*.

A verse like, "These are the accounts of the heaven and earth" in Genesis 2:4 may indicate some prehistoric, pre-Biblical written record.

"This is the book of the generations of Adam…" (Genesis 5:1) sounds even less like some oral lore, and more like an actual written record. Huge temple walls are required to carve out a chronicle in non-phonetic hieroglyphs.

Again, the person who reveres the Paleo Hebrew *Aleph-Bet*, and considers them sources of profound teaching must ask himself the following: Would the Creator have a letter ב *Bet* that 1) pictures nothing in the natural world, but that depicts the two lips and air flow that He designed? or 2) a crude image (images are forbidden) or glyph that depicts a house or בית BaYit?

In scenario 1, the word for house need not have existed before the square, Torah ב *Bet*.

In scenario 2, the word BaYiT already existed. Humans were just trying to devise a glyph to recapture the lost "B" sound. The human brilliance of this strategy is diminished with the prospect that there once existed a phonetic alphabet – but this was replaced by lowly people who couldn't deal with a letter that meant a number (40), and who wanted to name the letters after something they could see. (This compelling graphic imagination, a need even to see the non-material Creator of space, is called idol worship in Judaism and Islam.)

The Torah days of the week and month similarly had no names. They were numbered. Here too, along came the minds of idol-worshipers, like the Babylonians, Norsemen, Germanics, and Romans, who named the days and months after deities like the Sun, Moon, Thor, or Frig (wife of Woden), Janus or emperors like Julius and Augustus. Observant Jews will use Babylonian month names like Tamuz, a pagan deity. This is Biblically forbidden, but devotion to the time-honored errors of sages won the day.

It would appear that the so-called Paleo *Aleph-Bet* best fits an atheist world view, rather than one where a Divine Lawgiver carved (straight) letters in stone. When Moses was told to redo the second tablets, he chiseled them. He was not introduced to quill and inkjet technology for writing curvy glyphs – like a round *Ayin*, as opposed to an *Ayin* of straight lines which can not possibly depict an eye.

Again, Edenics does not depend on the demotion of the Paleo *Aleph-Bet* as a later, merely- human device. It is a hunch, not a thesis carved in stone.

EDENIC LETTERS ARE NUMBERS

Noah's ark-building measurements (Genesis 6:15) required a knowledge of the Edenic letters, which are also numbers. Either A) he was the genius who first developed numbers, B) Noah merely inherited the Edenic letters/numbers that were innately in his Edenic language program, or C) the whole story is a foolish fable – whatever floats your boat.

Only Edenic literacy explains the Joseph story. Joseph clearly had learned how to make mathematical notations and to keep precise records before he got to Egypt. The slave Joseph was only sold to a royal official in Egypt because his literacy made him a standout in the ancient world. He was not promoted to chief steward for his ability to memorize the elaborate inventories of his master's estate. He could already read and write. Literacy, writing, heiroglyphics, was a magic power only to be given to sacred scribes or חרטמים K[H]aRTooMiM, the royal sorcerers, literally inscribers (Exodus 7:22).

The Egyptians rightly venerated Joseph (*The Riddle of the Exodus* by James D. Long – Lightcatcher Books).

Ira Younger points to Exodus 41:49 for how Joseph counted grain that was amassed like the (uncountable) sands of the sea…"very much, until he stopped counting…" Joseph's mathematical ability was able to handle huge projects, not merely the running of an estate and a prison. יוסף Yo$aiF or Joseph's name is like הסיף HoaSeeYF (to add). This first Hebrew to venture into the outside world became the world's mathematical superstar.

And this wasn't because of so-called Paleo-Hebrew pictographs, which were not used as numbers.

Joseph had learned the wisdom of using the square, Torah letters. It is unlikely that his busy ancestors had invented a number system, even if Jacob counted sheep. We now use Arabic numbers, because the numerals of the dense Romans are so unwieldy. (They do look good on Superbowl T-shirts.)

The source of a number system appears to long predate Arabic culture. When considering the numerical aspect of the Edenic letters, it becomes less far-fetched to consider that Edenic letters/numbers may be from some pre-historic, even non-human source.

Literacy and prowess with record-keeping and economics remained an invaluable Hebrew skill in a largely illiterate world, well past the first European banking and brokerage houses begun by Jews in what the West would call the Dark Ages.

The too-often uniquely Jewish facility with counting and spelling, with their exotic letters (which gave rise to our Arabic numbers) were considered a form of magic.

This was not a good thing in a world where sorcerers were executed as dangerous criminals. It is the whitest of White "Magic" when a Jewish woman recites a Hebrew blessing over candles and a snowy tablecloth, closing her eyes and waving her hands in an alchemical event that transforms the weekday into Sabbath.

But this can look like scary Black Magic to a non-Jewish neighbor. Hearing Jews chanting a blessing over food, magically transforming the animal into the angelic, sounds unnerving. It is why some theorize that *abracadabra* is from "the blessing has been said" in a mangled Aramaic.

Only Hebrew has letters that are numbers, giving counters the ability encode numbers in words and words in numbers. In this chapter on letter shapes, note how number two resembles the second Hebrew letter, ב *Bet*. The two different ways of writing number four (4) are seen in different eras of writing the Semitic *Dalet* – ◢ – the triangular delta or upside-down h. These two fours may indicate that the Edenic *Aleph-Bet* and the Paleo-Hebrew scripts existed side-by-side, rather than one having evolved from the other.

The mathematic element of Edenics requires reading other books, but suffice it to say that Ph.D.s in Biblical literature who are unfamiliar with the numerical values of key Hebrew Bible terms are only skimming the surface of the text. The Edenic word for spelling out letters is the same for counting: *Sin-Pey-Resh* ספר $aPeR. An accounting (retelling) is like counting. We will see how liquids/tongue letters L and R interchange. It should no longer surprise you that SPELL, German or Yiddish *shpiel*, and a venerated accounting like the Go**SPEL**s are from ספר $aPeR, to count. [GOSPEL]

Historical linguists believe that Hebrew is a late Semitic language. They are right. Edenic is NOT Hebrew, but Pre-Hebrew.

Secular scholars have never considered the concept of an Edenic human language that predates terms like Semitic. It would not matter if the carbon 14 dating of Sumerian shards are earlier than Abraham's Late Bronze Age. And Abraham is the first known Hebrew speaker. Hieroglyphic systems are certainly older than any widespread use of Edenic writing. Edenic was not for pressing cuneiform wedges into

> The first time that an actual script is alluded to seems to be in Exodus 32:15,16. This is quite late even for a document that documents Akad, one of our oldest known cities. But this script was likely not unknown to Moses when he got the stone tablets. It certainly preceded the Egyptian experience because the Hebrew *Aleph*-Bet is far advanced from and nothing like Ancient Egyptian hieroglyphs.

clay tablets to record the sale of sheep. This would not be the only time in history that Edenic or Hebrew literacy would be an esoteric, underground discipline. Perhaps the *Aleph-Bet* was quietly passed down the generations, from Adam to Shem, from Shem and Eber to Abraham, from Joseph's teachers and students to Moses' and, finally, to today. Grade school kids in Tel Aviv learn conversational skills in Modern Hebrew, the spoken language closest to Edenic.

And so, perhaps it is not so far-fetched to presume that the concept of writing letters, words and numbers did not evolve over millennia by nearby Semites, and then got borrowed by Hebrews. There is no evidence of an older alphabet than the *Aleph-Bet*. Archeological markings prove greater use, not greater antiquity. The gift of Edenic literacy may go back to the dawn of history. It may be that the archeological evidence or various ancient Mideastern scripts speak of awkward attempts to simulate a primordial phonetic Edenic alphabet.

For lack of hard evidence, linguists are justified in assuming that Hebrew is a relatively recent West Semitic dialect. No secular king knew the Torah script to carve it into a stone stele to boastfully lie about some great victory. The writers of the Dead Sea Scrolls were more pious than learned. They wrote in the only script they knew, a Semitic *Aleph-Bet* of the masses. They may have copied sacred scrolls from the boxy Torah script, so as to render them readable to their fanatically pious, but not scholarly Essene community at Qumran. There exist certain Torah scrolls, such as one discovered in Prague, that retain peculiarities that allegedly date it to a copy of one of the early copies made from Moses' original scroll.

It is speculative to suppose that Abraham had literacy, when the first reference to letters and Torah writing is in the context of the Ten Commandments several centuries later.

Moses had to teach, and dictate laws, and the Torah calls itself a "book." It is unlikely, however, that literacy popped out of thin air at this time. It makes sense that earlier generations had to have literacy. But why would the earliest Hebrews need literacy if their traditions could have been handed down orally? Don't popular authors write about the Hebrew "nomads" as though they were illiterate desert shepherds with a penchant for storytelling?

In post-Biblical times, the belief that words are somehow pre-existent persists.

In the daily morning Hebrew liturgy is an important morning blessing of ברוך שאמר BaROOKH SheAMaR. It opens with: "Blessed is the One who but said the words to bring the world into existence." We can never fathom the mind of our Creator, of course, but plumbing the depths of Edenic words, roots and letters will offer insights into the richly complex workings of the Creator of all natural sciences. By the end of this century, there should be advances in geology and biology that were embedded in Edenic terms. By the end of this book, the reader will be more able to mine the Edenic riches in the Bible, which are barely strip-mined by the translators.

"In the beginning was the word." This is the Gospel of John's Greek echo of the Jewish tradition that these letters and words pre-existed, and were key instruments in Creation.

The concept may seem to be bizarre, but allow Edenics to make the case that this unique, primeval *Aleph-Bet*, may be the Keyboard of Creation.

The oldest letters of known alphabets are a stylized picture of an object to signify a specific sound. For example, if one wanted to record the "A" sound in the ancient Semitic alphabet of the 8th century B.C.E., one made a glyph depicting an *Aleph* (ox). The English A retains that graphic of a head and horns (though upside down).

It is also easy to see that in the boxy Torah scroll letters, the authentic *Aleph-Bet* (not the modern cursive letters) has an א *Aleph*/A which is NOT an ox or anything imagined by a secularist. Not enough of the traditional letters depict pictures of the objects represented in the evolved glyphs of Paleo-Hebrew.

Hebrew's round cursive is clearly from these earlier scripts. This was the script of the common people. The boxy sacred script has a different pedigree, is purely phonetic, and was only used by a handful of scribes.

This graphic difference between Hebrew script and Torah print does not prevent scholars from assuming that the Torah *Aleph-Bet* (called the Assyrian Script or כתב אשורית *Ktav Ashurit*) is also merely an evolved version of the ancient Semitic glyphs that academics call "Paleo-Hebrew." Lacunas in logic never sway those with religious (in this case anti-religious) bias. Convincing evidence that the ancient Semitic alphabets are the ancestor of the Torah *Aleph-Bet* is missing. Just as the Missing Link between Man and the apes remains missing.

Secular linguists are more concerned with semantics, what a word means **now**, than a word's history. So, then, does it really matter if a letter symbol is a sound by itself or if the Paleo-Hebrew glyph of an ox (an א *Aleph*) gave rise to the letter we use for the א *Aleph* sound? [ELEPHANT] [ALPHABET]

Practically, it doesn't matter. In this book it matters a great deal. You may liken it to the second of the Ten Commandments prohibitions against totems, physical representatives of the metaphysical. The authentic Torah letters don't merely represent sounds, they ARE sounds. Edenics may be summed up on one foot with the formula: *sound = energy*.

An intelligent designer seems to have engineered the human mouth to make these letter/sounds, and we shall be following the letter-shapes of these sounds and the patterned permutations of these sounds. A verse from Scripture that describes a creator of speech, calling for peace and healing to global speakers near and far, is Isaiah 57:19:

> "I create the fruit of the lips; Peace, peace to him that is far off, and to him that is near, saith the Lord; and I will heal him." (KJV)

In the next pages, it will be demonstrated how the Edenic letters may reflect anatomy (the engineering of the human mouth, and the sounds that it can make). Later we will see how these "atomic" particles, the Edenic letters, combine to form roots that echo some properties of physics and chemistry.

The phrase "Keyboard of Creation" indicates that language, from the *Aleph-Bet* up, is another ordered, natural science. Language was not evolved by humans who accidentally had their cranial cavities enlarged and a hyoid bone for speech grown in their throat. The word "Creation" is therefore relevant in a language field once abandoned to the chaotic liberal arts. "Keyboard" is a musical term, and the scientific principle that sound is energy means that human meaning is tickling the ivories of divine music. The letters are the notes of that music of meaning. Neither the shapes nor sounds of the *Aleph-Bet* letters are the result of human achievement, as per the conventional wisdom in our libraries and schools.

As with languages, words or writing systems, the current understanding of secular scholars is that the *Aleph-Bet* letters evolved from hieroglyphs, pictographs and finally phonetic symbols based on these previous forms. This chapter will explore a different scenario.

Secular linguists have noted and recorded some key patterns within this de-evolution that broke up the apparent All-Earth Mother Tongue at the dawn of time.

Proving that early writing systems were also a weakened form of some aboriginal *Aleph-Bet* may be impossible or unnecessary. Yet, there exists the belief that words are somehow pre-existent.

The Lord designed the human mouth to make these sounds, and we shall be following the letter-shapes of these sounds and the patterned permutations of these sounds. The verse from Isaiah 57:19 says, "I create the fruit of the lips...." ניב NeeYBH is mistranslated here as "fruit" by the literary but sometimes less accurate KJV. The Ben-Yehudah dictionary defines NeeYBH as "idiom, speech, dialect, and canine tooth." The non-accidental design in the initial diversity of world language is our point here, and "fruit of the lips" ignores the physical teeth and lips most relevant in this chapter. Can you hear the word NIBBLE in NeeYBH? In later chapters you'll encounter the reversals, like NB → BN, that which also let us catch the buck-toothed BUNNY.

Just as geneticists couldn't imagine a system so complex – yet elemental and modular – as the genome discovered in the 1990s, so linguists can't fathom the rich, economic, divinely engineered profundity in the building blocks of meaning in the *Aleph-Bet*. Geneticists are stunned to discover how few genomes separate a man from a mouse. Similarly, the change of one letter of the *Aleph-Bet* within the same root provides pure antonyms (opposites) or synonyms (of the same logical theme). Our study will also reveal how subtle sound shifts, often of a single root-letter, allow us to link similar words in languages never before linked.

In English, a much de-evolved, thus relatively simple and logical language, one can express a subject and verb with a tense (time frame) in only three words. For example: "We will go." In Edenic, it takes only three root LETTERS to do the same: *Noon-Lamed-Khaf*, N-L-KH, or נלך NeyLeKH. Humans are not capable of such economy and engineering. Certainly not cavemen, nor even a committee of Early Bronze Age elders chipping glyphs into stone.

Since much of this is in an essay from the Edenics website, let us reproduce a modified version of that essay here:

THE ABCS OF CREATION

In the decades of work on Edenics since the 1980s, it may be confirmed that sound is sense, and that human vocabulary (all variants of the original

Edenic – Biblical Hebrew and other proto-Semitic roots) is from the same Creator of the human brain and mouth, astrophysics or biochemistry.

The thesis is as old as Genesis 11, yet the work remains radical (pun intended). Edenicists are root doctors, digging for sub-roots. We follow the shifts of sound or space of each root letter. We mostly listen to phonemes, the sound of two root letters combined. If atoms are like letters, phonemes are the molecules. Anything longer than two letters is a compound, a combination of meaning elements, just as any substance which includes H_2O has been added to water (hydrogen plus oxygen).

Edenics has concentrated on the sound and sense of words, and has not done much with the history or shape of the Torah's alphabet letters or *Aleph-Bet*. There are books on the mystical symbolism and meaning of each letter, and I defer and refer you to them. They are largely homiletic, symbolic, or kabbalistic. For a cross between a scientific and kabalistic approach to the graphics of the Hebrew *Aleph-Bet*, visit the Meru Foundation's website.

Edenics should consider questions about the history and origin of writing, and of the design of the Torah's *Aleph-Bet* – from its more scientific perspective. Without competing with the bodies of work on the graphics of the *Aleph-Bet*, Edenics will offer observations that touch upon two important areas.

The historic confusion between the square or Torah letters and the "Paleo-Hebrew" hieroglyphs, the curvy, "cursive" Semitic *Aleph-Bets* of various eras. In Hebrew, TeYBHaH means box or word.

The formulation of a graphic-as-sound hypothesis which explains why like-sounding Edenic letters look alike. These sets of letters reflect the interchangeable quality of these letter sounds – and these letters show the anatomic mouth and air-flow positions of each sound.

For that first goal, let us theorize about pre-history. While Edenics believes that Adam and Eve, the first Cro-Magnons or modern humans, were neurologically gifted with speech when they were fashioned by the Creator, there is no evidence that they could read or write.

A verse like, "These are the accounts of the heaven and earth" in Genesis 2:4 may indicate some prehistoric, pre-Biblical written record.

"This is the book of the generations of Adam" (Genesis 5:1) sounds even less like some oral lore, and more like an actual written record.

But, without an artifact, the archeological evidence of antediluvian writing old enough for the period of Noah, Shem and Eber (or Ebher, whose language gave the name to *Ivrit* or Hebrew), all theories of the earliest written Edenic must remain speculative.

We have yet to find any ancient carvings that might be pre-Flood. Noah did have dimensions of the ark to measure. Perhaps if he had arithmetic, he had Hebrew letters (which are also numbers). But secular scholars would say that both the Hebrew system of letters/numbers and the flood "story" are later derivatives – rather than the precedents for later, inferior models of Semitic alphabets, and for the less detailed and weaker literary Gilgamesh epic of a Deluge.

This recalls our Chapter One dialectic between evolution and de-evolution. Finally, the evidence of a global proto-language did win out. Similarly, here with letters in Chapter Two, we must consider the scientific principle of entropy, and the possibility that a superior, pristine alphabet was the original one, and that subsequent systems are imitations and awkward attempts to amend it. When the Greeks borrowed the alphabet from the Phoenicians (a euphemism for Israelite Sea traders), they retained parts of the sequence. A-D and K-T are largely intact, but U-V-W had to added to make up for the maddening versatility of *Vav*. To make the alphabet more precise to their Yaphetic-Indo-European mind, the Greeks adding syllable letters to the Semitic alphabet they borrowed.

The Pentateuch refers to other ancient books that remain lost, but we shall only discuss literacy as it relates to the verified use of the boxy *Aleph-Bet*. The earliest Hebrews were named for speaking Hebrew, but we may never know if the patriarchs had the Torah's square *Aleph-Bet*. Modern Hebrew's cursive script is clearly from the older Semitic scripts. This cursive was never used for writing a sacred Torah (Pentateuch) scroll, while lesser scrolls, like Prophets or Writings, are found in antiquity. The Torah script bears little resemblance to the ancient picture-glyph alphabets of the Middle East. Yet secular academics presume that the boxy Torah *Aleph-Bet* is derivative, that is made by people.

The Torah's first mention of writing reinforces the idea that the traditional, boxy letters of Torah are not from human origin. Here's Exodus 32:15-16, just before those Divine letters are destroyed:

> "Then Moses turned and descended down the mountain, with the two tablets of testimony in his arm, tablets written [miraculously] on both sides, cut through but [visible] from both back and front. [Both the] tablets were the work of the Lord, and the script was **the Lord's script**; the letters inscribed on the tablets [were free-floating within the stone]."

This inscription was supernatural, so it is possible that this *Aleph-Bet* of Creation was first introduced to humanity at this time. Or, if the Edenic *Aleph-Bet* had been lost by most during the generations of slavery in Egypt, the Ten Commandments and the "book" written by the Lord (referred to later in Exodus 32:32) would serve to re-introduce it. It is not possible that the stone tablets were written in mere Semitic or "Paleo Hebrew" script. This script already involves curves for the quill, instead of only straight lines for hammer and chisel. The Semitic *Mem* is like an English W and unlike the Edenic *Mem*. It is not K[H]ayROOT or a free-floating, circular design that would fall out of the stone tablet were it not suspended miraculously.

On the surface, the taught chronology of the Semitic writing systems seems logical and defensible. Certainly, the Semitic 8th Century B.C.E. alphabet had wide currency and is far more evident in the English and Greek alphabets. (The Z and L letters are identical in Semitic and English, and not in Greek). Sometimes, the Semitic letter glyph must be rotated before an English reader can recognize it. For example, the glyph for an ox or

Aleph ✖ is simply an A that leans to the left. The *Gimel* ⅂ resembled a *Gamal* or camel; the *Dalet* ◁ depicts a DELTA-like tent flap or doorway, etc.

As pictographs of objects like the eye (*Ayin*), they were easy for ancient Semites to adopt as phonetic symbols of the *Ayin* sound. Any child could recognize the small circle **O** as an eye, thus the sound of *Ayin* (eye). For a more familiar example, the Semites, including most lay Israelites through the centuries, used a wavy line *Ɏ* for the M sound because it depicted MaYiM (water). That wavy line for water is still seen in the English letter M or m.

The Greeks who borrowed and modified the Phoenician alphabet did not have any word for water that sounded like "m," but using one symbol for one sound allowed for a revolutionary, truly phonetic alphabet that was far better than cumbersome rebus or hieroglyph systems. The Greeks now had history's latest and greatest writing system. Some Eurocentrists forgot that this was a borrowing from Semites.

An Indiana University website hails the "*1000 BCE PHOENICIAN ALPHABET,* used all around the Mediterranean for trade purposes. The first true alphabet: both consonant and vowel phonemes had symbols. All alphabets in the world (including Arabic, Hebrew, Ethiopic, Greek and Latin) are derived, directly or indirectly from this one." While "Phoenician" may be a euphemism for "Semitic" or "Israelite," the Indiana University professors do feel that the "600 BCE *BRAHMI SCRIPT*' probably derived from Semitic."

A website with graphics and more about global alphabets is *word2word.com*. (The site has many on-line language resources. Feel free to compare the shoddy etymologies to those of Edenics.)

These glyphic or picture-based *Aleph-Bets* were so common around the Middle East, that only the learned scribes among the Hebrews still used the sacred, boxy Torah letters (misnamed כתב אשורית *Ktav Ashurit*, Assyrian script – more on this later). The "Paleo-Hebrew" glyphs did evolve from pictures of word-sounds into a phonetic alphabet. The secular scholars want to establish that the Torah letters merely evolved from the primitive glyphs (which are clearly human constructs of Semitic speakers). This would prove that the Torah, too, is a human endeavor.

However, of all the letters from the 8th century B.C.E. alphabet, only *Koof* vaguely resembles the Torah letter. Nonetheless, these glyphs are called "Paleo-Hebrew," to mean the precursor of Torah letters. Academics like to date the writing of much of the Torah to the Babylonian exile, so it fits the secular agenda to call the boxy Torah letters an "Assyrian Script" – כתב אשורית *Ktav Ashurit* – as if this *Aleph-Bet* only came about in the time of Ezra and the return to Israel of the Second Temple period.

This canard is half true, in that the Torah letters were only able to emerge as dominant in that traumatic period of renewal and purification, when the assimilated Jewish masses had largely abandoned Hebrew for Aramaic (as the Hellenized masses later would for Greek). Authentic Hebrew was no longer written by the masses. If the average Jew of that period could write any Hebrew at all, it was in the common Semitic script WHICH DID EVOLVE from Paleo-Hebrew glyphs.

An illustration of Hebrew's loss to the masses involves the custom of reading an Aramaic targum, translation in paraphrase in the synagogue as the weekly Hebrew Bible portion was read. In Talmudic times, even synagogue goers in Israel and Babylon had lost their ability to understand – and certainly to write – Hebrew the authentic way. {The "ancient" curvy Semitic scripts were newer, feeble imitations of the pre-ancient, boxy Torah script.) This necessary custom of public reading of the Torah with the Aramaic translation was able to fall away with the revival of Hebrew in Ezras the Scribe's time. Aramaic was to give way to the popularity of Greek. This time it was Aramaic which was preserved by Jewish scholars.

What secular scholars mistake for older, Paleo-Hebrew was soon lost. It was survival of the genuine *Aleph-Bet*, not merely of the fittest. The culture war of the Hasmonean/Hanukah era dramatizes how deeply Hellenized the Jewish masses were. The average Jew who could write did so in Greek. The only Hebrew now used for sacred documents would be the scribe's authentic *Aleph-Bet*, termed the כתב אשורית "Ktav Ashurit" of Ezra the Scribe and his renaissance men who returned from Ashur (Babylon/Iraq). Let us refer to the boxy Torah letters as Edenic letters. The "cursive" *Aleph-Bet* is clearly a faster pen-and-ink way to write the classical *Aleph-Bet*, but letters like the Alef do indicate influence from the most ancient Semitic glyphs. The Edenic

Aleph, on the contrary, is nothing like the ox-head picture, and more likely influenced the Dead Sea Scroll script of the 1st Century.

When discussing the right-to-left direction of the first writing system, we saw how the boxy Edenic letters are from stone carving times. The rounded letters of even the oldest of the Semitic scripts reflects a later ink-jet technology of quill and papyrus. Beyond this evident technical-historical point, one can see by examination that the glyphs of Paleo-Hebrew letters did not evolve into the Torah letters. With ז *Zayin*, ט *Tet* and ק *Koof*, it appears that the English Alphabet letters Z, T and Q are far closer to the 8th Century B.C.E. Semitic letters than to the Greek. The Edenic ק *Koof* is harder to make than the Q-like oldest *Koof*. It is therefore not likely that the Edenic letter is later. It is more likely that the pictographs and their successors were influenced by those who had some familiarity with Edenic letters.

Take, for example, the oldest Semitic ב *Bet*. This later became the English "b," when turned on its head. It doesn't resemble an Edenic ב *Bet* at all. The H, N, M and T from the 8th century alphabet will also look familiar to English readers after some rotation. There may well be some memory of an Edenic literacy that inspired an alphabet and one or two letter designs. For the most part, however, the Paleo Hebrew letters do not depict an evolutionary chart that explains the designs of the Edenic letters. The secular, evolutionary theory remains a theory, and new theories must be considered.

THE UNDERGROUND HISTORY OF THE TORAH ALEPH-BET

Academics have every right to be confused about the "Assyrian Script."

The כתב אשורית Ktav Ashurit only seems to appear (or get standardized for public use) by Ezra the Scribe at the beginning of the 2nd Temple period. The secret history of the Edenic Torah script is best understood when noting the similar history of the Japanese alphabets. As depicted in the introduction of *The Word* (pg. 9), the original Japanese alphabet was phonetic (sound-based). This alphabet went underground when the country was dominated by Chinese culture, even though the dominant culture had an inferior, hugely complex pictographic writing system. Only the clerics retained the ancient phonetic alphabet. The comparison would have been perfect if Japan returned to their ancient alphabet, but the dramatic and perilous history of Hebrew is without parallel.

The original alphabet of India was also lost, and only used by clerics who kept up their Sanskrit. Americans can think of the Latin preserved by Catholic priests. In Eastern Europe, Old Church Slavonic has special historic value. Hebrew was unspoken, so was largely petrified within study and liturgy for millennia in exile, and now one must consider a similar phenomenon with its *Aleph-Bet* – but further back in history.

The Babylonian Talmud, in Sanhedrin 21b-22a, states that all the known alphabets were prefigured in the *Aleph-Bet*. If one looks at the Old Japanese alphabet in *The Word*, or looks at the graphics of the Sanskrit alphabet, one can see that this claim seems largely verifiable. At most, one has to rotate or invert the Semitic *Aleph-Bet* letters to see how the subsequently borrowed alphabets of the rest of the world resemble the Semitic ones. The graphics involved in such comparisons are those of the Semitic glyphs. The *Aleph-Bet* sequence, however, reflects the primeval and original (boxy) *Aleph-Bet* that we will soon posit as not of human origin.

A culture is enamored with a foreign culture at its own peril. Had the older, phonetic alphabet of the Japanese not been lost, its similarity to Semitic *Aleph*-Bets would probably be common knowledge. The world would have been more aware of its common, ancient or pre-Semitic culture. The masses unknowingly burdened themselves with a Chinese writing system where each word, not each sound, has its own graphic. Just as the Old Japanese alphabet was only kept up by secluded monks, only a minority of Jewish scholar-scribes used the original, authentic (boxy) Torah *Aleph-Bet*.

In most of its troubled history, Israelites and Jews largely tried to become something else. By the 1ˢᵗ Century, Aramaic and Greek culture was at least as attractive to the Hebrew masses as Chinese was to the Japanese. The Hebrew language itself was in danger, and Hebrew might have been recorded in Greek letters, were it not for the scribes. In exile, in learning if not in conversation, the scholars of the Babylonian academies were able to preserve Hebrew and finally to reassert the original (boxy) letters or "Assyrian Script."
The people returning to Israel with Persian King Darius' permission (thanks to Queen Esther) were no longer allowed to retain foreign spouses or to marry Hebrew with a

foreign alphabet. Ezra the Scribe's way, the authentic way, was now the only way. Ezra's original Alpeh-*Bet* was brought back from the Torah academies of Babylonia. Thus the name כתב אשורית "Ktav Ashurit/Assyrian script.

How could it be that the authentic Torah *Aleph-Bet* was known only to a few scribes, and that even the king and many Levites in First Temple times did not know the Torah *Aleph-Bet*? Look at II Kings 22:8 and read the shocking evidence that Torah scrolls were a lost artifact that had to be discovered by King Josiah when dealing with the High Priest (Hilkiah) and the scribe (Shaphan). Shapan the scribe had to read the scroll to King Josiah. Josiah was so unfamiliar with its contents, that "when the king heard the contents of the scroll of the Teaching, he rent his clothes" (II Kings 22:11 – JPS).

Today, there are tweens celebrating their Bat-Mitzvah by chanting the text of the Torah scroll (with punctuation and musical notes memorized). Yet, as difficult as it may be to imagine, Judean kings and most commoners could only read Hebrew from a variety of non-sacred Semitic scripts. However poor the Hebrew literacy level was in the Judean kingdom's time, it was far worse for the non-scholars in subsequent centuries. It is not conjectured that few Judeans could read or write, but that popular Semitic scripts had replaced the Edenic *Aleph-Bet* for a long time. For a long enough time, apparently, for scholars to assume that Ezra's prehistoric *Aleph-Bet* was new and the result of "evolution."

The miracle of Hebrew's survival over the millennia, with relatively minor changes, owes much to the fact that it became only a language of prayer and textual study, and not one of daily conversation. Nobody wrote love letters or laundry lists in the sacred Hebrew *Aleph-Bet*. The scholars who copied Scriptural scrolls and other apocryphal documents became a small, esoteric group who were charged with maintaining the authentic, boxy *Aleph-Bet*. The perfection and accuracy of these scribes, even today, is a well-known marvel. The positive side of the people losing the *Aleph-Bet* (until Ezra) and conversational Hebrew (until the 1930s) is that they were kept safe from inevitable corruption and outside influences.

Thanks to Ezra the Scribe, even gossip was printed in the traditional *Aleph-Bet*. Printers of movable type favored the boxy letters to the curvy cursive, so that even when pidgin or

Creole languages like Yiddish (a Hebraicized German) evolved, at least secular Jews read their Yiddish papers in the authentic font.

There is reason to celebrate the survival of this authentic *Aleph-Bet*. Much would have been lost if some of the Paleo-Hebrew alphabets replaced it. While it is hard enough to make the case for a supra-human origin of language and vocabulary, Edenics suggests that this particular alphabet, as well, is too extraordinary to be humanly evolved.

II

THE ALEPH-BET AS POSSIBLE GRAPHICS OF THE HUMAN MOUTH.

Unique among ancient writing systems, the Torah's *Aleph-Bet* appears to depict the shaping of each letter in the human mouth, or the air flow necessary to pronounce each letter. This sounds like only an intelligently designed system that could be called "The Keyboard of Creation."

Let's see and hear how this works. Have a graphic of the *Aleph-Bet* in front of you, and keep in mind that the graphic mouth depictions always face left. The graphics of these letters allow the reader to feel what is being pronounced. The letters ARE sounds. At the Revelation at Sinai as described in Exodus 20:15, "the people saw the sounds." If you direct your breath and mouth following the descriptions below you should be able to *see the sounds* of these unique letters.

The Anatomy of the Edenic Aleph-Bet
(which point, as they flow, from right to left.)

Alef (A) is a "weak" letter, functioning almost as a vowel. One could explain how the lines of these three letters depict the tongue in the mouth, resting laterally, dipping down to the throat, not striking the palate, not blowing through lips, not forcing air down the throat or pushing it past the tongue. It is therefore better to return to Alef at the end, to better define the voiceless Alef as NOT doing what the others are.

ב **Bet/Bhet (B/BH),** פ **Pey/Phey (P/PH)**

These letters are a graphic depiction of the human **lips**, or what linguists call a bilabial *plosive*. What is the only difference between the similar looking *Bet* and *Pey*? The *Pey* indicates muscular stress on the upper lip – precisely that which differentiates a P sound from a B.

The Edenic gutturals are ג **Gimel (G),** ה **Hey (H),** ח **Het (K[H])** כ **Kaph/Khaf (K/KH),** ע **Ayin (GH)** and ק **Koof (Q).**

These harsh **throat** sounds are made by air being forced out, and the Hebrew gutturals besides ג *Gimel* and ע *Ayin* all depict that with an enclosure that forces the exhaled air out harshly – but with importantly different exit strategies. The ה *Hey* and ח *Het* are most identical, and are easiest to sound out their difference. The ה *Hey* has a porthole to easily vent the exhalation. As the softest guttural, ה *Hey* is just a breath. Lacking that porthole to the side, the otherwise identical ח *Het* pushes the exhalation down to the throat more harshly. Pull down the leg of the ה *Hey* (toward the throat) and you get the even harder guttural, ק *Koof*.

The כ *Kaph* goes deeper in the throat to pronounce the harder guttural. The air is exhaled straight out, leftward, unlike the others. In its stronger and more direct air flow, it most resembles the open-mouthed plosives. The כ *Kaph* and Khaph also have a left-sided space for exhalation. While gutturals, they don't have the resonance of trapped air featured by ה *Hey* and ח *Het*. Whether a כ *Kaph* or *Khaf* (even harder for English speakers to reproduce) – it's evident that, when reversed to left-to-right, they gave Western alphabets the (hard) C.

The א *Gimel* and ע *Ayin*/[A] (sometimes a vowel) are graphically upside down opposites. The guttural ע *Ayin*/GH is a V of air going downward, while that of the ג *Gimel* is a V pointing upward. The ג *Gimel* depicts the upper and lower teeth growling, while the ע *Ayin* affects no parts of the mouth. The ג *Gimel* almost forms the same reverse hard-C as a כ *Kaph*, sounds most like a *Kaph*, and resembles a reversed K. The ע *Ayin* pockets air much like an upside-down ח *Het*, and the GH guttural of the ע *Ayin* sounds most like the ח *Het*.

ד Dalet (D) and ט Tet (DT)

are the next good pair of interchangeable sounds for comparison. In linguistics the D and T letters are called dentals. In both cases the tongue is stiffly vertical to the teeth ridge. The difference between ד *Dalet* and ט *Tet* is the exact nature of their tongue's engagement with the teeth ridge. As indicated by the ד *Dalet*'s T-like axis, the tongue lingers longer and heavier on the palette, as is reaches more horizontally across the teeth ridge. The ט *Tet*, in contrast, has the tongue strike the palette less horizontally, stressing the teeth ridge instead, with a lighter and quicker engagement. The ד *Dalet* uses no air pressure, and is fully open (to the left). The ט *Tet*, on the contrary, does use the air trapped within its two vertical lines.

In Chapter Four's more in-depth discussion of these letter/sounds, it will be discussed how easy it is to confuse the D-like ט *Tet* and the T-like ד *Dalet*. The "confusion" leads to the versatility Edenic needs to be the Earth's Mother Tongue. This also explains why in the pronunciation key to transliteration, ט *Tet* is a DT. (Languages like German or Thai have this DT.) Many ט *Tet* words will allow for English D or T words.

ל Lamed (L) and ר *Resh* (R)

Liquids (L and R) are interchangeable in linguistics – any Asian would be velly happy to confirm this – and so the ל **Lamed (L)** and ר *Resh* **(R)** nearly look alike (only in these Edenic letters). Both letters show the tongue curled upward towards the palate in an open mouth. The crucial difference between them is the ל *Lamed*'s small upward extension, indicating the tip-of-tongue stress on the roof of the mouth. The true Hebrew ר *Resh* rolls like a European R, rather than growling like an English R. The rolling ר *Resh*, therefore sounds and looks the lilting ל *Lamed*, and the roof of the ר *Resh* engages a greater surface of the horizontal palate.

מ Mem (M) and נ Noon (N)

The Edenic מ **Mem (M)** and נ **Noon (N)** both have the reversed-L graphic of a nose facing left. (Think of a longer Semitic nose, rather than a little Dutch one.) M and N are nose-sounds or nasals in linguistics. The מ *Mem* differs from the נ *Noon* in that it has a large, almost fully enclosed mouth to direct the airflow beyond that נ *Noon* or nose-like vertical stem. Unlike N, one needs a fairly closed mouthful of air ahead of the nasal to make the M sound. מ *Mem* is a vertical nasal, but it also has the horizontal "lips" of the ב *Bet* and פ *Pey*. The mouth is nearly closed though, because the air vibrates within, not blowing outward ("plosive") like the *Bet* or *Pey*. The *Noon* depicts no mouthful of air. No output of breath is needed to make the N sound.

ז Zayin (Z), ס Samech ($) and שׁ *Sin*/ Shin (SH/S)

Then, there are the whistling fricatives or *sibilants* such as ז **Zayin (Z),** ס **Samech ($) and** שׁ *Sin*/ **Shin (SH/S).** The tongue is vertically positioned for ז **Zayin,** looking most like the ד *Dalet.* (We will soon see how ז *Zayin* and ד *Dalet* interchange in the way Aramaic was spun off from Edenic, which is how AUDIENCE, an ADN term, came from AZN, אזן OZeN, the Hebrew ear.) Of all three sibilants, ז *Zayin* most strikes the palette (again, like the *Dalet*). The vertical tongue is less stiffly upright than the ד *Dalet,* however. The Z-like bend in the ז *Zayin* indicates that the tongue lets air whistle out without fully engaging the teeth ridge.

The tongue closes into a circle for the ס Samech, forcing air to whistle out more strongly than the other *sibilants* or fricatives. The whistling is softer for both שׁ *Sin* and *Shin.* Like כ *Kaph* and Khaph, שׁ *Sin* and *Shin* are the same letter, but only differentiated by a dot or diacritical mark. (Similar differentiation is seen in the Sanskrit alphabet, whose borrowing of Semitic numbers is even more evident.) The *Sin* has the dot on the left, or the SINister side. (One could probably add SINISTER to the unacknowledged borrowings in Chapter Two.)

In the שׁ *Shin* or *Sin,* the air whistles out from both vertical sides of the upraised tongue. Thus the graphic of the שׁ *Shin* /*Sin* depicts this divided air stream, directed upward – not downward like the gutturals or outward like the *plosives.* The שׁ *Shin* /*Sin* graphic depicts two air streams split by the upraised tongue in the middle of the mouth, resembling the top of a trident, or, non-coincidently, the Cyrillic (Russian) SH letter.

Yod (Y)

Yod is the tongue scrunched up small at the roof of the mouth. It is the most modest of consonants. There is no enclosure to trap air or outlet to direct any. As a sometimes vowel the י Yod is a barely heard complement of long e or ee. It is therefore the smallest of letters (and source of JOT).

In Chapter Four's elaborate documentation of *Letter Shifts*, י *Yod* is grouped with א *Aleph* as a voiceless vowel. א *Aleph* has been described as four Yods – two stretched out and slanted like an ornate back-slash rising to the left, and with two more י Yods above and below.

ת   Tahf/Thaf/Sahf (T/TH/S)

Tahf, like the צ *Tsadi*, is complicated because of its versatility as sometimes a dental and sometimes a fricative. One can see elements of the air pocket of ח *Het* within the *Tahf*, and elements of the teeth ridge engagement of the ד *Dalet* and the ע *Ayin*'s air pocket within the צ *Tsadi*. The *Tahf* greatly resembles an Old English letter called a Thorn. The Thorn had the TH sound of the *Thaf*. In the ת *Tahf* and Thorn one can see, to the left, the upraised tongue whose tip curls around the front teeth.

There have been recent alphabets designed for newly written languages, like Cherokee. None of these display the profound simplicity, and familiarity with the human mouth like this *Aleph-Bet*. One might conclude that this *Aleph-Bet* came from the desk of the same designer as the human mouth.

Grimm's Law

The secular linguists have certainly noticed the significance of the mouth, and how lip letters (bilabials), teeth letters (dentals), throat letters (gutturals), etc. are interchangeable, and have somehow been scrambled (often with much regularity) to break down parent languages into separate dialects. Following this sound-related diversification, Latin may easily be seen as Proto-Romance, the parent language of daughters: Portuguese, Spanish, Catalan, Provencal, French, Italian, and Rumanian. Students of Edenics trace such grandparents to Biblical patriarchs.

Grimm's Law was a formula of patterned letter changes recorded by the famous fairy tale collector, Jakob Grimm, in 1822. "The observed correspondences between cognate daughter languages as they derived from Indo-European parent languages" were rather like a fairy tale as far as consistency goes. (Linguists require absolute consistency from Edenics). But the somewhat-consistent patterns of *letter shifts* were a valuable contribution to the new field of historical linguistics. Of course, the patterns of *letter shifts* were only "consonantal," and did not involve vowels. The 19th Century linguists missed a clue. They would not consider that the shifting or versatility of letters had to do with Babel and the root letters of Biblical Hebrew or Proto-Semitic – whose roots involved no vowels, only those consonants.

Just as Hebrew has a פ *Pey* (P) and *Phey* (PH or F) as identical letters, differentiated only by a dot, Grimm noticed how P-words in Latin, like *pisces* (fish), often became an F-word in English – like FISH.

Just as Hebrew has a ת *Taph* and *Thaf* or *Sahf*, again differentiated only by a dot... Grimm records T shifting to TH, like the Latin source of "**tenuous**" becoming English **TH**IN.

Just as the Hebrew ק *Koof* is an elongated *Hey* (see above), Grimm saw Greek K-words like *kardia* (heart, source of "cardiac") shifting to English H-words like HEART.

Later on, we'll see that the Greek source is from Edenic *Het-Resh-Dalet*, חרד K[H]aReD (to tremble...the heart is the trembler. (Just feel under your left armpit, even if you aren't emotionally agitated). With Edenic letters like the ח *Het* transliterated as either K[H] or [K]H, it's easy to see the Biblical patriarch behind ancestral K-words and their descendent H-words. ק *Koof* and ה *Hey* are behind many other guttural shifts.

Just as Hebrew has both the פ *Pey/Phey* and the ב *Bet/Bhet* identical but for a dot (which is preserved by oral tradition, not written in Torah scrolls), Grimm observed how Sanskrit *bhara-mi*, (I bear), Greek *phero,* and Latin *fero* are all equivalent to English BEAR (to carry). In other words, all bilabials, as we saw when comparing the lip-looking ב Bet and פ Pey, are interchangeable. If one looks up the entries FERRY (to carry over) or OVER in *The E-Word CD*, they'll find many related B-R and F-R derivative words, from

BEAR to PHEROMONE. The patriarch of these ancestors of English is *Ayin-Bhet-Resh*, עבר [A]BHaR, over – a root with many extensions. [OVER]

Grimm's Laws continues with other examples documenting how all tooth-letters, dentals, throat letters, gutturals, etc. are all like one changeling letter when it comes to shifting sounds down through history.

It is unlikely that the Torah sages, who pored over every letter of Hebrew Scripture, didn't observe this same phenomenon of like-sounding letters interchanging.

Rashi's Law

רשי Rashi is the acronym of the premier Bible commentator, Rabbi Shlomo ben Yitzchak of Troyes, France (1040-1105). His essential, text-based commentary was first printed in 1470, and Rashi is always the first commentary printed alongside the text of the Pentateuch and Talmud.

In his commentary on Leviticus 19:16, where talebearing is prohibited, Rashi equates the Bible's רכיל RaKHeeYL (talebearing) with the Hebrew רגיל RaGeeYL (traveling about). This kind of circulating facilitates rumor-mongering. Rashi, as though merely stating a given, explains how the כ *Kaph* of one word can be shifted to a ג *Gimel* to offer us a fuller reading of the Biblical text. This was an observed guttural *shift* 400 years ahead of the West. He writes that "all letters that begin from the same place [in the mouth] interchange: ב *Bet* + פ *Pey*; ג *Gimel* + כ *Kaph*; and נ *Noon* + ל *Lamed*." (This last pair is beyond Grimm's Laws, but is documented and defensible).

Rashi and Grimm's Law will be essential to our ability to shift letter sounds, and find L/R changes [STYLE]; D/T changes [SPIT]; B/P changes [SPELT]; Z/S changes [SNAP]; G/K changes [SCURVY]; and N/M changes [ELM].

Fitting this possibly prehistoric, suprahuman, anatomical alphabet onto a seven-sound, *do-re-mi-fa-so-la-ti* keyboard for all human music and meaning, compatible with Rashi's Law, later Grimm's Laws of interchangeable letters.

We just saw that the *Aleph-Bet* letters uniquely are divisable by design into seven groups of sounds arranged according to the part of the mouth used to pronounce them: bilabials (lips), dentals (teeth), gutturals (throat), liquids (tongue), nasals (nose) and vowels (voiceless). These grouping are essential to Edenics because, after the Tower of Babel's confusion of language (or "Babel-babble"), an Edenic letter can and will morph into most anything in its range. These changes or *shifts* do not (at this early stage of Edenics) follow somewhat of a regular, predictable pattern, according to language family – like Grimm's Law letter shifts often do. This is why, despite overwhelming data regarding sound and sense, the linear-thinking linguists cannot easily accept the Edenics thesis.

From its very *Aleph-Bet*, Edenic is uniquely designed for letter and sound shifting, for diversity of pronunciation. (By similar design, the finch was given the ability to adapt to several different environments.) With the diacritical mark (or "dot") put in writing much later, a ב *Bet* is identical to a ב *Bhet*, a ג *Gimel* is identical to a (now rare) 'ג *Jimel*, the ו *Vav* could be any vowel or a V or W, כ *Kahf* is identical to כ *Khaf*, פ *Pey* is identical to פ *Phey*, ש *Shin* is identical to ש *Sin*, and ת *Tahf* is identical to ת *Thaf* or *Sahf*. Despite this fundamental fact, millions have no idea that Susan (Susanah) is from Biblical שושנה SHoSHaNaH (lily, rose).

Edenic words have already been diversified since the Tower of Babel. That altered, formerly-Edenic word then comes to the granddaddy of Latin or Sanskrit. The words in these new "ancient" languages subsequently break down into various dialects – often in a fairly regular way. Given all the letter shifts, etc. that have taken place since Babel, it is wondrous that tens of thousands of words in languages as young as English are traceable to Edenic. (Actually, words are getting simpler, dropping cumbersome grammatical elements. So, contrary to the established pessimism, it is getting **easier** to find the original human words.) Semantics (meaning or usage) shifts as well as do letters, so that one must expect to be dealt wild cards over the millennia of Babel-babble – especially compared to the mere centuries of language diversity since Grimm's Law.

For example, the word for *eight* in Romance languages comes from ח *Het*, the 8th letter French *huit* is an easy ח *Het*, but the Italian is *otto*, and the Spanish is *ocho*. One might expect other forms of ח *Het* to dominate global number-8 words, but it usually does not.

English EIGHT, Modern Greek *okto* or Japanese *hachi* do fit, but the Edenic cardinal eight, שמונה SHMOANaH, appears in Arabic *tsamaniya* and Czech *osm,* Polish *osiem* and Slovak *osem.*

Although Slavic is part of the Indo-European family of languages stretching from Ireland to India, Slavic languages often have different Edenic etymons (source words) than do Germanic or the Romance languages. It may take years before Edenicists work out the patterns of this word and letter shifting to rival the modicum of consistency in Grimm's Law. (Until then, readers must use common sense to decide between fictitious, often bizarre sources in our dictionaries or Edenic sources of similar sound and sense.)

Within the usual Grimm's Law, most Indo-European cognates (words from the same ancestry) are linkable by the simple shifting of letters taken up here. Edenics isn't inventing new or mystical letter-change schemes. The simple, usual shifts that differentiate French from Italian or German from English will suffice to see how Edenic (best demonstrated by Biblical Hebrew) underlies all Earth languages.

Grimm's Law, and all sensible aspects of secular linguistics, are helpful, even essential to the endeavor of Edenics. Knowing that Sanskrit *bhara* (bear, carry) often shifts to Greek *phero* and Latin *fero* only helps one find a ב-ר *Bet-Resh* Edenic etymon. The ב *Bet* of עביר [A]BHeeYR, transfer, carry across [FERRY] always shifts to all possible bilabials/lip letters (b,f,p,v), as we will note in this chapter on Letter Shifts.

The Trembling Heart

For example, take the Indo-European root *kerd* (heart). It is the laboratory-invented root that allows for HEART (from Germanic), CORDIAL (from Latin) and CARDIO (from Greek), and so forth. It is standard linguistics to expect this *KRD* root to shift to an *H* (guttural shift) and a T (dental shift).

Since a "proto Indo-Aryan" (sanitized to "Indo-European" after Hitler) language never existed, and its "root" words, like *kerd*, are only hypothetical estimates or "reconstructions" of what a prehistoric Aryan might have said, it would be better to find an actual ancient root that easily shifts from K to H, and which answers the never-asked question, *why* does K-R-D or guttural-liquid-dental mean "heart"?

The answer is with Edenics, our proposed primordial language. *Het-Resh-Dalet,* חרד K[H]aRaiD provides an actual etymon (ultimate word source) for H-R-D and K-R-D or C-R-D derivatives that mean *heart.* חרד K[H]aRaiD means "tremble." Dictionaries maintain that לב Le(V) means heart. לב Le(V), however, means the figurative, not the anatomical heart. לב Le(V) is better rendered "WiLL" (ל-ב *Lamed-Bhet* reversed – and don't forget that *V* is the same as *W).*

Now, put your hand under your left armpit. You can feel that the heart is the *trembler.* Words like HEART and CARDIO, or words of heart-beating emotions, like COURAGE, didn't evolve from nothing, or from a committee of academic cavemen at a language convention. Many other words of a fluttering heart are derivable from חרד K[H]aRaiD, but not listed under the IE root *kerd.* [CREED] [HORRID] [(S)CARED]

The anatomical nature of Edenic words was long noted by scholars. Many of them felt that the hand-related terms for possession or power spoke to the antiquity of Hebrew, but too few of them associated the designer of anatomy with the creator of this language and all language.

On other occasions, an Edenic source seems to be at least equally good, for *sound and sense,* as the reconstructed Indo European (IE) root. Certain words that were gathered by traditional linguists under the IE root *gerbh* (to scratch) allow for derivatives like CARVE and GRAPH – (note the shifts of guttural G to C, and bilabial BH or V to PH).

An Edenic etymon, however, is superior. Instead of being made up, it has ancient Biblical citations to confirm its meaning and antiquity. An etymon like גרב GaRaBH (itch) is closely related in *sound and sense* to a large family of words like גלב GaLaBH (to shave), נלב GaLaPH (to carve), חרב KHeReV (sword), קלפ QaLaPH (to skin or peel), גרף GeRePH (to sweep clean) or מגרפה MaGRePHaH (a rake, whose G-R-F root infers a scraper). [CARVE] [GRAPHITE] – note the shifts of liquids L-to-R and bilabials BH/V/PH.

Both the listing of letters and their shifts (below), and the transliteration key combine with this chapter's previous material to establish the unique versatility of these Edenic letters. By design, these letters, engineered for diversity, resemble the concept of Adam and Eve, or later, of Noah's family, having the genes to allow for subsequent millennia of human diversity.

Only Seven Letters

Skeptics are not impressed by economy of design. This is one way to interpret the D'VaRiM A[K]HaDin דברים אחדים (few or unique words) of Genesis 11:1. Historical linguists want older languages to be LESS economical, remember. The idea of the boxy Torah letters not evolving from primitive pictographs is not something a secular Western mind can conceive of. It requires thinking outside of the box.

They also cannot conceive of a Noah's ark containing all of the genes for our modern animals. Even an evolutionist cannot conceive of a time while Modern Man walked the Earth when there was only one proto-canine, for example. They see today's thousands of dog breeds, and so it's easier to assume that Noah's ark is malarkey.

They do not marvel at the *Aleph-Bet*'s versatility, and its ability to adapt or be "bred" into thousands of dialects. They can dismiss 30,000 bits of Edenics data, and complain that fitting world vocabulary to Edenic is simple because Edenics is only using seven primal letters. By the same token, it should be impossible to have infinite melodic lines in songs from a mere seven notes: *do, ra, mi, fa, so la* and *ti*.

The *Aleph-Bet*'s seven "musical notes," the menorah of seven branches which branched out to provide the vocabularies of the seventy ur-nations, appear in all the necessary variations. These "notes" are: 1) the bilabial *lip* letters, 2) the voiceless *vowel*s, 3) the throaty *guttural*s, 4) the toothy *dental*s, 5) the closed-mouth *nasal*s, 6) the tongue-rolling *liquid*s, and 7) the whistling *fricative*s or *sibilants*.

With so many variants possible, isn't it too easy to link unrelated words that happen to sound vaguely alike? Isn't Edenics playing tennis with the net down? So what if the planet has 30 "unrelated" wolf words that are variants of *Kahf-Lamed-Vav* or כלב KeLeBH (canine). Isn't it all too easy to find such links when so many wild cards are stacking the deck?

This is the leading argument of Edenics-deniers. However, one should throw into the mathematical equation the fact that languages have tens of thousands of words, and only one or two could mean *wolf.* See the chapter on animal names to witness the many cases of 1,000,000-to-1 odds that prove the primacy of Edenic. Positing a relationship between words based on sound alone is senseless. Especially if that sound is so versatile. But the subset of sound and sense is singular and significant.

It could also be argued that certain animal names are shared because of humanity's once-shared history in our dim prehistory. This point has been recently conceded by academia (see Chapter 1). This doesn't prevent opponents from disliking links between Edenic and remote languages like Fijian or Inuktitut (the language of the Inuit people of Alaska). Admitting that Proto-Semitic is older than Proto-Indo-European, despite anthropology's clear evidence, is too non-White and pro-Bible for academia.

The coincidence-criers most often complain about the alleged ability of Edenic to adapt BY DESIGN. Adaptation is supposed to be the province of accidental mutation, and survival of the fittest. It is unfair if there are only seven major categories of interchangeable human letters. No one is fool enough to take out two decades to prove it, but they claim that with such letter- shift versatility one can take *any* language and prove it to be Earth's Mother Tongue. The "unfairness" gets even worse for the Edenics-deniers. In later chapters we will soon see that the sequence of the root letters is also flexible.

But there are extraordinary examples of the sequence remaining steadfast. See the 30 languages that have dental-liquid-guttural words meaning way or road in the introduction here, from the DIRECTION entry in the *E-Word CD Dictionary*. Also, later chapters will explain the science of sub-roots, and how only Edenics contains built-in, designed synonyms and antonyms. Easier reading of the later chapters depends upon the reader mastering the simple letter shifts introduced in this chapter.

There are patterns beyond Rashi's Law and Grimm's Law within the various language families – but that's for a later study. Some well documented, regular shifts between Edenic and Aramaic, for example, do come up in the next chapter which documents the letter shifts. Why would a Semitic, Aramaic letter shift be of interest in a book for English readers? Because Aramaic was a world-class language at the dawn of Christianity, and Aramaic's influence is underrated.

Chapter Three ACTIVITIES

1. Current scholarship assumes that the boxy, Torah alphabet (*Ktav Ashurit* or Assyrian Script) evolved from the Paleo-Hebrew glyphs. Which letters seem to support this view, and which letters make this thesis unlikely?

2. What physical, technical evidence would favor the greater antiquity of square-like letters rather than curvy ones?

3. Describe with basic shapes how some Torah letters of the *Ktav Ashurit* appear to depict Bilabials (lip letters), Dentals (teeth letters), Gutturals (throat letters), Liquids (tongue letters), Nasals (nose letters) and Fricatives or Sibilants (whistling letters).

4. If prehistoric, why and how could the Torah letters be called *Ktav Ashurit*, as though they only emerged in The "Assyrian" period of Ezra the Scribe before the Second Temple period?

5. Looking at the *Aleph-Bet* charts either here or on page 9 of *The Word*, describe how the Phoenician script does or doesn't resemble the letters of the Torah's "print letters."

6. Looking at the *Aleph-Bet* charts at the beginning of this Chapter, then describe how the Phoenician script does or doesn't resemble the letters of the Greek and English letters. What indications in the Bible date literacy from what period?

7. What evidence exists that commmon Hebrews did not use the boxy Torah script? Why might no Torah scrolls exist in other Semitic scripts?

8. What reasons do secular linguists give for the diversification of letters and sounds along patterned lines?

9. Letters were to have shifted even from ancient languages by natural, human de-evolution, as seen in Grimm's Law. Present a sample of such letter shifts from an older language like Sanskrit then a younger one like Latin. How do they compare?

Chapter Four

Letter Shifts

These Seven Letters are ALL Letters.

For now, let us concentrate on those conservative Rashi's Law-Grimm's Law letter shifts that allow us to unmask the Edenic roots of English words. Below are examples of the letters' sound shifts within each of seven anatomic or part-of-the-mouth categories (with the key to Romanizations):

1) The interchangeable, **voiceless *vowels***: א *Aleph*/any Upper Case vowel, and the sometimes vowels – ה *Hey*/H; ו *Vav*/OO or OA; י *Yod*/Y and ע *Ayin*/ [bracketed Upper Case vowel] or GH.

2) The interchangeable Bilabial **(lip)** letters: ב *Bet*/B; *Bhet*/BH or [V] ו *Vav*/V; פ *Pey* /P and *Phey*/PH or F

3) The interchangeable Guttural **(throat)** letters: ג *Gimel*/G; ה *Hey*/H; ח H*et*/K[H] or [K]H; *Kahf*/K, *Khaf*/KH; ע *Ayin*/GH; ק *Koof*/Q

4) The interchangeable Dental **(tooth)** letters: ד *Dalet*/D; ט *Tet* DT; צ *Tsadi*/TS; ת *Tahf*/T or TH

5) The interchangeable Nasals **(nose)** letters: מ *Mem*/M; נ *Noon*/N

6) The interchangeable Liquid **(rolling)** letters: ל *Lamed*/L; ר *Resh*/R

7) The interchangeable Fricatives **(whistling)** letters (a.k.a. *Sibilants*): ז *Zayin*/Z; ס *Samekh* $; צ *Tsadi*/TS; ש *Shin*/SH; *Sin*/S; and when ת *Tahf* is read as *Sahf* (S)

As a T and S combined, the צ *Tsadi*/TS gets to dance at both weddings (dental and fricative). The sharp צֵן TSaiN (thorn) gave English TINE. The צנור TSeeNOAR (pipe) gave English SNORKEL and SNORE.

Do not confuse this breakdown of anatomical sounds with the number of *Aleph-Bet* letters. פ *Pey* and *Phey* (P/PH or F), כ *Kahf* and *Khaf* (K/KH) and ש *Shin/Sin* (SH/S) are *each* formed from *the same* graphic letter. When reciting from a Torah scroll, the reader has to know which letter is intended. (Of course, this allows for many of the double entendres and ironies that delights Easterners and vexes Westerners.) In non-sacred writing, or in the Israeli newspaper for new immigrants, diacritical marks are added to aid pronunciation. As mentioned above, an added dot differentiates the above letter pairs. A dot in the middle of the letter means more distinct sound, and less vibrating air. (ב *Bet* פ *Pey* and כ *Kahf*, instead of *Bhet, Phey* and *Khaf*).

For the ש *Shin/Sin* pair of sounds, however, the differentiating dot is above. It is on the right side for the *Shin*, and on the left for the *Sin*. Now you know why SINISTER means "on the left." There is something "not right" about the left, but superstitions about evil southpaws are baseless.

This dot digression about Edenic letters has impacted our Alphabet. The Japhetic (or Indo-European, Western-trained mind does not tolerate ambiguities – and their penchant for "precision" demanded that an *H* follows *P* or *S* to indicate the sounds *PH* or *SH*. The Semitic sensibility, on the other hand, which the Edenic Bible is predicated on, thrives on the wordplay and multiple entendres available in these richly versatile symbols of sound and sense. Here is a good rule to remember in either linguistics or Bible Studies:

Where the Japhetic sees mind-numbing contradiction, the Semitic sees mind-provoking paradox.

The believing Bible reader is willing to plumb the infinite depths of words that spring from an Infinite Sensibility. The typical agnostic bible scholar at a secular university demands a simple reading from the archaic text of the simple humans that he presumes wrote a patchwork mess called the bible, using an evolved, flawed alphabet.

As we move from this last more theoretical chapter of *The Origin of Speeches* to the chapters that concentrate on documentation, it is hoped that both kinds of readers, those predisposed towards or against the Edenics thesis, remove their books from the table, and carefully taste-test the pudding for possible proof.

Rashi was not the first to observe the fact that letters shift according to similar sounds from the same part of the mouth (like nasals M and N). His commentary anthologizes established rabbinic traditions, so that knowledge of these Grimm's Law-type shifts probably existed long before the 11th Century.

Before documenting the Rashi-Grimm's sound/letter shifts as applied to Edenic, let us give Letter Shifts some teeth with an example of what happened at שנאר Shinar/Babel to the Edenic word for "tooth."

At the TINE entry in the *E-Word CD Dictionary*, one sees how *Tsadi-Noon*, צן TSaiN, thorn, is a source for the many D-N DENTAL (tooth words) in Indo-European. Here again, the צ *Tsadi* is a swing letter that can become a dental (carrying the T "gene") or a fricative (carrying the S "gene"). At this entry we see the sharp, biting צן TSaiN (thorn) closely related by sound and sense to the sharp, biting שן SHeN (tooth). Just within the (whistling) fricatives of *Shin-Noon*, we can amass quite a few interesting spin-offs.

Derivatives of שן SHeN
display the range of fricatives.

Post-Babel spin-offs of Edenic ש-ן *Shin-Noon*, שן SHeN (tooth)
– fricatives: CH, S, TS, Z; nasals M, N

Edenic	tooth	SH e N
Arabic	tooth	S I N
Chinese	tooth, horn similar	CH 'ih
English	irregular tooth	S Nag
Finnish	tooth – reversed	S a MMha
German	tooth	Z ah N
Italian	tusk, fang	Z a Nna

Japanese	horn, antler	TS u No
Korean	ivory	S a Nga
Malay	tooth	S/CH N
10 dialects have this common element reverse		
Tupi Indian Brazil	tooth	S ai Nha
Swahili	tooth – J is like SH	J I No
Yiddish	tooth	TS oh N

Note: This chapter could have only contained one consistent (and boring) facet of displaying letter shifts. Ranging to examples and topics beyond just letter shifts in Edenic-to-English etymology gives this chapter more variety and spice.

Now the intrepid reader, especially those willing to think outside the box of a Western education, are invited to investigate specific letter shifts in the seven (like the menorah or week) letter/sound categories. There are countless examples of these Letter Shifts. This chapter will try to cover at least one example of the major shifts, usually just with Edenic to English:

To quickly find the relevant entries in order to check for a Biblical citation, the so-called "Indo-European root," or English and foreign cognates, digitally search the *E-Word CD Dictionary*. If the data appeared in 1989 it could be found in *The Word*, whose index leads one to the required entry . The planned Edenics dictionary (after 2011) should have full indices. Words can also be researched in a search engine at *edenics.net*.

Voiceless Vowels

א *Aleph /*any Upper Case vowel

The sometimes vowels – ה *Hey /*H, ו *Vav /OO or OA,*

י *Yod /Y* and ע *Ayin*

Note: The English "sometimes vowel" Y helps us understand the intention here. ה *Hey* (H) is the softest guttural, and is easily unvoiced or dropped. ו *Vav* is a V/W consonant, but also an OO/OA vowel. ע *Ayin,* likewise, is often pronounced as a vowel when not functioning as a guttural GH. Edenic grammarians call ה *Hey* (H), ו *Vav* (V/W), and י *Yod* (Y) "weak letters," because they drop out of their three-letter root in tense changes.

The two-letter sub-roots introduced in this second edition will always ignore these "weak letters" that appear in Hebrew dictionaries. As merely "sometimes consonants", ה *Hey*, ו *Vav*, ע *Ayin* and י *Yod* join א *Aleph* here as vowels.

The 12th century Spanish grammarian and scholar, Ibn Ezra, only condones letter changes between the א *Aleph*, ה *Hey*, ו *Vav*, and י *Yod*. In the several regular changes between Edenic and the later, more cumbersome Aramaic, the א *Aleph* and ע *Ayin* often interchange.

The 19th Century Bible commentator who made Edenics possible, Rabbi Samson Raphael Hirsch (SRS) documents the interchangeability of these "weak letters." For example, in the ל-ט *Lamed-Tet*/L-DT word pair below, it makes no difference if the middle letter is a ה *Hey*/H or ו *Vav*/V. L-DT words of covering up and secret arts are לוט/להַט LaHaDT/ LOADT. [LID]

In Ashkenazi – or Germanic – pronunciation, א *Aleph* and ע *Ayin* are both voiceless. Especially in the etymology of Germanic words, the ע *Ayin* often drops out or goes unheard. Unlike *Hey*, *Vav* or *Yod*, the ע *Ayin* has a "regional" factor. [RAVEN]

These unvoiced vowels are easily dropped after Babel.

א *Aleph* can become any vowel, but can also be ignored altogether.

   The best known example might be the Edenic mother, אמא *Aleph-Mem-Aleph*, EeMAh. In English MA or MAMA, that first א *Aleph* gets no respect. *Aleph-Bet-Yod-Resh*, אביר ABeeYR, means a powerful, wealthy man who does get respect. In a word like BARON, however, the א *Aleph* is ignored (the initial א *Aleph* is dropped). [BARON]

It is not wrong to speak of an Ashkenazi or Sephardic *Ayin*. But the guttural and vowel *Ayin* variants are thought to be only historical, about regional dialects in Sepharad (Iberia) and Ashkenaz (Germanic lands). Global cognates prove that these variants are designed and prehistoric.

א *Aleph* can shift to Y or H

Edenic אזוב AyZOABH became *hyssops* in Greek and *ysope* in Anglo-Saxon (similar in Old French) before it is rendered HYSSOP in English. (In this unacknowledged borrowing, note not only the א *Aleph* to H and Y shifts, but how Edenic Z became S, and the BH morphed into a P). Why care about an obscure Biblical plant that is probably a Hebraism anyway? Because the HYSSOP was the first known cleanser, and is probably behind the word SOAP. HYSSOP and SEEP are discussed at the end of this chapter.

ה *Hey* (H) can be as voiceless as a vowel

הר *Hey-Resh is* HaR, mountain [OROLOGY.] Yet the mother of all Biblical mountains is Ararat. The *Hey* has melted away. המון HaMOAN means a crowd of MANY. See the **numerous M-N amounts** at MANY – the *Hey* here does not count.

In the middle of Edenic words, the *Hey* (H) can drop out like a voiceless vowel. נהג NaHaG means to lead, conduct or drive. A spouse can be a NAG, or a rider could continually cajole his old horse. [NAG]

Certainly נהג NaHaG is a better source than the given one, Old Norse *gnaga* (to bite). The *Hey* (H) of NaHaG has dropped out, or at best, become a voiceless vowel.

Hey (H) often drops out when we shall go on to discover the two-letter Edenic sub-roots behind the traditional three-consonant roots of Hebrew. For example, בהל BaHaL is frightened, dismayed, confused. We will soon be familiar with the B-L sound and sense of a BALL of confusion. [BALL] BaHaL is a member of the B-L BALL family because the *Hey* (H) drops away.

ו *Vav* (OO or OA) can shift to another vowel or disappear

In *Dalet-Vav-Dalet*, דוד DOAD, beloved, beloved male relative, like uncle, the *Vav* as vowel could shift to appear in words like DUDE. But even on the rare occasions when *Vav* is a consonant, it can be dropped. *Vav-Resh-Dalet*, ורד VeReD is a rose. But the *Vav* is trimmed off in the word ReD.

In קו QaV, *Koof-Vav*, (a line) the *Vav* is a prominent Bilabial. After Babel-babble a word meaning "line" was used by the ancestors of Latin and English in the guise of QUEUE or CUE (a line, as when Brits QUEUE up to wait in line). Notice how the *Vav* has shifted from a bilabial to a vowel. [QUEUE]

י *Yod*, too, can lose its voice and presence

Yod-Lamed-Dalet, ילד YeLeD, means a boy. But the *Yod* has run off in the derivative LAD. [LAD] *Yod* can shift to various vowels, so it is more noticeable in the borrowing *IOTA* – the tiny Greek *Yod*-like letter.

י *Yod* (Y) to voiceless vowel in Borrowings

Yod or *Y* names like ישמעאל *Y*ishmael, יצחק *Y*itschak, and ישראל *Y*israel are commonly rendered as Ishmael, Isaac and Israel. These are mere Hebrewisms, but it is significant that Western ears heard the Y as an I. (Also note the fricative shift when the *T*S of Yi**ts**chak was rendered as an S in I**s**aac.)

י *Yod* (Y) to J is not a shift, but another foreign rendering of the Y sound.

For *Yod* bearing both **J**OT and **I**OTA, I and J, see below at the dental shifts.

Some Edenic *Yod*/Y words, like ירושלים **Y**erushalayim, are routinely spelled with a J, as in **J**erusalem. We discover that first-person pronoun "I" is a non-borrowing from Edenic *Yod* with some help from the first-person French pronoun *je* (I). In past tense a *Yod* is the crucial suffix element to indicate first-person. For example, הלכתי HaLaKHT**ee**Y means "I went." Also, *Lamed* means "to" And לי Lee**Y** means "to **me**." So French *je* (I) is from this first-person Edenic *Yod*/Y.

Once alerted to this, we can see how the English pronoun "I" is also from the Edenic *Yod*/Y as first-person marker. This is not a borrowing, and is relevant to this sub-section of *Yod*/Y shifting to a vowel.

The actual Edenic subjective pronoun for "I" is אני ANeeY. We'll get to nasal shifts below, N-to-M, but this is the source of the objective first-person pronouns in French and English: *moi* and ME. French pronouns get noticed easier because "we" is *nous,* just like Edenic אנו ANOO (we). Like the older English THEE and THOU, the second-person pronoun in French is *tu,* a ringer for אתה ATaH (you).

' *Yod* (Y) to voiceless vowel

Edenic *Yod-Gimel-Vav-Noon*, יגון YaGOAN, great pain, gave us AGONY. [AGONY]

If the Edenic letters may be called the Keyboard of Creation, then these seven-letter categories may be likened to the Creation week. יום *Yom* [YoWM] is day, but is the source of Greek *aeon* and English EON. Again, *Yod* (Y) has shifted to a vowel, just as יעקב Y'[A]hQoaBH is rendered *Jacob* in English or the Italian *Iacobos*.

ע *Ayin*, as Voiceless Vowel, can diappear

The Edenic Ta-Q-[A]h, תקע *Tahf-Koof-Ayin*, means "to stick in." The ע *Ayin* has turned voiceless or dropped off as it gave English the word TACK. [TACK]

Many Sephardic Edenic-speakers (largely in the Middle-East since the Spanish Expulsion) think it's erroneous to pronounce the ע *Ayin* as a voiceless A, as in the Ashkenazi or Germanic way. But many letter "A" entry words in the *E-Word Dictionary* CD come from ע *Ayin* etymons. See ANTIQUE for one example.

ARBOR, from *Ayin-Resh-Bhet-Hey*, ערבה [A]RBHaH, willow or other leafy tree (Leviticus 23:40) is another example of an ע *Ayin* word that gave English an A word.

In the ROOF entry, one sees one of the many examples where the ע *Ayin* has become voiceless in Old English *hrof*, before being dropped altogether by the time Modern English has the words ROOF.

The ע *Ayin* as a soft H doesn't always disappear. We still hear that H when the ע *Ayin* from עדנה [E]DnaH (pleasure) and עדן [A]iDeN] (Eden, mankind's pleasurable first home) became Greek *hedone*, pleasure. This came into English as **HEDONISM**. (Did it take Edenics to make you consider that Adam and Eve were placed in This World, a Garden of "Hedonism" – that is, of pleasure?)

The ע *Ayin* as H also drops in Anglo-Saxon words like *hraefn* (raven), source of RAVEN, as it comes from the Biblical raven, עורב [O]Rai[V]. [RAVEN] There, one finds that ע *Ayin* as near-voiceless H is an "Ashkenazic" thing by Germanic peoples like the Anglo-Saxons. Mediterranean peoples (equivalent to the Sephardic designation) render ע *Ayin* as a guttural consonant. Witness the Latin raven, *corvus*, or the French *corbeau*.

The most obvious example of an *Ayin* becoming a voiceless vowel involves the meaning of עין [A]YiN itself, an *eye*. The Middle English eye is *eyne*, while the Old Teutonic is *augon*. [EYE]

ע *Ayin* as a guttural is not even a shift, but the more common, Sephardi (from the Spanish Diaspora) way to pronounce the ע *Ayin*. Gaza, source of the GAUZE pad, is from the place called עזה *Ayin-Zayin-Hey*, GAZA. Those who learn the Ashkenazi (Hebraic German) pronunciation have trouble remembering the fact that ע *Ayin* is primarily a guttural, just as some Israelis have trouble recognizing the legitimacy of a voiceless (Ashkenazi) ע *Ayin*.

Much of Edenics, especially the etymological aspects of it, require one to be more flexible than one's particular linguistic background or teaching. The RAVEN entry is a good place to note the planet's Ashkenazi and Sephardi ע *Ayin*. It is not merely an accent variant or *shibboleth* of Edenic speakers.

The ע *Ayin* can interchange with a guttural in Antonyms

Tsadi-Ayin-Koof, צעק TSa'[A]hQ, cry is the built-in, sound-alike opposite of *Tsadi-Het-Koof,* צחק TSaK[H]aQ, to laugh.

All the vowels interchange within related Edenic words; the look-alike *Vav* (V) and *Yod* (Y) are good examples

A question was asked whether Eve's name, see Genesis 3:20, was supposed to be *Het-Yod-Hey,* חיה [K]HaYaH (living thing, creature) rather than the Bible's *Het-Vav-Hey,* חוה [K]Ha[V]aH (Eve). The *Vav* looks like an elongated *Yod*. So, asked the questioner, perhaps the *Vav* of חוה [K]Ha[V]aH was a mistake due to a scribe's overly long *Yod*?

Unlikely. Most such "scribal errors" are intended multiple entendres. As we learned previously about the purposeful design behind nearly identical bilabials *Pey* and *Bet*, the *Vav* is a longer *Yod* to evoke comparisons between these comparable sometimes-vowels. Both the meaning of Eve as Life-Giver, as if it were spelled with a *Yod*, and the sound of *Het-Vav* are intended. Actually naming the first woman חיה [K]HaYaH or "creature" would negate the fact that humankind was not an animal. Woman, especially, was formed from a man rather than an animal. (And it shows.) As for the *Het-Vav* sound, it echoes the *Khet-Bhet* family of terms of endearment and close connection: חביב [K]Ha[V]eeY[V] is dear, חבר [K]Ha[V]eR is friend, חבק [K]Ha[V]aQ is to hug, etc.

Biblabials (lip letters)

ב *Bet* (B); *Bhet* (BH or V); *Vav* (V); פ *Pey* (P)/*Phey* (PH or F)

The *Mem* is enough of a lip letter to be called a "bilabial plosive" in linguistics, but is not enough to be considered a bilabial along with ב *Bet* and פ *Pey*. Graphically, too, the *Mem* has more in common with the other nasal (nose word), *Noon*, than with those *bilabials* that better resemble lips. True, the *Vav* has a sound but not the shape that fits here. We had the vowel *Vav* above, and remember that as a consonant the *Vav* is a V or W. (The two are commonly interchangeable in Europe.)

The normal pattern of bilabial shifts is that B=BH or V=P, PH or F. The interchangeability of this lip sound (or all seven of the part-of-the-mouth sounds) is more profound than just a way to notice cognates or even descendents. The English bilabial words Bet, Faith, Void and Wedding all share a theme, in sound (bilabial-dental) and sense, of FiDelity or legal promises. Void means the opposite, legally invalid. There is no reconstructed root that could include these five words. But the ט-ב *Bet-Tet* subroot includes both בטח BeDTa[K]H (assurance) and its opposite, בטל BaDTeL (invalid). There is more on sub-roots and built-in antonyms (certainly not evolved by humans) later, but here let us note how *Bet* begat a range of bilabials: the B of BET, F of FAITH, V of VOID and W of WED. [AFFIDAVIT] [BID]

The P sound was not in the example above, so let us examine the ultimate source of PURE and FRESH. The P-word PURE is a Babel-babble (in this case a bilabial shift) of בר BHaR, pure, clean clear, the source of *pure* (Psalms 24:4). The *Bhet* shifted bilabials to P. More at entries like BARE, BERYL, PURE and BORAX (A). P from B is a rather common shift. Sometimes it's a default shift. For instance, Arabic has no P sound. When thirsty in Egypt ask for a "Bebsi." So, let's look at an Edenic P etymon that gave us F derivatives, as the PR root of "purity" touches fruit with the word FRESH.

The Western European words for FRESH are *frais, fresco,* etc. Though also from Latin, Rumanian has seemingly shifted bilabials to *proaspat,* now, ironically, sounding more like the Edenic PR etmon בר BaR meaning pure, thus newly harvested and unpreserved. The German for FRESH is *frisch.* The Scandinavian words are predictably similar. The Dutch, however, has shifted bilabials to *vers.* When contemplating an actual source word for these F, P, and V words, rather than reconstructing a fake one, we must suspect that the Proto-World (read: Edenic) etymon should be some bilabial plus *R.* That bilabial is most likely a ב *Bet* or B because the Indonesian word for FRESH is *baru.* Of course the creators of IE roots are not allowed to search globally. This would upset the older, sacred belief that peoples and languages evolved from different monkey groups, or the newer theory that some primitive Whole-Earth language that evolved was diversified solely by natural means.

The study of bilabial shifts, like B to P, also are significant in noting the relationship between like-sounding and like-meaning Edenic words. (The term "synonym" infers accidental cognates and redundancy, so the term can only be used loosely for the divinely engineered language of Edenic).

Birds of a feather flock together. Thus, צפור TSiPOAR, bird, is akin to צבור TSeeBOOR, congregation, group. [SPARROW]

Other *Bet* to P words, Edenic to English:

PIPE is from אבה ABHeH, reed, which doubled the *Bet/Bhet* in אבוב ABOOBH, tube and in the nasalized (extra M or N) Akkadian *imbubu* (flute, pipe). [OBOE] Playing this same double-plosive note on rhe Edenic reed, you can hear the FIFE as well as the PIPE and more obvious OBOE. Moving away from musical reeds to sheet music, consider how the earliest PAPER was made from PAPYRUS. Now you can hear how these P words are from hollow, bendable but sturdy Edenic *Bet/Bhet* source words, along with more obvious B-B words like BIBLE or BIBLIOGRAPHY. [BAMBOO]

APACHE (enemy in Cree) is from איבה AiBHaH, enmity, and אויב OWYeBH, enemy.

LUPUS (wolf) is from כלב Ke*LeBH* (dog, canine). The same *Bhet* of כלב KeLeBH gave Samoan its only wild dog name: fox is *alope.* [LOBO]

More *Bet*/B or *Bhet*/BH-to-P shifts at entries like LEOPARD and ASPIRE, from Edenic *Bet* etymons like ברד BaRoaD, spotted, and שבר SaBHaR, to wait, hope.

Bet, B shifts to V, W

VACCINE is from Latin *vacca* (cow), ultimately from Edenic בקר BaQaR, cattle. [BUCKAROO] In Navajo, cow or cattle is *waga.* To hear the ending-*Resh* (R) restored to בקר BaQaR, go to the word from Arabic you've seen on tuna cans: ALBACORE. (*Al* is an Arabic article familiar to you from the chapter on borrowings.)

Besides the *Bet-Resh* and pure B-R clarity above, the *Bet-Resh* phoneme or sub-root offers much more. ברי BaReeY, clear, and ברור BaROOR, evident, gave us Latin *veritas,* (truth, things held to be self-evident) which gave us VERIFY, VIRTUAL, VERY, and so forth. [VERY]

More *Bets* or *Bhets* becoming W include: CRAW from קרב QeRe[V], animal stomach; ROW from ריב ReeY[V], quarrel; SWITCH from שבט SHe[V]eDT, rod, stick; and SEVER and SHIVER, break, as in "shiver me timbers" from שבר SHaBeR, break. Combined with Liquid (L/R) shifts, there's also WELL from באר B'ER, water source, and WEAR from בלה BaLaH, to wear out.

Bhet (BH) shifts to F

בתר BHaTAR, after, is a good example of Biblical Aramaic that qualifies as Edenic. [AFTER] עברה ABHaRaH is a **f**erry, which ferries one over water. [FERRY]

Bhet, **BH or V, shifts to P**

Edenic חרב [K]HeRe**BH,** sword, allowed Greek *harpe* (sickle), then the English HaRPoon. בוץ BoaTS, mud, tar, is the ultimate source of PITCH. [PITCH]

Bhet, **BH or [V], shifts to W**

WIZENED (shriveled) is from Anglo-Saxon *wisnian* (to become dry), from יבש YaBHaiSH, dry, to become dry (Genesis 8:14); [WIZEN] *Bhet* is closer to a V, but it gives WITH its W. [WITH]

Besides a bilabial, *Vav* can be a vowel (see above)

Vav/V shifts to B

The letter *Vav* means a hook. The V-V shifts to B-B to give us the hairpin called a BOBBY pin. Lexically, the *Vav* is also a "hook," a conjunction like "and" or "with" (which fastens phrases together).

Vav/V shifts to W

This is so common that Edenics renders *Vav* as a V or W right in the pronunciation code. Europeans often pronounce V as W. The borrowing SCHWA (the "ah" vowel) is from the Edenic שוא SHVAh, *Shin-Vav-Aleph*. Within Semitic, it is typical that the name דוד DaViD should be Da*W*oud in Arabic. A husband in Arabic is a *zaWg*; while the Edenic couple is זוג *Zayin-Vav-Gimel.* [ZYGOTE] It is more significant that the pronoun *hoo*, הוא *Hey-Vav-Aleph* (meaning, *he* - the male personal pronoun), is *houWa* in Arabic. This impacts more on English pronouns like *he, whom* and *who*. This *Vav* shift is harder to pick up where the V is merely a vowel in the Edenic etymon.

On rare occasions (in English) the *Vav* seems to shift to R. See MORTAL where the מות *Mem-Vav-Tahf* meaning "death" may be providing the R in mo**R**tal words. *Vav*, a bilabial when not a vowel, shouldn't be shifting to R, a liquid. The answer to this mu**R**der mystery probably lies in the WR combination (dipthong). The R words in "MORTAL" probably did shift to W or WR after Babel, but they got "corrected" to R in time..

Pey, P shifts to B

Edenic פה PeH (mouth) gave us the following mouth words: Latin *bucca*, Hausa *baki* and Spanish *boca* (Boca Raton means "mouth of a rat," but I guess the weather in that Florida town is a source of pride).

Phey, F shifts to W

Iowa (weary in Sioux) from עיף [A]YeF, tired. The *Phey* shifted bilabials to a V in the fairly similar version in Samoan *iva* (sleepy). V and W are similar.

Phey, F shifts to V

The V in AVIATE is from עף *Ayin-Phey*, [A]F, to fly [AVIATE]

Evo (*nose* in Cheyenne) is from אף *Aleph-Phey*, AF, *nose* [OBOE]

146

Guttural (throat) letters:

ג *Gimel/G*; ה *Hey/H*; ח *Het// K]H or K[H],

כ *Kahf/K*; *Khaf/KH*; ע *Ayin/GH* and ק *Koof /Q*

Watch various gutturals go in front of the *Bhet-Lamed* sub-root of mixed strands: The meaning intensifies as we move up the *AlephBet* keyboard from

1) *Gimel-Bhet-Lamed*, גבל GeBHeL (plait or braid), to
2) *Het-Bhet-Lamed*, חבל [K]HeBHeL, HBL (rope or string), to
3) *Kaph-Bhet-Lamed*, כבל KeBHeL, (strong cable).

Going up the keyboard of intensity with gutturals *Het* and *Koof*, allows us to understand that נקמה NeQaMaH (revenge) is a harsher form of נחמה NeK[H]aMaH (consolation). In these examples, note that changing gutturals turned the volume knob, more than it changed the tuner to a different frequency (or meaning). Another example of going up the guttural keyboard involves Genesis 47:28. The text should have just had Jacob **being** in Egypt – *Hey-Yod-Hey*, היה HaYaH (to be). Instead, the point is made with ויחי יעקב VaYiK[H]eeY Yaakov, living, not merely existing, that Jacob was able to חיה *Het-Yod-Hey* (**live**) in the Diaspora and maintain his cultural identity. One can ascend the guttural scale further, as *Koof-Yod-Mem*, קים QaYaM, is to **endure forever**, the highest form of being or living. The guttural-plus-*Yod* is the core sub-root for observing this "scale" as we move from existence, to life, and to persistence.

Moreover, putting these gutturals before the *Mem-Resh/Mem-Lamed* (nasal-liquid) sub-root of loads, one sees the swift גמל GaMaL (camel) and the plodding but stronger חמור K[H]aMOAR (donkey – the two common beasts of burden in the Middle East). Relevant to *Het* and ע *Ayin* burdens, a חמר K[H]oMeR (pile) may involve heavy lifting, but עמל GHaMaL (labor, toil) is harder work. [AMERICA]

Whether guttural *Het* or *Koof* precedes צ *Tsadi*, they share the sound and sense of exteriority. חוץ K[H]OOTS means outside and קצה QaTSeH means extremity. [EXIT] [COAST]

Hey/H and *Khaf*/KH can be interchangeable. לֹהֵן LaHaiN is "therefore" (Ruth 1:13), as is לכן LaKHaiN (Genesis 2:24) . The gutturals have slightly shifted, but the meaning is the same.

Of the seven Edenic "tones," the gutturals can often be lower or too throaty for some peoples to hear, recall or otherwise reproduce.

Gutturals are the easiest of the consonants to drop

The *Het* runs off from חמור [K]HaMOAR], donkey, before we get English MARE, and MULE, where a shift of Liquids turned the *Resh* to an L.

Kahf is emphatic in a word like כל KoL (all), but it is left out by the time English has the word ALL.

Ayin (Edenic עסיס [A]ee] means SAUCE, but we don't *taste* or hear the *Ayin* in SAUCE or SUSHI – sauce in Japanese).

Gimel to J or Y

The *Jimel – Gimel* with a dot, is preserved by the Yemenites. Edenic *giv'ah* גבעה [GiBH[A]H, hill, shifts to *jebel* (hill) in Arabic. The "j" is pronounced like a D and J together, approximating the Polish or Slavic "dz." *Gilah* גלה [GiLaH] (*gladness*) gives us joyous J-L words like Jolly and Jollity.

Gimel (G) to hard C or K

עגול GHaGOOL, *Ayin-Gimel-Vav-Lamed*, means round or a circle. CYCLE is from a root spelled with a K. This harsh guttural in CYCLE requires a *Gimel* guttural shift to hard-C. Avoid confusion by visualizing hard-C as a K.

Within Edenics' sound-alike synonyms, גרד GaRaD and קרד QaRaD both mean to scrape (whence to CARD or GRADE). סכר $aKaR, to shut, echoes סער $aGaR, to close.

The Edenic letter *Gimel* (G), in reverse, looks like a K, and often becomes a K in sound. The גמל GaMaL (camel) not only got spelled *kamelos* in Greek, but also got pronounced *kamal* or *jamal* in different Arabic countries. The *Gimel* of גדי GiDeeY, goat, gives English KID. The dental shift allowing the D after G to allow for the English GOAT is further down.

It is therefore no surprise that Greek rendered a *Gimel* (G) as a K, giving English a hard C, as in the source of OCEAN, from Greek *okeanus,* from אעם AGaM, body of water; CORAL from Greek *korallion,* ultimately from גורל GoRaL, pebble, lot; COLOSUS from Greek *colossus,* from the Biblical name גלית GoLiaS, Goliath.

In Arabic, *akbar* means great. The *Gimel* of גבר GiBoR, mighty or great, need not have shifted gutturals to a K, as with Edenic GaMaL, camel and Greek *kamalos* (camel). Already within Edenic, GiBoR has a like-sounding synonym, כביר KaBeeYR, great (Isaiah 16:14), the source of Arabic *akbar*.

Gimel (G) to X

נגד NeGeD, in front of or before, is the source of NEXT, requiring a mild T from *Dalet* (dental) shift, but for the guttural to harden from G to X. [NEXT] X is more often from a whistling fricative [Xenophobia]. [XIPHOID]

Gimel (G) to Hey (H)

גבב GaBHaBH means to *heap* up. Besides the *Gimel* (G) shift to H, you should have heard the *Bhet* (BH) shift to P. If you look up the Indo-European roots beginning with a G, you'll find several H words in English. Anything an invented root can do, Edenic can do better – and with more authentic documentation.

Once *Gimel* (G) shifts to a soft H, it might be expected to be dropped altogether. This is especially so when an initial *Gimel* has moved to the end, as in the full reversals common to the American Indian and Asian words from Edenic. The LLAMA is the native Peruvian name for their camel-like beast. CAMEL, seen above, is from *Gimel-Mem-Lamed*. Reverse גמל GaMaL to **LaMaG**... but take off that end *Gimel*.

Hey (H) to hard C

CITRUS and CITRON came from hard-C words in Greek and Latin, but they came from an Edenic *Hey*. The lemon-like fruit described as הדר HaDaR (noble) is used for the Tabernacles/Sukkot ritual of Leviticus 23:40. We spoke of how easily a lead-*Hey* might be unvoiced or dropped, and thus when Semitic languages were spun off from Edenic, the Assyrian citron became *adaru*. This golden fruit word sounds like ADORE, and הדור HaDOOR, the source, means adorned. [ADORE] The same *Hey* of הדר HaDaR shifted to harder gutturals in Greek, *Kedros,* and in Latin, *cedrus.* (These missing links are hard to find. Who would have extracted the essence of CITRUS by way of Latin or Greek, and ultimately, Edenic with a guttural shift.)

Hey (H) to G

An example of this rare shift is הב HahBH (give!) and GIVE (whose Indo-European "root" is *ghabh* (to give, receive). This shift occurs often in Slavic. A Russian speaker pronounces *H*ello like *Gh*ello, and Russian history books record the name *H*itler as *G*itler. So, an Edenic *H*-word like הר HaR, mountain, source of HiLL after a shift of liquids, becomes *gora* (hill) in most of Slavic. In Czech, though, the word for hill stayed at *hora*.

Igloo may well be from *Aleph-Hey-Lamed*, אהל OHeL, tent or hut – with the *Hey* (H) shifting to a G.

Hey (H) to CH

Kachinas (priest, ancestral holy men of the Hopi indians) from Kohen כהן KoHaiN, (where there are *Kahf-Hey-Noon* priest words in Haitian, Japanese and Maya as well.) [KHAN]

English H words are from *Het* than from *Hey*. English speakers routinely pronounce the throaty *Het* as an H.

Het ([K]H) to vowel

See entries like ADORE or ACUMEN, and the vowel section above. *Het-Vav-Tsadi*, חוץ K[H]OOTS, out, is shifted to a vowel in giving us the E and O- words like EXIT, EX- and OUT. [EXIT]

The guttural *Het*-to-vowel shift is more common in languages where consonants are dropped, like Chinese. Edenic חן [K]HeN means "grace." After Babel, Chinese "grace" became *en* X157. In contrast, the Japanese hardened the *Het*, and reversed חן K[H]eN to *onkei* in their word for grace and favor.

Het (K[H]) to hard C

The city of Haifa, Israel is etymologically twinned to **Cape**town, South Africa – in that Haifa is named for being a חף [K]HaiF, cape, on the חוף [K]HOAF, sea shore.

Het (K[H]) to G

The noun GORE is initially from an Anglo-Saxon word for dung and filth, from Kara חר [K]HaRA], excrement. [GORE] Also see GAZE and GOAD for G-words from a *Het*.

The *Kahf* (K) and *Khaf* (KH) do not shift much. If their English derivatives have a C, K or Q this is due to the serendipity of English spelling – not a shifting to another guttural sound. Spelling in all normal languages (all but Edenic) is a haphazard human thing. Shifting to another sound IS worth noting.

Kahf (K) to H and vowel

In the ancient Anatolian of Troy, sheep was *howi*. The Latin sheep, *ovis* (source of EWE) also is ultimately from Edenic כבש Ke[V]eS, sheep. [OVIS]

"Yes" in Edenic is כן KeN, while in Mohawk (American Indian) it became *hen*. At the HEARTH entry, The H in HEARTH, fireplace is from כ *Kahf* (K) of כור KOOR, furnace, oven.

Kahf (K) to G

In the etymology of GOVERN, the cited source is Greek *kybernan* (to steer, direct, guide). כון KeyVaiN means the same, is in the Bible, has the same guttural shift, and needs no bilabial shift (Greek B to V). [GOVERN]

Ayin is not only Sephardic:

It is not wrong to speak of an Ashkenazi or Sephardic *Ayin*. But the guttural and vowel *Ayin* variants are thought to be only historical, about regional dialects in Sepharad (Iberia) and Ashkenaz (Germanic lands). Global cognates prove that these variants are designed and prehistoric.

Brian Beckman writes, "In Arabic, the GHaRBeeyeen are the westerners or occidentals; the maGHReB is MoRoCCo or the westernmost part of North Africa; also the sunset, which is in the West. Arabs spell these words with an *Ayin* that has a dot above. The Arabic word for ARaB is spelled with the other kind of *Ayin* that doesn't have a dot overhead in the Arabic/Nabatean alphabet."

Thus we see the two variants of *Ayin* established in Arabic, not related to the location of Jewish communities. The harder *Ayin* dominates in the Mediterranean, and the softer in Germanic lands, but both variants exist everywhere.

Ayin (GH) and *Hey* (H)

Only a drop of the *G* in *Ayin* separates the two.

For the harsh, guttural *Ayin* becoming a C, see CROW at RAVEN. See the MaGHReBH, the Arabic west, at EUROPE.

Below is an entry from the *E-Word* that focuses on the ע *Ayin* becoming an *H*:

SER(OW)   שער   **Sah[E]eYR**

ROOTS: A SEROW is a goat antelope of Eastern Asia. It is from the native Tibet or Sikkim name. שעיר Sah[E]eYR or SaGHeeYR means goat, "goat-demon" or "satyr" (Isaiah 1 3:21). שעיר Sah[E]eR or SaGHeeR means hairy (Genesis

27:11). Pulling together 1) hairy 2) sacred goats 3) the land of Sair and 4) a hairy twin brother is the Bible's Esau.

> **BRANCHES:** Pulling the thread of Sin-Ayin-Resh might lead to English HAIR. There is no earlier source for HAIR than Middle English heer, so the Ayin-to-H shift might have come from Semitic, like the Arabic shaar (hair) version of the Edenic above. The initial S would have been trimmed off. Ayin is already GH, so becoming just an H is hardly a shift. That Ayin-to-H change is seen in borrowings as when the Ayin of עברי [I]BHReeY (Hebrew) is rendered as the H of HEBREW.

Other *Ayin* (GH)-to-H changes include:

- Dutch, Danish and Norwegian *hals* (neck) from *Ayin-Lamed*, על GHoaL, yoke. [COLLAR]

- French *hier* (yesterday) from עבר *Ayin-Bhet-Resh*, past. [OVER]

- HAMADRYAD (a wood nymph) from Greek *hama* (together, with) plus *drys*, tree [TREE] – *hama* is from *Ayin-Mem*, עם GHeeM, with – a likely source for HOMO- and HOMEO- words as well.

- HARLOT, lewd woman, servant, from *Ayin-Resh-Lamed*, ערל GHaReL, uncircumcised (Exodus 12:48) - (churl, via Old French); ערלה GHaReLaH came to mean a gentile woman.

- HEATHEN and HEATH from *Ayin-Tsadi*, עץ GHaiTS, forest, wood. [LUTE] The theoretical Indo-European root for these words is also a harsher guttural, *kaito* (forest).

- HEDONISM, *Ayin-Dalet-Noon*, עדן [A]iDeN, pleasure. [HEDONISM]

- HELIX, spiral (Greek) from *Ayin-Gimel-Lamed*, עגל GHaGoaL, round [CYCLE] with other GH-G-L terms switching places (by metathesis) to HL, plus the other guttural. This appears in a word like HELICOPTER.

- HERD from *Ayin-Dalet-Resh*, עדר GHeDeR, flock, herd. [HERD]

- HERMES, originally the Greek god of "cunning" (*Webster's*) from *Ayin-Resh-Mem*, ערם GHaRahM, subtle (KJV) or cunning (Genesis 3:1).

153

- HONEY, *Ayin-Noon-Gimel*, ענג GHoNeG, delight [HONEY]. The immediate source here is German *honig*, honey, so the Edenic, ultimate source is stronger than it looks.
- HOVER from *Ayin-Phey*, עף GHahF, to fly [AVIATE]
- In Basque, a baby, *haurra* is from *Ayin-Lamed* words like עולה GHOOLaH, suckling, infant (Isaiah 49:15) and עולל GHOALaiL, child, infant (Lamentations 2:11). [GIRL]
- Basque finger is *hatz*, shortened from *Aleph-Tsadi-Bet-Ayin*, אצבע ETSB[A]h, finger (Genesis 8:15).
- Basque village, *herri*, like *hiri* (city) is from *Ayin-Yod-Resh*, עיר [E]eYR, city, settlement (Genesis 4:17).

Koof (Q), like hard K, to soft gutturals like CH

Note what Babel-babble does in shifting the *Koof* (hard *K* sound of *Q*) of יקר YaQaR, dear, expensive (the initial *Yod* is dropped). There is still a hard K sound in Latin *carus*, dear, and English CARE. But, somehow, *carus* later or יקר YaQaR earlier also gave us the softer French *cher* (dear) or the English CHERISH. Other derivatives of the ק-ר *Koof-Resh* of יקר YaQaR include Spanish *caro,* Finnish *kallis,* Modern Greek *akrivos*, and Arabic *ghal*. (The *Resh-*to-L liquid shifts come up below.)

Koof-Mem-Resh, קמר QaMaR, vault/arch, is behind the semi-circular, vaulted things [CAMERA] and one of its derivatives has shifted softly to CHAMBER. If we bend the *Resh* (R) to the other liquid, *Lamed* (L), we can exchange *Koof* for another guttural, the *Gimel* (G), and get zoology's vaulted, heaped up or humpbacked creature – the גמל GaMaL or CAMEL

Koof renders H words:

Many H words have ascribed roots beginning with a K: HEAD from IE *kaput* (head), HEAT from Greek *kauter*, burning, or HORN from Latin *cornu* (horn).

These are ultimately from קדקד QoDQOAD, head [HEAD], קדח QaDa[K]H, to kindle [CAUTERIZE] and קרן QeReN, horn [CORONET].

קוה QaVeH, to hope is the source of HOPE. Besides the *Koof* /Q to H guttural shift, note how the *Vav*/V has shifted bilabials to P.

There is a list of H-from-*Koof* (Q) words at the HEAD entry.

Guttural summary:

A good *E-Word* entry to recap the wide range of gutturals available from Edenic *Khaf* is MARKET. One can see *Hey, Het, Kahf* and *Khaf* among related Edenic words, and C, CH, H, K and X among the derivative words in other languages. These words include Latin *merx* (merchandise) and *mercari* (to trade), the "Italic root" *merk* (aspects of commerce), COMMERCE, COMMERCIAL, MARKET, MART, MERCANTILE, MERCENARY, MERCER, MERCHANT, MERCURY and MERCHANDISE – all from מכר *Mem-Khaf-Resh* (to sell). Latin *merces* (pay, reward, price) matches up with מחיר MiK[H]eeYR, pay, price in (II Samuel 24:24). מכר MeKHeR is a price or sale; מכר MaKHahR is to sell or to *MARK*ET (Genesis 37:36) and מכר MOAKHaiR is a seller or *MERCH*ANT. Not only do we have *Khaf* and *Het* sandwiched by *Mem* and *Resh* in these MERCENARY terms, but the *Hey*, a third guttural, is represented too. מהר MoHahR is a dowry or bride price (Genesis 34:12). Other commercial *Khaf-Resh* words at HIRE.

Dental (tooth) letters

ד *Dalet* (D), ט *Tet* (T or DT), צ *Tsadi* (TS or TZ), ת *Tahf* (T or TH)

Interestingly, the Edenic *Dalet* (D) looks like a T, and double-*Dalet* words like דד DooD (uDDer or TeaT) and דוד DOAD (lover, beloved) gives us double-T terms of endearment like TooTs and the TaTa – variant of DaDDy and DuDe.

Archaeology has confirmed the Genesis record that the first agricultural development was in the Middle East. Surely the goat would be one of the earliest of herd animals. Without letter shifts one could see the Edenic גדי GiDeeY and not recognize a goat. A dental shift of *Dalet* to T allows one to hear the GOAT.

The T in JOT or IOTA is derived from Greeks bearing away the gift of the tiny Edenic *Yod* י – its final letter, *Dalet*, shifting dentals from *D* to *T*. (*Yod* rendered as a I or J is seen above.)

Can you hear the T in words like TRACK, GATHER and METER in Edenic words with *Dalet* (D) like דרך DeReKH, road, גדר GeDeR, fence, and מדה MaDaH, measure? (Note: In British English or New England regional pronunciation, the R-sound in METER is barely pronounced as an H; meter or metre is reduced to "metuh.") The entries to check these for a Biblical citation, the so-called "Indo-European root" or cognates are DIRECTION, GATHER and METER.

Dalet (D) may provide an ST as if it were a Tsadi (TS)
    CAUSTIC (burning, later stinging) is from Greek *kaustikos*, and is a cognate of another K-ST-sounding word, HOLOCAUST (wholly burnt), and a K-T-sounding word CAUTERY. [CAUTERIZE] The K-T involves the common dental shift, *Dalet*-to-T, but the other words suggest that *Koof-Dalet-Het*, קדה QaDaK[H], to kindle, has allowed for the K-ST burning words. This would mean that the *Dalet* has dental shifted to ST, normally the role of the *Tsadi*/TS. In Asian and Amerind languages that ST is TS., and words are often the reverse of Edenic etymons. It is therefore not surprising that "hot" in Mayan Indian is *tsoko*.

Dalet (D) providing T words as seen at the AT entry.
    Edenic עד [A]hD] means "up to this point" – the *Ayin-Dalet* is the transliterated source of Latin *ad*, until; the dental shifts of D to T for English *at*, and even for the *et* locative suffix (for a place) that ends words like Massachus*et*ts in the local American Indian dialect.

Dalet (D) can provide a TH (a softer dental).
    דרום DaROAM, south may be behind Greek *thermos*, warm. [SOUTH]

Dalet (D), *Tet* (DT), *Tsadi* (TS or TZ) and *Tahf* (T or TH) interchange

Het-Resh-Tet, חרט K[H]RaDT, *Het-Resh-Tsadi*, חרץ K[H]RaTS, and *Het-Resh-Tahf*, חרת K[H]aRaT as seen in Exodus 32:16, all mean to etch, engrave, and chisel (cut in). Add to these dental variants in this ר-ח *Het-Resh* family of engravers the guttural variants of *Gimel-Resh-Dalet*, גרד GeReD, to scrape and *Koof-Resh-Dalet*, קרד QeReD, to scratch. These five sound-alike "synonyms" indicate that the "S" of *S*CRATCH was a later, non-historic scratch-in. [SCRATCH]

Tet (DT) sounds like a T, but can shift to D

The Edenic *Tet* ט (DT) looks like a backward D, and you can hear D words like DIVINE and SHIELD in Edenic *Tet* words like טוב DTOA[V] (good) and שלט SHeLeDT, shield of leather, and later, any signboard or SLATE. [SHIELD] In the DIVE entry one sees several D bilabials (DAB, DABBLE, DAP, DIP and DIVE) from the *Tet-Bhet* root of dipping and immersing.

Tsadi (TS) is more commonly a fricative, but the S drops in D entries like: STRAND, TOMENTUM, TOM THUMB and TUMOR.

Tsadi shifts to T

In EXIT, as חוץ K[H]OOTS means outside. The *Tsadi* shifts to T in Czech, where *tvra* means form or shape like צורה TSOORaH, a form (Ezekiel 43:11); *tvor* is a creature as is יצור YiTSOOR. [STYLE] (Note how the vowelized *Vav*/OO is the consonant *Vav* or V in Czech.)

Tsadi shifting to the softer dental TH may be seen as ארץ AReTS (land) gives us EAR*TH*. חלוץ [K]HiLOO*Ts*, vigor, gives us HEAL*TH*. [EARTH] [HEALTH]

Th is not from a dental shift, but a legitimate rendering of *Tahf* as *Thaf*

Shifts that affect Greek will often impact upon words that become English. TH is often from Edenic *Tahf*, pronounced as *Thaf*. (Sephardic or modern trained Hebraicists dislike *Tahf* as *Thaf* or *Sahf*, but they are all historically important variants.) BOO*TH* (a small housing) ultimately comes from בית BaYiT, house, pronounced as BaYiTH. (Hebraicists wince at names like Temple Beth Shalom or BETHLEHEM, or the shorter BEDLAM as corruptions by English speakers. But these are more than mispronunciations; the TH is a post-Babel form of *Tahf*.

The old Anglo-Saxon "th" letter called *Thorn* (Þ) both resembled a *Tahf* and had the TH sound. [ARITHMETIC]

Tahf (T, TH) can shift dentals to D

A *Tahf*-to-D dental shift in English occurs in DOE, where the etymon is *Tahf-Aleph-Vav*, תאו T'OW, antelope. [DOE]

The D of DOLLAR is from the *Tahf* of תלה TaLaH (to suspend, thus weigh) terms of weights and values like Sanskrit *tula,* Greek *talanton* (a TALENT of silver), the Samoan currency *tala,* English TOLL (a tax based on weight) and that dental shift seen in **D**OLLAR. The D of DOLLAR is seen in other English words of "suspense" that are not monetary, like DELAY and DALLY. [ATLAS]

Tahf/T can be a *Sahf* (S) in Germanic.

This is normally heard (with disgust by Israelis), and dismissed as part of the Ashenazik accent of Germanic Jews. But words like German *sehr,* (very/much) before an adjective or adverb (adapted by Yiddish) are from יתר Ye(S)eR, exceedingly. [SURPASS] The Ashkenazik *Tahf* /T as *Sahf* (S) long predates Jews in the Rhineland. The Proto-Germanic people got the *Tahf*/T as *Sahf*/(S) at the dawn of history (Shinar, or The Tower of Babel).

Nasal (nose) letters:

מ *Mem* (M) and נ*Noon* (N)

English *me* is from אני ANeeY, *first-person pronoun*. There are well over a score of such pronouns among the world's *me* words. They involve one of the two nasals with a vowel before or after it. [ME]

Mem (M) shifts to Noon (N) in Edenic synonyms

מעון [Mah[O]WN] means almost the same as מקום MahQoaWM. Both *Mem-Ayin-Vav-Noon* and *Mem-Koof-Vav-Mem* words mean "place." This also documents the interchangeability of gutturals *Ayin* and *Koof*.

Noon (N) shifts to Mem (M) in Edenic antonyms

נכר NeyKaR is strange, while מכיר MaKeeYR is to *be* familiar with. [MARK] [More on the unique, built-in synonyms and antonyms of Edenic in Chapter Seven and Eight.]

Mem (M) shifts to N

Illinois means "warrior men" or "masculine warriors" in Algonquian – which is ultimately from חיל [K[H]aYaL, soldier, and מת MaS, masculine. [MASCULINE] The "IL" element of *ILL*inois is from *Het-Yod-Lamed*, with the *Het* and *Yod* becoming voiceless as seen above. The "NS" suffix of illi*NoiS* is from the מת *Mem-Sahf* Edenic word of Deut. 3:6.

A *Mem* (M) similarly is behind the many words for five, or hand, which have an N in them. Why *hand* for five? Just count your fingers. Whether it's QUINT, French *cinq*, Spanish *cinco* or Chinese and Japanese *chen*, they all come from a *Mem* to *N* shift in words like חמש K[H]aMeSH, five and קמץ QaMaTS, hand measurement. [QUINTET] Along with the nasal shift, a look at these words for *five* will include guttural shifts, and more soft C/hard C confusion.

Edenic מטה MaDTaH means down, below or under. Various NT and ND words fall [Be]*Nea*TH this etymon. [NETHER]

Noon (N) shifts to M

In Genesis 4:12, Cain is put into MoTion as a נד NaD, wanderer. The M-T of MOTILE is from the *Noon-Dalet* of נד NaD. Besides the shift of nasals, notice the dental shift (*Dalet*/D to T). There are several nasal-dental motion terms at the NOD entry.

MORON is from נער Nah[A]hR (*youth*). Greek *moros* is foolish; *moro* is a baby. Yiddish *narishkeit* means *foolishness*, but literally it means childish. *Narishkeit* is acting MORONIC. The MORON-youth/childish connection should be painfully clear to so-called mature adults.

אילן ILaN, shade tree, gave English the **ELM**.

Above, at the *Yod*/Y shifts, we encountered אני ANeeY (I) becoming "me" in English and French *moi*. Edenics will win the respect of academia when we figure out why, for example, the Edenic *Noon*/N shifted to M in French, English, Gaelic and Yoruba (West Africa), but there are N-vowel forms of first-person pronouns in American Indian, Australian Aborigine, Basque and Korean.

Liquid (rolling) letters
ל *Lamed* (L) and ר *Resh* (R); and sometimes, נ *Noon* (N)

No two Edenic letters look more alike in their original boxy or square form than the liquids *Lamed* (l) and *Resh* (r/r), and it's not just Asians who confuse L's and R's.

Why does קול קורא במדבר QOAL QOARAy B'MiDBaR, "a voice crying in the wilderness" (Isaiah 50:3) work as poetry? Because *Lamed*/L and *Resh*/R are the same tone, liquids.

Just as within Edenic a שרשרת SHaRSHeReT and a שלשלת SHaLSHeLeT both mean a chain, there is a clear link between דלף DaLaPH and **drip**, מלט MeLeT and **mortar**, סבל $oBHeL (to suffer) and **suffer**, and גלגל GaLGaL (wheel) and **gear** or **gyre**.

Resh/R **also provides English with** *L*, **as seen in examples like:**
HiLL from הר HaR (hill or mountain), HoLe from חר [K]HoaR, and TeLL from תאר Ta'ER, describe. There is also SPeLL or German *spiel* (story) and GoSPeL from the verb ספר SaPeR, to count, recount, narrate and the noun ספור $eePOOR, story, account. [GOSPEL]

Mea culpa, fault, blame, and CULPABILITY are from חרפה K[H]eRPaH, reproach, shame.

LO! (behold!) is from ראה R'AyH, behold [LO!].

The interchangeable liquids (L, R)

The interchangeable liquids will help us understand that LUST had a far nobler origin. In German *Lust* means pleasure and delight, not just LUST. Moreover, the antonym *lustlos* (dull, spiritless) makes it more clear that L-ST is a liquid shift from *Resh-Tsadi* words like RaTSaH, to want, desire and רצון RaTSOAN, will, desire. What was focused will in Eden lapsed to a spiritless LUST in later usage. [ROTATE]

History's first literary "Rosetta Stone" or multi-lingual text is in Genesis 31:47 where Jacob's Edenic and Laban's Aramaic (a.k.a. Syriac or Chaldee) are juxtaposed. Jacob calls the cairn of rocks they build a גל GahL (heap) while Laban calls it a *yigar* (heap). The Edenic L has shifted to R in a nearby Semitic tongue, and such liquid shifts from Edenic are global.

Among many liquid-based built in antonyms are the hot/cold KL/KRs of:

קלי QaLeeY, roasted or toasted grain – [ALKALI] – English CALORIE, Spanish *calor* and *caliente* (heat and hot).

קר QaR means cold, source of English CooL [CRYOGENESIS] where one finds words like Japanese *kori* (ice), and Edenic קרח QeRa[K]H (ice). True, ice isn't from this guttural-liquid family, but try a word like GLACIER.

Something cold enough to have congealed like GeLaTiN usually means adding a dental to this guttural-liquid family of cold words. Thus, in Semitic languages like Arabic, *galid* is snow, and גלידה GLeeYDaH was available to become the modern Hebrew word for *ice cream*. Ice cream is *glace* in French, like English GLACIER.

An example of liquid shifts in Edenic synonyms is רפה **RaPHaH** and עלפה **[E]eLPHeH**, both meaning *weak*.

There are few liquid shifts involving the initial letter of a word.

RAZZ (to ridicule) from לץ **LaTS**, to mock, may be a rare exception. It also involves fricative *Tsadi* (TS) shifting (mildly) to Z.

Far more common is the liquid shift at the ends of words. Latin *auxilior*, to help, is linked to עזר **[O]ZehR**, to help. [RAZZ] [AUXILIARY]

It's easy to see how ארז **OReZ**, rice, gave us Spanish *arroz* (rice), and English RICE. There seems to be a shift of liquids when stirring rice in Navajo: *aloz*. But, as likely in Samoan rice, *alaisa,* these might be borrowings spelled the way that the new word is heard.

Resh/R can shift to W (normally a bilabial) in the Cwazy Wabbit Rule, see below. WR is an R sound. [WRONG]

The ר *Resh*/R as WR that may provide for a W or V word is explored in entries like WEAK from רך **RahK**, soft, tender. Many Chinese W words come from Edenic *Resh*/R words (George Shen).

Fricatives (whistling) letters (a.k.a. sibilants):
ז *Zayin* (Z); ס *Samekh* (S); צ *Tsadi* (TS or TZ); ש *Shin* (SH)/*Sin* (S);
and at times, ת *Tahf* (T or TH) as *Sahf* (S)

Pedants who sanctify spelling are upset to discover that the energy of sound trumps the exactitude of spelling. For example, among the fricatives, both ח-ר-ס *Het-Resh-Samekh* (Jeremiah 19:2) and ח-ר-ש *Het-Resh-Sin* (Jeremiah 19:1) can mean pottery.

Within Hebrew one can see the interchangeability of the fricatives by the three spellings of the word meaning to rejoice. [EXULT]

1) *Ayin-Lamed-Zayin*, עלז GHaLaZ, to exult rejoice (Harkavy – Psalms 28:7),

2) *Ayin-Lamed-Samekh*, עלס GHaLa$, exult (Job 20:18)

3) עלץ GHahLaTS, exult, rejoice (Habakkuk 3:14 and Old South Arabic).

Fricatives ז *Zayin* (Z) and ש *Shin* (S) are closely related. Both רגז RoGe**Z** and רגש ReGe**SH** mean agitated. [RAGE]

Zayin (Z) shifts, Z to S

SAKE (benefit) is traced to a family of *Zayin-Koof* and *Zayin-Khaf* words like זכות Z'KHOOT meaning merit or credit. [SAKE]

SEAMY (depraved) is from זמה ZeeMaH, lewdness. [SEAMY]

SEETHE, like the boiling beans than Esau sold the birthright for in Genesis 25:29 is from זיד ZeeYD, to boil.

SEEP is from a *Zayin* word, זב ZahBH; the entire SEEP entry is reproduced below. (There was also a bilabial shift of ב *Bhet*/BH to P.)

At SEISMIC (A) the *Zayin-Zayin* etymons of movement include זוז ZOOZ, to move – related to *Samekh-Vav-Samekh*, סוס OO, horse.

Zayin (Z) shifts, Z to SH

SHAG is ultimately from זקן ZaQahN, beard. [SHAGGY]

SHACKLE is ultimately from זיק ZaYQ, the fetters or chains of Psalms 149:8 [SHACKLE]

Zayin (Z) may provide an ST as if it were the other fricative, Tsadi.

זרע ZaR[A]h means to STREW or scatter. So does the *Zayin-Resh* in פזר Pa**ZeR** [STREW] In the entry above, STRETCH, there are built-in synonyms using every fricative, including *Zayin*.

Samekh ($) rarely shifts to another fricative.

The *Samekh* (or "$" to differentiate it from *Sin* "S" – but they're both pronounced the same) is indeed usually an S, but it can shift fricatives to a Z, as seen in the OOZE entry. The *Samekh* appears to be identical to the *Sin* in sound. The *Samekh* is apparently connected to the soft C/hard C problem and the Greek X as something between a fricative and a guttural. Further study of *Samekh* shifts may emerge, as Edenics research continues, to enable us to separate the fricative sounds of the *Samekh* and the *Sin*.

For example, Greek *xiphos* (a sword) was forged from *Samekh-Yod-Phey*, סיף $aY iPH, sword. [XIPHOID] קרס QeRe$, clasp, should be behind French *croix* and English CROSS. [CROSS] סיני If $eeYNeeY means Chinese (in the Bible), one must explore further possibilities of *Samekh* rendering CH.

The all-purpose fricative is the versatile Tsadi (TS).

TS is always switched to ST in "Indo-European" languages. Often one of them drops, leaving just S or T (a dental); and sometimes is behind a TH, CH, soft C, SH or Z [EXIT] from חוץ K[H]OOTS), for a *Tsadi* word whose S has dropped OUT.

Only two ST entry words in the *E-Word CD Dictionary* are from another fricative plus a dental. The others are all from *Tsadi* words in Edenic, now pronounced ST instead of TS (which is harder to pronounce). One of many *Tsadi* (TS) to ST words is seen when STRESS comes from צרתה TsaRoT, TSaRoTH or TSaRo(S) meaning *oppressing troubles.* [STRESS]

Tsadi shifts to S and more

Between S or T, this is by far the more common shift for *Tsadi*. See entries like SEAM, SICK, SIDE, SIGN or SPARROW.

Tsadi to CH

בץ BOATS, bitumin, gave us PITCH.

Tsadi to *soft C*

רץ RahTS, to run, gave us RACE

Tsadi to J

As with JOKE from צחק TS'[K]HoaQ, joke, laugh, [CHUCKLE] is not really a shift, but an alternative way to record the TS sound. The Cherokee alphabet uses J for the same TS sound as the *Tsadi*/TS.

Tsadi as S is normative. (SS is one of the Arabic, thus legitimate Semitic varients) SADDUCEES are a rendering of צדוקים TSiDOOQeeYM. [SYNDICATE]

Tsadi to SH

The same Edenic etymon above, as used in Genesis 41:14, where Joseph is being RUSHED out of prison for an audience with Pharaoh: ויריצהו vah-y'ReeTSooHOO, "and they rushed him".

Tsadi to TH

The reconstructed Indo European (IE) root is *andh*, bloom. The factual etymon is Greek *anthos*, flower, and the Edenic ultimate source is נץ NaiTS, blossom, or נצה NeeTSaH, flower, (Isaiah 18:5). [CHRYSANTHEMUM] ארץ AReTS gave us EARTH and חלוץ [K]HiLOOTS gave us HEALTH. [EARTH] and [HEALTH]

Tsadi shifts to T

Zayin/Z-to-D shift, via Arabic, is seen at AUSCULATE. The Hebrew צב TSaBH, lizard, is identical to the Arabic *dab*. צוק TSOOQ is to press upon; Arabic *dayqa* is narrow. צלע TSeyL[A]h, side or slope, gave Arabic *dali'a*, bent, curved. ארץ AReTS, earth, gave Dutch *aard*, earth, as in the earthpig or AARDVARK [EARTH]. קץ QaiTS, posterior [COAST] gave Latin and English the CODA (end).

Tsadi seems to be behind X (normally KS) in Amerind.

Maya *k'ix,* a verb to finish or conclude, is from קץ QaiTS, end. [COAST] One knows that the X is from ץ *Tsadi* because Maya *k'ix* is also a noun meaning "sting" (insect). This is from עקץ [A]**QeTS**, sting. [STING]

Tsadi does not seem to provide English with Z words,

But then there are so few Z words in English. One exception may be BRAZEN. Like BRA**SH,** BREA**CH** and FIR**ST,** all these fricatives come from the *Tsadi* of פרץ PeRe**TS,** to burst forth. [BREACH] [PROSTITUTE]

צאצא TSETSE means children or offspring; the *Tsadi-Aleph* sub-root means that with goes out (from one). In Swahili *uzazi* means birth. *Zi* means both children and bullets in Chinese. [EXIT]

זהר ZoHaR, brightness, צהר TSoHaR, light, (Genesis 6:16), and צהל TSoHaL, to shine (note the Liquid *R/L* shift) have influenced *sol (*sun) words. These engineered "synonyms" show how *Zayin* (Z) and *Tsadi* (TS) are interchangeable fricatives.

The versatile *Tsadi* dances at 2 weddings, as both a fricative and a dental. The *Tsadi* in מלץ MaLaTS, sweet, is the source of both fricatives like the S in MOLASSES, and dentals like the D in MOLDY, sweet-smelling decay. [MOLASSES]

Most English S words are from *Shin* (SH) or *Sin* (S)

The word SHIBBOLETH became a borrowing from Biblical Edenic because pronouncing it with a *SHeen* (SH) or Seen (S) gave away the locale of the speaker. It is then clear that some letter shifting to create regional dialects even happened in at least later Biblical Israel. This is another reason why the word "Hebrew" is not the same as "Edenic."

All Edenic words with a *Shin* (SH), even when Edenic names are merely transliterated into English, seem to be heard as an S rather than an SH. Note how SHimon, SHoSHana, and SHimSHoan became Simon, SuSan(ah) and SamSon (or SimpSon).

It's not much of a leap from these names to other words like SCOPE from שקף SHaQaPH, to view, or SPILL from שפל SHaPHeL, to bring low.   [SPILL] Applying these whistling fricative sound shifts to the Edenic number six, שש SHeSH, is it any wonder that the French six is *SiS*. [SIX]

Sin (S) never provides an *SH* word in English.
If BUTCHER is from בשר BaSaR, meat, then BUTCHER came to English via Old French *bouchier*, and the CH is not quite an SH.

שעיר Si[E]eYR (storm) does allow for the word SHOWER, but the H is from the soft, Germanic *Ayin* and not the initial *Sin* shifting. [SHOWER]

The *Shin-Bhet* subroot of returning has related words when one switches fricatives to *Zayin-Bhet* or *Samekh-Bhet*. [SWIVEL] Also see the *Shin-Bet* article in the "Many Edenic Documents" section of the *Edenics CDIII*.

SH to Amharic (Ethiopic) S and ST
This SHoSHaNaH to SuSaN(ah) shift is not just common for English speakers, it can be seen in the fellow Semitic language of Amharic. (Like Ancient Egyptian, this is a Hamitic, African people whose language is Semitic.) Numerals 3, 5, and 6 in Edenic are שלשה SHaLoSH, חמש [K]HaMeSH, and שש SHeSH.   The Ethiopians pronounce these numbers soowuST, amST and sidST.

Fricative and other sound/letter shifts from Edenic to Aramaic are taken up at the end of the chapter. Shifts that are particular to various language groups are noteworthy, but will have to taken up later. For now, we'll concentrate on those shifts that help us understand how the Edenic sources of English have been hidden all these millennia.

Shin shifts, SH to TH

רשם RaSHaM is to record. This gave us ARITHM(ETIC). [ARITHMETIC]

Greek *orthos* (straight) gave us ORTHODONTURE, a crooked post-Babel form of ישר YaSHaR, straight; also note the *Yod* becoming a vowel. CATHARSIS is from Greek *katharos*, pure, ultimately from Edenic's pure כשר KaSHeR or kosher (ritually pure – thus *fit* or *proper*). Popularized as a rare borrowing from American Jews, now even an Irish District Attorney in Indiana might investigate if a charitable group is really KOSHER.

THIN is from *Samekh-Noon*, סן $ahn, sharp, like a סנה $NeH, bramble. [TINE]

Other Fricative shifts:

Shin (SH) to CH: CHAFE and CHANGE; for *Shin* to X, see XENOPHOBIA.

You may not think Swahili has much in common with Greek, but both shift the Edenic *Shin* (SH) to a TH sound. Swahili snow is *THeluji* instead of שלג SHeLeG (snow), while the THYROID is from Greek *THura* (door), a form of Edenic שער SHa'[A]R, gateway. (Genesis 23:10)

Sahf /(S) from *Tahf* is not just an Ashenazik variant.

The IE base of SMIRK is *smei* (to smile, be astonished). The AHD's SM base for "astonishment" may be from תמה TaMahH, to be astonished (Habakkuk 1:5) – which may be rendered (S)aMahH. Like the *Ayin* variant (as a vowel), this *Tahf* variant (as an S) is too globally verified to be limited to Ashkenazik Jews.

Non-Grimm's Law letter shifts include: *Lamed* (L) to N. Other letter shifts to be studied are likely to be specific to the Babel-babble of particular language groups.

Edenic to Aramaic Shifts

Beyond Grimm's Law and Rashi's Law, there are regular letter shifts that happened at Babel to divide the most ancient of vocabularies. (The grammatical patterns that broke up the languages are beyond the current parameters of Edenics. Semitic languages are closer grammatically than they are lexically.)

The set of shifts noted earliest were between Edenic and it's close Semitic relative, Aramaic. Some of these shifts are not familiar as derived from the same parts of the mouth, and so we can see that language diversity, even within Semitic, was a divine, not simply a natural, phenomenon. Letter shifts continued to "naturally" break up languages, such as Latin *pater* (father) shifting to Dutch *vader* (Skywalker's daddy) and to English *father*.

But Edenics, based on Genesis 11, presupposes devolution for all of language diversity, including letter shifting. Even if the patterns of letter shifting from Edenic to Aramaic seldom apply to other languages, they are important to note as 1) indications of other letter shifting patterns yet to be discovered in other language groups, and 2) there are English words that developed by way of Aramaic which can now be traced.

Aramaic, one of the languages in Israel at the time of Jesus, was at one time the most widely spoken language shared by the known world. Ask Mel Gibson. His *Passion* movie had the Pharisees speaking Aramaic. It is no wonder that these non-Grimm's-Law letter shifts have wider implications than for merely a few "West Semitic" languages.

As a language of trade, numbers would be of significance. English retains, for example, some influence of Aramaic three, *tlath or tlas* (note the dental and liquid shifts), even though one has to link THREE or TRIO to Latin *tres*, three. See the *TIRZA RIMA* entry. Latin gets its *tres* from Aramaic *tlas*, which before Babel was the Edenic שלש SHaLoSH, three. We have learned about the easy fricative shift from SH to S, but now we find a *Shin* (SH) shifting to a T. This common Edenic-to-Aramaic shift echoes the Sephardi/Ashkenazi difference between the *Tahf* (T or TH) and *Sahf* (S – the softer version of *TH*).

The *Shin*/SH to T fricative-to-dental shift resembles the *Zayin*-to-D shift from Edenic to Arabic. For example, Edenic זהב ZaHaBH, gold, becomes Arabic *DaHaBH* (gold).

Edenic Shin (SH) shifting to Aramaic T – and roping academic bull

The Edenic שור SHOR (bull) became the Aramaic TOR (bull). This is how Latin and Spanish got words like TAURUS and *toro*. [TAURUS]

Skeptics always ask why, just because there's a correspondence between Edenic and another word, should one assume that the Edenic is from an older, original world language of Eden? Scholars, who have never looked at language holistically, assume that Edenics must be pure, chauvinistic bull on the part of those annoying Edenicists. Let's grab this bull by the horns, shall we?

TAURUS has no close T-R relatives that suggest a profound word family, reflective of natural (creation) science. Edenic שור SHOR, on the other hand, is clearly yoked to the concept of the bull's unique significance. Only the bull naturally plows in a straight line, a שורה SHOORaH, and ישר YaSHaR, source of SHEER and SERIES. *Boustrophic* is a Greek term for writing in lines that follow the bull's innate plowing pattern.

A horse or donkey can plow, but the farmer must work hard to get the animal to plow straight. As will become more evident as we encounter large word families, Edenics does not have accidental homonyms with the same sound or spelling. Accidents are a sign of corruption, and the chaos of human input, especially the whims of spelling conventions. Order is a sign of non-human engineering. What about a SH-R word like שירה SHiRaH, poetry? Surely, poetry is not related to a bull. Not *all* poems are bull. But a poem is all about the writing of lines, שורות SHOORoaT, as is the work of bulls. A line or section in the Koran is a *sura*.

The *Shin* to T shift happened to other Semitic languages too. In Arabic number two is *'itnen*, and eight is *taemaenyae*. Edenic two (2) is שנים SHNaYiM and eight (8) is שמונה SHMOANaH.

If *Shin* shifts to T in Aramaic, it shouldn't be shocking to find a *Shin* shifting to the other dental, D, in another language group. The data is building a case for a *Shin*/SH to D shift in distant languages. For example, the *Shin*/SH of נחש NaK[H]aSH, snake, seems to become the D in *anaconda* (Singalese snake) and *inada* (Cherokee snake).

Edenic to Aramaic shifts include

Zayin (Z) shifts to D: אזן OZeN, ear, gave us AUDIENCE, the Z-to-D, or D-from-Z, shift is common in Arabic as well as Aramaic. [AUSCULATE]

The *Zayin*-to-D shift via Aramaic allows us to identify the Spanish pig, *cerdo,* as the Biblical חזיר K[H]aZeeYR, pig. *Het* gives us the hard C, and *Resh* gives us the R of *cerdo.* The shift allows the D to come from the *Zayin.* But the D is the 3rd consonant in Spanish, and the *Zayin* is the 2nd in Edenic? We'll learn about metathesis soon (letters switching location).

Cerdo = pig < M132 חזיר K[H]aZeeYR, pig (Z shifted to D via Aramaic) [HYOSCYAMIE]

Conversely but more rarely, *Dalet*/D can shift to a Z

Spanish *Corizon* (heart) < חרידי K[H]aReYDeeY, trembler [CARDIAC]

Noon (N) shifts to R

This is a rare shift in Indo–European. You may know BaR as the Aramaic *son,* from the term *Bar Mitzvah.* The Edenic word for son is בן BeN, as in BENjamin, *son* of my right [hand].

Another Unusual Shift – *Resh* (R) to W

WR is pronounced as an R, so just think of the R-to-W shift as merely a WR without the R. *Resh-Ayin* is often mistranslated as "evil." Evil can be seen as a satanic force independent of human behavior, and as such there is no "evil" in Hebrew Bible philosophy. Importantly, *Resh-Ayin* or רע WRahGH is the source of WRONG. A person's decisions can be wrong, but one is not inherently evil. The WR from *Resh* and the G from the GH of *Ayin* are fine, but where did the N of WRONG come from? Nasalization, adding a non-historical N or M to a word, is discussed in the next chapter.

Some of the letter shifts may have sounded like speech defects. The *Resh*/R-to-W shift is the *Cwazy Wabbit* phenomenon that pre-existed cartoon character Elmer Fudd. One can hear the *Resh*/R shift in these examples: WASH from רחץ Ra[K]HaTS (to rinse); WEAK from רך RaKH, tender, weak; WET from רטב RaDToaBH, moist; and **WOM**AN and WOMB from רחם Re[K]HeM, womb.

For non-Indo European examples of the *Resh*-to-W shift, Arabic *khawi* (empty) is from either ערה GHaRaH, to pour out, or a reversed ריק RayQ, empty. *Wehka* (far), in the El Salvador Indian dialect of Wahat, is likely from *Resh-Het-Koof*, רחוק RaK[H]OAQ, distant.

For an example in a Japanese metathesis, *Yod-Koof-Resh* or יקר YaQaR, dear, became *kawaii* (dear, lovely).

The *Vav* (V, W) also can render an R. See ESTROGEN, NEW, OR, REGAL, WEAK and WRONG for *Resh* shifting to W and *Vav* shifting to R.

This is not restricted to Indo-European languages as they were spun off of Edenic. At the FERRY entry one sees how "bring" is *bawa* in Indonesian – from the Edenic *Bhet-Resh* root of carrying something over.

In general, if there's a lisp or other speech defect affecting a pattern of shifting, it shows up in Edenics. Similarly, dyslexia will have much bearing on metathesis, where root letters switch their order.

Most W words are from Edenic bilabials like *Bhet* (BH) and *Vav* (V). Other entries where the English W comes from the Edenic *Resh*/R include WET, רטב, and רמה WORM.

Perhaps the most important application of this shift involves the subject of evil. EVIL is a human trait, the English word coming from עול [A]VeL, injustice. [EVIL] The Lord did not plant a tree of good and "evil" in Eden. "Evil" as some sort of absolute beyond human choice or Free Will is **not** in the Garden of Eden. The fruits of the garden of This World where Man must pick his metaphorical fruits, are about 1) what is divine and good, and 2) what is wrong and ungodly.

That first mistranslated tree in Eden is about *Tet-Vav-Bhet*, טוב DTOA[V], good – or **div**ine. Transliterate it as DToaBH to better see the Slavic "good," ***dob***re. We have removed evil from Eden, but what English word *does* come from that second tree, *Resh-Ayin*, רע R[A]GH, bad? The *Resh* sometimes becomes WR, also an R sound, in English. The *Ayin*/GH can just as easily shift to a hard G as a soft H (as seen above). We will soon learn about nasalization, the adding of unhistoric nasals (M or N). So, we have W up front, G at the end, and now an N in the middle. We can now discard the dangerous, external concept of "evil" which makes human choice and morality meaningless. We now have an Edenic garden with fruit trees to choose… or the individual Free Will, the ability to act **DIV**INELY or to do what is **WR**ONG. More at DIVINE and WRONG.

A chapter on important Biblical mistranslations was planned, but like many topics here, could be the subject of a future book.

The best way to say שלום SHaLOAM, goodbye, closure, peace, to a chapter on letter shifts is to invite the reader to shift one, two or all three letters of this familiar word. The fricative *Shin* (SH) shifts to S, the liquid *Lamed* (L) to R, and the nasal *Mem* (M) to N. There are easier ways to get from SHaLOM to SOLEMN, grand SLAM (completion in games), and SO LONG (an acknowledged borrowing from Semitic), but one should never overlook SERENITY.

Some Shifty Afterthoughts

Two shifts within one word are common. *Sachem* and *sagamore* are two names for tribal chiefs among Algonquian Native Americans. Both are from זקן ZaQaiN, tribal elder – related to the Arabic *sheik* and the Iranian *shah*. [CHECKMATE] Did you notice how the *Zayin* (Z) has shifted fricatives to S, and the *Noon* (N) has shifted nasals to M?

All three radical syllables can shift in one word. For a *sweet* example, look at Edenic דבש D[V]aSH, honey (Genesis 43:11). When we read the root letters reversed it's SH-V-D. Now use your new knowledge of letter shifts (fricative, bilabial and dental) to read it as S-W-T. *Sweet*, isn't it?

In German, *gerade* (direct) is דרך DeReKH backwards. (*Khaf* shifts gutturals to G).

If searching HONEY in the *CD Dictionary*, HONEY is taken up with other full reversals at the QUARTER entry.

Chapter Four CONCLUSION

Not a mere chapter, but a large book is required to more fully document the significant letter shifting within Edenic, and those shifts which allow us to see the many millions of global words (descendants) from our sparse, primeval Edenic roots (patriarchs).

Later chapters will offer further ways to see how the *Aleph-Bet* letter shifts offer deep insights into Edenic word families and the fuller understanding of Biblical words (unknown to translators).

Letter shifts are crucial for noting all the like-sounding synonyms and antonyms intelligently designed for each Edenic word. More on this later, but here is one example where all three root letters shift to provide a synonym:

Shin-Koof-Tet, שקט SHeQeDT means silent. Another fricative-guttural-dental term of keeping silent is ס-כ-ת *Samekh-Kaph-Tahf* in Deuteronony 27:9. [QUIET]

Chapter Four ACTIVITIES

Read the SEEP entry below, and answer the following questions after you follow the letter shifts from the *Zayin-Bhet* or fricative-bilabial Edenic root:

SEEP		*Zayin-Bhet ZaBH*
ZAHV	זב	**[Z-BH → SP]**

ROOTS: Old English *sypian* (to drip, seep) is traced to the IE root *seib* (to pour out, sieve, drip, trickle). זב ZaBH, easily shifting to *S-BH*, then to *S-P*, is to ooze or flow out as in "a land *flowing* milk and honey" (Exodus 13:5).

Less clean SEEPAGE involves the man or woman with a sexual discharge called an "issue" or flow (Leviticus 15:33) – the male זב ZaBH or female זבה ZaBHaH.

BRANCHES: Cognates of SEEP at IE *seib* are SAPONATE, SAPONITE, SIEVE, SIFT and SOAP. Edenic can now wash its hands of a borrowing from Latin, since SABON (SOAP), came from Edenic. The flowing SAP (from a tree) belongs here too. SOAP and Greek *hyssopon* (hyssop) relate to the cleansing אזוב AyZOABH. [HYSSOP]

זבל ZeBHeL (*dung*) provides the Edenic etymon for SWILL (only traced back to Swedish *slime*), SEWER, and SYPH [ILIS] after normal shifts of the Edenic זב/*ZB* root's (whistling sibilant) fricative and bilabial (lip-made).

SEEP and SIP are like-sounding opposites because שאב SHoABH, to draw (Genesis 24:19, absorb, suck in) is an SB antonym of Z-BH (to flow out). שפע SHaPH[A] is to flow; while שפך SHaPHaKH is to pour. A substance like SAP was used to waterproof, to prevent SEEPAGE, of baby Moses' ark in Exodus 2:3. The Edenic word for pitch or tar, זפת ZePHe*TH* or ZePHe*S*, fits our fricative-bilabial family as a typical built-in antonym.

French *suer* or *sver* (to sweat) leads one to believe that German *schweissen*, Yiddish *shvitz* and English SWEAT are other bodily issues ultimately from this Edenic *S/Z-PH/BH* root.

PUS might result from reversing our *Z/S-BH/P* root. A metathesis also reveals similar זב ZaBH words like Altaic *pusu* (squirt out) and Sumerian *pes* (semen). *Suupee* means running, nasal mucus in Proto-Eastern Polynesian. The difference between a runny nose and a mighty running river is one of mere volume, so the S-P river word in Algonquian found in MISSI**SSIPPI** (the river and state) is related. After the Tigris and Euphrates, the greatest rivers in Iraq are the Greater Zab and the Lesser Zab. [BISON]

זאב Z'EBH, the wolf (Judges 7:25), is related to the זב ZahBH, the person with an emission dripping from his body that makes him ritually impure (Leviticus 15:25) and to the land "flowing" with milk and honey (Exodus 3:8). All canines uniquely drip saliva. The salivating, **seep**ing wolf gave us the expression "hungry as a wolf." Yes, food stimulates the flow, but dogs sweat through their mouths.

1. List ten English and/or foreign words that record the Edenic ז *Zayin* (Z) in the featured etymon (ZaBH) shifting *fricatives* from *Z* to *S*.

2. List ten English and/or foreign words that record the Edenic *Bhet* (BH) in the featured etymon (ZaBH) shifting from *BH* to *B* or *P* or *W*.

3. What is gained by citing more Biblical Edenic words, and other Semitic ones, when we already have one good Edenic word to establish the root?

Looking through the *E-Word CD Dictionary* (or finding a new one elsewhere):

4. document a guttural shift that was not noted above.

5. document a dental shift that was not noted above.

6. document a fricative shift that was not noted above.

7. document a *vowel/voiceless* letter shift that was not noted above.

8. Examine the AFTER entry, and record the shifts from the Edenic originals to words in Semitic, Hamitic, and Indo-European (read Japhetic).

9. The DIRECTION essay is also in chart form, allowing you to see the shifts easily. Document these shifts not by language, but by the 7 sound-letter categories.

10. Using your own books, and the foreign language of your choice, find and record three different letter shifts that are not in the *E-Word CD Dictionary*.

Chapter Five

Nasalization

(added Ns and Ms)

Nasalization is a very common, universal phenomenon in linguistics. It is one of the simplest but most effective ways to disguise the Edenic origin of words. It merely involves the adding of a Nasal, an N or M, in the middle of words. It should be considered a man-made form of language corruption, as it makes words easier to pronounce and/or to be distinguished. Metathesis and reversals, taken up later, are NOT signs of human corruption, but from a neuro-linguistic scrambling..

Edenic חרד [K]HaRaD is to dread, leading to an adjective meaning dreadful. English has both HORRID and the nasalized form, HORRE[N]DOUS. Spanish also has both a nasalized and a non-nasalized form of חרד *Het-Resh-Dalet* (dreadful): *horrido* (horrid) and *horrendo* (horrendous). This importantly illustrates how nasalization is part of the normal, human corruption of language. Extra Ns and Ms were inserted simply to aid pronunciiation and/or to differentiate words. They are not part of the neurolinguistic Babel-babble that diversified Edenic, hurling humanity into our multi-lingual history.

Instead of thinking of HORRE[N]DOUS as a **horrible** or **horrific** corruption of a pure word that we once shared, we should appreciate how it helps us to recognize H-R scary words as Edenic, even if the end-dental (D,T) was butchered in the **horror**-mystery of language usage.

INTRODUCTION TO NASALIZATION

The most often used word in the English language is AND. AND is a known corruption of the earlier "and" term of French and Latin *et*. If *et* was nasalized, shouldn't e.t. with an added Nasal be ENT or EMT? Yes, but it's easier to say AND, or Germanic *unti* then German *und*, with shifting vowels as well as the Dentals shifting from T to D. The ease of pronunciation is behind almost all language corruption. No matter how extensive nasalization may have been in Babel's Big Bang of language dispersion, it has continued to turn cognates (words with the same ancestry) into the unrecognizable terms of different dialects.

Et is the Latin granddad of AND, and its Hebrew patriarch or ultimate source is one of two Vowel-Dental words that are not conjunctions, but mean much like "AND." 1) *Aleph-Tahf*, את ET (Genesis 6:9), the Lord walks "together with" Noah. 2) *Ayin-Vav-Dalet*, עוד [O]WD, further, also the source of ADD. Japanese *to* means "and." This is further evidence that the Vowel-Dental conjunctions above are likely from a primeval term meaning "in addition," and that AND has been nasalized.

Even though nasalization still happens today, it appears to have begun millennia ago. Even venerable peoples like the HiNdus, who settled the INdus Valley, seem to have a nasalized name. INdia is referred to as הדו HoeDOO (no N) in the opening line of the Book of Esther. Unlike mere regional variations, like calling a Persian king Darius or the Biblical דריוש DaRYaVeSH, the Bible would not have dropped the N from India. Therefore, words like HINDI, INDUS, INDIA, INDIAN and the American slang INJUN shows how far a term can stray from its original HD form.

The word for listening in the so-called isolate language of Basque is *e[n]tzun*. In Edenic to hear is האזין H'EZeeYN. You aren't hearing a coincidence, but a nasalization of Edenic in a unique language that may well be one of the original spin-offs after Babel.

GRA[N]D is a nasalized GREAT, but they are not linked by scholars. The Dental shift of D/T shouldn't bother you, and soon you'll be suspicious of Ns and Ms that seem to insinuate their way into a word's final syllable.

Both QUASH and QUENCH mean to subdue or put down. Our current dictionaries have no clue that QUENCH is a nasalized כבש Ka(V)aSH, to conquer, the source of QUASH. [KIBOSH] [QUASH] [QUENCH]

Unaware of how pervasive this mode of corruption is, even the fine work of historical linguists misses some obvious nasalization*s*. The Latin and English BRACHIUM is the arm, shoulder to elbow. Greek *bracchion* is the arm, whence words like BRACE and

BRACELET. The obvious sense of the BRK sound is of breaking off into extensions from a single trunk, as heard in ברך BeReKH, knee **and** פרק PeReQ, joint, crossroad or FORK. See the large BREAK entry; later we'll fully explore the large family of bilabial-liquid-guttural breakers.

Instead of recognizing the BRONCHUS, the limb-like branches of the windpipe, as a nasalized branch of the BRK breaker family of words, the Indo European (IE) root for BRACHIUM, etc. is *mregh-u* (short). The main arteries to the lungs are as FORKED as BREECHES, but non-holistic scholars who don't spot nasalizations can congest our reference books with etymological BRONCHITIS.

Nasalizatiom Predated the Bronze Age

Here's an entry from the *E-Word CD Dictionary*:

BRO(N)ZE	**BaRZeL**	***Bet-Resh-Zayin-Lamed***
Bar-ZELL	ברזל	**[BRZL→ BR N Z]**

ROOTS: BRONZE, like its alleged cognates BEAR, BRUIN, and BROWN, is thought to come from IE root *bher* (bright, brown). The olive brown metal we call BRONZE (now used for a copper-tin alloy) was apparently known in the Bronze Age. A metal term from the Bronze Age with a B,R and Z ought to be considered . If there were a metal term with a BRZ in Latin, nobody would doubt that BRONZE was merely a nasalization (extra N) of the Latin term. A BRZ term in the Bible, however, will not be considered by those who feel that linguistic theories are sacred and infallible, while the Bible is human and fallible.

נחשת NiK[H]oaSHeT means copper, while ברזל BaRZeL means "iron." The two are together, "copper and iron implements," in Genesis 4:22.

LA(N)GUAGE itself is a nasalization.

A language is a tongue, and a tongue is a language. "To tongue" or "to lick" presents an obvious L-K source for LANGUAGE, once the liquid-guttural (LK or

LG) is nasalized with an extra N. LICK is said to be from Greek *leikhein* and the IE root *leigh* (to lick). לקק LaQaQ is to lick (I Kings 21:19), and עלע [E]eLaGH is to lap or swallow. Ugaritic *lhk* is to lick. The Arabic tongue is *lougha*, the same word, naturally, for language.

Nasalization has kept us from recognizing our aunt:

Czech *teta* (aunt) and Finnish *tati* (aunt) ultimately came from Edenic דודה DoDaH, aunt. This double-dental term of endearment fits many relatives and loved ones. [TOOTS] Later, German, French, some Slavic and Yiddish speakers nasalized the double-T word for "aunt" into *taNte*. By the time English comes around, who's going to know that AUNT, which dropped the initial T of *taNte*, was once a nasalized ד-ד *Dalet-Dalet* term in Edenic? It's no wonder that the IE root for AUNT is the vague *amma* (various nursery words), which includes Latin *amita* (aunt) but also several AMATORY words one would not associate with one's aunt. To see where these etymologies went wrong, see MAMA and AMITY.

English itself is a *nasalization*:

Those Yiddish speakers above had also nasalized words straight from the Hebrew Bible. The best example is how they turned יעקב Ya'[A]QoBH (Jacob) into the pet name YaNkle. The propensity for nasalization is likely from Eastern Europe, because Sephardic (Spanish then Middle Eastern) Jews have Koby as the pet name for Jacob.

The middle position in the word, right before a Guttural, is a common place for nasalization, and one can hear how the Anglo-Saxons nasalized Hebrew עקל [A]QeL, crooked, into words like A[N]KLE (the angle at the end of our leg) and A[N]GLE. It just so happens that the Germanic Angles got their name from an angular territory on the continent from which they staged their invasion and occupation of what came to be called ANGLE-LAND, then ENGLAND. So, ENGLISH itself is a nasalized form of עקל [A]QeL, angular, and is related to the ע-ק *Ayin-Koof* name of Jacob – which is also associated with the ankle or heel. The reader will decide if the association of the English with crookedness is appropriate or not.

Being attuned to the nasalization of Yiddish speakers allows one to discover the nasalization behind SYNDICATION. The accepted etymology assumes that SYNDIC is a combination of Greek *syn* (together) and *dike* (justice), and the ancient SYNDIC was a judge or advocate. But a nasalization of צדק TSeDeQ, justice makes more sense than "together justice." Add the slight fricative shift from TS to S. The צדיק TSaDeeYQ is a saintly man of justice, and the one who would settle arbitration. The spiritual "godfather" at circumcision ceremonies is the סנדק $aNDiQ. This Late Hebrew term is said to derive from the Greek, but, typically, it is a disguised Edenic term. In this case it is a nasalized צדיק TSaDeeYQ, just, righteous or holy man. [SYNDICATE]

THOSE LONG SEMITIC NASALS

Some Hebraicists think a נ *Noon* was dropped in Hebrew, but only for the singular form of נשים NaSHeeYM, women; אשה EeSHaH is a woman; בנות BaNOAT, daughters; בת BaT is a daughter. Importantly, there is no example of Biblical Hebrew adding a nasal. Nasalization is clear evidence of a later addition, a corruption, and it is very evident in all other Semitic languages. Akkadian *maNzazu*, is a doorpost. The Biblical doorpost is the מזוזה MeZOOZaH. [MEZANINE]

Akkadian embellishes כזב KaZeBH, to lie, with *kuNzubu*. Akkadian expands Edenic ניר NeYR, light, to *naMaru*, to give light. Especially seen in Aramaic's cumbersome suffixes, every other language, including Semitic tongues, adds to the comparative scientific economy of Edenics.

A venerable but post-Tower of Babel Semitic language like Aramaic will often nasalize Edenic words. פנים PaNiM, face became *aNpin;* [PANE] חטה [K]HeeDTaH, wheat, became *hiNta* [WHEAT]; and אתה ATaH, you, became *aNtah* [THOU]. Again, the historical dates of Hebrew speakers (the Late Bronze Age) are irrelevant; we are dealing with a Prehistoric, Pre-Hebrew or "Edenic" – which is best preserved in early Biblical Hebrew.

The Syriac palate is *kheNka* instead of חך K[H]aiKH. The ancient Egyptian *ankh*, their sacred totem of life, is a nasalization and (typical reversal) of חי K[H]aiY, life.

[HYGIENE] *Chi* (as in *TAI CHI*) is the Chinese life force. Even though Semitic languages are considered the most conservative and slowest changing, they too are post-Babel corruptions of Edenic. Of all Semitic languages, nasalization is the easiest to see in Arabic.

TA[M]BOURINE is one of the many English borrowings from Arabic. The nasalization already comes from the Arabic hand-drum, a *taNbur*. The Edenic is תף ToaPH and also note the shift of bilabials. [TAP]

Speaking of nasalization, the Arabic nose is *aNf,* instead of אף AF. [OBOE] Reversing the פ *Pey* and vowel of the Edenic allows for פה PeH, mouth or any opening. [OPEN] The nasalization suffocates our awareness of the engineered profundities within the divine terms for anatomy.

The Arabic pig is a *haNzir*, instead of a חזיר [K]HaZeeYR – the animal that is חוזר [K]HoZeR, returns, to its leavings. [HYOSCYAMINE] Both Jews and Moslems refrain from eating swine, but K[H]OAZaiR is to return, and the nasalized pig doesn't embed the meaning that hogs return to their excrement for dessert.

Edenic משור MaSOAR is a saw. The Arabic Nasalization is *miNshar*. [SAW] Ethiopic turns MSR into *moshart*. An Arabic *minshar* may cut just as sharply, but one won't see the link to the German knife, *messer,* or to the Luftwaffe warplane, the **messer**schmidt.

Aramaic *ANTE* (you) or Ethiopic *eNt* is clearly a later corruption of את AT and אתה ATaH, you - source of Latin and French *tu* and English THEE and THOU.

Edenic wheat, [K]HeeTaH, becomes *hiNta* in Arabic. The nasalization makes it harder to see the historical connection between WHEAT and WHITE.

English has the world's richest vocabulary, and nasalization helped to create its much nuanced lexicon. For example, CRI[M]P, CRA[M]P, CRU[M]PLE and CRU[M]PET are all known nasalized cognates of CRAFT. [CRIB] Suspect any longer word ending in MP.

When looking up NIMBUS clouds and NEBULA, lexicographers will acknowledge the clear nasalization, and the IE root will echo the NB words as more historically authentic. There are nasalizations in the IE Roots themselves, however, as they cannot know about Edenic roots. SLING, for example, is seen at the IE root *slen(w)h,* to slide, sling, throw. An older and not nasalized Edenic root is שלח SHaLaK[H], to send away, release, throw. [SLOUGH]

Even obvious borrowings from the Hebrew Bible get obscured by borrowings.

For a good example let us see the SABBATICAL entry in the *E-Word CD Dictionary:*

SABBAT(ICAL)	**SHaBaT**	***Shin-Bet-Tahf***
Sha-BUT	שבת	**[S(H)-B-T]**

A SABBATICAL, paid leave-of-absence, like other rest-day forms of SABBATH, are obviously a Biblical borrowing from שבת SHaBAT. See some hidden forms of שבת SHaBaT at STOP. Just to note the diversity of borrowings of the same Hebrew word, it is interesting to note words for Saturday like: Arabic *al-sabt,* Czech and Polish *sobota,* Indonesian *Sabtu,* Italian *sabato,* Modern Greek *Savvaton,* Russian and Serbo-Croatian *subota,* and Spanish and Portuguese *sabado.*

There are nasalizations like Hungarian *szo**mb**at* and Rumanian *si**mb**ata.* Once morphed into S-M, one would never know that French Saturday, *samedi,* and German *Samstag,* are really from שבת SHaBa(S) "day."

Here are some simpler Nasalizations in English. To sniff out the historical trail back to their given roots, and their not-yet-known but ultimate Edenic roots, see the entries.

ARRA[N]GE is now given the IE root *sker* or *ker* (to turn, bend). You might prefer to consider it a nasalization of words like ערך [A]RaKH, to arrange and EReG, to weave. [ARCHITECT] [ORGAN]

BA[M]BOO אבוב ABOOBH, pipe, reed; source of PIPE, FIFE and OBOE.

BU[N]T is a nasalized cognate of BT words like BEAT, BAT and BUTT. If you know American baseball and football, you can see how BUNT is to BAT as PU[N]T is to BOOT. That is, they are nasalized but clearly related in sound and sense. Even in the more muted sport of golf, a precise strike is a PUTT (not nasalized like BuNT and PUNT). *The American Heritage Dictionary of Indo-European Roots* doesn't have a bilabial-dental root for all these, but the Hebrew Bible does. See בעט Ba'[A]DT, to kick out, at and a family of BT and PT words at BEAT.

CA[N]TEEN is a nasalized guttural-dental receptacle like CADDY and KETTLE. כד KaD is the water pitcher or bucket of refreshing Genesis scenes. [KIT]

DU[M]P, like so many words ending in "MP", is a nasalization of an Edenic word. טבע DTaBH[A]h in Exodus 15:4 is to sink or drown. It means immersing in liquid, so it is the source of dental-plosive words like DIP and DIVE. Nasalize dental-plosive to get DUMP. So, you might say the Egyptian chariots were drowned or dipped into the Sea of Reeds, or even that they were DUMPED there.

FRA[N]K is a nasalized FREE. If one is too frank, and speaks out too freely, one might be considered a FREAK. FaR[O]oah or FaRGHooah means unrestrained.

KI[N]DLE, CA[N]DLE, INCA[N]DESCENT and INCE[N]IARY are all nasalized forms of older guttural-dental burning words like Greek *kauter* and, earlier, Edenic terms like קדח QaDa[K]H, to kindle. [CAUTERIZE]

JU[N]CTION, JU[N]TURE and JU[N]TA are nasalized forms of cognates like JUXTAPOSITION, YOKE and YOGA. Edenic יחד YaK[H]aD or Ya[K]HaD, together, allows for JKT, JT and YK or YG words, as you'll recall from your Chapter Four knowledge of *Yod, Het* and *Dalet*. The provided Latin and IE root cannot hold all of them together. [JUXTAPOSE]

LA[M]P is a nasalized IE root *lap* (to light, burn), but better linked to the more lamp-like לפיד LaPeeYD, torch. (Genesis 15:17)

PI[M]PLE is a nasalized BUBBLE or BUBO (inflamed swelling, like the BUBONIC plague.) The oldest source is Anglo-Saxon *piplian*, to blister. A plague of Egypt, boils, was אבעבוע AB[A]BOO[A], Exodus 9:9, also rendered blister, pimple or wart. [BUBBLE]

PRO[N]TO is a borrowed Spanish word is thought to be from Latin *promptus*, brought out… at hand. It may be a nasalized *PROTO-* (first), related to PRESTO and FIRST. The proto-word may be פרץ PaRaTZ, to quickly appear or make a BREACH. [BURST] [PROTOTYPE]

SI[N]K and SAG are alike enough to share the IE root *seng(w),* to sink. They are better traced to שחה SaK[H]aH or שקע SHaQ[A], to sink, calm down, set as the sun. [SAG]

SPE[N]D is said to be from Latin *dispendere*, to weigh out. The etymology is forced, but SPENDING does involve giving money. ZeBHeD is a present or gift (Genesis 30:20). Shift the fricative *Zayin*/Z to S and the bilabial *Bhet*/BH to P, and add an N.

SWA[M]P, like all words ending in MP, sounds like a nasalization. The IE root for SUMP and SWAMP is *swombho* (spongy). A soggy marsh Semitic etymon for all these words should be סוף $OOPH, reed, rush. *Samekh-Vav-Phey* easily accommodates SWP, which would be nasalized to SW[M]P. Moses is set adrift in the spongy, riverbank marshland or סוף $OOF in Exodus 2:3, and variations exist in Egyptian and Arabic. Reinforcing the SWP etymon is צוף TSOOPH, Tsaddi-*Vav-Phey* (in Syriac as well). It means to overflow or float.

Following the AHD, note the many cognates that are nasalized at roots ending with a bilabial. The "root" *skerbh, skerb* (to turn, bend) lists derivatives like CRAMBO, RIMPLE, RUMPLE, RAMP, SHRIMP and SCRIMP.

185

Chapter Five CONCLUSION

The last chapter on Letter Shifts plus this one on nasalization will help you out of the post-Babel linguistic JUNGLE. There couldn't be an Edenic source for the word JUNGLE, because there isn't a JUNGLE anywhere near the Middle East. Right? Wrong! Edenics is not about history or the original flora or fauna of some ancient homeland of jabbering post-simian bipeds. It's about pre-history, and the neurologically engineered (and then dispersed) computing language installed into the blown-out cranial cavity of the original modern humans, Adam and Eve, by our Creator.

It can be assumed that there was no need in Eden for a term meaning JUNGLE. After Babel, one of the 70 like-speaking clans migrated eastward to the Indus Valley. All these migrations were hastened by the new breakup of the single Earth landmass (perhaps the Atlantis of legend) which helped to isolate and consolidate the development of these linguistic clans into what would become proto-languages and embryonic peoples. Much later, they would form national groups.

The clan that reached what is now India spoke the now-extinct langue of Sanskrit. This venerable language de-evolved over the centuries to ten derivative dialects, one of them called Hindi. Hindi gave English the word JUNGLE. Hindi *jangal* came from Sanskrit *jangala*, but these people who needed a name for the thick vegetative growth they encountered did not coin a word out of thin air, or get inspired by an echoic source.

Despite the years and miles: one can take the humans out of Eden, but you can't take the Edenic out of humans. The closest thing to a jungle in the Near East would be a forest of trees. Forest in Edenic is יער Y[A]'aR or YaGH'aR, *Yod-Ayin-Resh* (Deuteronomy 19:5). The nasalized YGR became *jangala, jangal*, then JUNGLE.

Why not Yungle or Jugre or something closer to Ya'ar? Yes, language is a jungle that we weren't meant to fight our way out of until these times. Let's revisit the letter shifts of Chapter Four. The *Yod* is often rendered as a J in Indo-European, like YiTROA and YOABHaiL being rendered Jethro and Jubilee. The more normative *Ayin* is the Sephardic, Guttural GH or G. The *Resh* often shifts Liquids from R to L, like AReeY (lion) to LEO.

Now we have our J, G, and L. And this chapter explains the added N. Now you know that a JUNGLE, the Hindi *jangal,* is a nasalized and twice letter-shifted Edenic forest. Sorry for testing you with this complex example, but if you made it through JUNGLE, you're on your way back to the Garden of Eden.

Chapter Five ACTIVITIES:

Link these 10 nasalized words to their cognates in English or other languages. If one of them is not nasalized, point this out as a significant proof. Indicate any Semitic sound-alike, mean-alike terms that reinforce the ultimate Edenic origin, citing a verse in the Hebrew Bible when available. Look them up in *The Word's* index, (or search if you have the *E-Word* CD).

A[N]TIQUE	DaTZ (to leap, rejoice).
DA[N]CE	NoEPHeT (adulteress).
HA[N]KER	SHooPH (to rub, polish).
NY[M]PHET	SaPHaK (to clap or strike by hand).
RI[N]SE	TS-B root of stubble
SHA[M]POO	ATiQ (ancient).
STU[M]P	SOOaKH (to bend down),
SHA[N]K	SHoaK (leg)
SI[N]K	RaGH (bad).
SPA[N]K	HaQeH (to anticipate).
WRO[N]G	RaHaTS (to wash).

C h a p t e r S i x

Metathesis

Root Letters Switching Places

Metathesis is another common, universal phenomenon observed by Western linguists. It involves root letters switching places, appearing in a different sequence. The usual Edenic root has three-consonants. Vowels are not part of these root letters, so be vigilant in ignoring vowels. In *The Word*, metathesis is often called a "letter flip." You'll find many hundreds of examples in dozens of languages by searching "letter flip" in the pre-1989 2/3 of the *E-Word CD Dictionary*.

As we discovered with nasalization, metathesis is not more than something that helped corrupt parent languages, forming the changed vocabulary of a new dialect. Metathesis also was used in the Babel-babble of Edenic vocabulary into the world's disguised spin-offs. We will encounter various ways to scramble the sequence of an Edenic word by metathesis.

Words borrowed by other languages and cultures can be rather mangled in the word's new incarnation. But it won't be subject to a shifting of letter sequence (metathesis). If a word as likely to be borrowed as a number turns up in a scrambled form, it can be assumed that the word **wasn't** borrowed. Polish number eight is *osiem*. Perhaps it is mere coincidence that the Edenic eight is שמונה SHMOANah, with a similar S and M like the Czech, Polish and Slovak. The Upper and Lower Sorbian number eight is *wosym*. Rather than making *osiem* look less connected to SHMOANah (8), it becomes more evident that ש-מ-ו-נ-ה *Shin-Mem-Vav-Noon-Hey* lost the *Noon-Hey* ending, and had the *Vav* as vowel or as V/W consonant moved to the front, before the *Shin-Mem* or S-M This W or O moving from third place in Edenic to first place in Slavic is called an M312 metathesis. This is an uncommon metathesis pattern for Edenic's formation of the roots of English. [EIGHT]

The most common way that the Edenic root letters switched places after Babel-babble to create the roots of the world's words (some of which eventually ended up in English) is when the 1-2-3 Edenic sequence became the 1-3-2 sequence of the new word. We shall then call this pattern of metathesis simply M132.

This is how Latin *merx*, merchandise, came from *Mem-Khaf-Resh*, מכר MaKHaR, to sell. [MARKET] On the home page of *edenics.org* there is a flash movie of *Mem*, *Khaf* and *Resh* rearranging themselves and morphing into the M,K and R of MARKET. Neither Latin, nor its theorized Etruscan predecessor fell from the sky, and the Indo-European (IE) root, *merk-2* (commerce) is a laboratory concoction. Words like COMMERCE, MERCHANT and MERCENARY came from this MKR → MRK metathesis.

Among the cognates of MARKET listed in the *American Heritage Dictionary* is, of all things, MERCY. Our language experts are so clueless as to the source of our words, that they will even link MARKETING and MERCY simply because they sound alike.

This makes no sense. MERCANTILE or MERCENARY pursuits are not noted for their MERCIFUL qualities. But the establishment linguists are often guided by similar spellings, not by the marriage of sound and sense required by the more demanding standards of Edenics.

WOMBMATES BY METATHESIS

Edenic *Het-Mem-Lamed*, חמל K[H]aMaL means pity and compassion. [CLEMENCY] A KML→KLM Metathesis, another M132, seems a likely source for CLEMENT (lenient). This is close to the meaning of MERCY, but we don't have to derive MERCY from חמל K[H]aMaL with an M231 metathesis plus a liquid shift. A better source for MERCY involves a different Edenic source word and a different metathesis. One can see how *Het-Mem-Lamed*, חמל K[H]aMaL, pity, compassion, is designed to be similar to *Resh-Het-Vav-Mem*, רחום RaK[H]OOM, merciful. [MERCY] [WOMAN]. Both have a *Het*, *Mem* and liquid (L or M), and awareness of metathesis helps us to see that חמל K[H]aMaL and רחום RaK[H]OOM are congenital wombmates. An M312 metathesis of

מ-ח-ר *Resh-Het-Mem* allowed MERCY to be born. (מ-ח *Het-Mem* warmth in רחם *Resh-Het-Mem* mercy is taken up in the AMITY entry.)

In this chapter and in the next we shall see that metathesis is not just a way to link words to Edenic, but to see how Edenic words are linked to each other.

"Wombmates" was not a flippantly chosen term. רחמים **RaK[H]aMaNOOT** appears as early as Genesis 43:14 in its plural noun form, meaning mercy. It is famously related to the identical מ-ח-ר *Resh-Het-Mem* root for "womb" (Genesis 20:18) because the concept of mercy is a byproduct of the maternal instinct to protect the weak and helpless. An Intelligent Designer is behind the related words of MERCY, CLEMENCY and WOMB, and is also behind Swahili mercy, *huruma* – an M213 metathesis.

(If the words for such things may be designed, surely the natural source for compassion, even for secular humanism, may have been designed. Atheists musk ask if this divine maternal instinct, and the human ability for kindness to strangers, was an aberrant mutation or extended great ape behavior that is somehow advantageous to survival).

It is far less common, but there are English words that come from a M312 metathesis, where the initial Edenic root letter reappears in the third (root consonant) position in the later word. The word WORD is a good example. German *vort*, word, is from the *Dalet-Bhet-Resh* of דבר Da[V]aR, word, thing, (Genesis 11:1). דבר D[V]R changes position to V-R-D (the dental shifting from Edenic *Dalet* to German T, and back again to D for English). In the 1989 publication of *The Word*, there were too few examples of M312 metathesis to include an entry for the word WORD among the 22,000 more conservatively derived words in the index. More examples of metathesis follow, but first more on the concept.

Metathesis is most often noted as a reason for a word variant, especially in a closely related dialect. Metathesis is largely overlooked, however, as a way new words may come from a parent language. It is especially never considered that a metathesis from an "unrelated" language could be useful in tracing a word's origin. Even the cutting-edge historical linguists that now accept the concept of a Proto-Earth overlook metathesis as a way in which languages got diversified.

The Spanish pig, *cerdo*, looks completely unrelated to the German pig *Schwein*. But both are a metathesis of the Edenic pig, חזיר K[H]aZeeYR, ה-ז-ר *Het-Zayin-Resh* (the "weak" letter *Yod* doesn't count). *Cerdo* is an M132, with the Aramaic-related *Zayin*-to-D letter shift. *Schwein*, like English SWINE, is from a M213 with a *Resh*-to-W shift (Cwazy Wabbit rule). See the *Het-Zayin-Resh* porker at HYOSCAMINE.

To better follow where the Spanish and German little piggies went, let us better illustrate the two metathesis paths from 1) *Het* 2) *Zayin* 3) *Resh*.

Spanish **cerd**o (K-R-D) from 1) *Het*, 3) *Resh* and 2) *Zayin* or M132
German **Schwei**n (S-CH-W) from 2) *Zayin* 1) *Het* and 3) *Resh* or M213

Perhaps the Spanish D-from-*Zayin*/Z shift indicates that *cerdo* has origins in ancient, pre-Latin Iberian – which may have had Aramaic influence. *Cerdo* doesn't smell like Latin *porcus* (pig). Future Edenics research will help to trace the genealogy of words and their speakers.

In English, in recent centuries, metathesis is the given reason why "flutterby" became BUTTERFLY, "bridd" became BIRD, "crul" became CURL and "thrid" became THIRD. THIRD is easier to pronounce. Occasionally a post-Babel metathesis does make the new, post-Edenic word easier to pronounce. But mostly disguise, not ease of pronunciation, is the result, and apparent motive, of metathesis.

The examples of metathesis within English often involve vowels, and are otherwise not strictly about root consonants swapping place. English-from-Edenic metathesis is far more consistent. Words like butterfly (where a dairy product goes airborne) is part of the weirdness that allows thinking people to assume that language is human and chaotic. No matter what form an English or etc. word turns out to be after metathesis and/or some other aspects of Babel-babble, it's original, Edenic form can be demonstrated to have been profoundly designed…as better seen in the next two chapters.

Linguists think that any metathesis was similarly a mistake that caught on because the new form was easier to pronounce, or had some element that helped it stick in speakers' minds. There are words in Biblical Hebrew that appear to be accidental variants from speakers of different regions or from alleged scribal, copying errors. Secularists want very much to portray the Bible as typically human and flawed. While metathesis of Edenic words appears even in ancient Semitic languages, the case can be made that these Biblical spelling variations are built-in and purposeful rather than mistakes by human authors and copyists.

A well-known spelling variation occurs in the word for the Biblical lamb. When Jacob is breeding them in Genesis 30:32, the lamb is always a כשב KeSeBH, *Kaph-Sin-Bhet*. In Leviticus 4:32 the lamb is a כבש KeBHeS, *Kaph-Bhet-Sin*. This reshuffling of root letters looks like an accidental metathesis. A Western-trained mind looks at כשב KeSeBH and כבש KeBHeS and crows at the "contradiction." This looks like evidence of an all-too-human input in the Bible.

Consistency is the hobgoblin of little minds, and Edenic was arguably engineered by the Creator of minds, by an Intelligent Designer of profound subtly and paradox. When Jacob came to Laban as a penniless refugee, he was preoccupied with amassing wealth. כשב KeSeBH echoes כסף KeSePH (bilabial shift of *Bhet* and *Phey*) which means 1) desire (Psalms 17:12, as in the lion's desire to pounce on prey), and 2) money (Genesis 20:16).

(Non-Edenic words for money are about weights and measures. They were not coined by the Intelligent Designer who minted human psychology.)

The giving of animals to the altar is far more than sacrificing one's desired wealth. A penitent wishes to conquer his character flaws, to grow from willful, animalistic sinner to obedient lamb – and כבש KaBHaSH means conquer. And so the two nearly similar "lamb" words, כבש KeBHeS and כשב KeSeBH, are as different as redemptive innocence and a costly tray of lambchops.

A slight fricative shift from KeBHeS the lamb gets one to כבשן KiBHSHaN, a furnace. Moreover, כבס KaVa$ (fricative shift from *Sin* to *Samekh*) means to wash. Who brings a כבש KeBHeS, sacrificial lamb, at the altar wants the self-conquest of cleansing fire.

In Leviticus 14:8-14, כבס KeeBHe$, washing and כבש KeBHeS, lamb occur four times, making their connection strong and clear. Bible critics work on the premise that Biblical devices like alliteration and repetition are mere literary flourishes. But these scholars knew far less than you do now about sound and sense in Biblical Hebrew.

Only in the language of the Bible is the gentle lamb and the theme of conquest linked by an identical root. This is why the cowed or domesticated lamb is suited for sins of passivity. (Rams are brought to the altar for misdeeds of an active nature.)

Militant pacifists should take note that Latin *pax* (peace) only results from כבש KaBHaSH, conquest, subjugation. Peace is only derived with an M213 metathesis of Edenic ש-ב-כ K-B-SH, becoming ש-כ-ב BH-K-SH, which shifts bilabials to PKS or *pax* (Latin, immediate source of PEACE). Sadly, many violent uprisings must be "pacified" (which means put down by force, not pandered to by the terrorized.)

Bible critics have no clue that Edenic words seemingly corrupted by metathesis are actually carrying multiple, intelligently designed entendres. They are mistakenly taught that the Bible is just a book, and that the Biblical Hebrew of the Pentateuch is just a language. As Edenics improves, seminaries may require such uninitiated scholars to master the fundamentals of Edenics before they can be called doctors of divinity.

In addition to the engineered innuendos for listeners and readers of Torah text, the variations of כבש Ke[V]eS/כשב KeSeBH have important functions in giving the world different sheep terms. כבש Ke[V]eS allowed Latin *ovis*, sheep. Initial gutturals are prone to dropping, as seen in Chapter Four. From this slight letter shift or drop allowing Edenic כבש Ke[V]eS to become Latin *ovis*, English would get words like EWE, OVINE and OVIBOS. [OVIS] With a similarly dropped initial *Kahf*, most Slavic sheep words have an O,V or W, and a soft C. Polish and Czech sheep words are *owca* and *ovce*.

English SHEEP, from Anglo-Saxon *sceap*, and like Danish *schaap*, is more likely from a common M213 metathesis of כשב KeSeBH. The first and second root letters swap places, so that K-S-BH becomes S-K-BH. This becomes S-K-P with the simple *Bhet* shifting bilabials to P. Linguists with insomnia can better count sheep thanks to the Edenic variants-by-metathesis of כבש Ke[V]eS and כשב KeSeBH.

שלמה SaLMaH and שמלה SiMLaH are both Biblical words for dress. Most scholars presume that this "doublet" reflects human error, as they do for the sheep variants above. But SaLMaH has the *Shin-Lamed-Mem* of שלמות SHLayMOOT, fullness, and so it means an entire outfit, an ensemble. [ASSEMBLE] [ENSEMBLE] The SLM variant stresses wholeness. שלם HaLeM is complete. At the SLAM entry, there is the SLM verb, the completion of action – like a "Grand slam" in bridge or baseball.

שמלה SiMLaH is more like the סמל $eMeL, figure, image, design of a garment. As usual, the link between these like-sounding words are suggested by the Biblical text itself (Deuteronomy 4:16). S-M words of sameness and similarity are taken up at the SEMANTIC entry. So, שמלה SiMLaH is more formal and theoretical, like "outfit," while שלמה SaLMaH is actually one's full ensemble. [SIMULATION]

Edward Horowitz's *How the Hebrew Language Grew* (N.Y., 1960) calls such variants "doublets," and he is sure that such variants are the typical pronunciation and spelling errors (metathesis) that come with languages that evolved normally. Of course, Hebrew did get somewhat corrupted by human use, but even insightful scholars like Horowitz could not imagine that Hebrew is the closest we have to the Intelligently Designed Edenic.

Another set of "doublets" or words that Edward Horowitz calls "mixed up" is אמץ AhMeyTS, be strong and עצם [A]TSahM, be strong. The core root of ע-צ *Ayin-Tsadi* is related to the trunk of a tree: עץ [A]iTS. [LUTE]

A similar word, אמצע EMTS[A]h, means "middle." You can hear "midst" and the Greek "bone" at the OSTEOMA entry. The *Aleph-Mem-Tsadi* word, on the other hand, means "encouraged" or "bold." The same root means adoption and determination. In Joshua 1:9, Moses charges Joshua with being "strong and resolute" (JPS). אמץ AhMeyTS shares music and meaning with אמת EMeT, truth. [ETYMOLOGY]   So, עצם [A]TSaM is physical strength, while אמץ AhMeyTS is emotional strength.

Sure אמץ AhMeyTS and עצם [A]TSahM have similar sound and sense. But they are far from identical or "mixed up." Edenic sound-alikes are NOT accidental doublets that happened when two different source words were used (like "shirt" and "skirt" in English), or when some tribal chieftain with a speech disorder created an instant variant.

Metathesis is, in every normal language, a sign of the corruption and chaos of language that allows linguists to assume that languages grew or evolved accidentally. This is unlike the Intelligently Designed metathesis found in Edenic, where the similar words are NOT the result of identical cognates or mispronunciations. The engineered Edenic variants then morph into the well-disguised sources of world vocabularies. No one would imagine that both EWE and SHEEP come from metathesis-driven variants of the "sheep" word of Biblical Hebrew.

Those who assume that Edenic variants imply corruption are unaware that there are far more than a score of such "doublets." A look through the *E-Word CD Dictionary* reveals that most 3-root consonant Edenic terms have like-sounding "synonyms" and "antonyms" built into it. Some of this was seen in the chapter on letter shifts, and more of this phenomenon will be documented in a later chapter.

Terms like "synonyms" and "antonyms" are only used loosely when applied to Edenic. All later languages have words of similar sound and meaning due to shared cognates, or words of similar ancestry, which have changed differently over the miles and millennia. Only Edenic's words, or molecules of meaning, with similar letters or tones, in variant pitches or spellings… result from supra-human design, not from human error.

Metathesis drives many of the observable Edenic "synonyms" and "antonyms," usually working with letter shifts – so that their existence has been a secret from linguists who don't know enough Hebrew, and from Hebraicists who don't know enough linguistics.

There are few fully anagrammatic opposites or metathesis-driven "antonyms" which do not also involve letter shifts. Two of these are:

מ-ע-ד   *Mem-Ayin-Dalet* (to slip)

ע-מ-ד   *Ayin-Mem-Dalet* (to stand firm)

ת-ל-ש   *Tahf-Lamed-Shin* (to uproot)

ש-ת-ל   *Shin-Tahf-Lamed* (to plant)

Built-in opposites with the exact same spelling also exist. שרש SHoReSH means root, source, origin. שרש SHeyResh is a verb of uprooting. (Yes, you know of the *Shin*-to-S shift and you **did** just hear the source of SOURCE.)

As we discover more about the Edenic two-letter sub-root at the core of the established three-letter Semitic root, we must be open to rethinking what we know about the structure of words. Examining some of these Edenic synonyms-by-metathesis and letter shifts forces us to think about sound and sense being more important than spelling.

In *E-Word CD Dictionary* entries like CARDIO (the heart is the trembler), DREAD, HORRID, RATTLE, and TERROR one finds a few Edenic words for trembling with fear. The first three all contain a *Resh, Dalet* and a guttural, but metathesis has shifted the letter sequence, and the letters have shifted sounds. No wonder no one has recognized the words below as designed "synonyms."

1) חרד [K]HaReD, *Het-Resh-Dalet*, to tremble, to be afraid (Genesis 27:33)

2) ערץ [A]RahTS, *Ayin-Resh-Tsadi*, to dread (Deuteronomy 1:29)

3) רעד R[A]'ahD, *Resh-Ayin-Dalet*, to quake in fear (Exodus 15:15)

Very close to these are

4) רדט RaDTaDT, *Resh-Tet-Tet*, to tremble (Jeremiah 49:24), and

5) Aramaic דחל Di[K]HaL, *Dalet-Het-Lamed*, to fear.

With all these majestically similar Edenic terms for being rattled with a shaking fear, Modern Hebrew has coined a new word, sounding like *TerrROAR,* that simply imitates the English.

There are designed synonyms-by-metathesis which involve the exact same letters, rather then letter shifts. This is beyond what Hebraicists assume were accidental "doublets" or scribal errors. Two examples of this are:

נשף NaSHaF, to blow or breathe

נפש NeFeSH is a breath or soul

בגרת BiGeeRooT, puberty

גברת GiBHeeRoot, adulthood

Importantly, the meanings are similar, but not exact. This is not like English, where cognates of the same *angh* root for "painful constriction" developed semantically, by usage, to give us ANGINA, ANXIETY and ANGER – see חנק [K]HeNeQn, to strangle, at HANG. There are no exactly duplicative homonyms in the pristine, Intelligently Designed original human language program called Edenic.

Shifting letters allows these anagrammatic (from metathesis) "synonyms" and "antonyms" to belong to different roots and word families. But, we should expand what we now understand as word families. We shall employ what we have learned about metathesis and other techniques of Babel-babble to discover such wider word families in Chapter Nine. Of course, we are also pushing the envelope of language families, and perhaps by the end of this book you will feel more related to the planet's human family.

METATHESIS FOR LEXICAL INREACH AND OUTREACH

It is far more crucial to Edenics that root letters can swap places externally (etymologically) than internally (for similar and opposite words). For the internal applications of metathesis, the crucial two of the three root letters cannot be moved without causing damage to the meaning and family network of any Edenic word. Externally, though, non-Edenic words have no known meaning beyond semantics (whatever meanings they are used to convey). So linking the word to a scrambled Edenic word is a plus.

For example, the Indo-European root reconstructed for NECK is *ken-5* (to compress, something compressed). It is no problem that our N-K might have come from a K-N. Metathesis happens. Edenic has words like ענק [A]NaQ, necklace and חנק [K]HeNeQ, to strangle (II Samuel 17:23) [NECK] [HANG] The Old English (an actual word, not a fiction) for neck is *hnecca*. ק-נ-ח *Het-Noon-Koof* is the stronger source word. Even if one wants to employ the metathesis with the Edenic etymons, they explain better than *ken* why NECK is spelled with a CK (two gutturals). The Edenic gutturals, *Het* or *Ayin* and then *Koof*, may well have undergone a metathesis, rather then a simple dropping of the initial guttural. (ק-נ-ח *Het-Noon-Koof* minus *Koof* is the simplest NECK/compression.) Either way, the Edenic path to Old English *hnecca,* Swedish *nacke,* Hungarian *nyak* and English NECK stands head and shoulders above the "Indo-European" dream words of the White Power of the Ivory Tower.

To further see the advantage of exchanging a reconstructed, imaginary root with a documented, Edenic one, let us see the first part of the WORD entry. A strange anagram is involved, but decide if you know more about WORD after noting the secret metathesis in its background or when only reading what the dictionaries now know.

WORD	Da[V]aR	*Dalet-Bhet-Resh*
Dah-VAHR	דבר	**[DVR→WRD]**

ROOTS: The proposed Indo-European alleged root for WORD is *wer-6* (to speak), allegedly the source, as well, for IRONY and RHETORIC. More likely, the German *Wort,* or the older Yiddish *vort* (word), is from the *Dalet-Bhet-Resh* of דבר Da[V]aR, word, thing (Genesis 11:1). Getting W-R-D from *Dalet-Bhet-Resh* requires a M312 metathesis. The initial Edenic Dental (*Dalet*/D) follows the Bilabial-Liquid core-root (*Bhet-Resh*/[V]R), instead of preceding it. Perhaps the dental shifted from Edenic *Dalet*/D to Germanic T, which then shifted back again to D for the English WORD.

דבר Da[V]aR meaning both "word" and "thing" echoes the thesis of Edenics and of Ralph Waldo Emerson who wrote that "words are signs of natural facts." Words as creations is a concept beyond the field of secular linguistics. In Edenics the word IS the thing, rather than a human convention to infer a thing.

The two-letter sub-root of ד-ב *Dalet-Bet* is found in דבה DeeBaH, report (Genesis 37:2) [TAB]

The opposite of a factual report is the reverse, ב-ד *Bet-Dalet*, בדה BaDaH, to invent, concoct or lie.

Shifting to *Bet-Tet*, BeeDTooY means uttering, pronouncing or expression.

Let us observe an example of linguists dealing with known instances of metathesis. The made-up Indo-European (IE) root of words like INSPECT, SPECTACLE, and SPECULATE is theorized to be *spek* (to observe). The Germanic and Latin etymons favor this S-P-K root, even though the Greek is *skeptesthai* (to examine, consider). The Greek suggests that the sequence is S-K-P, not S-P-K. Either the Germanic or the Greek has jumbled the letters of this observation word.

Words like EPISCOPAL, SCOPE and SKEPTIC are merely filed at the end of the entry by the *American Heritage Dictionary* as a "suffixed *metathetical* form." Not only do Latinate languages like Rumanian and Italian have S-K-P observational terms, but the Edenic *Shin-Koof-Phey* word, שקף SHaQaPH, to look out at, is recorded as far back as Genesis 26:8. [SCOPE] השקפה HaSHQaPHaH means outlook, overview and point of view, more in line with SCOPING something out.

In would appear as though the AHD got it wrong. SCOPE and SKEPTIC retain the correct letter sequence from the true, ultimate etymon. It is the S-P-K words like SPECULATE that underwent the metathesis. The historical, Greek etymon trumped the Germanic, Latin and invented IE source words. The Biblical Hebrew has allied with the Hellenic to defeat pre-Nazi, Romantic notions about the superiority of the Germanic and Roman. Modern linguists began in 19th Century Germany; maybe their chauvinistic speculation is showing. It's all about השקפה HaSHQaPHaH, philosophical perspective.

In the example above we saw that metathesis is certainly observed in reference books. Our dictionaries may catch or miss many instances of metathesis among cognates, but without the compass point of Eden-Babel they get lost. Instead of using metathesis as a way to unify the world's words under an original tongue, the lexicographers only use it to further display language as an accidentally corrupted mess.

Since Babel-babble is ongoing, much metathesis has occurred well after the Big Bang of language dispersion. Our focus here is on the many primeval anagrams that we can find if we play cosmic word search. In the examples below, we will see how a metathesis of Edenic provides a strong source for a word, especially when there is no real or invented etymon of equal value.

Letter shifts and nasalization are the more common and more straightforward methods of Babel-babble, which disguise the Edenic origin of human words. Metathesis, while ranking third, will nonetheless prove to be a significant contributor to the "confounding" of languages. Our Edenic language program is hardwired in the brain. More than a pronunciation error, or like accidentally spelling TYPO as "tpyo," the primeval metathesis from the Tower of Babel can be seen as a neurological wire switch.

Here is an essay on metathesis first printed in a syndicated column in the *Jewish Post & Opinion* chain of Midwestern U.S. newspapers (disrupted by a threatening Dr. Noam Chomsky), and then in the Jerusalem-based ROOT & BRANCH website.

When the World Had Dyslexia

Go ahead, AKS me how the original words of Edenspeak [Edenic] could have been corrupted. No, that's not a typo. AKS is a contemporary corruption of ASK – one that is standard in non-standard English. AKS happens because it is easier to pronounce than ASK. When letters switch places, like the S and K here, it is called metathesis. These letter switches happen to some people all the time, in a neurological condition called dyslexia. Neurologists have noticed that this reading disability seems to be lessened when the letters flow from right-to-left, as in Semitic.

In the early 1980s it was alarming when my inner-city student approached me and said: "Teacher, I wanna AXE you." (At least, that's the way it sounded.) By now, legitimate KS etymons have emerged for words like ASK. [SEEK] So, perhaps ASK is really the metathesis, and the slang got it right. (SLANG is a metathesis of לשון LaSHOAN, language. [SLANG]

Even wasps get these dyslexia-like wire crossings in the brain. In fact the word WASP (the insect, of course) comes from the Indo-European root WOPSA, according to our dictionaries. Notice how the root letters have changed position from WPS to WSP. But too few English words are recognized to be the results of prehistoric corruptions like metathesis.

In the following list, note how both English words share the same sound and meaning, yet the root letters seem to reverse:

Sample reversals	Edenic source	[entry]
aLTo and TaLL	תלל TaLaL (heaped high)	[TALL]
CaSe and SaCK	כסוי Ki$OOY (covering)	[ENCASE]
	שק SahQ (sack)	[SACK]
CaVity and VaCuum	נקב NeQe(V) (cavity)	[CAVITY]
DRaG and GRaDe	גרד GaRaiD (scratch)	[GRADE]
LaPse, SpiLL (and FaLL)	שפל SHaFaiL (to lower)	[SPILL]
FoLio and LeaF	לבלב LiBHLaiBH to blossom	[LEAF]
LoVe and PhiLo	לבב LeeBaiBH (charm the heart)	[LOVE]
NuMber and aMouNT	מנה MaNeH (to count)	[AMOUNT]
PaT and TaP	תפף TaPHaPH (to beat a drum)	[TAP]
RoTary and TiRe	דור DOOR (circle, wheel rim)	[TIRE]

There are many more, but they are not as obvious. For example, there's CeLL and LaCuna and HoLe and LoCH. Without looking them up, however, few would know that all these guttural-liquid and liquid-guttural words are synonymous with LaKe (a large, water-filled HoLe).

Even before looking up the more evident reversals and anagrams in *The Word* book or *E-Word* CD, you may be aware that some of these words came to English via different parent languages. You may have recognized PHILO as Greek, and hopefully remembered that PH and V are interchangeable bilabials. Cognates (words with shared ancestry) like LOVE and LIBIDO are from Germanic and Latin. FOLIO (a page or leaf) came to English via Latin; MORPH (form or shape) came from Greek. All these strangely reversible words have predictable ancestors, but in Edenics we deal with the always reversible Edenic patriarch. At the TALL entry, for example, it is normal to reverse *Tahf-Lamed* to get words like ALTITUDE. After the scrambling of what our prehistoric record (Genesis) calls the Tower of Babel, it is not unusual that "tall" in Arabic is *tawil,* while in Romance languages like Italian, Portuguese and Spanish, "tall" is *alto.*

Those of us who are committed to current linguistics theories might presume that the reversed synonyms above are mere coincidences. Did one of the cognates of each set get scrambled by accident? Perhaps, but only with Edenic can one tell which was scrambled, un-scrambled, or re-scrambled. For example, TAP is much like the original *Tahf-Phey* word of beating or striking as in a hand-drum, while PAT is the metathesis of that *Tahf-Phey* etymon seen at TAP.

What can be seen from the Edenic patriarch is usually not apparent from the parent languages (Greek, Latin, Germanic). Unlike the relatively easy list above, most English synonyms from different sources do not share enough commonly spelled letters to appear linkable. For example: both GALAXY and LACTOSE are milk words. One is from Greek *gala;* the other is from Latin *lac.* They are both from Edenic חלב K[H]aLaBH (milk). The Greek merely shifted *Het* to G, and dropped the *Bhet* at the end. The Latin didn't shift the guttural-liquid very much, but the KL was reversed to LK.

The unique architectonics of Edenspeak [Edenic] is full of such patterns, but most linguists would see nothing in common between LACTOSE and GALAXY. The fact that both are milk words means little to disciples of a faith that denies the idea of intrinsic meaning, and strongly rejects a hypothesis leading to an ordered, non-human source of human thought and speech.

Edenspeak [Edenic], on the contrary, sees metathesis as one of the fundamental ways that humanity was made multi-cultural. Words were neurologically scrambled at Babel, and were enabled to subsequently keep on diverging. This global "dyslexia" helped the language of Eden get בלל BaLaL, confused (BALLed up in the mixing BOWL of Babel-babble) in the scenario of Genesis 11. As in a salad bowl, the once-whole vegetables could be painstakingly reconstructed, if people are willing to work a long time and to get their hands dirty.

The above just touched on reversals in English. Words that mean the same backwards or forwards (letter shifts allowed) in any language are being collected. Reverse synonyms signify a designed "confusion," not natural corruption.

The essay above does not imply that all of us post-Eden humans have learning disabilities. Homo Sapiens still *sapiens*, or think, with their factory-installed programming language. The software still functions well. We still think with Edenic whether we speak Chinese, Swahili or English. The scrambling only affects the output stage. Maybe Babel-babble was something like having one's floppy disk jumbled by an airport X-ray scanner.

If a pre-Hebrew (older than a proto-Semitic) or Edenic is the elusive Proto-Earth language, and if large-scale neurological scrambling did happen, then we should be able to find the ore-Hebrew sources, most verified in Biblical Hebrew, for many thousands of synonym and cognate pairs like those above. We should and we are. (Your help welcome).

Since the first edition of this book, our world-wide examples of a single word continue to grow. Consider the following:

THE <u>CA</u>SE OF THE REVERSIBLE <u>SACK</u>

Global words for vessels or structures of concealment are guttural-fricative (throat-whistling) or fricative-guttural (whistling-throat) sounds. [ENCASE] [SACK]

קש SahQ	SACK, bag, sackcloth garment	*Sin Koof*	SAC, SACK (bag + dress)
צקלן **TSeeQ**LoaN	SACK		
כסה Ka$aH	to cover, conceal, en**case**		
כיס KeeY$	pocket, SlipCASE		
חסוי K[H]ee$OOY	shelter, purse		
סכה SooKaH	hut, temp. house		
קשקשת QaSHeSHeT	scales covering fish or men (in armor)		
Afrikaans	*sak*	bag, sack	
Akkadian	*kusu*	to cover	
Akkadian	*kusitu*	garment	
Akkadian	*shaqqu*	sack	
Albanian	*kasa*	a money case, safe	
Albanian	*kasolle*	hut	
Albanian	*qese*	bag	
Albanian	*saksi*	flower pot	
Anglo-Saxon	*sacc*	sack	
Arabic	*kasa*	he clothed	
Arabic	*makhsan,* from verb *khaza,* to store	storage area; *khaza,* store	MAGAZINE
Arabic	*sak*	bag	
Armenian	*k'sak*	purse	
Azerbijani	*kisa*	handbag	
Basque	*hasiera*	house	
Belarussian	*miašok*	sack	
Bulgarian	*kosh*	chest	
Catalan	*sac*	sack	
Chinese	*xiang*	case, box	
Chinese	*xing*	baggage	

Coptic	*sok*	bag, sack	
Czech	*kazeta*	box	
Czech	*mesec*	purse	
Czech	*sacek*	bag	
Danish	*aeske*	box	
Danish	*kasse*	chest, cash-box	
Danish	*saek*	bag, sack	
Dutch	*kas*	greenhouse	
Dutch	*kist*	coffin	
Dutch	*kast*	cupboard	
Dutch	*zak*	box, sack, pocket	
English words not treated elsewhere: briefCASE, CASEMENT	CAISSON CACHE CASHIER CASING CASQUE	CASSETTE CHEST (box and breast) Cul de SAC ENCASE	RuckSACK SAC/SACCULE SACK coat, SACQUE
Farsi	*kisah*	bag	
Finnish	*kassi*	bag	
Finnish	*sakki*	sack	
French	*sac*	Box, bag, sack	
French	*casserole*	Covered slow cooker	CASSEROLE
French	*chuassette*	sock	
Gaelic	*casag*	long coat	CASSOCK
Gaelic	*sack*	sack, load	
Gaelic	*sacraidh*	baggage	
Galician	*saco*	bag, sack	
German	*Haus*	house	
German	*Kiste*	wooden box	
German	*Sack*	box, sack	
German	*Schmuckkassette*	jewelry box	
Gothic	*skohs*	shoe	SHOE
Greek	*Askos, kystis*	sac, bladder	ASCUSO, CYST
Greek	*sakoula*	box	

Greek	*sakkos*	sack	
Hungarian	*haz*	house	
Hungarian	*zsák*	sack	
Icelandic	*skasr*	shoe	
Indo-European	* *kus, *keus*	to cover, hide	
Indo-European	*(s)keu*	to cover	
Indonesian	*kasut*	shoe	
Indonesian	*kaus*	socks	
Indonesian	*saku*	pocket	
Irish	*saic*	sack	
Italian	*casa*	house	
Italian	*cassaca*	long coat	CASSOCK
Italian	*casino*	little house	CASINO
Italian	*sacco*	box, sack	
Japanese	*kasa*	umbrella	
Korean	*sang-ja*	box	
Late Latin	*sacellum*	money bag	SATCHEL
Latin	*casa*	house	
Latin	*saccus*	sack, bag	
Lithuanian	*karstas*	coffin	
Lithuanian	*kastonas*	chestnut	
Middle French	*casque*	barrel, helmet	CASK
Middle French	*casset*	box, chest	CASKET
Norwegian	*eske*	box	
Norwegian	*kasse*	Box, case	
Norwegian	*kiste*	coffin	
Norwegian	*sekk*	sack	
Old English	*socc*	sock	SOCK
Old Frisian	*hus*	house	HOUSE
Old French	*cacher*	to hide	CACHE
Old French	*chasse*	box, receptacle	CASE
Old Saxon	*hosa*	leg coverings	HOSE (socks)
Polish	*kieszen*	pocket	
Portuguese	*caixa*	case, cashier	

Portuguese	*casa*	house	
Portuguese	*saco*	bag, sack, purse	
Romanian	*caseta*	box	
Romanian	*sac*	bag, sack	
Russian	*meshoc*	sack	
Slovac	*kosel'a*	shirt	
Slovac	*saek*	sack	
Spanish	*casa*	house	
Spanish	*casco*	visor	CASQUE
Spanish	*casilla*	box-office	
Spanish	*castana*	chestnut	CASTANET
Spanish	*casucha*	hut, hovel	
Spanish	*saca*	box	
Spanish	*saco*	sack	
Swahili	*kasah*	turtle (covered)	
Swedish	*ask*	box, packet	
Swedish	*hus*	house	
Swedish	*säck*	sack	
Swedish	*sko (Dan., Norw.)*	shoe	
Thai	*sawng*	pocket	
Turkish	*kazak*	tunic	
Turkish(Arab.)	*kese*	bag, pouch	
Ukrainain	*mishoc*	sack	
Welsh	*sach*	sack	
Yiddish	*Schiech (Ger. Schuh)*	shoe	
Yiddish	*zak*	sack	

In Fernando Aedo's 3 language groups below, the meaning precedes the word. As this new chart grows, more data will be divided by language family. Other Edenics team members on this project include: Jonathan Mohler, Isaac Mozeson, Kinneret Pau and Regina Werling.

Amerind		
Araona	basket	*ziqui*
Dakota	container, case	*ožúha*
Dakota	sheath, bag, holder	*ožúha*
Skiri Pawnee	sack, bag	*kásii'u'*
Ojibwa: Algonquian	MOCCASIN	*makisin*
Timicua	scales of fish	*qeche*
Mayan: Aguacatec; Ixil	net, bag ;	*c'ach*
Mayan:Chorti	net, bag	*chijl*
Achuar Shiwiar	chambira bag	*shiikiar*
Quechua P.	bag made of chambira	*shikra*
Quechua P.	bag	*tsaka*
Capanahua	a weaved bag	*jisin*
Nomatiguenga	bag	*tsagui [thagui]*
Yanesha Amuesha	backpack, bag	*oshaquets*
Bora	coat, cape, jacket	*tsuucoja*
Piro Yine	recipient, vase	*swaga*
Dravidian: Kanada, Telugu, Malayalam	a sack, a bag	*saci (c=ch)*
Waigali	bag	*kuchok*
Tamil	netted bag	*chiko*
Bihari	sheath of maize cob	*kosa_*
Prakrit	sword sheath	*ko_si*
MBh.	sheath	*ko_s'a*
Pali	sheath, cocoon,	*ko_sa*
Sinhalese	sheath	*kos*
Sanskrit	to cover	*sku*
Vedic	box	*kos'a*
Sindhi	leather bucket	*kosu*
Gujarati	leather bucket	*kos*
AV.	case, cover	*ko_s'a*
Tamil lexicon	receptacle	*ko_cam (c=ch)*
Bantu: Kiga-Nkore (Taylor)	bag(s), sack(s), pocket(s), purse(s), fund(s)	*sháho*
Venda Murphy	box, case	*gese*
Yao Ngunga	bag; bellows	*n- saku*

| Masaba Siertsema | pod | *soka* |

COMMENT:

Three words are known to be near-universal. Those who deny the monogenesis of language have no explanation. "Mama" and "papa" words, they guess, are from baby talk. That is crazy talk. At least half the words for a parent should be "gaga."

And there is no sound for a SACK or CASE, nor any reason that most S-K and K-S words should all mean "concealment." Unless, God forbid, sound and sense, music and meaning was hard-wired into the homo sapiens brain when the species had a Proto-Earth language program at some primordial "Eden."

SOCK is universal for the SACK worn on our feet. SOCKS may have been developed by one culture, and borrowed by others. But it is absurd to think that the bag or sack was invented by anyone, and had to be borrowed…like the word "radio."

The *Random House* online dictionary on SACK:

> "large bag," O.E. *sacc* (W.Saxon), *sec* (Mercian), *sæc* (Old Kentish) "large cloth bag," also "sackcloth," from P.Gmc. **sakkiz* (cf. M.Du. *sak*, O.H.G. *sac*, O.N. *sekkr*, but Goth. *sakkus* probably is directly from Gk.), an early borrowing from L. *saccus* (cf. O.Fr. *sac*, Sp. *saco*, It. *sacco*), from Gk. *sakkos*, from Semitic (cf. Heb. *saq* "sack")

A score of KT-TK bag words were left out. Some of these might belong here, as Latin Taurus (bull, ox) and Aramaic *toar* (bull, ox) had come from the Edenic SHOAR (bull, ox). But there is a Hebrew Bible KD word for a leather bag or "pitcher," so guttural-dentals were left out. They belong with entries like KIT and CADDY.

Metathesis is trickier than reversals. It can be hard to spot when it is in effect together with the more common letter shifts and nasalization. A grand example involves the word GRAND.

210

GRAND	**GaDoWL**	***Gimel-Dalet-Vav-Lamed***
gah-DOLE	גדול	**[GDL→ GDR→GR (+N) D]**

ROOTS: There is no reconstructed Indo-European root available for GRAND. Latin *grandis* means full grown or large. גדול GaDoWL means large or great (Genesis 1:16). In legal terms it means one who has attained majority. Following the bracketed diagram above, 1) *Gimel-Dalet-Lamed* shifts liquids to GDR. 2) It then undergoes metathesis from GDR to GRD. 3) Finally, GRD is nasalized from GRD to GR(N)D.

Sorry if that was more grind than grand. The only way to find such well-disguised Edenic etymons is to focus on the meaning. Grand meant large, not glorious. Nasalization can be a stealth confounder, so you are more likely to uncover the metathesis that made GREAT emerge from גדול GaDoWL. (Here there is also a dental shift, *Dalet*/D to T.) If you then see a similarity between GREAT and GRAND, then you have sniffed out the nasalization.

Fortunately, these triple-threats are rare in English. The *E-Word CD* has more examples of these metathesis-nasalization-letter shifts. The hard-core Edenics fan can go, for example, 1) to the ARCHAIC entry, for the Australian Aborigine cognate from אחור A[K]HOAR, rear; 2) to the CADDY entry, and the Thai cognate from כד KahD, vessel; and 3) to the EACH entry with the Mohican cognate from אחת AK[H]a(S), one, once. Actually, of the three examples, this last, of the Mohican, requires only a nasalization and a metathesis for e*nska* (one) to come from AK[H]a(S). Different language groups display different patterns of Babel-babble, patterns which shall emerge in the subsequent decades of Edenics discovery.

It is hoped that some readers find such a gaming challenge, not a daunting task nor a mine of fools' gold. The haystack is full of needles. Languages have few words that even mean wider things like "one" or "large." "Large" in Russian is *bolshoy*. You may recognize the Bolshoi Ballet. Looking in a Hebrew dictionary for "large" is no help, but a fruit that is ripe, or large, is בשל BaSHeL, [BOLSHEVIK] Perhaps Russian B-L-SH large and Edenic B-SH-L large is just a coincidence. But then one has to throw into the equation other "large" terms from unrelated languages, like Malay *besar* (large).

The Edenic etymon searcher and researcher must be prepared for the possibility that root consonants letters can be out of sequence. Usually only two of the three letters have swapped places. But remember SWEET and דבש D[V]aSH, date honey, from Chapter Three? In that case all three letters have reversed and shifted, dental-bilabial-fricative to fricative-bilabial-dental, Edenic 123 to English 321.

At the ASININE entry one can find Greek *onos*, source of ONAGER (wild ass). It is a M132 metathesis of אתון ASOAN, ass or she-donkey. When moving on to חמור K[H]aMOAR, donkey, we need a M213 metathesis to saddle the Rumanian *magar* and Serbo-Croatian *magarac* donkeys.

At BASIL one can taste the metathesis of Edenic בצל BaTSaL, onion, in Yiddish *tsibele*, as well as the *cipolla, zwiebel, cebula, and sipuli* (onions all) that Italian, German, Polish, and Finnish mamas have cried over for centuries. In Estonia it's *sibul*, while in Latvia it's *sipol*. *Tipula* is an onion in Basque, the so-called "isolate language with no affinities." (The Basque is not borrowed from either neighbor: Spanish *cebolla* nor the French *oignon*.)

Typically, as an entry goes on, as letter shifts allow one metathesis to spin off a dozen variations, expect letters to peel off of the root like the leaves of an onion: Drop the *Lamed* of BaTSaL to get CHIVE, from Latin *cepa* (onion) – the *Tsadi* and *Bet* are still reversed. Now drop the *Bet* of בצל BaTSaL to get *sol,* an onion to Kiowa Indians.

Another M213 metathesis involves the word for speech and language in Hebrew and Sanskrit. The Edenic word for speech is *Sin-Phey-Hey*, שפה SaPHaH (Genesis 11:1). The Sanskrit word for language is *bhasaha. Phey* easily shifts bilabials with BH. Simply switch the order of the first and second consonant, and *bha-sa-ha* becomes *sa-bha-ha*, which is much like Edenic שפה SaPHaH, language, (harden the *Hey* to hear the possible source of SPEECH).

Within Indo-European languages, finding a metathesis from Edenic is easier. The eight examples below are all M132. You don't have to be a scientist or a whiz at anagrams to match the English words in column A with their Edenic sources in column B.

A	B
BeSeeCH	בקשה BaQeSH, request, beg
HaLT	חדל [K]HaDaL, cease, stop – note the Dental shift D to T
DaRK	קדר QeDaR, black, sad
DeGRee	דרגה DaRGaH, step, grade
MaRKet	מכר MoaKHeR, to sell
GRiD	גדר GeDeR, fence
STERN	רצין RiTSeeYN, serious
TiNKer	תקון TiQOON, correction

Of course, English words are all from something else. These matchups would have been harder if you only had the French source of MeRCHandise, the Greek source of TeCHNology or the Russian suffix in LeninGRaD.

We have seen letter shifts or a nasalization make a metathesis get harder to spot. Here is an example of something as simple as a *Yod* rendered as a J helping to hide the Biblical origin of jurisprudence.

English JURISPRUDENCE initially comes from Latin *juris*. Extending the Edenic *Shin-Resh* sub-root meaning straight [SHEER], we get ישר YaSHaR, straight, as in honest, upright and just. The term gets corrupted after Babel-babble with a M132 metathesis, so that honest or just in Latin becomes *juris* (as in JURISDICTION) instead of a JSR term. By the time the S at the end is dropped, and we get words like JURY, it's no wonder that this ר-ש-י *Yod-Shin-Resh* word can't get a fair trial.

It is also possible that the devotees of subjective, man-made law are not fond of the idea of jurisprudence originating in a place like I Kings 9:4.

METATHESIS IN OTHER LANGUAGES

A small team of Edenicists are collecting specimens from the world's vocabularies. They should look for patterns, such as which kinds of metathesis are found in which areas. Beyond sound, one has to keep in mind the sense of the culture one is working in. One has to keep in mind that different language groups "hear" and "mispronounce" the Edenic etymon their own way. There is a cultural ear as well as an aural one.

Edenicists are not currently doing much in Semito-Hamitic languages, because any discovered links will not raise eyebrows. But Edenic research in African and Middle Eastern languages are welcome, and important in understanding what happened at the ground zero of language diversity in old Iraq.

A foreign metathesis can reinforce an Edenic-English link. Is SALVATION from Edenic שלוה SHaLVaH, physical safety from harm? The Modern Greek word for "safe," *asfalis,* is among the foreign words that back up this proposed link. This, even though *aSFaLis* is an M132 metathesis of שלוה SHaLVaH. [SALVATION]

Since war is Arabic is *harb*, one might mistake Hungarian war, *haboru*, for a borrowing. But borrowed words are not usually recast in M132 form. Nor did anyone hav to borrow a word for war. Hungarian *haboru* (war) is thus a post-Babel form of Edenic חרב [K]HeReBH, sword... also used to mean war.

Arabic Metathesis from Edenic

If the Babel scenario is going to be documented and proven, there had better be examples of Semitic words also coming from the Edenic (Proto-Semitic). Most of the clearest examples of this are in Arabic. Let's begin with Arabic words familiar to English speakers, and with the strange etymology given for GIRAFFE. There is no Z to G letter shift, but the French *giraffe* was somehow attributed to the Arabic word *ziraf*. As with most animal names, this term has no known meaning (more in Chapter Ten).

The GRF of GIRAFFE, instead, was more logically named for the creature's scruff or back of the neck, the Edenic ערף GHoReF or *Ayin-Resh-Phey* [SCRUFF] It is possible that the Arabic ZRF giraffe name also came from the front of the neck. Arabic *ziraf* could be a M132 metathesis of צואר SaVAhR, neck or throat. (There is also a bilabial shift from V to F.)

ELIXIR (sweetened alcoholic solution mixed with a drug) is one of hundreds of English words that came via Arabic. This is one of several that can be traced back to Edenic via a M213 metathesis, as *iksir* is from שכר SHayKHaR, alcoholic drink – the source of Japanese *sake*. [SAKE]

MONSOON is the seasonal wind of S.E. Asia. The name came from Middle Dutch *monssoen* and Portuguese *monceo,* from Arabic *mausim* (time, season). An M231 metathesis of זמן Z'MahN, a period of time, (Ecclesiastes 3:1) blew into the language center of the Proto-Arabic speakers at Shinar (Sumer), and the final *Noon* got changed to an M with a dental shift.

SAFFRON (the bright orange color, as worn by Buddhist monks) is from Arabic *za'afaran.* This is an M132 metathesis from שרף SoRaiF, burning (the flame-like orange color). The Seraphim are fiery angels, something the spiritual monks are emulating. [SAFFRON]

Edenic Metathesis In Arabic Proper

Through trade and Islam, Arabic became a widely influential language. Further examples of metathesis in Arabic, therefore, make it clear that, ultimately, the diversity of Edenic at Shinar (later Babel) is more significant than the military, economic and religious power that drove Arabic borrowings from Damascus and Mecca.

> *atzb*, sweet – M132 from דבש D'(V)aSH, date honey (Exodus 13:5). (Add to the M132 metathesis letter shifts of the dental and fricative.)

Boursa, stock exchange – M132 from בשר BaSaR, flesh … the leather of a purse … then the money receptacle of the BOURSE. [BURSAR (A)]. The results of this M132 metathesis have provided BOURSE terms for much of Europe.

Merakh is Mars, the red planet (*merah* in Malay) M312 from חמר K[H]eMaR, clay, thus red. [MAROON]

Raqaba, neck – M213 from גרף GHoRePH, neck, note shifts of guttural and bilabial. [SCRUFF]

Sajama, flowed – M213 from גשם GeSHeM, rain. [COSMOS (A)]

Sadika, quiet, calm – M132 from שקט SHaQaiDT, quiet, calm. [QUIET]

Sanaha, stench – M132 from צחן TSa[K]HaN, stink. [SKUNK]

Sarody, he placed one after the other – M132 from סדר $aDeR, to order. [SORT]

Tazik, fresh – M312 from חדש K[H]aDaSH, new (Psalms 103:5) Note how all three letters, the dental and the guttural shift.

Tsouban, snake (all tail) – M132 from זנב ZaNaBH, tail. [SNAP]

Zakad, charity – M132 from צדק TZeDaQaH, charity. [SYNDICATE]

[Note how the metathesis where the Edenic 1-2-3 root letter becomes the first-third-and second consonants in the derivative – or M132 – predominates from Edenic to Arabic. But, as with other languages, one leading metathesis pattern must not mean overlooking the occasional M213 and M312.]

For several more of these, let's see the historically significant MASTABAH entry in the *E-Word CD Dictionary:*

MASTABAH	MaTSayBHaH	*Mem-Tsadi-Bhet-Hey*
Ma-tsay-VAH	מצבה	[M-TS-B → MSTB]

ROOTS: MASTABAH means an oblong tomb or mortuary chapel in Arabic. This symbolic house for the dead is found in ancient Egypt. It is architecturally equivalent to the dolmen or cromlech (one large top stone laid across base stones) found in pre-historic burial sites throughout Eurasia.

In Hebrew dictionaries a מצבה MaTSayBHaH is defined as a tombstone or monument. The מצבה MaSTayBHah that Jacob builds over Rachel's grave is wrongly translated "pillar" in Genesis 35:20. Jacob didn't build a simple grave marker but a 'house" for his lost, beloved wife. The מצבה MaTSayBHaH was really a MASTABAH, a funereal "house," such as seen in the large, above-ground tombs of wealthy peoples.

The structure over Rachel's tomb today, then, is more architecturally accurate than is the lexicography of Bible scholars who did not link the *Tsadi-Bhet* root to words like STABLE. מצב MooTSaBH means military post, elevation or monument; יצב YaTSaBH means to set up, stabilize. For more on the *Tsadi-Bhet* sub-root of stability, see STABLE and STUBBORN.

BRANCHES: Arabic, as all Semitic, can preserve Edenic roots lost to Hebrew. But Arabic, like all Semitic languages, is post-Babel, with "confusions" like the metathesis above. Further illustrations of Arabic from an Edenic metathesis include:

ams (yesterday) from Edenic תמול (S)'MOAL or T'MOAL, yesterday [ETERNAL]

asfar (yellow) from פז PahZ, gold. [PHOSPHORUS]

bouhayra (lake) from ברכה B'RayKHaH, pool. [BROOK]

faida (interest for loan) from עדף [O]aDeF, excess. [ADD]

kalmia (word) from מלה MiLaH, word [MELODRAMA]

souf (wool) from כבש KeVeS, lamb. [OVIS]

yahgsik (wash) from רחץ RaK[H]aTS, wash. [WASH]

217

In these seven examples, one would expect to read them backwards, in order for us to see Arabic and Hebrew as mere dialect variants… fitting the theories of Semitic scholars who presume that both Arabic and Hebrew are later dialects of an earlier Proto-Semitic. These examples suggest otherwise, that the source of Arabic was spun off of Edenic no less than the sources of Sanskrit or Quechua (Inca). This does not make Arabic and Hebrew any less intimately related within the Semitic family, in grammar or in vocabulary.

Unlocking Arabic Metathesis by Way of Hungarian

LOCK itself is allegedly from IE root *leug-1* (to bend, turn, wind), a cognate with the LOCK of hair. This is so weak, that we are forced to return to Edenic נעל NaGHaL, lock, (Judges 3:24), to reverse it and to drop the *Noon*. This gets us to a better "lagh" than the IE root doctors. *Laka[t]* (lock) in Hungarian sounds better as a נעל NaGHaL, lock derivative when we consider other "lock" words. Finnish *lukko* is related to the Hungarian, and confirms that it is an LK word. Turkish *kilit* reveals that the guttural ע-ל *Ayin-Lamed* seems to be out there in the Near East.

Now, Arabic *kaloun* is unlocked as an M312 metatheis of נעל NaGHaL.

Hungarian, related to Finnish and not Indo-European, has some interesting links to Edenic via metathesis. *Lamed-Bhet-Shin*, לבש L'[V]OOSH means clothed. [VEST] Hungarian retains the *Lamed* that Latin doesn't use. There is an M231 metathesis seen in Hungarian *visel* (wear – pronounced *vi-shel*).

REVERSALS

If there are only two root letters involved, an inversion in letter sequence is better seen as a simple reversal rather than a metathesis. לא *Lamed-Aleph* means "no"; אל *Aleph-Lamed* means "don't." (An echo of No and UN-, but the L/N shift isn't taken up here.) The most easily observed two-letter reversals involve the Edenic MA and PA words: reversed to the vowel-first EM, mother. [MAMA] and ABH, father. [ABBOT] *Tet-Vav-Bhet*, טוב DTOABH, means good. Because the middle *Vav* is a weak vowel, we should expect it to be dropped. The BT of BETTER (more good) is a reversal of the Edenic, not a full metathesis.

A high percentage of Asian and American Indian (Amerind) words are the reverse of Edenic words. With many letters not pronounced, a reversal of a two-letter element is bound to be more common than a three-letter metathesis. The Peruvian beast related to the camel, the LLAMA (from Quechua or Inca) can be called a metathesis of גמל GaMaL. camel, if the *Gimel* was replaced by an unvoiced guttural. If the *Gimel* is merely dropped, the link to Edenic is better called a two-letter reversal.

Does the Hebrew Bible like reversals?

Look at Genesis 6:8. Noah (*Noon-Het*) found חן K[H]eN, *Het-Noon* (grace) in the eyes of God. The next time there is a similar phrase in is Genesis 38:8. Here, ער [E]R, *Ayin-Resh*, (Judah's son) was רע R[A]h, *Resh-Ayin* (evil) in the eyes of God. Reversals are an intrinsic part of the art of Biblical prose-poetry. If the Drivers and Strongs had no clue that Biblical Hebrew contains significant reversals, it may be time to reverse your opinion of such back-seat, weak scholars.

Another good example of Biblical poetry and related, reversed letters is in the *Shin-Resh/Resh-Shin* wordplay of Numbers 21:35. In this verse there is SH'eeYR, remain, שריד **SaR**eeYD, survivor, and ירש Ya**RaSH,** to inherit. These all figure is entries like RESIDUE and REST (as in remainder).

Reversals have become a far larger component in the Babel-babble of language diversity than was first thought. The *American Heritage Dictionary* has NECK coming from a so-called Indo-European (IE) root called *ken*-5 (something compressed). They do not apologize for KN reversing to NK. It is evidently an acceptable part of historical linguistics. As the global Edenics documentation of reversals piles up, reversal will be accepted as a common factor in word diversity, rather than an unusual neuro-linguistic phenomenon akin to dyslexia. If a metathesis involves three root letters, that M321 can be termed a "full reversal."

Chinese is a problem because there are so few words that are three consonants long. They are harder to link up with Edenic roots, which usually have three consonants. With such languages, one has to consider whether a metathesis involves a switch of the first two or last two root letters. The Edenic two-letter sub-root should be established as having its own meaning – often done with like-sounding Edenic synonyms. (More on this in the next chapter.)

Chinese has short words because it has exchanged many letters with rising or falling accents. Although one is forced to work with Edenic two-letter sub-roots, and to record two-letter reversals instead of the more certain three-letter metathesis, you should see some compelling links below.

Examples (from the work of George Shen):

Key: Meaning – transliterated Mandarin – Edenic etymon that was reversed – Cognates or entry in *The Word* or *E-Word CD* to note (when available, otherwise a Biblical citation is given).

Except (conj.)	*chu*	אח AKH,	only, but;
		<u>aka</u>	but (Hawaiian)
Falcon	*sun*	נץ NaiTS,	falcon (Jeremiah 48:9).
		Ts'om,	buzzard (Mayan)
		NaZA	hawk (Aramaic)
Father	*ba*	אבה ABH	father
		Latin *avus*	grandfather
		ABBOT	
Field	*dong*	(in place names)	
	tian	אדמה ADaMaH	land or country
		DEMOCRAT	

| Flesh, meat, skin | r'ou | עור [O]WR – CORIUM CARNI(VORE), | |
| | caro | Latin, flesh –CHROME | |

Fly, flying bird, hover, flutter, float

	fei, fu	עף [A]F	to fly
		עף [O]aF or GHoaF	bird, fowl, fly
	vuka		fly (Fijian)
	kupu		butterfly (Malay)
		AVIATE	

| Fog | wu | עב [A]BH | cloud |
| | | EVENING | |

Japanese has far more consonants, and reversed Edenic is less common. Among the scores of reversals in our word-base are the following:

KEY: The first word defines both the Japanese and Edenic word

Aroma	kaori	ריח RaYaK[H]	REEK
Distance	kyori	רחק Roa[K]HaQ	REACH
Empty	akeru	ריק RaiYQ	KARATE
Happy	ureshi	אשר ASHeeR	RICH
Kindle	taku	קדח QaDaK[H]	CAUTERIZE
Prayer	inori	רנה ReeNaH	RUNE
Seat	seki	כסא Kee$Ai	CHAISE
Woman	yoshi	אשה EeSHaH	EACH

Japanese has some three-letter metatheses as well:

The word for "open space," *hiroba*, is a M213 of רחב Ra[K]HaBH, broad expanse (Job 36:16,18) or an M231 of its letter-scrambled counterpart רוח ReVa[K]H. space, interval. (Genesis 32:17). [AIR]

221

Fujin (lady, wife) is an M321 or a full, three-letter reversal of נקב NeQaiBHaH, female (Genesis 5:2). English QUEEN is an M231 of the same *Noon-Koof-Bhet* source. Sadly, the Japanese lady and the English queen are mere cognates of **CAVITY**, as if they were "female" components in electronics NOOK.

With more consonants than other Asian languages, there should be more examples of metathesis with Japanese-from-Edenic words. The fact that there are so few suggests that Japanese is one of the original 70 spin-offs from Edenic, and reflects the many centuries of Japanese isolation when the language changed little. In a more rare example of a metathesis below, the three Edenic root letters come out third, first, and second (M312):

Supporter   *mikata*   תומך ToWMaiKH   (Isaiah 41:10)

M312s are not as rare as one might assume. Two of the most common words in the world fit this pattern of Babel-babble: WORD and WORLD. Of course, English words must be discussed in a historical context, so let us move to German *Welt* (world) and *Wort* (word). Even better, let us use the Yiddish *velt* (world) and *vort* (word) to preserve an older pronunciation.

Eliminate vowels (the first step in accurate historical linguistics), and VLT and VRT are remarkably similar. With only the L/R liquid shift differentiating them, it would make sense that a similar neuro-linguistic phenomenon diversified them from their Edenic original.

VRT is an M312 scramble of דבר Da[V]aR, 1) word (Genesis 11:1) 2) statement – the word used by the KJV to render the Ten Commandments (Exodus 34:28) with literary license. [WORD]

VLT is an M312 scramble of תבל Te[V]eL, world (Isaiah 14:17). [WORLD]

While both sound similar in earlier Germanic, they end up with different English spellings. *Velt*, but not WORLD keeps the Edenic *Tahf*/T. WORLD takes on both Liquids (L and R) from the Edenic *Lamed*. *Vort* has only changed from דבר Da(V)aR with the initial M312, and with a dental shift of *Dalet* to T. By the time we have WORD, the bilabial has shifted, V to W, and the re-shifted dental restores the original *Dalet*.

The M312 metathesis isn't bull.

Let's note the beginning of the CARIBOU entry.

CARIBOU	BaQaR	*Bet-Koof-Resh*
Bah-CAR	בקר	[BQR → QRB]

ROOTS: The CARIBOU (reindeer) is the Canadian French take on the native name for the only beasts similar to cattle in the Arctic. Fur trappers borrowed the term from Russians who once owned and hunted these lands. The Russian cow, *karova*, got Frenchified.

Neither CaRiBou nor KaRoVa resemble the Biblical Hebrew cow, פרה PaRaH, but the more generic cattle term, בקר BaQaR (Genesis 26:14). In what is called a M312 metathesis, *Bet-Koof-Resh* in the language of Eden gets reshuffled, after Babel-Babble to Q-R-B. Or to KRV or hard C-R-B.

The Phillipino water-buffalo, the CARABAO, is not related to reindeer or CARIBOU. But they also named this animal with the scrambled Edenic word for cattle. Only someone with the reasoning of a cow could chalk up these long-lost Edenic cognates as coincidences or borrowings.

BRANCHES: The Russian cow gets leaner in Polish krowa or Czech krava. With the initial Bet out of the way in Germanic, it's easy to get German kuh, Dutch coe or English COW by simply pronouncing QR in the clipped fashion of a New Englander. (Folks in Manchestah, Nah Hampshah don't heah Rs at the end of words.)

E.D. Klein has the "epithet of the bull-colossus" in Akkadian as *karibu*. Similar to the "cow" words which reverse the *Koof* and *Bet* of בקר BaQaR, the Latvian cattle word is *gvous*.

The *Bet* or *Bhet* did survive the creation of the Romance languages, but the end-R, again, is trimmed off. Variations of *vaca* (Spanish, Portuguese, Roman) are familiar to you from the Latin source of VACCINE. For more on בקר BaQaR, and to meet the Mexican-Spanish term that best echoes the Edenic. [BUCKAROO] For the other reindeer herders, of northern Sweden, see BEAST.

The water buffalo of the Phillipines, the CARABAO, is also an M312 of בקר BaQaR. The Spanish spelling is a Spanish rendition of the Malay *karbau*.

The Andean ALPACA is just *paco* in native Peruvian. Their staple cattle is another bilabial-guttural form of בקר BaQaR, with the *Bet*/B shifted and the *Resh*/R dropped.

In Numbers 23:22 there are the "lofty horns of the wild-ox." (JPS) The KJV translators render the ראם R'EM as a "unicorn." Swedish *ren* gave us REINDEER, a mere nasal shift from R'EM. These deer with the large, magnificently curved antlers most likely had not yet retreated to arctic Scandinavia in antiquity.

Another *E-Word CD Dictionary* entry features an M231 in the beginning and end:

KITCH(EN)	SHaK[H]aDT	Shin-Het-Tet
Sha-KHUTT	שחט	[SH-K-T → K-T-SH]

ROOTS: The *American Heritage Dictionary*'s recipe for the Middle English word KITCHEN involves the real Latin word *coquere* (to cook), a pinch of Sanskrit *pakva* (ripe) and the inedible concoction of *pek(w)* to cook, ripen, as their so-called Indo-European root.

The Hebrew kitchen is the מטבח MiDTBaK[H]. This literally means the place of טבח DTeBHaK[H], slaughter, in preparing meat (Genesis 43:16). *Matbah* is also an Arabic kitchen, where the word *tabakha* came to mean any cooking, not just killing animals. Before frozen food the kitchen was an even messier place. The other Biblical word for slaughtering animals, especially for sacrifice, is *Shin-Het-Tet* שחט SHaK[H]aDT. Isaac was nearly killed with this verb in Genesis 22:10. The verb means pressing and squeezing too. In Genesis 40:11 grapes are squeezed into juice with bloodless *Shin-Het-Tet* food preparation. With no easy Western source for KITCHEN, one can do worse than sliding over from טבח *Tet-Bhet-Het* slaughter to שחט *Shin-Het-Tet* slaughter, and then sliding שחט SHaK[H]aDT into a fine **KITCH**EN with an M231 metatheis. The CH is from the initial *Shin*, and the "K.I.T." echos *Het-Tet* or the ט-ח K[H]aDT end of שחט SHa**K[H]aDT**.

The second element in SHaK[H]aDT also echoes חד K[H]aD, sharp. [ACUTE] KITCHEN as a double-guttural is explored at CAKE.

> **BRANCHES:** Alleged cognates under the "root" *pek(w)* include: **APRI**COT (see
> פרי PReeY, at FRUIT), BISCUIT, COOK, CONCOCT, CUISINE, CULINARY
> (see כלי KayLeeY, utensil, at CULINARY, DYSPEPTIC, KILN, PEPO, PEPTIC,
> PRECOCIOUS, PUKKA, PUMPKIN and RICOTTA.
>
> To cook in Hungarian is *szakacs,* recalling *Shin-Het-Tet.* H and the (related)
> Finnish kitchen, *keittio,* reinforces the thesis that English **KIT**CHEN isn't just an
> aberrant "cook" word like the KK kitchens of Germanic. [CAKE] It is possible
> that only the English retained the T and the CH, and the pronunciation of that
> even post-Babel *Het-Tet-Shin* was butchered by the pre-Romans.
>
> Back to the *Tet-Bet-Het* kitchen (the מטבח MiDTBaK[H]), we expect the Turkish
> Kitchen to contain a slight shift like *mutfak.* It is less clear why in Rumanian (a
> Latinate language), *bucatar* is to cook, and *bucaterie* means a kitchen. Perhaps
> they are from an M231 metathesis of this primeval טבח *Tet-Bet-Het* cooking
> term, and they never took to Roman cuisine.
>
> Latin *victima* meant an animal for sacrifice, and so gave us VICTIM. טבח
> DTe[V]aK[H] means slaughtered cattle (Genesis 43:16.) An M231 metathesis
> and some sensitivity gets **VICT**IMHOOD even from the culinary sense of טבח
> DTe[V]aK[H].

In Chinese: *peng* (X499) means to hold in both hands, and a double handful. An M312 metathesis gets *peng* from חפן [K]HoaFahN. In the Bible this hand word is used to measure a handful. [FIN]

Other M312: M312 with a *Resh*-to-W shift: Japanese *kawaii* (dear, lovely) from יקר YaQaR, dear. [CHERISH]

Always involving some letter shifts as well, there are some full reversals, where the 1ˢᵗ, 2ⁿᵈ and 3ʳᵈ Edenic root consonant become 3ʳᵈ, 2ⁿᵈ and 1ˢᵗ in English. Many of these are at the QUARTER entry. There you will see how רבע Re[V]aGH, a FOURTH (1/4) reversed to **QUAR**T, **QUAR**TER and **SQUARE**; גדש GaDeSH, to heap up, reversed to STACK; דבש D[V]aSH, date honey, reversed to SWEET; and גלש GaLaSH, slide, reversed to SLEIGH and SLOG. GULF has been linked to פלג FeLeG, a break-up. [FLAG] These full reversals, like an M321 metathesis, also seem to be rare in most non-IE language families.

METATHESIS PATTERNS

Metathesis patterns, as might be suspected, are usually particular to language groups. At the DEGREE entry, Romance and Germanic languages have GRD word from an M132 metathesis of דרגה DaRGaH, step, degree. Instead of the European pattern, Swahili has an M312 metathesis for its DEGREE word *kadiri*.

Metathesis patterns also function to separate vocabulary within a language superfamily. The authorities do not link Greek *megalo* (great) with *gammel* (old) in the Scandanavian tongues. But Edenic גמל GaMaL means "weaned" in Genesis 21:8, in other words "great" or "large" or "old" enough for an infant to be independent of its mother. גמל GaMal, camel, is the greatest or largest beast in the Middle East, so *Gimel-Mem-Lamed* is clearly more about size than about suckling. [MEGALOMANIAC] So, the Greek had a M213 metathesis happen to it at the Tower of Babel, while the Swedish, Danish and Norwegian equivalents experienced no change. Any slight semantic (usage) shift was quite natural – see BIG for the large-mature equation.

Most M213 metatheses are in foreign words. But entry words with this metathesis are also seen in entries like FENESTRATE (נפץ), SNACK (נשך), SUCCOR (עזר), and VIGOR (גבר).

Once metathesis sets in, cognates from the same language group can be hard to spot. French *hiver* (winter) is a relatively easy M132 metathesis from Edenic winter, חרף [K]HoReF (Genesis 8:22). This is the source of **HIBER**NATE (stay the winter). Other winter words in nearby languages have changed much from the Old French. Looking just at Spanish *invierno,* Italian and Portuguese *inverno* and Rumanian *iarna*, one could never dig out a ח-ר-ף *Het-Resh-Phey* etymon.

Can the same Edenic word spin-off a few variations in different languages via metathesis?

Certainly. At the SPIN entry we see that צ-נ-ף *Tsadi-Noon-Phey*/TS-N-PH is the verb of winding round, and a noun of a turban (both in Leviticus 16:4). In Greek we have the *stephanos* (wreath) that gave English the STEPHANE (ornamental headdress of ancient Greece) and the name Stephen/Steven. This involved an M132 metathesis. To SPIN or a SPINDLE also was formed from an M132.

Arabic *nasif* is a veil, another garment that is wound around the wearer. This metathesis is an M213 from צ-נ-ף *Tsadi-Noon-Phey*.

To wind around in Japanese is *mawasu*. After nasal and bilabial shifts, one can see how nasal-bilabial-fricative came from Edenic fricative-nasal-bilabial, or an M231 metathesis.

Chapter Six CONCLUSION

Here is an apt example to conclude a chapter on metathesis. The word ETYMology describes the endeavor of tracing the ancestry of words. The etymology of ETYMOLOGY goes back to the Greek *etmos* (truth). The suffix *-os* may be eliminated to reveal the core root, or etymon, as ETM. Truth in Edenic is אמת EMeT, instead of ETM or ETYM.

How do I know that אמת EMeT, *Aleph-Mem-Tahf*, is the older "truth? " How is Edenic truth more truthful than some Hellenic ancestor of Greek? Why isn't the Biblical Hebrew the metathesis? Two reasons: 1) א Aleph as a prefix means "not" (as in English A-), and מ-ת *Mem-Tahf* means death. [CHECKMATE] So, as a compound, א-מ-ת *Aleph-Mem-*

Tahf means **UN**dying, eternal… as truth. 2) The *Aleph* leads the *Aleph-Bet*, the *Tahf* ends it, and, in the middle, is the *Mem* – just as truth always resides, between the extremes.

After this metathesis-driven etymology, the name for that aspect of Edenics involved with the source of words in subsequent languages may be called **Emetology**.

Chapter Six ACTIVITIES

The following ten words came from a metathesis of the Edenic source found at a given entry. In each case, spell out the Edenic etymon, document it with a Biblical citation or a Semitic term, and identify if it's a M213, M132, or M312 metathesis:

1. DEGREE and דרגה DaRGaH, step, rank [GRADE]

2. DELIC(ACY and דקל DeQeL, edible date [DELICACY]

3. CERAM(IC and חמר K[H]aMeR, clay…material see "CERAMIC, A]

4. RISE and זרח ZaRa[K]H, sunrise [RISE]

5. ARCHAIC and אחור AK[H]OAR, rear, back [CARRACK A]

6. DENSE and דשן DaSHaN, fat [DENSE]

7. TUNIC and כתנת KiToNeT, shirt, garment [COTTON]

8. HASTATE, spearlike and חץ [K]HaiTS, arrow [HASTATE]

9. SCREEN and שמר SHoMeR, protection [SAMURAI] – note shifts

10. SIMILE and משל MaSHaL, proverb, parable, poetic example [SIMULATION]

Chapter Seven

The Chemistry and Physics of Edenics

This book is about sound and sense, not your father's "linguistics" as we know it.

Sound is energy.

In the Theory of Word Relativity E= S+S. The combined *sound* and *sense* of words forms the *energy* that drives Edenics.

INTRODUCTION:

We could not arrive at this chapter without previously learning about the Letter Shifts and other ways to unmask disguised Edenic. Nor could we go on to note extensive word families (in Chapter Nine) without this chapter's perception of what we'll call the Chemistry and Physics of Edenics.

Within the sound and sense of Edenics, the "Chemistry" involves the modular, compound – component structure of Edenic's three-letter words. This is comparable to dividing H_2O into hydrogen and oxygen. One phoneme, or sound made from two of the three root letters combined, tends to contain the core root or sub-root. As we compare the Edenic root to a chemical compound, that sub-root is the key molecule containing the important two root letters or atoms.

Within the music and meaning of Edenics, the "Physics" relates to the ways in which these roots and sub-roots extend to nearly opposite and completely opposite "antonyms." This is reminiscent of such laws of physics that cover equal and opposite reactions, such actual substances as positive and negative charged ions, and more theoretical substances like matter and antimatter.

It might appear as though this chapter, which delves into the *internal* nature of the new science of Edenics, has little to do with the *external* nature of Edenics – that which involves etymology and how Edenic appears to be the source of world languages. Rest assured, however, that this chapter's glimpses into an Intelligent Design of Edenics, discovering a non-human, perhaps supra-human architectonics of Edenics, makes the linkages to other languages that much clearer and easier.

The *chemistry of Edenics*, isolating the inner two-letter sub-root, enables a link between Edenics and a foreign language. Take, for example, the Hawaiian *hula*. There is no guttural-liquid-vowel three-letter word meaning a similar dance. Miriam and the Israelite women did dance at the Reed Sea while striking a tambourine (Exodus 15:20). In Edenic this dance is a מחלה Ma[K]HoaLaH.

The initial *Mem* is a prefix letter (more on this later), and ח-י-ל *Het-Yod-Lamed* means to shake (Micah 4:9). The חל *Het-Lamed* sub-root is the perfect source word for the writhing Mideast belly-dance of celebratory Israelite women, and of Hawaiian women similarly shaking in place and telling a story with their arms during a *hula* dance.

With the *physics* of Edenics, the law of built-in, sound-alike opposites also can help one find the Edenic etymon of words. As seen by CAPRICIOUS (whimsical) or to CAPER (to frolic like a "goat or lamb" – *Webster's*), Latin *capra* (a goat) must have been named for frisky, young animals. The closest Edenic word is פיר K'PHeeYR, a young lion (Judges 14:5). The sound correspondence is good, and the sense is notable because the young of ruminants is *exactly the opposite* of the young of their predators. As seen at the CAPRICORN entry, an appropriate Edenic word for the young of ruminants was found. *Ayin-Phey-Resh,* עפר [O]aPHeR of Songs 2:9 is usually translated to mean the young of deer or gazelles. But the *physics* of Edenics leads one to understand the word as the young of ruminants, as the engineered opposite of the עפר [O]aPHeR, of prey for the predatory כפיר K'PHeeYR. Now it is clear that one should read the *Ayin* as a guttural, so that עפר GHoPHeR lines up with Latin *capra* or with the theoretical Indo-European root *kapro*, which includes deer as well as goats.

After observing some of the uncharted science of Edenics, a reader may be more likely to conclude that Edenic vocabulary is unique, is far closer to natural science than any "normal" language, and is more fitting to be the world-class original Proto-Earth that scholars like McWhorter despair of ever finding.

Ironically, it is just the global aspect of Edenics that allowed, even demanded that the new field of Edenics work with the long-neglected concept of two-letter sub-roots (a primary rule of the *chemistry* of Edenics. A good example of linking several English words to a clearly established two-letter Edenic root is seen in the entry below:

STUB(BORN)	(Nee)TS'BaH	*Noon-Tsadi-Bet-Hey*
(NEE)TSIB-BAH	נצבה	[TS-B → ST-B]

ROOTS: The dictionaries have trouble with STUB and STUBBLE, which they connect to the theoretical Indo-European root (*s*)*teu* (to push, stick, knock, beat). They are addressing the sense of "stubbing" one's toe. Middle English *stoborne* (stubborn) ought to connect to STUB, but the authorities are not sure how to do so.

A ticket STUB and **STUBB**LE in the field is that which **STUBB**ORNLY remains firm after cutting or harvesting.

The **STUBB**ORN Hebrews have a two-letter ב-צ *Tsadi-Bet*/TS-B root of standing firm. This is seen in נצב Nee**TSahBH**, standing (Genesis 18:2), root נצב Nee**TSaBH,** handle, hilt (Judges 3:22), and נציב Ni**TSeeYBH**, column, (the "pillar" of salt that Lot's wife was petrified into in Genesis 19:26). More lasting architecture at STABLE. Closer to the emotionality of STUBBORNESS are נצב Nee**TSBaH,** resoluteness, steadfastness, and יתיצב Yi(S)Ya**TSayBH,** to "stand up to" someone or to **stubb**ornly oppose them. (Deuteronomy 7:24).

BRANCHES: OBST INATE may belong here with צ-ב *Tsadi-Bet* resiliency, instead of being placed with STABILITY and STU(M)P (nasalized STUBBLE) at an IE "root" called *sta* (to stand). These physically enduring ST-B words are from the צ-ב *Tsadi-Bet* sub-root. יצב Ya**TSaBH** is the formal verb meaning "to set or stand up." [MASTABA] [STABLE] Latin *stabilis* means "standing firm" and *stipula* is a (sturdy) stalk or stem. Deuteronomy 29:9 is insufficiently translated as "standing." נצבם NiTSaBHiM conveys the endurance, the stubborn stability of the eternal people, not merely their being in a vertical position.

In the STUMP, or remaining tree trunk that stubbornly persists, there is a nasalized (extra M) added to the צ-ב *Tsadi-Bhet*. STUMP is from Middle Low German *stump,* a cognate of STAFF (stick), STALAG, STAMP. STAMPEDE, STAPLE and STOOP at the IE "root" *stebh* (post, stem, to support, place firmly on, fasten). The P of STUMP is from a bilabial shift of the ב *Bhet*/B. The same bilabial shift from a *Bhet* to an F is seen in STIFF. STIFF is another form of **stubb**orn resistance … all from our צ-ב *Tsadi-Bhet* sub-root.

Reversing to ב-צ *Bet-Tsadi*: בצר BeTSeR means strength, related to fortification words. For ב-צ *Bet-Tsadi* instability, the built-in opposite of צ-ב *Tsadi-Bhet*/TS-B, see בץ BoaTS, mud, mire (Jeremiah 38:22) at PITCH.

Isolating the צ-ב *Tsadi-Bhet*/TS-B molecule of meaning within the compound of Edenic and English words involves the *chemistry* of Edenics. Reversing to ב-צ *Bet-Tsadi*/B-TS for built-in synonyms and antonyms involves the *physics* of Edenics.

Let us again demonstrate both the *chemistry* and the *physics* of Edenics within one set of words, a set which will also provides the sources of English words that we all know. Note the חל *Het-Lamed*/[K]H-L common "health" theme below, a proposed sub-root. Traditional Hebraic scholars object to the medieval notion of two-letter sub-roots. Whether you have academic tenure in previous theories, or you have never encountered ancient Semitic words before this book, you are asked to first taste the pudding, and **then** to judge the alleged proof.

Here is the "HEALTH" entry from the *E-Word CD dictionary*:

HEALTH	[K]HeeLOOTS	*Hey-Lamed-Tsadi*
HEAL-OOTS	חלוץ	[HL+TS → HL + TH]

ROOTS: Old Norse *heill* means healthy; the theoretical Indo-Euopean (IE) root is *kailo* (whole, uninjured, of good omen – cognate with "holy").

The IE root is a wannabe כל KoaL, all, whole (Genesis 13:10).

Edenic provides better sound and sense for health words. חלוץ [K]HeeLOOTS means strength and vigor (Isaiah 58:11), similar to it's ח-ל *Het-Lamed* built-in synonym חיל [K]HaYiL, active or capable. (Genesis 47:6) חיל [K]HaYiL as strength and military power is similar to the Syriac ח-ל *Het-Lamed* word. חיל [K]HaYaL is a soldier. Power and vigor is the issue, not being uninjured. Even English HALE is more about vigor than wholeness. HEALTH can come from the *Het-Lamed-Tsadi* of חלוץ [K]HeeLOOTS, health, just as TH of EARTH came from the ץ *Tsadi* of ארץ AReTS, earth.

The Woman of Valor or חיל [K]HaYiL in Proverbs is praised for vigor and strength, not for her military prowess. חלם [K]HaLahM is to be healthy and strong; Syriac חלים [K]HaLeeYM is healthy and firm.

BRANCHES: Teutonic names like HILDA do convey the military sense of *Het-Lamed*.

CELIBATE, CURE, HALE, and HEAL are alleged cognate of HEALTH.

Antonyms of ill-health like **AILI**NG and **ILL** are from sound-alike ח-ל *Het-Lamed* opposites such as חלא [K]HaLAh, ill, diseased; חלה [K]HaLaH, ill, sick,weak, (II Kings 13:14); חלה [K]HoaLeH, sick; and חלי [K]HoaLeeY, illness (Deuteronomy 29:21); חלש [K]HaLahSH, weak (Joel 4:10); חיל [K]HeeYL and חל K]HahL means writhing in pain or childbirth.

CHOLERA, mentioned at "GALL," is a ח-ל *Het-Lamed* antonym of illness. חלי רע [K]HoLeeY R[A]h means a grievous illness. The "CHOLY" in MELAN-**CHOLY** also reflects this ח-ל *Het-Lamed* of illness. Greek *chole* (bile) is from געל Ga[A]hL, nausea. [GALL]

Ola is health in Hawaiian; *ahul* is weak, feeble or debilitated in Basque. Sick in Polish is *chory*, involving a liquid shift (L to R).

See ALL and HAIL. English HELLO or German *heil* are not mere greetings, they are ח-ל *Het-Lamed* wishes for another's health.

So, even though there is no word with just ח-ל *Het-Lamed*, and even though these *Het-Lamed* synonyms and antonyms contain other letters, Edenics sees ח-ל *Het-Lamed* as a sub-root of health. This two-letter sub-root is not a lucky accident. It is representative of a common design feature in Edenic vocabulary. Admittedly, this particular example is unusually obvious, and does not involve any letter shifts or reversals.

Again, we are using two natural sciences as a metaphor. Isolating a two-letter sub-root of distinctive sound and sense (like the ח-ל *Het-Lamed* above) involved the *chemistry of Edenics*. Charting the ח-ל *Het-Lamed* **positive** health words like HALE and HEALTHY, along with the **negatively charged** ח-ל *Het-Lamed* health terms like ILL and AILING involves the **physics of Edenics**. A future chapter or entire book should be devoted to each aspect of Edenics, but at least this book offers an introduction.

Sound and Sense, in both the Chemistry and Physics of Edenics, can also be noted in two key words of Passover: חמץ [K]HaMeTS, leavened bread and מצה MaTSaH, **un**leavened bread. (Exodus 13:7). Like physics, like matter and anti-matter, the two opposites contain nearly identical components (root letters). One is *Mem-Tsadi-Hey*, while the other is ח *Het* (closest relative of *Hey*)-*Mem-Tsadi*.

Like a chemist, we now isolate the molecules of meaning within חמץ [K]HaMeTS: 1) ח-מ *Het-Mem*, and 2) מ-צ *Mem-Tsadi*. The halachic or legal criteria for creating prohibited חמץ [K]HaMetz are 1) baking for over a minimum length of time, and 2) exposure to any liquid that might set off the leavening process. ח-מ *Het-Mem* or חם [K]HaM means heat, and מיץ MeeYTS involves liquid. (It usually infers the extract of juice, and is a possible source of MOIST. [MASS] [MEAD]

MOIST conveys the liquidity of מיץ MeeYTS, but חם [K]HaM doesn't easily resonate with English speakers. The heated warm words that derive from it have shifted to emotionally warm terms like AMOROUS. [AMITY] Noah's son is חם [K]HaM, but his name was Anglicized to Ham. Ham was warmer than his esthetics-driven and publicity-driven brothers, Japheth and Shem, but sometimes his heat and passions got him into trouble. Relevant to like-sounding, related terms and to this patriarch of peoples of color, חום [K]HOOM means the warm color of brown.

It is easier to feel the heat of חם [K]HaM outside of English. To boil for the Maidu Indians of California is *hom*. To hear the K in חם K[H]aM, seek Asian religious words like Japanese **Kamikaze** and Sanskrit **Kama** *Sutra*. (Spirituality is only the opposite of amity and desire for Westerners.)

Once the reader is more familiar with the KH-M and M-TS molecules of meaning within חמץ [K]HaMeTS, one is more easily able to appreciate the chemistry of its sound and the physics of its sense. Most of the discussion above centered on the chemistry of Edenics, the modular composition of חמץ [K[HaMetS and מצה MaTSaH, but remember that the *two are opposites,* Passover matter and anti-matter, and so this was also about the physics of Edenics.

Most dissections of Edenic three-consonant words do not involve two distinct two-letter sub-roots combined (as in חמץ [K]HaMeTS). Usually there is a recognizable, controlling two-letter root, and one can isolate the one remaining letter (fore or aft) with steers that 2-letter sub-root (fore or aft) like canoeing upstream.

This chapter shall further explore both the chemistry and the physics of Edenics in isolation, but see entries like GOOD, GATHER, JUXTAPOSE and YOKE – with their *Gimel-Dalet* and *Het-Dalet* sub-roots which both isolate and unify, to see both the chemistry and physics of Edenics working together.

HOW EDENIC DID NOT GROW

Last chapter we encountered Edward Horowitz' 1960 book entitled *How The Hebrew Language Grew*. The book uses Hebrew orthography, but at least it is written in English. Like Ernest David Klein's dictionary, he opens up Hebrew to English readers – to those who can read Hebrew. Horowitz's classic of the previous generation may well record some of the grammatical growth that did expand from usage, from later people needing to express the core Edenic roots with more complex applications.

But it is absurd to accept the accepted thesis that one clan of West-Semitic speakers in the Bronze Age developed a language with a profound economy not seen even in allegedly earlier or definitely later Semitic dialects. Germanic Neanderthals didn't "evolve" words this way, so it's pure chauvinism to assume that only Hebrew "evolved" or "grew" in an ingenious, economical, and orderly way. Adding the observations of Edenics to what is known about Hebrew, it is obnoxious to assume that Hebrew was developed by the Hebrews. It's totally non-chauvinistic to assume that this orderly language was designed by something higher than humans, was given to the first pre-historic humans (belonging to the planet, NOT to any one people), and that this Edenic then got diversified to create our multi-national history.

Horowitz, like the better dictionaries, will note how the newly-coined Modern Hebrew words משב MoSHa[V], collective settlement, and משבה MoSHaBHaH, a colony, came from the Biblical term ישב YaSHaBH, to dwell. This is undeniable. But the original stock of Edenic letters (like atoms) and phonemes (two letters combined to form one molecule of meaning) did not evolve, as Horowitz and the linguists of his generation guessed, from echoic or imitative sounds.

Current dictionaries assume that the Hebrew root ישב YaSHaBH evolved from Akkadian *washabu* (to sit, dwell). The ש-ב Shin-*Bet* sub-root of dwelling and sitting does not appear in Maya *shukba* (to sit) *or* Japanese *suwaru* (to sit) because of 1) a coincidence, or 2) because sitting-dwelling somehow "sounds like" SB or BS.

But something doesn't sit well with the given concept of the static ישב YaSHaBH root of sitting still or remaining in place. ש-ב SHaBH means "to turn away," and סבב $aBHaBH is "to walk about, to turn around" [SWIVEL] and Arabic *wathaba* means "he jumped." שבי "SHeBHeeY" is when the losers in battle are taken away to captivity (the opposite of שב SHaBH, to return home). On *Shin-Bet-Tahf*, the שבת Shabbat (the Sabbath, or the week – a returning cycle of seven) one can lose the workaday world and *Shin- Bet*, בש SHaBH (return) to one's soul.

It is logical, in a scientific way, to have opposite words that sound nearly alike, but it's downright impractical, anti-semantic.

These sound-alike antonyms in Edenics reveal that language in its pristine form is like physics, a natural science.

We will encounter many instances of synonyms and antonyms from the same root. For example, רש RaSH means poor, while ירש YaRaSH means to inherit wealth, and עשר [A]SHeeR means wealthy. (If you thought of reversing the sound to get RICH, you should be עשר OSHeR, happy.) [RICHES] Like matter and anti-matter, such data demonstrates how Edenics resembles physics.

Secular Hebrew scholars were trained by secular linguists not to see anything special in the Hebrew language that they worked with. The Hebraists of the 19th and 20th centuries were busy turning a sacred language into a mundane, usable one for a dreamed-of secular Hebrew-speaking state.

Intelligent Design in language, or in anything demonstrated to not be made by humans, is not merely the province of Evangelicals. It fits the prevailing agnostic philosophy called Deism. Such Deistic thinking suited America's Founding Fathers. This does not prevent some from deeming anything supporting I.D. to be unconstitutional. Any studies considered anti-Darwinian will guarantee no tenure or employment according to the strict code of Academic Freedom.

A well-trained Hebrew grammarian or secular Hebrew Bible critic would not dare even link ישר YaSHaR, straight and שורה SHOORaH, row, line. [SERIES] Yes, both words contain a ש-ר *Shin-Resh* sub-root, and both words are about something linear and straight. But according to the grammar books they lack the conventional prefix or suffix to suggest a shared root. There is much good thinking inside the box, but not much vision. ש-ר *Shin-Resh* straightness even informs the naming of the שור SHOAR, bull or ox, that innately plows in straight lines. The ש-ר *Shin-Resh* common sub-root of the words above is self-evident to someone with a creative aptitude in science or literature.

The Hebrew Bible is full of verses that yoke words of similar sound and sense which are not considered related, and which contain multiple entendres that don't fit conventional understanding. Biblical exegetes have produced scores of commentaries to plumb the infinite depths of what they see as superhuman writing. Biblical grammar, spelling and vocabulary has set parameters, but these are constantly stretched to vex the creative reader into new, intended innuendos. Western-trained grammarians and bible critics think with a linear logic very foreign to the Biblical mindset, are they not famous for creativity either in science or in literature.

Since Edenics is both a science and a poetics of sound and sense, the student of language must employ the inner ear beyond conventional spellings. Let us notice some more of the dynamics of the S-R Edenic root of straightness and strictures, allowing this segment from the SWERVE entry to open us up to this particular music and meaning, in synonyms and antonyms carefully regarding then disregarding the way they are spelled:

SWERVE	$WooR	*Samekh-Vav-Resh*
SVOOR	סור	**[SVR]**

ROOTS: From the theoretical Indo-European root *swerbh* (to turn, wipe off), SWERVE means to turn aside from a straight line or course. סור $OOR or $VOOR means to turn aside precisely this way.

Deuteronomy 2:27: *I will keep strictly to the highway, **turning off** neither to the right nor to the left.*

There is also *Sin-Vav-Resh*, שור SwooR or SOOR, to turn aside (Hosea 9:12). The "wiping off" in the IE root is from הסיר *(Hey)*$eeYR, to remove, put aside, related to the same S-R Hebrew root. ז-ו-ר *Zayin-Vav-Resh*, ZVR, also means to turn away. סרר $oReR is perverted, rebellious (Deuteronomy 21:18).

ס-ר *Samekh-Resh* is also the built-in antonym of not swerving, not deviating. אסור A$OOR means bound, imprisoned, later prohibited. All mean restricted from deviating (SWERVING off the straight and narrow). Genesis 39:20 has both the verb and the *Samekh-Hey-Resh* noun, סהר $oaHahR, of prison. מוסר MOO$aR is ethical teachings (Proverbs 1:2).

Moving to *Shin-Resh*, ישר YoSHeR is justice. [JURISDICTION] Restrictions, teachings and laws are all S-R opposition to deviation. The ש-ר *Shin-Resh* built-in opposites of straightness are at SHEER.

> **BRANCHES:** שור SOOR, with a ש *Shin* not ס *Samekh*, also means to turn aside or depart; its ש-ר *Shin-Resh* antonymic counterpart is שורה SHOORaH, line, row. [SERIES]. For a sense of S-R stricture with the other fricative, *Tsadi-Resh*, see צר TSaR, narrow, the companion of straight at STRESS. צרר TSaRahR is bound up or straightened (Joshua 9:4).
>
> One doesn't have to be claustrophobic to sense that there ought to be a link between the words "wall" and "narrow." In Edenic, following the S-R theme in entries like SERIES, SHEER, STRAIT and SWERVE, we can hear the relationship between צר TSaR, narrow and שור SHOOR, wall. In mankind's original computing language we can hear the similar opposites just as clearly.

To discover many more of the built-in sound-alike antonyms of Edenic, search "antonym" and "opposite" in the *E-Word CD Dictionary.*

Here is another entry (*E-Word CD*) that makes a clear point about similar opposites, again involving both the *chemistry* and the *physics* of Edenics:

MEL(T)	**MaLa[K]H**	*Mem-Lamed-Het*
Ma-LUKH	מלח	**[ML]**

ROOTS: There is no source older than the Old English *melten,* to melt. The IE root is *mel* (soft, softened). [MILL]

מלח MaLa[K]H is to vanish, pass away (Jeremiah 38:11,12 in plural or Isaiah 51:6 in the Niphal tense). With no older etymon, any legitimacy for the T has melted away.

The most common sense of מלח MeLa[K]H is salt. Lot's wife and the region of Sodom turns to salt, Genesis 19:26, as an eternal reminder. The ברית מלח BReeYT MeLa[K]H of Numbers 18:19 is not a salty covenant, but a perpetual, eternal one. מ-ל-ח *Mem-Lamed-Het*, like so many Edenic words, has a built-in opposite, because the Engineer of words and minerals created things paradoxically with similar opposites. When one has to MELT the ice on steps, salt will make it melt, vanish or pass away. When one wants to preserve or salt away foods, one also uses מלח MeLa[K]H.

A related *Mem-Lamed* word of breaking down a substance is מלל MaLaL, usually an abrasive rubbing and scraping. (Job 18:6)

THE CHEMISTRY OF EDENICS

Taking apart Edenic root words longer than two consonants, to isolate and reveal the word's working sub-root, is the primary task in the chemistry of Edenics. This involves noting the molecules of meaning within the chemical compound or word. A single letter has multiple, very general meanings too, but like splitting an atom, trying to use one-letter roots can be dangerous. Such "roots" are so amorphously general as to discredit the entire enterprise of Edenic chemistry. Edenics is too SOUND to hear one letter clapping.

A single letter can be a useful prefix or suffix before or after the two-letter core of the typical three-letter root. (See the end of this section). But it takes two consonant root letters to form the minimum molecule of meaning. Linguists call this minimum sound a *phoneme*.

Perhaps the best entry to mark a sub-root is to follow the bouncing *Bet-Lamed* at the BALL entry:

BALL	BahLahL	*Bet-Lamed-Lamed*
BALL-UL	בלל	**[BLL]**

ROOTS: The theoretical Indo-European root of BALL is *bhel,* to blow, swell. בלום BaLOOM, swollen and בלט BaLaDT, to protrude, address a BL root of filling or expanding. [BLOAT]

Other Hebrew words match the rolling, mixed up sense of being all BALLED UP in a BALL of confusion. בלל BaLaL is to confound (as human vocabulary was in Genesis 11:9 with the BABBLE of Babel); בלול BaLOOL is to mingle together (Leviticus 2:5) and בלבול BiLBOOL means confusion.

Bilabial-liquid related words include ערב [E]eRBaiL, to mix, confuse, and *Ayin-Resh-Bet* terms of mixing, confusing and swarming. Rolling and mixing occurs on both the BALLFIELD and BALLROOM.

A B-L antonym which prevents overlapping is גבול GiBHOOL, border (Genesis 10:19).

Edenic words containing the sub-root *Bet/Bhet-Lamed* imply a mixing of elements: גבול GiBHooL is a border between two countries; חבל [K]HeBHeL, a string, is threads twisted together, (גבל GeBHeL, braid and כבל KeBHeL, strong rope are taken up at CABLE); טבל DTeBHeL is to immerse one thing in another. [DIP]

מבול MaBHooL, the flood of Genesis, was a cataclysmic geological mixture of biblical proportions; the נבל NaBHaL is an impious fool who mixes the sacred and profane (Isaiah 32:5) [VILE]; שביל SH'BHeeYL is a path that links different areas (Psalms 77:20).

There is an argument, going back to medieval Hebrew grammarians, whether the basic root is made up of two or three letters. Both sides are right. For basic grammar, for using verbs in tenses and most practical applications of language, the tri-consonantal root is standard. However, when micromanaging vocabulary, taking Edenic words apart to reveal their undocumented relationships to both other Edenic words and to those distant global cousins separated at birth since the Tower of Babel, one must look to the two-letter sub-root or core root. Since sound is energy, we must be prepared to hear and see that two-letter sub-root even when it has shifted to related letters, or when it has been disguised by metathesis or *nasalization*.

Edenics needs to work within the conventional wisdom of normative Hebrew grammar and the three-letter root.

Edenics is not a violent revolutionary movement, and eventually academics will be less threatened by it.

Edenics merely wishes to build on past scholarship, and to take the field to the new level needed in the coming era of lexical, then cultural and theological globalization – a state of "one consent" brought about by all peoples realizing that we all have the same Intelligent Designer. The limitations of grammar, together with secular assumptions about language as being man-made has pushed linguistics into a humanities discipline. At best, present-day linguistics can be categorized as a soft science. Edenics strives to reshape linguistics into a hard science – like chemistry and physics. The hardening process may take many years.

PREFIX AND SUFFIX

For verbs, Hebrew grammar always involves set prefix or suffix letters before and after the root.

In Genesis 12:1, for example, there's the single word *Aleph-Resh-Aleph-Kaph.* אראך AREKah means "I will show you." The three-letter root is ר-א-ה *Resh-Aleph-Hey*, to see. Here, the *Aleph* prefix is added in front of the root (first person, future action), while the *Kaph* suffix is added at the end of the root (second person receiving the action). In the unique economy of the language of the Bible, we then have the entire sentence, "I shall show you" in one four-letter word (whose essence is but *Resh-Aleph*).

The use of prefix and suffix letters in Hebrew is common, and can be studied in many standard Hebrew books.

The MIRROR entry, for example, demonstrates how several unexpected words are built from that *Resh-Aleph-Hey* root of seeing. The chemistry of Edenics however, will greatly extend word families, by isolating the two-letter sub-root, and allowing it to naturally expand into related sounds. Music and meaning are followed, not textbook rules. Similarly, the physics of Edenics allows the root's meaning to extend to words of thematically similar or opposite meaning.

Even the conventional Hebraicists have noticed the *Bet-Noon* operating in words like בנה BaNaH, to build; בנין BiNYaN, a building; building materials like the אבן EBHeN, rock or building stone; and לבנה LiBHaiNaH, the brick. The Biblical text around the Tower of Babel, Genesis 11, typically plays a symphony, theme with variation, with this *Bet-Noon*, B-N theme. Only the exceptional scholars of Hebrew have understood that בין BaYN, between, is the crucial B-N mortar that allows us to fit those BN rocks or bricks together.

The scholars are distracted by the *Yod* between the *Bet* and *Noon* in the spelling of בין BaYN (between), even though we had classified the *Yod* as a "weak" or easily ignorable letter. Conventional wisdom also misses out on בינה BeeYNaH, wisdom, as a B-N relative here, not understanding that בינה BeeYNaH is precisely that deductive wisdom that is derived in the synthesis בין BaYN (between) two factors. What about בן BeN, a child? A child is the building block between other members in the generational wall of the familial or national edifice. Generation building is societal bricklaying.

The Hebrew Bible exegetes use the formula "don't call it בניך BaNahYiKH (your children), but בניך BoaNaYiKH (your builders). They understood that the *Aleph*/A before אבן EBHeN (stone) was no impediment to linking children and building blocks.

More certainly, no one has connected the English BONE to this B-N family of building and interconnecting things. Suspiciously, nobody has dug up an older source for BONE than Anglo-Saxon. Surely, BONES are the interconnected building blocks of the larger animals.

After the first edition of *The Origin of Speeches*, synonyms and antonyms related by letter shifts, reversals and/or metathesis began to be collected.

Another set of sound-alike 1) synonyms and 2) antonyms involves the way guttural *Khaf* (K) interchanges with guttural *Ayin* (GH):

כנף KiNaF, wing, [CANOPY] is much like another guttural-*Noon-Pey*, ענף GHaNaF, branch (Leviticus 23:40). Both a wing and a branch are extensions, like the wing of a building, or a branch office of a corporation.

Also see the כפיר K'FeeYR, young predator, and the young of prey (the choicest prey), the *Ayin-Phey-Resh*, עפר GHoaPHeR, fawn. [CAPRICORN]

In the chemistry of Edenics, we are not satisfied with merely calling something water. We observe the hydrogen and oxygen molecules that combine to make up the compound we call water. The easiest way to isolate molecules of meaning that suggest connections to "unrelated" words is when a common two-letter sub-root contains the exact same letters. The second way is to see and hear relationships that are here in Edenics but absent from standard Hebraism. Hebrew scholarship is based on spelling; Edenics is based on sound.

For example, מטר MaDTaR means falling precipitation, whether rain (I Kings 17:1), fire and brimstone (Genesis 19:24) or hail (Exodus 9:23). Alexander Harkavy's dictionary states that the initial *Mem*/M is a prefix, so that the core root is *Tet-Resh*, DTaRaH, moist. But fire and brimstone is hardly moist. Is appears as though falling down is more important in this word, and that the word can be divided better. מטה MaDTaH means down or below like UNDER*NEATH* in the NETHER entry (nasal and dental shifts). This would give *Mem-Tet* a more logical meaning.

The *Tet-Resh*/DT-R second element sounds much like טל DTaL, dew (Genesis 27:28), a mere liquid shift away.

Tet-Resh or dental-liquid also reverses, with a dental shift, to רד RaiD, go down. [ROOT] Mechanical reactions to spelling may not offer as much analytical dissection as a more creative, sound-based method.

We can see the *Shin-Noon* sub-root in the verb שנה SHaNaH, to change. [CHANGE] The noun שנוי SHiNOOY, a change, is clearly related. The word for a solar year, שנה SHaNaH, is also spelled *Shin-Noon-Hey*, but this is merely a coincidence from the chaos of human-evolved language – or so think the professional professors. Think again. The *Shin-Noon* sun must also be thought of as an agent of time and change. שנם SHaNiM, years, may be rendered figuratively as suns or solar years (just as months are "moons").

The SN of SUN, and to a lesser extent, the SL of *sol* and SOLAR, seems to have ripened and changed under the Edenic sun. The SN of SUN reflects both שנה SHaNaH, year and שמש SHeMeSH, sun – M and N being interchangeable nasals.

The years, the effects of time, are the primary agents of change (*Shin-Noon*). The sun will change a grape into a raisin, and, after שנם SHaNiM, years, a youth into a SENIOR. A young congressman can become a SENILE SENATOR. These SN words are from Latin *senex*, old, and ultimately from Edenic ישן (Ya)SHaN, old.

We can even change overnight, after "sleeping on it.*" ישן (Yo)SHaiN is to sleep. [INSOMNIA]

On to other "unrelated" fricative-nasals, the שן SHaiN, tooth, changes and breaks down food to a form we can swallow and digest. The significant quantitative change is when one becomes two – שנם SH'NaiM. שני SHayNeeY, the second, is any individual's significant other.

One thing is only significant when compared to a second thing. *Sin-Noon* means "hated" in the sense of feeling second-class, as happens to the second wife in Deuteronomy 21:15. XENOPHOBIA is fear and loathing of the other, the second, or the stranger. So

Greek *xenos* (strange) is also from נ-שׁ *Shin-Noon*. The ז-נ *Zayin-Noon* core of זנה ZaNaH, idolatry or adultery (source of SIN) is also about an aberrant change, of taking a second, SINister turn off the right path.

It appears as though our reference books may have missed some things about the roots of CHANGE.

Here's the first section in the *E-Word CD Dictionary* that first conveys the conventional etymology:

CHAN(G)E	**SHaNaH**	***SHin-Noon-Hey***
sha-NAH	שׁנה	**[SH-N → CH-N]**

ROOTS: Old French *changie*r is said to come from Latin *cambire* (to exchange, barter). The IE "root"s offered are *skamb* or *kamb* (to curve or bend). Yes, the S before a guttural is often expendable (*skamb* means *kamb)* and a French CH from a Latin hard C is common, but a G (change) coming from a B (*kamb*) is not acceptable. For the source of IE *kamb* see CAMERA.

The Hebrew שׁנה SHaNaH, to change, alter, be different is the more logical etymon. "For I am the Lord, I have not *changed*" – שׁניתי "*ShaNeeYTee.Y*" (Malachi 3:6). Difference happens when one becomes another, or two (both "another" and "two" or שׁני SHayNeeY).

"Yom שׁני SHayNeeY," the 2nd day, is in the 8th verse of Genesis. It is possible for the G of CHANGE to come from the ה *Hey* of שׁנה SHaNaH.

ENHANCING SLEEP THROUGH EDENICS CHEMISTRY

Dormir in Spanish, French and Latin means sleep. To sleep in Edenic is רדם RaDaM. The *Resh-Dalet-Mem*, 1-2-3 letters, seem to have moved to the 2-1-3 position in the Romance languages (an M213 metathesis). You know this word from DORMATORY, even if sleep is the last thing you did in your college DORM. To DREAM originally meant to sleep.

Why would R-D-M be an older or better sleep word than D-R-M? Just because some long-neglected Biblical theory says so? Latinate DRM means nothing, so the secularists appear to be right about vocabulary being full of senseless chaos, with a word only having meaning because society understands that sound to have a set meaning. Edenic RDM is something else entirely. Like every phoneme, or sound, or molecule of meaning in Edenic, the phoneme R-D within R-D-M has its own meaning. רד RaiD means to go down – see ROOT – roots grow down.

Similarly, the D-M second element has a meaning. דממה DiMaMaH means silent. See DIM at DUMB. Therefore, רדם RaDaM or sleep, means "going down into silence."

Every three-letter Edenic word works something like this, a chemical compound composed of the interaction of two molecules of meaning. Most three-letter words can not be broken down as elegantly as רדם RaDaM. Often there is a prefix or suffix element, and sometimes a molecule has to be derived by the various Edenics methods that we have described here.

The chemistry of Edenics allows us to have a litmus test for the legitimacy of reversing a foreign word by metathesis and finding a superior etymon. We can now restore order and meaning to the seemingly chaotic world of words.

In the TIME entry of the *E-Word CD Dictionary*, note how different T-M and dental-nasal words in Edenic, with opposite meaning, provide an etymon (ultimate source) for TIME.

There is a range of T-M TIME words in Edenic. תם TahM is to be ended, finished, to be destroyed, to cease, or to be "spent" in Numbers 26:20. Inverting the letters brings *Mem-Tahf*, מת MaiT, to die and מתי MaTahY, when? Combining T-M and M-T terms of completed time, is צמת TSaMaT – 1) to put an end to, and 2) paradoxically but typically, to assign in perpetuity (Leviticus 25:23). Other temporal T-M time words include: תמל TiMoaL, formerly or yesterday (Genesis 31:2); and, yet another antonym is תמיד TahMeeYD, always or continuity (Exodus 28:29).

Globally, there are T-M time words like *tuma* (a period of time) in Bambara (African), while *thing* is to stop or pause in Cantonese. *Tamam* means finish in Farsi. Japanese reverses the dental-nasal to M-D for *madeni* (by the time…and two similar M-D words). In the excerpt above, both isolated sub-roots and creative semantics (meanings) brought the chemistry and physics of Edenics to bear. This despite the fact that there is no precise Edenic T-M word meaning "time."

This is significant in the Emetology (true etymology) area of Edenics, where sometimes there is no clear Edenic term with which to establish an etymology – but there is a clear group of sub-roots than capture the relevant *sound and sense.*

For example, there is also no Edenic like-sounding word that can mean HAS. There is אחז A[K]HaZ, to hold, and the related אחזה AKHooZaH, a holding or possession, which speaks to HAS. Other words with *Het-Zayin* are not supposed to be related, but they help get a hold of HAS. These include חזור [K]HaZOAR, to return to what one has or where has been; and חזקה [K]HaZaQaH, strong claim based on possession. An etymological connection is even strengthened by a like-sounding antonym: *Het-Samekh-Resh,* חסר [K]HaSe,R to lack or have not.

When the gutturals were taken up earlier, we noted how the harsher gutturals, going up the *Aleph-Bet* keyboard, made the same *Bet-Lamed* sub-root stronger. In this chapter, let us now note the unchanging sub-root, the *Bet-Lamed* of mixture. The mixed strands grow from mere folds to strongly intertwined in the three words below.

1) גבל GeBHeL is a plait or braid
2) חבל [K]HeBHeL is a string or rope
3) כבל KeBHeL is a very strong rope or cable [CABLE]

Bhet-Lamed by itself is not a word, but it clearly means the mixing of two separate strands. This is not only apparent from a deduction of the *Bhet-Lamed* group above. The words בלול BaLOOL means mixture, and בלבל BiLBaiL means to confuse. [BALL]

There are more B-L sub-roots at the Aleph-negative-prefix below.

Built-in antonyms also have the same sub-root. One of these is גבול G'BHOOL, a border. A border sets up the boundary between jurisdictions, and prevents overlaps and mix-ups. This example of the *physics* of Edenics is also recorded in the BALL entry.

In Merritt Ruhlen's *The Origin of Language* (Wiley, NY, 1994) one can see this B-L element appears in the word for "two" in the vast majority of earth's language families. The Edenic sub-root is deep within the human brain. Our inner *Bet-Lamed* allows the concept of two different objects, a mixing, to become the word for "two" when many migrating tribes from Sumer (later Babel) picked their brain for a word for "two.*"*

We already encountered many three-consonant Edenic words, where a two-letter sub-root was isolated. A more dramatic and rare feat involves Edenic words that are seen to have two overlapping sub-roots (as with רדם RaDaM above, the source of DREAM).

DOUBLE ROOTS

Some 3-Letter Words are from Two Overlapping Sub-Roots.
Xy + Yz = Xyz

This phenomenon is called **Double Roots**. (The documentation of this has expanded greatly since the first edition of this book.)

There are scores of these three-letter words that display 2 overlapping two-letter sub-roots, rather than the more common three-letter Edenic word that features a two-letter sub-root plus prefix or suffix letter. If hundreds more of these double root words are found, the unique modular engineering of Edenic will be established.

If a word in *Tanach* has four or more root consonant letters, they are more obviously combinations of words or the dominant parts of words that we might call sub-roots. An example of this is the חלמיש K[H]aLaMeeYSH, flintstone, silex (Deuteronomy 8:15). This rock is struck to make fire. The *Het-Lamed-Mem* is from הלם HaLahM, to strike; the *Yod-Shin* recalls אש AiSH, fire. For pedants who require *exact* spellings, rather than echos of sound and sense – nothing will catch fire.

249

But there are at least scores of **three-letter** words that display two overlapping two-letter sub-roots, rather than the more common three-letter Edenic word that features a two-letter sub-root plus one prefix or suffix letter. Simple examples of these 1+2 three-letter roots are the מ *Mem*-prefix letter in מגן MaGeN, shield, that which גן GahN, protects; and מקל MaQeL, walking stick, that which allows קל QahL, acceleration. Lesser known is the מ Mem-prefix of the מלאך MaLaKH, agent or angel, and the מלך MeLeKH, king – one who is made to לך LeKH, go, and the other who is the executive go-maker.

I had only previously heard the imperfect examples of שמים SHahMaYim (sky) meaning שם SHahM (there) [is] מים MaYiM (water), and שמש SHeMeSH (sun) as the combination of שם SHahM (there) [is] אש AiSH (fire). Only in 2010 in the *Zohar* did I come across another, better example of double roots. שושנה SHOASHaNaH, lily, was of שש SHEeSH, six (petals), and in its life cycle it שנה SHeeNaH, changes (colors). שושנה SHOASHaNaH (lily) technically has five letters, but two are "weak," so this so far is the closest I've seen to the Edenics treatment of double roots in three-letter words with no initial or final letter acting as a prefix or suffix.

We begin with the two early and simple examples from the Edenics slide show (at edenics.org). Let us first dissect the Edenic dog and flower. כלב KeLeBH, dog, is at the LOBO entry with other L-B canines, and פרח PeRaK[H], flower, is at the FRUITY entry with other P-R and F-R fruits or botanical items. At these entries one sees how KLB (dog) is a compound made up of two overlapping two-letter sub-roots. First, there is כל KoL or K-L, all, combined with L-BH לב LeBH or L-BH, heart. [LOVE]. The dog is the one animal famous for its loyalty, emotionality and courage. Compare a dog to a fickle, scaredy cat if you need help understanding why only a dog is "all heart."

Similarly, פרח PeRaKH, flower, is the chemical combination of a פר P-R (or F-R) element FRUIT plus a R-K[H] element ריח RaYaK[H], scent. [REEK] Sure some shrubs smell nice too, but the quintessential botanical object of scent is the flower.

It is effective to see this graphically. In the PowerPoint Edenic slide show there is a flower graphic and the *Pey-Resh-Het* of פרח PeRaKH (flower). One can see the פר *Pey-Resh* of words like PeRoT (fruit) being circled, and then the רח *Resh-Het* of ריח RaYaK[H] (smell). REEK did not originally mean a bad smell. It was about a smelled burning, much like a ריח RaYaK[H], odor, that wafts in the רוח ROOaK[H], breeze/wind.

In the dog graphic for the *Kahf-Lamed-Bhet* כלב KeLeBH (dog), first the *Kaph-Lamed* of KoL (all) is encircled. Then the *Lamed-Bhet* of LeBH (heart) is isolated. In high school you saw sub-sets marked off this way. In the slide show these 2 overlapping two-letter sub-root combinations are referred to by the formula XY + YZ = XYZ. The chemical formula for the Edenic flower is PR + RK = PRK.

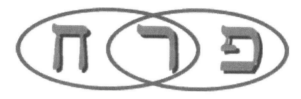

The canine genome may be expressed formulaically as KL + LB = KLB.

Combining these two overlapping sub-roots, one must then ask oneself 1) how the dog was named, in only three letters, "the creature who is all emotion? " and 2) how the flower was named "the botanical, fruit-related (all fruits bare flowers) scent-giver" *in just three letters!?* Was this by the evolved genius of a grunting, grooming gorilla, or was this the Intelligent Design of a supra-human engineer of botany, zoology, neurolinguistics, and all of the natural sciences?

In the **Double-Root words** below, words where two sub-roots appear to be combining like the examples above, a capitalized word [in brackets] again means an entry in the *E-Word CD Dictionary* or Edenics dictionary in some other form.

ONE אחד	EKHahD	*Aleph-Het-Dalet*	
אח *Aleph-Het*	AKH	an individual, a brother or countryman	[EACH] Genesis 4:8 Genesis 13:8
+ חד *Het-Dalet*	[K]HahD	single-pointed, thin, sharp	[ACUTE]
Aleph, the first letter, is a natural "one" – see the entry with article "A".			

ASHES, אפר DUST עפר	1) [A]FahR 2) AyFHeR	nose-affecting particles, ashes (Genesis 18:27)	flying particles
פר *Pey-Resh*	פרורים PeyROORiM	crumbled, tiny specks; crumbs	[FRIABLE]
+ אף *Aleph-Phey*	AF	nostril/nose	Genesis 2:7
עפ *Ayin-Phey* sub-root means to fly (Genesis 1:20 – "AVIATE"). Ashes are burnt particles that mostly impact our sense of **smell,** while dust is **flying** particles.			

WARRIOR/HERO גבר	GeBheR		*Gimel-Bhet-Resh*
גב *Gimel-Bhet*	גבה GaVah	high, mighty	[GIBBON]
+ בר *Bet-Resh*	אביר ABiR	male, a man of substance; brave	[BARON]
VIRILE – Literally having the upper hand; also used for Rooster or Cock			
SLIDE, GLIDE, SKI גלש	GaLaSH	*Gimel-Lamed-Shin*	[GLISSADE]
גל *Gimel*-Lam	גלל GaLaL	to roll	Genesis 29:3
לש *Lamed-Shin*	לשד LiSHaD	juice or sap	Psalms 32:4
+	לשון LaSHOAN	a tongue (which makes slick, smooth and wet)	Judges 7:5
A reconstructed Indo-European "root" for Slimy and Slippery words is *slei*. Reverse SL for LS and our *Lamed-Shin* sub-root. Does "rolling" + "wet" have to do with skiing?			

FLAG, or pennant with tribal symbol	דגל DeGeL		Numbers 2:3
דג *Dalet-Gimel*	DahG	fish (waving motion)	[GADOID]
+ גל *Gimel-Lamed*	GahL	wave	[GALE]
A flag is like a waving fish in a (wave) gale of wind			

חבל *Het-Bhet-Lamed*, **[K]HaBHeL,** a rope [HOBBLE] has two sub-roots that are treated at length in the *E-Word CD Dictionary.* A חבל K[H]aBHoaL, pledge (Ezekiel 18:7) binds lender and borrower. The first ח-ב *Het-Bhet* element is in חוב K[H]OABH, debt [OWE], while the ב-ל *Bet-Lamed* theme of mixing is found at BALL. [CABLE, CAPILLARY]

The XY element or first root in our XY + YZ = XYZ formula is *Het-Bhet.* חב [K]HOABH is a debt-like relationship tying the debtor to the lender – as seen at the OWE entry. The חבר **[K]HaBH**eR, friend, is bound as with a rope or חבל **[K]HeBH**eL, rope [CABLE] with his חבק **[K]HaBH**aQ, hug [HUG] of חבה **[K]HeeB**aH, love.

The YZ element, or second sub-root (בל/BL) in the formula is seen at BALL. Edenic words containing the subroot *Bet/Bhet-Lamed* imply a mixing of elements: גבול G'**BHooL** is a border between two countries; חבל [K]He**BHeL**, a string, is threads twisted together – (Ge**BHeL**, braid, and Ke**BHeL**, strong rope, are taken up at CABLE); טבל DTe**BHeL** is to immerse one thing in another [DIP]; יבל Ya**BHahL** is a stream of flowing waters; מבול Ma**BHooL,** the flood of Genesis, was a cataclysmic geological mixture of biblical proportions, where the dryness and seas mixed; the נבל Na**BHaL** is a churl who lacks propriety, an impious fool who mixes the sacred and profane (Isaiah 32:5) [VILE]; נבל Na*BHaL* is also a lyre (Psalms 150:3), on which, like a harp, notes are mixed – rather than the plucking of single notes; שביל SH'**BHeeYL** is a path that links different areas (Psalms 77:20).

BARREL/CASK/VAT	חבית [K]Ha[V]eeYT	The י *Yod*, a "weak" letter, doesn't count	
חב K[H]-*Bhet*	חבא [K]HaBAh	to hide, cover	Genesis 3:8,10
+ בת *Bet-Tahf*	בת BahT	liquid measure*	I Kings 7:26
Aramaic חבתא [K]Ha[V]iTAh and Arabic *habiya* can be traced to Edenic *anglicized as a BATH.			

SWADDLE; BIND (a turban); BANDAGE (a wound)	חבש K[H]aBHahSH		Exodus 29:9
ח-ב *Het-Bhet*	חבק **K[H]aBHahQ**	held close; hug	[OWE] [HOG]
+ ב-ש *Bet-Shin*	לבוש Li**BHOOSH**	clothes	

LEAVENING	K[H]aMeTS	*Het-Mem-Tsadi*	
חם *Het-Mem*	K[H]aM	heat	[CALM] [AMITY]
+ מץ *Mem-Tsadi*	מיץ MeeYTS	juice extract	[MOIST]
Jews search for חמץ, leavening, before Passover. Two of the principal halachic or legal ways for grain to become prohibited *Hametz* or fermented leavening involves 1) heat (not just baking, but even heated by the sun), and 2) moisture (even concerning standing grain and natural rainwater). לחם Le**K[H]eM** (bread) below.			

חנף K[H]a NeF, (flatterer, seducer, hypocrite – Isaiah 9:16) is one who tries to blow up or magnify a positive, likeable veneer. The ח-נ *Het-Noon* element is the חן K[H]eN grace or charm that this faker lusts after (נאף Noon-Alef-*Phey*), or is blowing the coals of נפח Noon-*Phey-Het*) or fanning and waving (נוף Noon-*Vav-Phey*). א פ ו *Aleph, Phey* or *Vav* are "weak" letters that help round out the theme of the נ-פ *Noon-Phey*, second element.

KINDNESS	חסד K[H]e$eD		Genesis 21:23 [CHASTE]
חס *Het-Samekh*	חוס K[H]OO$	to spare, pity have mercy	Deuteronomy 7:16
+ סד *Samekh-Dalet*	יסד Yee$ahD	to found/establish	I Kings 5:3
Thus חסד K[H]e$eD is the establishment of pitying or showing mercy.			

COVERING	חפש K[H]oaPHeSH	as for horseback riding – Ezekiel 27:20	
ח-פ *Het-Phey*	חפא K[H]aPHAh	to cover; cover/case canopy, bridal canopy	II Kings 17:9
	חפה/ חופה/ K[H]ooPaH		Joel 2:16
	חפה K[H]aPHaH	to cover or veil	
+ פש *Pey-Shin*	פשה PaSaH	to spread	Leviticus 13:5
This is an OUTSPREAD covering.			

WAR, SWORD, DESTRUCTION	חרב [K]HeReBH		[GUERRILLA]
חר *Het-Resh*	חרה [K]HaRaH	heated	[CHAR] and [IRE]
+ רב *Resh-Bhet*	ריב ReeYV	contention; quarrel	[RIFT]
Several words beginning with *Het Resh* carry the meaning of desolation, to lay waste, destruction, and aridness			

SHARP, BITTER, PUNGENT	חריף K[H]aReeYPH		
חר *Het Resh*	חרה K[H]aRaH	to burn	[CHAR]
+ רפ *Resh-Phey*	רפה RaPHaH	to be weak	[THERAPY]
Pungency is a "mild burning" sensation			

CRACK	חרך K[H]aRaQ		
חר Resh Het	חור K[H]OAR	hole	[HOLLOW]
+ רך *Resh-Khaf*	רך RahKH	slight, weak	[WEAK]
a CRACK is not a cavity, but a slight or weak hole			

TO LOVE & DESIRE	חשק [K]HaSHeQ		Genesis 34:8, I Kings 9:19, Isaiah 21:4
חש *Het-Shin*	חוש [K]HOOSH	quick, internal instinct, feeling, emotional appetite	Eccl. 2:25
+ שק *Shin-Koof*	תשוקה TiSHOOQaH	desire, longing	Genesis 3:16
	שקק SHaQaQ	greed, thirst	Psalms 107:9
SEEK			

255

THINK (verb)	חשב K[H]oaSHaiBH		[HASTY, GUESS, HUNCH]
חש *Het-Shin*	חוש [K]HOOSH חשש [K]HaSHaSH	hurry, hasten; quick instinct, intuition	Job 31:5 Eccl. 2:25
+ שב *Shin-Bet*	שב SHahBH	return, repeat, repent; bring back	Deuteronomy 30:3

TO THINK is hasty intuition plus mulling over the idea thoroughly; deliberating deliberately.

MILL, GRIND, CHEW PULVERIZE	טחן DTaK[H]aN	Moses "*ground* the golden calf to powder" in Exodus 32:20	
טחן *Tet-Het* = dental-guttural	דק DahQ דקק DaQaQ	fine, very small; crush into fine particles	Exodus 16:14 [TALCUM POWDER]
+ חן *Het-Noon* = guttural-nasal	כן KaiN	the biting bug of the 10 plagues, the louse	[GNAW] Exodus 8:12

There are also Hebrew, Aramaic and Arabic N-G words of biting. ח *Het* can also go silent, the biting and chewing goes well with the earlier crushing to make טחן DTaK[H]aN a fine root for tooth and DENTAL words [TINE].

HONOR, RESPECT	כבד KaBHaiD	guttural-bilabial-dental	
כב K-B	כבש KaBHahSH	to subdue	[HEFT] [KIBOSH]
+ בד B-D	עבד [A]BHahD	to serve	[OBEDIEDIENCE]

Whether an indentured servant or a loving child, giving honor and respect involves subduing one's ego to be in a position of serving another.

MONEY, SILVER	כסף KeSeF	Genesis 42:35	
כס K-S	כסא KeSEh כס Ke$eH	appointments and the silvery moon	Proverbs 7:20 Psalms 81:4
+ סף S-F	אסף A$aF	gathering, accumulating	Genesis 29:7

[SAVE]

כתב K'**TaBH** means writing (Exodus 34:1). K'TaBH is a combination of two roots that means making Hebrew words, or cutting out rectangles. כת the KT element, infers cutting or engraving. (See the CUT entry, where Aramaic כת KahT is a sect, a special group **cut** away from others, and where several guttural-dental words are CUT terms). The second, תב T-BH element is seen in תבה TayBHaH, a box, ark or word. This illustrates the box-like or rectangular shape of Hebrew letters. The boxy Hebrew letters were first cut or engraved into stone before pen-and-ink technology was invented. Scientists now agree that literacy began in the Middle East. It is not surprising that the word for writing should be about (1) cutting (2) words.

LICK	לחך LAK[H]aKH		Numbers 22:4
לח *Lamed-Het*	לח LahK[H]	moisture	Numbers 6:3
+ חך *Het-Koof*	חך K[H]aiKH	palate	Songs 7:10
It's a bit wet and messy, but baby animals love a good licking.			

BREAD, FOOD	לחם LeK[H]eM	Exodus 25:30	
לח *Lamed-Het*	לח LahK[H]	moisture	[LIQUID]
+ חם *Het-Mem*	[K]HaM	heat	Genesis 18:1
Bread requires the baking of moist dough. See חמץ K[H]aMeTS (leavening) above.			

REBELLION	מרד **MeReD**		Genesis 14:4
מר *Mem-Resh*	MaR	bitter	[MOROSE]
+ רד *Resh-Dalet*			ROOT for R-D "down" words
A bitter movement aimed at bringing **down** the power structure.			

CONSOLE, COMFORT	נחם NaK[H]aM		Genesis 38:12
נח *Noon-Het*	Na[K]H	rest	Exodus 23:12
		cease	I Samuel 25:9
		appease, calm down	Ezekiel 5:13
	[K]HaM	heat	Genesis 18:1
+ חם *Het-Mem*	חמה K[H]aiMaH	hot anger	Deuteronomy 29:28
Consolation is a cooling down from earlier agitation.			

DISPERSE, DRIVE AWAY נדף NaDaF		as chaff, smoke or a leaf in the wind (Lev. 26:26)	
נד *Noon-Dalet*	נדה NaDaH	removal; wandering	II Kings 17:21
+ דף *Dalet-Fhey*	דחף Da[K]HaF	drive on, impel with haste	Esther 3:15
Together, נדף NaDaF is not an orderly retreat or simply a hasty one, but one of panicky scattering, i.e. wandering of the banished קין Cain in Genesis 4:12.			

FEMALE	נקבה NiQaiBHaH		
נק *Noon-Koof*	נקיק NiQeeYQ	crevice/cleft	[NOOK]
+ קב *Koof-Bet*	קבה QoaBHaH	womb	[CAVITY]
In electronics, a wall socket is *female*.			

BLOSSOM	סמדר $MaDaR		Songs 7:13
סם *Samekh-Mem*	סמים **SahMiM**	spices, aromatics	
+ דר *Dalet-Resh*	דרור DROAR	freedom, release	Leviticus 25:19
Blossoms release aroma.			

REBELLIOUS	סרב $aRahBH		Ezekiel 2:6
סר *Samekh-Resh/$R*	סרר $oReR	perverted, rebellious	[SWERVE]
	סור $OOR	turning aside	
+ רב *Resh-Bhet*	RahBH	a lot	[RIFE]
Rebellion is a lot of turning aside from an expected path.			

HERD, COMMUNITY	עדר [A]iDeR or GHaiDeR		
ע-ד *Ayin-Dalet*	עדה [A]iDaH or GHaiDaH	assembly, community	[HERD]
+ דר *Dalet-Resh*	דר DahR	live, dwell	[ARSENAL]
Herd animals live in a community.			

258

HELP / AID	עזר [O]ZeR		[AUXILARY]
עז Ayin-Zayin	עז[O]aZ	strength	[GESUNDEHEIT]
+ זר Zayin-Resh	זר ZahR	foreign, someone else	Proverbs 27:2
Assistance means outside strength.			

IDLE, SLOTHFUL SLUGGARD	עצל [A]TSahL עצל [A]TSeL		Judges 18:9 Proverbs 6:6
ע-צ Ayin-Tsadi	עצה [A]TSaH	shuts down	Proverbs 16:30
+ צל Tsadi-Lamed	צל TSeL	shade	
Instead of making hay while the sun shines, he shuts down in the protective shade.			

עצם [E]TSeM The Biblical "[E]TSeM of the day" (essential, middle part of the day) speaks of both a small, select time, and a significant part. Both are evident when dividing עצם [E]TSeM into its sub-roots. עץ Tsadi-Mem/TS-M means **SM**all, shrunken (SMALL shares the fricative-nasal with TOM Thumb). עץ [E]TS means "tree" in the sense of its trunk or ST**EM**, its wooden core. Not its roots, branches or fruits. So, the Torah phrase "bone of the day" refers to the brief but core part of the day, when the extraordinary events were visible to many. [ESSENCE], [OSTEOMA].

SMOKE	עשן [A]SHahN		Genesis 15:17
ש-ע Ayin-Shin	עשש [A[SHaSH	decay, to be consumed	Psalms 6:8, 31:11
+ ש-ן Shin-Noon	שנה SHaNaH	change	I Kings 14:2
Smoke signifies chemical change, whether by burning fire or decay.			[CHANGE]

ENCOUNTER; MEET	פגש PaGaSH		Genesis 33:8
פ-ג Pey-Gimel		chancing upon	[GAFFE]
+ ג-ש Gimel-Shin		approaching	[GEISHA]
This is a chance meeting.			

LEAP, JUMP, DANCE	פזז PeeZaiZ		II Samuel 6:16
פ-ז Pey-Zayin	פחז Pa[K]HahZ	leap, run, hasten	
		or the wantonness of Jeremiah 23:32	
+ ז-ז Zayin-Zayin	זוז ZOOZ	to be prominent	
These combines well to describe the public athleticism of פזז PeeZaiZ.			[PIZAZZ]

UNRULY, RIOTOUS	פרע PaRA		[FREAK]
פר Pey-Resh	פרד PaRaD	to spread	[SPREAD]
	פרץ PaRaTS	to break forth, breach	[BURST]
+ רע Resh-Ayin	Rah	bad behavior	[WRONG]

פרץ PaRaTS, *Pey-Resh Tsadi*, means to break through rapidly, the source of words like BURST, BREECH, FIRST, PRESTO and the nasalized Spanish *pronto*. In Genesis 38:29 baby Paretz earns his name by a bursting, breeching first birth, even though his twin brother seemed to be the firstborn.

The פר *Pey-Resh* sub-root is all about breaking down and separating from, as seen in פרור PeROOR, crumb, [FRAY] and other FRIABLE fragments, even אפר AyPHeR, dust and עפר [A]PHahR, ashes.

The רץ *Resh-Tsadi*, second two-letter sub-root, means to run, and is the source of RUSH. Joseph was RUSHED out (*Resh-Tsadi*) out of prison to meet Pharoah in Genesis 41:14. מרוץ MayROATS is a running RACE (Ecclesiastes 9:11). [ROTATE.] פר *Pey-Resh* + רץ *Resh-Tsadi*, therefore, adds up to 1) breaking in a 2) hurry, as in bursting.

SUDDENLY	פתאום Pee(S)OWM		Numbers 12:4
Pey-Tahf/Sahf	פת PoaT	opening;	Num. 35:22
	פתע PeT[A]h	opening of the eyes,	
	פתח PaTa[K]H	twinkling (thus a moment)	[PATIO]
+ ת-ם Tahf/Sahf-Mem	TaMahH	astonishment	[SMIRK]
Suddeness is the wonder of an eye-opening moment.			

JUSTICE	צדק TSeDeQ		
צד *Tsadi-Dalet*	TSahD	side	[SIDE]
+ דק *Dalet-Koof*	דיק DeeYaiQ	finely ground, exact, worked over diligently;	[TACTICITIAN]

Edenic "justice" or צדק *Tsadi-Dalet-Koof*, is therefore the pursuit of exact precision in determining the right verdict between "sides" or plaintiffs. [SYNDICATION]

WOOL	צמר TSeMeR		Leviticus 13:47
צ-מ *Tsadi-Mem*	צמח *TSOMAH*	to spout hair; grow	[SUMAC]
מ-ר *Mem-Resh*	מרא EeMahR	lamb	[Ezra 6:9]

Your sweater grew on a sheep skin.

צפון TSaPHOAN, *Tsadi-Phey-Noon*, means north. This compound can be divided by 1) צפ *Tsadi-Phey* and 2) פנ *Pey-Noon*. The *Tsadi-Phey* molecule in the צפון TSaPHOAN chemical compound has its own meaning, appearing in words meaning to float or to overlay. The *Tsadi-Pey* phoneme as a separate word צף TSahPH means to float atop or just TOP, while צפה *Tsadi-Pey-Hey*, is a verb or noun of putting a cover or layer on top, or a covering or TOP.

The פ-נ *Pey-Noon* element indicates pointing, a direction. פנה PaNaH is to turn to or from. The large PN Pointer Family is seen both at the POINT entry, and is fully charted in Chapter Nine's word families. Even if you do not know Biblical words like צפוי TSaPHOOY, an overlay or coat (as with gold) and פנה PaNaH, to turn to or point towards, once you see what they mean and how they combine you probably can hear English words like TOP and POINT. You can then go back to צפון TSaPHOAN and add up the molecules of meaning. This makes צפון TSaPHOAN (north) "the top pointer." TS-PH-N = TS-PH + PH-N

צפון *Tsadi-Pey-Noon* TSAPHOAN, north, and צפון TSaPHOON, concealed, display similar, modular construction. Both have double roots (XY + YZ = XYZ), using different nuances of צפ *Tsadi-Pey* TOP and פנ *Pey-Noon* POINT. צפון TSaPHOON, concealed, XYZ, is XY, the צפ TOPPING or coating, concealing the YZ, פנ PANE or surface. So,

צפון TSaPHOON, concealed, is the Edenic way of indicating "hidden under a covered surface." (Al L. Ansley)

GRAVE	קבר QeBHeR		[CAVITY] and [VACUUM]
ק-ב *Koof-Bhet*	קבה QaiBHaH	stomach	
	נקב NeQeBH	indentation	
	נקבה NiQaiVaH	female	
	יקב YeQeBH	wine cellar	
+ ב-ר *Bhet-Resh*	בור BOAR	a pit (noun)	[BORE]
		bore (verb)	
A GRAVE is that which is hollowed out in the size of a pit			

קצף QaTSaPH, to cut or pluck off; a splinter or fragment of wood, etc (Hosea 10:7) is different than קצץ QaTSaTS, to cut into pieces (Exodus 39:3). קצף Qa**TSahPH** is a cutting at the TOP, from the second sub-root צף *Tsadi-Pey*. This sub-root is seen above, and the many guttural-dental CUT words appear here [CUT].

So, קצף QaTSaPH is a top or surface cutting.

CRUST, SKIN, MEMBRANE	קרום QROOM		
ק-ר *Koof-Resh*	קרן QeReN	hard; horn	[UNICORN]
	קר QahR	cold	[CRYOGENESIS]
	קרח QeRaK[H]	ice	
+ ר-ם *Resh-Mem*	רם RahM	raised up	[RUM]
The coagulation of CREAM, etc. is a membrane that rises to the top.			

רחם **RaK[H]ahM** is a WOMB (Genesis 49:25), and רחם RaK[H]eM is to have mercy and compassion (Genesis 43:30). Famously, it is said that humans only have compassion because of the womb, and the woman's maternal instinct. [MERCY] רחם RaK[H]eM has two sub-root components. 1) *Resh-Khaf* (close to *Resh-Het*) is weak, tender, said of young children and cattle (Genesis 33:13). 2) חם *Het-Mem* is heat, passion and warm compassion seen at the AMITY entry. Even with literal heat [CALM], the womb is a place to keep the vulnerable embryo warm. And passionate care for the weak is compassion.

רחף Ra[K]HaiPH, to HOVER (Genesis 1:2) shares a *Resh-Het* with רחם RaK[H]eM, to have mercy (I Kings 8:50). This compassionate HOVERING-over-birdlings theme is expressed in the double-root found in רחף Ra[K]HaiPH. While *Resh-Het* echos *Resh-Khaf*, רך RaKH, weak… a young child [WEAK]. The second sub-root, *Het-Phey*, means "covering." חפף [K]HaPHahPH is to cover, protect, shield (Deuteronomy 33:12).

PAVEMENT	רצפה RiTSPaH		II Chronicles 7:3
ר-צ *Resh-Tsadi*	רץ RaTS	run	[RACE]
	ארץ AReTS	ground	[EARTH]
+ צפה *Tsadi-Phey-Hey*	צפה TSipPaH	cover; overlay, coat	[TOP]
We know from Aramaic, Syriac and Arabic that *Resh-Tsadi-Pey* is about inlaying stones to pave a walkway.			

PATH	שביל SH'BHeeeYL		[SWALLOW]
ש-ב *Shin-Bet*	שוב SHOOBH	again	
+ ב-ל *Bet-Lamed*	בלה BaLaH	to wear out	[WEAR]
So, the footpath, the שביל SH'BHeeYL is that which is WORN by REPEATED trips.			

שבר Sa[V]aR with a *Sin* seems to infer careful consideration. The Biblical Aramaic and the Syriac are spelled with a Samech, סבר $i[V]aR, and mean thinking, supposing and having an opinion (Daniel 7:5). There is also a difference between the kinds of "thinking" in the two spellings when a double root is considered. The second, ב-ר *Bet-Resh* element suggests an ultimate clarity: ברור BaROOR, lucid and ברי BaReeY, certainly. [PURE] [VERY] The "thinking" stage, before this clarity, is either ש-ב *Shin-Bhet* returning, repenting, or doing away with [alternatives] or ס-ב Samech-*Bhet* turning [thoughts] around. [SABBATICAL] [SWIVEL]

שבת SHaBaT, *Shin-Bet-Tahf*, is the Bible's sacred sabbatical, the origin of the weekend. After a שבוע SHaBHOO[A]h, week of שבע SHeBH[A]h, **sev**en (days), we can שב SHahBH **return** to being truly human – a creation not a creator – when not busily scrambling for a living on the Sabbath. We also reconnect with family. שבת SHaBahT is to rest; ישב YaSHahBH is to sit. *Shin-Vav-Bhet* means to reunite (Genesis 43:18). The *Vav* in SHOOBH is a "weak" letter. The sometimes-vowel *Yod* is likewise negligible in the next word. בית *Bet-Tahf* is the BaYiT, home (both the common "house" and in Exodus 1:21 "household" or family. So שבת SHaBaT, *Shin-Bet* + *Bet-Tahf* can mean 1) return 2) home.

BLACK	שחור SHaK[H]OAR	
שח *Shin-Het*	שח SHahK[H]	sunken; depressed
+ אור *Aleph-Vav-Resh*	אור OWR	light
Black is the depressed mood of sunken light.		

שכן The two elements of שכן SHaKHaN (to dwell), S-K and K-N, establish the double root. First, there is the שׂ-כ *Shin-Khaf* of שׂך SoaKH, enclosure, dwelling (Harkavy – Lamentations 2:6). Second there is the כן *Khaf-Noon* of כון KOON, to establish, (Numbers 21:27). These combine to make SKN, source of ESCONCE, sound cozy, safe and settled. The S-K and K-N elements are enlarged with sound-alikes at ENSCONCE. These include סכך $aKHaKH, to cover, and חנה [K]HaNaH, to encamp, incline or settle. The שכינה SHiKHeeYNaH, the Divine Presence, embedded in the משכן MiSHKahN (Tabernacle) and Temple, may be said to be an enclosed dwelling, a nesting and embedded force within sacred space.

שלט SHeLeDT is a shield in II Samuel 8:7 and II Chronicles 23:9. We can take apart *Shin-Lamed* and *Lamed-Tet* to try to get a meaning to add up. For *Shin-Lamed* there is: שלה *Shin-Lamed-Hey*, to be secure (Jeremiah 12:1); שלו SHaLahV, to be at rest (Job 3:26); שלו SHaLaiV, tranquil (Jeremiah 49:31); שלוה SHaLVaH, tranquility, ease (Proverbs 1:32); שלום SHaLOAM, well-being, safety (Exodus 18:7); שלי SHiLeeY is rest, quiet (II Samuel 3:27). [**SALVATION**]

A *Lamed-Tet* לט L-DT sub-root of defensive words emerges when considering **לוט** LOOT, to cover, conceal (I Samuel 21:10), לוט LOAT, a cover, veil (Isaiah 25:70; פלט **PLaDT,** to be saved, to escape (Ezekiel 7:16); פליט PaLeeYDT, refugee, fugitive, escapee (Genesis 14:13) and the person of לוט LOADT (Abraham's nephew). Lot is rescued from the Biblical world war (Genesis 14) and is a shielded escapee from the destruction of Sodom (Genesis 18). [LID].

SUN	שמש S(H)eMeSH		Deuteronomy 4:41
שם *Shin-Mem*	שם SHahM	there	Genesis 2:12
+ אש *Aleph-Shin*	אש AiSH	fire	[ASIA]
"Fire is there," in the SUN. In the same way, SHaMaYiM (heavens – Genesis 1:1) can mean "there is water."			

LOW; LOWLY	שפל SHaFahL		[SIMPL]E
ש-פ *Shin-Phey*	שפי SHiFeeY	height	
+ פ-ל *Phey-Lamed*	נפל NaFahL	to fall	[FALL]
Lowly is that which has fallen from a height			

WHISTLING	שריקה SHiReeYQaH		Judges 5:16
ש-ר *Shin-Resh*	שיר SHeeYR	song	[SIREN]
+ ר-ק *Resh-Koof*	ריקה RaYQaH	empty	Genesis 37:24
Whistling lacks the lyrics and harmony of song; it carries the mere melodic line of song.			

to CLOSE, SHUT OUT	שתם SHahTahM		[SHUT]
ש-ת *Shin-Tahf*	SeT	closing	[SET]
+ ת-ם *Tahf-Mem*	TaM	completion	[TIME]
Thus Edenic "closing" is setting completion.			

תולעה TOAL[A]yaH is a worm (Isaiah 14:11). To see why this worm is more accurately translated as a caterpillar which dangles from a filament, note the ת-ל T-L element. תלה ToaLeH means to suspend (Job 26:7). [ATLAS] The second, לע *Lamed-Ayin* element, means chewing. לוע *Lamed-Vav-Ayin* means a jaw, speaking rashly (jawing) or chewing/swallowing (Proverbs 20:25). Adding the two elements for another double-root, the תולעה TOAL[A]yaH, caterpillar is the "suspended chewer."

STITCH; SEW TOGETHER	תפר TaPHahR		[FRIABLE]
ת-פ *Tahf-Phey*	תפש **TaPHaS**	grabbing hold	
	תפס **TaPHa$**	grab	[THIEF]
+ פר *Phey-Resh*	פרורים **PeROORiM**	crumbs, pieces	
reversing פ-ר	טרף **DTaRaF**	torn; ripped apart	[TROPHY]
Stitching is the grabbing hold of that which has been torn or frayed.			

The historical linguists think that language evolved over a gazillion years of simian social activities like grooming. There IS evidence that Language came from Licking:

LICK	**LaK[H]aKH**	*Lamed-Het-Khaf*
LAH-UCK	לחך	**[LHK]**

ROOTS: LICK is said to be from Greek *leikhein* and the reconstructed Indo-European (IE) root *leigh* (to lick). A better reason for the double guttural (C and K) of LICK is found in לחך LAK[H]aKH, to lick (Numbers 22:4). The Edenic liquid-guttural-guttural compound may be seen as a combining of two shorter elements or sub-roots: לח LahK[H], moisture, and חך K[H]aKH, palate.

לקק LaQaQ is to lick (I Kings 21:19), and עלע [E]eLaGH is to lap or swallow. Ugaritic *lhk* is to lick. The Arabic tongue is *lougha*, the same word, naturally, for language.

BRANCHES: Cognates of LICK include ELECTUARY and LECHER. Although Latin *lingere* is to lick. Latin's *lingua* (tongue) words such as LANGUAGE, LINGUIST, etc. are listed instead at the tongue-twisted IE "root" *dnghu*. This proposed IE "root" may link up with *Tet-Ayin-Mem*, טעם DTaGHaM (to taste).

Tongue and LANGUAGE are synonyms. To lick is "to tongue," as many nouns are tied to verbs, and sophisticated nouns (as easily seen in Semitic) are derived from parts of the body. LINGUAL words are clearly a nasalized (extra N) form of the Semitic liquid-guttural terms above.

See the "LIQUID" and "**SLA**NG" entries at ww.edenics.net or in whatever form the Edenics word-base is available in when you read these words. Perhaps by now you can see how לישון LaSHOAN, tongue or language, LSN, became SLN, as in SLANG, after an M213 metathesis.

The last phase of our brief glimpse into the chemistry of Edenics involves the isolating of initial letters of the three-letter root, and conceiving of these as "prefix" letters serving the two-letter sub-root. There are, of course, prefixes and suffixes built upon Edenic roots as in any language, but Edenics proposes that a *single letter within a three-letter word* can function as a prefix or suffix.

Without any prefixes or suffixes, the essential root is only two-letters in the non-grammatical, purely lexical view of Edenics.

Only three letters are needed in Edenic, *Noon-Resh-Dalet –* נרד NeReD, to convey the complex sentence: "We shall descend." Only three letters contain 1) a third-person subject, 2) the tense, and 3) the verb. Keeping this is mind, is it any wonder that a logical person must question if this economy of design is from human engineering. Furthermore, it now seems more possible that a single Edenic letter within a three-letter word can function as a prefix or suffix?

THE MEM/M PREFIX מ-

The *Mem*-prefix, as מפעל (Mi'PHa[E]L), facilitator, added to a three-letter root is well known to students of Semitic. (Can you see **FACIL**ITATOR in the *Phey-Ayin-Lamed* F/GH/L of מפעל Mi'PHa[E]L?)

For example, כסה KHa$eH is the verb "to cover." [ENCASE] Adding the *Mem*/M prefix, מכסה MiKHa$eH means "that which covers" or simply "a cover" (Isaiah 14:11). The word may have walked a few miles before we got that foot covering called a MOCCASIN or that housing in a gun that we call a MAGAZINE. The glossy storehouse of reading matter came much later.

We know this same M-prefix appears in Arabic MINARET, a high light tower akin to the smaller מנורה MiNOARaH (candelabra). In both cases the M-prefix clearly precedes נר NeR, candle, or *noor,* light.

This *Mem*/M prefix within a three-letter root, however, is not always recognized, except for very obvious examples like מגן MaGeN, shield. *Gimel-Noon* or גנן GaNaN is the verb of defending, below and a score of others where a "weak letter"* from a three-letter word is seen as dropping away:

> * The "weak" letters, are seven according to the early grammarians: ה *Hey*/H, א *Aleph*/A, מ *Mem*/M, נ *Noon*/N, ת *Tahf*/T,Th,(S), י *Yod*/Y and ו *Vav*/V. – Rabbi Major Yehoshua Steinberg.

But separating an initial *Mem*/M from what is thought to be a three-letter word fits the modular, molecular approach of Edenics. The prevailing grammarians favor three-letter roots, and merely acknowledge that there are several two-letter roots.

Koof-Lamed, קל QahL means swift, light or easy (source of Latin *celer,* swift as seen at the ACCELERATE entry). Thus *Mem + Koof-Lamed,* מקל MaQeL, a walking stick, is the same *Koof-Lamed* root with a *Mem*/M prefix that makes the walking stick or cane a man's primitive accelerator (that which allows for swifter, easier walking).

> מטה MaDTeH (rod, staff – Exodus 4:2) is the *Mem*-prefix added to הטה HeeDTaH, to lean. A third walking stick or staff is the משענת MiSH[E]NeT (Exodus 21:19), another *Mem*-prefix extension, this one of שען SHa'[A]hN, lean, support (Genesis 18:4). – Rabbi Major Yehoshua Steinberg

מלך MeLeKH means king (Genesis 14:2). מלאך MaLaKH means angel, messenger or agent (Genesis 16:7). They both have the *Lamed-Khaf* sub-root of לך LeKH, go! They both have the *Mem*/M prefix. They are similar, built-in opposites. The מלך MeLeKH, king, is the "go" maker. The מלאך MaLaKH, agent has been charged "to go."

In מבול MaBOOL (the Deluge), the flood was that which caused *Bet-Lamed*, the two-letter root of mixing together. [BALL]

מגן MaGeN is a shield. That which is *Gimel-Noon* ג-נ, defends [JANUARY]. The "How the Hebrew Language Grew" crew are likely correct in assuming that the word מגן MaGeN (shield) evolved naturally from the להגן verb of defense when the shield was invented. But what about words like מלאך MaLaKH (angel) and מבול MaBOOL (the Deluge) which may not have been invented by humans? (Although most secular academicians would suppose that Genesis is a fable.)

A מרד MeRED, rebellion, is that which brings down a regime. (רד RaiD) [ROOT] (It may also be a double-root word – see above.)

Three-letter *Mem* words like מנה MaN[A]h. to withhold, מפל MaPahL, that which falls off, and מצב MaTSaBH, stand, station, are not seen as two-letter words with a prefix *Mem*/M since Hebraicists did not consider connections to non-Semitic words like NO, FALL and **STAB**LE.

In Edenic words of four or more letters, an initial *Mem* may be a prefix or part of a combination of two overlapping two-letter sub-roots, as we have seen above. Some rabbinic commentaries like to divide מדבר MiDBar, wilderness, as *Mem* prefix plus דבר DaBeR, to speak, like the דבר DaBHaR word that we saw. This is of homiletic value, since the מדבר MiDBaR, wilderness, is seen as the setting for revelation. But, more scientifically, Edenics would divide the *Mem-Dalet-Bet-Resh* of מדבר MiDBAR as מד MaD, a measure of [METE] + בר BaR, uncultivated or wild land [BARRIO].

A *Mem* or M- prefix is relevant in Edenics' quest to link the world's words to their Edenic roots. A good entry in the *E-Word CD Dictionary* to illustrate this is MIGRATE.

(MI)GRA(T)E	GaR	*Gimel-Resh*
GURR	גר	**[GR]**

ROOTS: Latin *migrare* is to change one's place of living. No T. The theoretical Indo-European root only addresses the M element, as *mei-1* is to change, go or move. "M" like an initial *Mem*, is often a prefix, so the G-R element is more important. This entry will attempt to demonstrate how the AHD sinned by not loving the G-R. גר GaR is to dwell temporarily (Genesis 35:27). גר GaiR is a stranger (Genesis 23:4), who MIGRATED from elsewhere. The noun and verb forms are together in Exodus 12:48. מגורים **MiGOOR**eeYM means sojourn in the *Ben-Yehuda* dictionary.

> BRANCHES: A theological newcomer or convert is a גר GaiR. Hagar's name means "The Convert." Gershom, the "stranger in a strange land" is also named from this root (Exodus 2:22 – KJV). The GR stranger term shifts to GL in the Irish town of Galway (stranger's town). Nasalize MIGRATE and there are IMMIGRANTS and EMIGRANTS, with some MIGRANT workers MIGRATING more often than geese.
>
> One who "sojourns in her house" is מגרת ביתה **MeeGaRa**T BaiTaH in Exodus 3:22.
>
> Japanese *magari-(nin)* is a roomer or lodger who is *magari (suru)* renting a room.
>
> *Gimel-Vav-Resh* is the formal infinitive of dwelling. A dwelling or tent is *ger* in Mongolian. Dwelling is *ghar* in Hindi. *Gari* is a settlement or town in Hausa (Hamitic).
>
> For GR circling around, see GYRE.

THE ALEPH/A PREFIX - א

Aleph-Yod, אי EeY, is a standard negative prefix, added on to words with a hyphen. Here it is proposed that the initial Alef/A letter alone, within a three-consonant root, can sometimes function in this same way.

In English the prefix A- means "not," as in ASYMMETRICAL.

The Indo-European (IE) root for A- is *ne* (not), just as the Hebrew prefix, *Aleph-Yod* or אי EeY- is believed to be a short form of אין AiYN, not Sanskrit has both *a-* and *an-*. [INSOMNIA]

The negative prefix *Aleph-Yod* is found in I Samuel 21:4. A baby boy is named Ichabod to say איכבד Eey-KaBHoaD, "there is no" honor. In Phoenician the negative prefix is also אי EeY. In Modern Hebrew, איפשר EeY-EFSHaR means "impossible."

It is not impossible that *Aleph* alone can mean "not" without being an abbreviation of אין AiN (not). Just as *Aleph* can be an article, like "A" meaning "one exists." [A] This chapter is all about the existence of negative images, of anti-matter, like negative numbers in the perfect, designed world of mathematics. *Aleph*/A should therefore also be able to infer that "none exists." Such is the science of Edenics, "the thing and its opposite" in terms of Hebrew studies. So think of this proposed *Aleph*/A prefix as an anti-article.

In an important component of the ancient Semitic languages that add to our knowledge of Proto-Semitic or Edenic, Akkadian, *ai, e* or *i* is this negative prefix. There is no *Yod* or Y, nor any indication that it is an abbreviation of a longer negative term. Moreover, *I* and *ii* mean "not" in Saami (Lapp).

There are several Edenic words that begin with *Aleph*, where the *Aleph* alone can mean negation. No negative prefix is employed or intended. Nonetheless, when one analyzes the Edenic word as a chemical compound, with modular elements of meaning, a one-letter (*Aleph*) element of negation emerges to "negate" the two-letter sub-root. Here are ten examples:

1) אבל ABHaL, *Aleph-Bhet-Lamed*, but, only (Genesis 42:21). *Bet-Lamed* means a mixture of components [BALL]. A + BL could mean NOT mixed together with others – as in "but" and "only."

2) The other *Aleph-Bhet-Lamed* word is pronounced אבל ABHeL, meaning: a mourner or the verb to mourn. [OWL] [WAIL] The noun of mourning is אבל AyBHeL. Once again the two-letter sub-root is B-L togetherness seen at BALL and the world's most popular sound for "two." Mourning is about feeling the isolation of losing the two-ness, the relationship with a loved one. The *Bet-Lamed* mix or relationship has been negated (*Aleph* prefix) by death.

3) אגוז EGOAZ, *Aleph-Gimel-Zayin,* means a nut, that which is אגז AGahZ or bunched together [ZYGOTE]. גזז GaZaZ means cut, shear, separate. A + GZ could mean that which is not separated.

4) אדם ADaM, *Aleph-Dalet-Mem,* means man, Adam, man of earth or earthling. *Dalet-Mem* means silence [DUMB]. A + DM could mean the one species (Man) that is "NOT silent," as the world's only speaker.

5) אדמה ADaMaH, *Aleph-Dalet-Mem* means earth, land. [DEMOCRACY] *Dalet-Mem* also means liquid. [DAMP (A)]. A + DM could mean the dry land, or that which is NOT wet on this blue planet.

6) אדון ADOAN, *Aleph-Dalet-Vav-Noon,* means lord or master. [ADONIS] *Dalet-Noon* means law. – [DAMN] A + DN could mean the one entity NOT under the law, in someone else's jurisdiction (מדינה MiDeeYNaH). [MADONNA]

7) אכל AKHaL, *Aleph-Khaf-Lamed,* to consume, finish off, thus eat. *Khaf-Lamed* is the sub-root of completeness. (WHOLE at the ALL entry) At the EAGLE entry of this eminent destroyer and eater one sees the *Khaf-Lamed* word of completing a creation. This wholeness and creation is negated with the *Aleph* prefix.

8) אמת EMeT, *Aleph-Mem-Tahf,* means truth. [ETYMOLOGY] *Mem-Tahf* means death. [CHECKMATE] A + MT could mean that which is undying (truth).

9) אסר A$aR, *Aleph-Samekh-Resh*, is to harness, tie, forbid or imprison (Genesis 40:3). *Samekh-Resh* means to turn aside or stray. [SWERVE] A + $R could mean confined and NOT allowed to stray.

10) אשכול ESHKOAL, *Aleph-Shin-Kaph-Vav-Lamed*, means a cluster or group. [SCHOOL] שכול SHiKOOL, just the *Shin-Kaph-Vav-Lamed*, means bereaved [SINGLE]. A + SHiKOOL could mean NO individuals lost from the group (of children or grapes).

11) אשם ASHahM, *Aleph-Shin-Mem*, means guilt. [ASHAMED] *Shin-Mem* shifts nasals to Name, fame and reputation (Genesis 4:17). A + SH-M means the loss of face, of good name, of reputation that comes with shameful guilt.

If the solo *Aleph* as negation (negative "prefix" letter) thesis does not get enlarged and accepted, at very least these *Aleph* words all provide built-in sound-alike antonyms, a staple of the physics of Edenics. These properties often came up in the previous pages, but let us now focus more exclusively on reversals and antonyms.

THE PHYSICS OF EDENICS

Back in the chemistry of Edenics section, we began with the *Resh-Aleph-Hey* word, ראה RAhaH, to see. The core root is ר-א *Resh-Aleph*. If we reverse to א-ר *Aleph-Resh*, we get אור OWR, light. (The *Vav* here is a "weak" letter, as was the *Hey* in RAhaH.) A basic fact is that sight and light are profoundly related. Even the new night-vision technology requires some light. Reversing or shifting letters for a synonym or antonym (or global cognate) involves the physics of Edenics, rather than the isolating of molecules of meaning from a longer word-element – which involves the chemistry of Edenics.

When finding a metathesis to link a derivative word to Edenic, or to find a synonym or antonym of an Edenic etymon, it is hoped that some readers don't accuse us of engaging in alchemy. While sounds are as easy to bend as spoons are for a psychic, it is hoped that Edenics' loyalty to the meaning of words distances it from any accusations of magic or mischief. It would hurt were Edenics accused of being as imaginative as the *American Heritage Dictionary of Indo-European Roots*.

Nonetheless, all these pirouetting letters can make one's head spin. This dynamism helps the core Edenics thesis (that language was designed), rather than weakening it. The patterns of shifting letter-sounds and letter-sequence within words is a very poor strategy for the semantic utility of an evolved, human language. Does the speaker or writer mean one thing, or its very opposite? The answer to this problem is that Edenic, the one language displaying this "anti-matter" phenomenon, this black hole in Darwinian thought, did NOT evolve.

The usual thinking about evolved language does not fit the language with the most evidence for being the global, primary language. We are not talking about primitive Semites who lacked the Germanic orderliness to use set negative prefixes (like un- or non-) instead of having the same vowel-less letters that, foolishly, could signify something or its very opposite.

If a Semitic gardener is given a written note to work on *Shin-Resh-Shin*, roots, the poor fellow has to figure out from the context if the SRS meant to root or to uproot. Similarly, *Samekh-Ayin-Phey* means both a branch, and to take off branches. In English, and more clear languages where the priority is to eliminate ambiguity, there are prefixes like uproot, untangle, deplane or disbar.

Surely the English "grasshopper" is more neatly descriptive and precise than Edenic ארבה ARBeH, the locust of the plagues. Perhaps, but neither "grasshopper" nor "locust" has the *Resh-Bet* sub-root implying both a multitude, רב RaBH, and a famine, רעב Ra'[A]hBH. [RIFE] [RAVENOUS] Only ארבה ARBeH can display *Resh-Bet* opposites implying both plenty and lack of plenty. Only ארבה ARBeH conveys the vast swarms and devastating consequences of this creature, displaying uncanny but typical oxymoronic design. There also may be intriguing profundities within the words GRASS, HOP or LOCUST, but this would only be accessed by looking up their Edenic sources.

SIMILAR OXYMORONIC OPPOSITES

Contrary to theories about words evolving for semantic clarity, Edenic has several oxymoronic couples of the same letters (no letter shifts needed). These are examples of what the sages called דבר והיפוכו – the thing and its opposite.

These most non-human, paradoxical words include:

אזרח EZRa[K[H, a citizen, native (Leviticus 16:29). An alien or stranger is a זר ZahR (Leviticus 22:13). זר *Zayin-Resh* is the core of these built-in opposites

אפס APHai$: The פ-ס *Pey-Samekh* opposite of אפס APHai$, running out of something (like money in Genesis 47:15), is the abundance of פסה Pee$aH, (like the corn in Psalms 72:16).

ברח BaRaK[H], flee (Genesis 31:22). בריח BaReeYaK[H], a fugitive. The built-in opposite of all this breaking out and escaping is בריח BaReeYa[H]K, a bar or bolt to prevent escape . The opposite of בר BahR as obstruction is seen in terms like בר BahR, open field, suburb and ברור BaROOR, clear. [BARRIO] [BARE].

גרף GaRaF means both to sweep away and to gather. [PURGE]
חלץ [K]HaLahTS is to gird (also Syriac). Its built-in opposite is the identical חלץ [K]HaLahTS, to draw off, withdraw, to loosen. [LOOSE]

חסד [K]He$eD is grace (II Samuel 9:3). חסד [K]HaSahD is disgrace (Leviticus 20:17).

טמום DTaMOOM means stupid or senseless; טמטם DTiMDTaiM is to make stupid; נטמה NiDTMaH (Job 18:3) is to be stupid. טעם DTa'[A]hM, wise, (Proverbs 26:16) is a like-sounding antonym.

מוש MOOSH can mean touch or feel [MASSAGE] and the opposite, to withdraw [MISS].

מלח MaLa[K]H means to rub small, to reduce to dust (Harkavy –Isaiah 51:6), but also מלח Mala[K]H is the noun and verb of salt or salting, a preservative which prevents organic material from breaking down (Exodus 30:35). [MILL]

מלך MeLeKH, king)is the Go-Maker. He makes people LaiKH (go!). A מלאך Mal'AKH, angel, is an agent told to go.

מסך Ma$ahKH is to mix (Proverbs 9:2). [MIX] Paradoxically, the same מסך Ma$ahKH means curtain, screen [MASK]; that which separates space, and prevents areas from mixing..

נחם NaK[H]ahM means both to grieve, regret and to be comforted, consoled. [AMITY]

נכר NeeKahR means both to be recognized and נכר NeeKaiR, to treat as a stranger (Genesis 42:7) [MARK]

נצח NeeTSayaK[H] means both to beat and to be beaten. [SANGRIA]

Samekh-Phey, סוף $OAF, end, and הוסיף HOA$eeYF, to add. [PHASE OUT] *Samekh-Phey* spacial ending has its opposite number in, סף $ahPH, a threshold (a beginning of space).

עד *Ayin-Dalet*, עד [A]hD is eternity (infinite) or it means until, up to a certain point (finite). [ETERNAL] Similarly, עוד [O]aWD, further, still, is the opposite of finiteness. [ADD]

עולם [O]aWLaM is This World , our visible reality (Ecclesiastes 3:11) where the spiritual reality of our Creator is עלם [A]LahM, hidden (Leviticus 4:3).

עור [O]WR, our sensitive skin is the source of AWARE. [CORIUM] [ORIENTATION] Read slightly differently, *Ayin-Vav-Resh* also provides the opposite of awareness — blindness. [UMBRELLA]

עזב [A]ZahBH means both to leave and forsake (Genesis 39:13), and to strengthen, fortify and build up (Nehemiah 3:8).

ערבה [A]RaBHaH means both a dry desert (whence Arab) and a willow tree (that grows near water). [ARBOR]
פנים PaNeeYM means both interior and exterior [PENETRATE] [PANE]

רב RahBH means plenty, much, many [RIFE]. רעב Ra'[A]BH is a famine, time of scarcity. [RAVENOUS]

ר-פ *Resh-Phey* words are for both healing and ill health: רפא RaPHAh is to heal or cure (Exodus 15:2); פות RiPHOOT is health in Proverbs 3:8; רופא ROAPHAy is a doctor. תרופה T'ROOPHaH, treatment [THERAPY] is the opposite of תורפה TOORPaH, weakness [TORPID]; רפה RaPHAh is weak (Jeremiah 49:24) and רפיון RiPYOAN, weakness (Jeremiah 47:3).

שבות SH'BHOOT means both captivity and repariation. [SABBATICAL]

שד SHahD is a nurturing breast or teat (Lamentations 4:3), and the name of the deity as hidden, natural nurturer is שדי SHaDahY (Exodus 6:3). Yet, the same *Shin-Dalet,* שד SHoaD, means robbery and oppression (Psalms 12:6), and שד SHaiD is a destructive demon (Deuteronomy 32:17). [SHADE]

שחר *Shin-Het-Resh*, SHaK[H]oaR means dark or black, and SHaKHahR means light or dawn. [SWARTHY]

שנה *Shin-Noon-Hey* means both to change and to repeat. [CHANGE]

Conventional Hebraicists who believe that Hebrew "grew" or evolved only with semantics or human usage have long noted, and have made peace with a few oxymoronic pairs that make sense in context. Like having the identical letters of a word mean both "root" and "to uproot." But the list is longer than they know, and identically spelled words which mean something **and its opposite** does not reflect a human coinage for unambiguous communication, but the non-human design of an intelligence subtle enough to reflect the paradoxical aspects of things.

גרם GaRaM as bone, and to crush bone

סעיף $a'e[E]YF is a branch, and סעף $ay[A]aiF is to lop off branches. [PHASE OUT]

סקל $aQahL is to stone, and סקל $eeKail is to clear of stones. [SILICON]

עצם [E]TSeM is a bone, and עצם [E]eTSaiM is to break bone. [OSTEOMA]

ערף [O]ReF is the neck, and [A]RahF is to break the neck. [SCRUFF]

שרש SHoReSH is a root and to uproot. [SOURCE]

Pairs like these are as natural as to SKIN a rabbit or to BONE a fish. They certainly must have come from human usage. The set of oxymoronic pairs, and the hundreds of opposites which are separated by a letter shift of two, appear, instead, to be engineered — perhaps by very clever chimps or cavemen.

The physics of Edenics invites us to not only follow the S-N sound and sense (explored with CHANGE above) to derive related synonyms, but to find like-sounding antonyms as well. The opposite of the S-N theme of CHANGE, is שנה SHaNaH, to repeat, to do the same (without change). שנן SHaNaN is to repetitively drill a lesson to students. The SHaiN, tooth, can either be a pickax of change or a drill of repetition. Teeth are the only body parts of which we grow a second set –שני SHaiNeeY (second). Even the number two, שנם SH'NaiM, can infer another, similar one, not only a second, different one. Here is another aspect of Edenics images and their mirror opposites. There are more English and foreign terms in the CHANGE entry, but it is hoped that the organic, sometimes paradoxical concept is clear. While this entry is exceptionally full of illustrations of S-N sub-root extensions, this design pattern applies to every word in the intelligently designed language we'll call Edenic.

It is harder to see similar patterning in English, but opposites LIGHT and DARK share structural similarities. Both have a dental (D/T), liquid (L/R) and guttural (GH/K), albeit in different order and tonality after Babel-babble. This similarity of opposites in this pair of English words is only possible to detect because their Edenic etymons are designed antonyms: *Dalet-Lamed-Het* and *Dalet-Lamed-Koof*: דלח DaLaKH, foul, dark, קדר QeDaR, dark (M312 metathesis) and other Semitic "dark" words are seen at the DARK entry. At the LIGHT entry you'll find *Dalet-Lamed-Koof* and *Lamed-Hey-Tet*: דלק DaLaQ, to burn, and להט LaHaDT, to light. Also at that entry, there is yet another example of similar opposites – something that occurs from word engineering, NOT from survival of the semantically clearest. Moving to fricative-liquid words for LIGHT, the entry adds that the opposite of שחור SHa[K]HoaR, black is שחר SHa[K]HaR, dawn, light (Genesis 19:15).

In non-Edenic, one needs luck to be able to shed light on such mysteries from the Edenic sources. Too often, the sands of time and semantic usage can obscure the ancient Edenic footprints, unless they were petrified in the lexical fossil record. It seems impossible, for example, to link HOT and COLD. But the CL of COLD could be echoed in CLOT and cold, coagulated things like GELATIN. A similar guttural-liquid "hot" word, CALORIE, goes back to Latin *calor*, heat. You may know Spanish heat, *caliente*. Latin *calidus*, warm, sounds suspiciously like COLD. What could be behind this? What else? In Edenic קר QaR is cold, while קלי QaLeeY is toast. It is normal for Edenic opposites to be so similar, in this case a liquid shift away.

Centuries of Hebraists are familiar with Hebrew's unusual number of seemingly built-in antonyms, the principle of דבר והפכו Da[V]aR V'HeePooKHOA – "the thing/word and its opposite." None of these scholars suggest a parallel with the laws of physics. Ironically, the medieval Torah commentators are closer to the principles of linguistics —

which they have intuited — because of their religious belief in the Hebrew language not being of human origin.

Western-trained Hebraists could not consider, for example, ץ-ל-ה *Hey-Lamed-Tsadi* (vigorous) and ש-ל-ח *Het-Lamed-Shin* (weak) to be built-in antonyms. In the HEALTH words explored above, these similar opposites were overlooked by scholars in the post-dictionary age because the exact spellings are not alike. Modern Hebraists with PhDs know a great deal about things like interchangeable gutturals and fricatives, and most are familiar with basic chemistry and physics, but old school scholars consider it ludicrous to think across disciplines. Renaissance men went out with the Renaissance. We live in an era of specialists. Lost is the awe and creative curiosity to observe a wondrous phenomenon (like similar opposites in words) and to holistically make connections to other, to all natural sciences.

It would have been near impossible for an English-speaking historical linguist to know that HALE (healthy) and AIL (to be in poor health) are from the same root (or sub-root) in an "irrelevant" Semitic language. The unity of opposites would be dismissed as some Eastern, mystical notion of no applicability.

In non-Edenic, the evidence DOES point to only the human input in language. After their initial spin-off, from past Eden to present Babel, there was a natural selection of successfully communicative words based on their semantic utility. Survival of the fittest terms. Man was the single arbiter of what he'd say. Clarity, successful communication is the goal of all human languages.

Does all this paradoxical engineering of built-in "synonyms" and antonyms" have at least a literary use, even if some verbal confusion is possible when the context is unclear? Yes, the purposeful entendres make the Hebrew Bible, which is verbally chanted as well as studied in a text, infinitely rich. To open Genesis 41:53, for example, the listener hears ותכלינה Va'TiKHLeYNaH …that the seven years of plenty had "come to an end." The next verse opens ותחלינה Va'TiK[H]eeLeYNaH… that the seven years of famine had begun. The music plays on the opposites, with תחל TiK[H]aL meaning "to begin" while תכלית TaKHLeeYT means "end, completion." In this chapter we would see the ח-ל *Het-*

Lamed and ל-כ *Kahf-Lamed* as built-in, similar opposites. The Edenic for "famine" above is ב-ע-ר *Resh-Ayin-Bhet*. The word for plenty is רב RahBH, ב-ר *Resh-Bet*. (As seen with above with the *Resh-Bet* locust from Exodus.)

The infinite architecture of Hebrew was engineered to house the Hebrew Bible. Sadly, you who read this book know more about Edenics than many thousands of "experts" in language, Bible or religion.

Another good entry in the *E-Word CD Dictionary* to illustrate why the intricate, seemingly discordant music of meaning in Edenics is important is "TABOO."

TABOO	ToW[A]iBHaH	*Tahf-Vav-Ayin-Bhet-Hey*
TOE-AYE-BHA	תועבה	[T-A-B(H)]

ROOTS: תועבה ToW[A]iBHaH is translated "abomination." But it couldn't be that "every shepherd is an *abomination* unto the Egyptians" (Genesis 46:34), or that the "*abomination* of the Egyptians" is to be sacrificed to God in Exodus 8:22. EDK renders it "horrible deed." The new JPS Bible's rendition, "untouchable," is far better. "Untouchable" is the basic meaning of the Tongan word TABOO. Sheep were TABOO to the Egyptians, and various misdeeds in Biblical law are TABOO – off limits, but not outrageous or abhorrent. The "off-limits" sense of תועבה ToW[A]iBHaH is best seen in Deuteronomy 7:26 where it is compared to a חרם [K]HayReM, devoted thing, proscribed thing. [HAREM] תועבה ToW[A]iBHaH is an extension of תעב Ta'[A]hBH, to abhor (Deuteronomy 7:26). A like-sounding "synonym" is איבה AYBHaH, hatred (Genesis 3:15), while like-sounding opposites are אוה AVaH, desire (Psalms 132:13) and its synonym-by-metathesis אהבה AHaBHaH, love (Genesis 24:66).

BRANCHES: Japanese love, *ai*, is like Edenic א-ו *Alef-Vav*, while the Modern Greek love, *aga'pi* (with an H-to-G guttural shift and a *Bhet*-to-P bilabial shift), is more like Arabic *houb* and Edenic אבה AhaBHaH.

TABOO is spelled *tabu* in Polynesian; *tapu* means consecrated. The Edenic extensions of love and hate get to the essence of TABOO. While תאב TayAyBH is to loathe, תאב Tah'ABH is to desire or long for. To Eve, the forbidden fruit was a תאוה TahAhVaH, lust, passion or delight (Genesis 3:6). תאוה TahAhVaH sounds too much like its opposite, תועבה ToW[A]iBHaH, to be a coincidence. Edenic thus captures the psychological complexity of TABOOS like incest, simultaneously revolting but desirous, mixed emotions deep in the depths of abnormal psychology.

Edenic isn't human. It is better described as a language designed by the designer of humans. The words of the Pentateuch (five scrolls of Moses) are not merely human (until they are flattened by translation). Early Hebrew Scripture is purposely to dense to skim for mere content. The media is the message. It offers infinite innuendos, and multiple entendres, including the phenomena of chemistry and physics outlined here. The Torah doesn't strive for unambiguous "clarity," a Western, Occidental virtue. On the contrary, it constantly vexes the serious reader into unearthing a myriad of intended hidden meaning, as if the Writer were encoding microchips of data, volumes of messages, within the smallish confines of the Pentateuch. Later Biblical Hebrew is fine for its drastically lower level of inspired history, and one can order a falafel sandwich in Modern Hebrew. Only in our post-Babel languages can we hope to understand, say, a mortgage broker.

If this chapter's applications of the chemistry and physics of Edenics applies only to English, than perhaps this is all an elaborate trick with smoke and mirrors. Babel-babble was to have spun off Edenic into 70 original (proto) language super-families, which continued to break up into all the thousands of subsequent dialects on Earth. Edenics must show that the patterns suggested here can apply to many, even to all different languages.

To conclude, let us briefly apply this chapter's patterns and methods to a non-English language.

In Japanese, the initial dictionary offering for "sharp" offers no prospects for linkage to Edenic words like חד K[H]aD, sharp, חדק K[H]aDaQ, thorn or חדד K[H]aDaD, to be sharp [ACUTE]. The third Japanese word given for "sharp" does have some promise, however. *Togatta* means pointed, the "*atta*" appears to be a suffix, and ח-ד *Het-Dalet* can render a T-G after both a guttural and a dental shift. There's a reversal too, but keep in mind that most American Indian and Asian words reverse the Edenic root. (Or, if you prefer, they "read" Edenic from left-to-right). Another relevant GT term in Edenics is גת GaT, a winepress (Judges 6:11).

To pursue a possible "tog-" link to ח-ד *Het-Dalet*, we need a Japanese-English dictionary, and not just an English-Japanese one. (This goes for any budding Edenicsts out there, who, it is hoped, will go on to pan for gold in even the most remote streams.) Going to the t-o-g section of the lexicon, we find eight words: 1) *togameru*, find fault, 2) *togarashi*, red pepper, 3) *togatta*, pointed, sharp, 4) *toge*, thorn, prickle, 5) *toge,* high mountain pass, 6) *togeru*, accomplish, 7) *togireru,* break, and 8) *togu*, sharpen, grind. Number 6 we can dismiss as unrelated. 1, 5 and 7 are not quite sharp enough to justify a reversed link with two letter shifts. Words 2, 3, 4 and 8, however, are sharp enough to establish a strong link of sound and sense between Japanese T-G and Edenic ח-ד *Het-Dalet*.

Many of the concepts of this chapter are demonstrated in the section below. It appears that our species was gifted with an exquisite, intelligently designed language program, with the language softwear carefully based on the language hardware in the human mouth.

Chapter Seven ACTIVITIES

1. In the HANG entry, there is no NK Edenic word that specifically means NECK. What sub-roots emerge to mean NECK?

2. In the GATHER entry, how might GATE be traced to the Edenic etymons?

3. In the LOBO entry, similar to the FRUCTIFY and TALCUM POWDER entries, there are three-letter root words broken up into two overlapping two-letter elements of music and meaning. Explain the modular design behind the Edenic כלב KeLeBH, dog, and פרח PeRaKH, flower.

4. Synonyms from differently spelled words are not acceptable in normative language study. In the SIMULATION entry, how is a two-letter word like *Shin-Mem*, שם SHeM, name, linkable to Words spelled ס-מ-ל *Samekh-Mem-Lamed* (symbol) and צ-ל-ם *Tsadi-Lamed-Mem* (image)?

5. In the ACUTE entry what words containing a guttural-dental sub-root are synonyms?

6. In the same entry, present a guttural-dental antonym.

7. English has an oxymoron like freezerburn. Similarly, in the BURN and FROST entries, what BR and FR terms are sound-alike opposites?

8. In the SACK-1 entry and at an entry like HOUSE, what evidence is there that casings and enclosures are both guttural-fricatives and, inversely, frictative-gutturals?

9. There is no Edenic word with precisely the sound and sense of CUT. List at least eight differently spelled words that make up for this, and provide a sub-root as etymon.

10. חוש K[H]OOSH, to GUESS and נחש NaHaSH (interpreted as serpent and necromancy) are not considered related by scholars, despite the same ח-ש *Het-Shin* sub-root in both terms. The snake is nature's most instinctual animal (few senses but a heat-seeking capability), and the sorcerer or necromancer (Genesis 64:15) uses instinctual guesswork. Explain why חשב [K]HoSHeBH, to think or reason, is an antonym of this ח-ש *Het-Shin* sub-root, and why and how HUNCH might have come from it.

11. In Exodus 16:21, the שר SHiR, song of Moses at the sea is followed by the שר SHiR, song of Miriam. Immediately, the freed slaves come to the wilderness of שור SHOOR, wall. A skilled Bible reader might notice an alliterative poetic device, but the student of Edenics might hear and see far more. What similarities and contrasts emerge to you from the clash of these SH-R terms?

Chapter Eight

Synonyms and Antonyms

This *internal* evidence of a *sound-based human language program* is an important complement to the vast *external* evidence involving other languages linked to Edenic. This document offers a brief example of data found throughout the entries of the vast Edenics text base. The new science of Edenics demonstrates that in the premier human language, Edenic or Proto-Semitic, *sound* extends relationships beyond mere spelling. If some Hebraicists dismiss these as variants and "scribal errors," the point is still made that Hebrew and all language is attuned to sound, not merely the overrated convention of spelling.

SYNONYMS

The extensive word families in *The Origin of Speeches* and some entries have many sound-alike synonyms – and some antonyms – where the same sub-root is involved. Examples: synonyms of dividing, פרש פרס **PaRa$** and **PaRaSH** or ח-ל *Het-Lamed* antonyms of health: חלץ [K]HaLaTS, vigor and חלש [K]HaLaSH, weak [HEALTH]. Both cases require a fricative shift. This document involves synonyms that are only recognized, scientifically-based via letter-shifts, therefore eluding centuries of Hebrew scholars who only based the relationship of words on spelling – and the allowance of minor variations.

Bible scholars have long noticed the incremental repetition and other extensive poetic wordplay in the Five Books of Moses. Now that Edenics is leading Hebraicists to the study of sub-roots, and built-in synonyms and antonyms that use the standard letter shifts, we can also appreciate this wordplay as linguistic architectonics. In one early, famous example of this, in Genesis 18:27, Abraham describes himself as אפר [A]FahR and עפר AyFeR, "dust and ashes." These are not merely two words with repetitive poetic effect. *Aleph* and vowel *Ayin* are interchangeable; the פר *Pay-Resh* sub-root means particles, crumbs (פרורים). See מות MaVeT (death) and תום TOAM (completion) below for another example where hidden synonyms appear together in a verse.

Here are bilabial-fricative, fricative-bilabial "blowers" from the ASPIRE entry:

> The SP or fricative-bilabial two-letter root of breathing is established in Hebrew by nasals שאף SHahAhPH, to pant, gasp, aspire (Jeremiah 14:6) and the synonyms נשף Nee*SHaiPH*, to breathe, exhale (Exodus 15:10) and reversing to PS, נפש Ne*PHeSH*, breath, spirit, character (Genesis 2:7); shifting bilabials B to P, נשב Na*SHaBH*, to breathe or blow (Isaiah 40:7) and the blowing סופה *S*OOFaH, storm, tempest, whirlwind, hurricane (Jeremiah 4:13).   More TEMPEST at TIME. **PASS**ION may be a reversal of the breathy S(H)-P sub-root. [SPIRIT]

Note how נפש NePHeSH, breath of life (Genesis 20) and נשף NaSHaPH, to blow, breathe (Exodus 15:10) are built-in synonyms via an M132 metathesis. The same phenomena that allow Edenic to reclaim external relationships with long-lost descendants allow it to amass an impressive, internal family of designed synonyms and antonyms.

ANTONYMS

Hebrew scholars know that the same root often provides דבר והיפוכו "the thing and its opposite." Examples include ערף [O]ReF, neck, and ערף [A]RaF, to break the neck. SHaNaH שנה can mean to change or to repeat the same; and עשב [E]SeBH, grass, and עשב [E]eSaiBH, to weed . The same letters of פנים can mean either "face" (as in face, facet or façade… exteriority) or within, "inner" (interiority). More at the end of this longer list of non-identical opposites.

When the spelling has changed a word to another root, Hebraists lose sight of Hebrew's architectonics. The sound-based system of linguistic science was unknown and is still of no use to traditional Hebraicists. Just as historic linguists who do not know Semitic are at a great loss, Hebraicists who do not know and use the letter shifts and metatheses of scientific linguistics are missing much.

KEY TO THE SYNONYM/ANTONYM CHARTS

Letter Shift Codes – A menorah of only 7 sounds, as all music is from 7 notes

All **VOWELS** are interchangeable, no letter shifts need be indicated.
S-B = bilabial shift [interchangeable lip letters: B, F, V, W]
S-F = fricative shift [interchangeable whistling letters: Soft C, S, TS]
S-G = guttural shift [interchangeable throat letters: Hard C, G, K, Q]
S-D = dental shift [interchangeable tooth letters: D, T, TS]
S-L = liquid shift [interchangeable tongue letters: L, R]
S-N = nasal shift [interchangeable nose letter: M, N]
M = metathesis [root letters switch places]
Example: an M213 metathesis is French *blanc* coming from Edenic לבן LaBHaN (white)
REVERSE the (root letters of) the Edenic word
[UPPER CASE] word is an entry in the Edenics dictionary entry.

The above effects are important in linking Edenic with all languages. An important exception is nasalization (adding N or M). Such as deriving *dance* from DahTS (to leap exultantly). This is from natural, human corruption and not from the neuro-linguistic event that spun off the (traditionally 70) original languages from the language of Eden. Nasalization is about corruption, to ease pronunciation. It is not about our sound-based design for comparing and contrasting words. There are no nasalized words (only) in Edenic.

Note: Some designations could go either way. For example, אהל OHeL, tent, could be seen as a *synonymous* housing term with היכל HeYKHaL, palace, or the humble tent may be seen as an *antonym* of the lavish palace.

The following charts are first divided into what seems to be the dominant effect which differentiates the words with comparable music and meaning. S or A designates similar or opposite meanings. Other shifts which may apply to the word are in Column Three, followed by the relevant entries in the E-Word Dictionary cited in Column Four.

VOWELS

S or A = Synonyms or Antonyms

S A	All VOWELS are interchangeable	More Shifts	Entry to see
A	אב AhBH, father, originator (source of pronoun OF) אב AiBH, young sprout, shoot		ABBOT

A	אב AhBH, green, fresh
	אבד ABHaD, lost; "perished" (Numbers 21:30)
	עבד [A]hBHahD, to work
	    From a nasalized (extra N or M) אבד ABHaD comes
	    ABANDON, loss of will to keep working.
			VIVID
			
			OBIT
			OBEDIENCE

S	אגר AhGahR, to gather עגור AGOOR, amassed		GROW
A	אהבה AHaBHaH, love איבה AYBHaH, hatred		
A	אור OWR, light, enables sight עור [E]e(V)eR, blind		AURA (R. Sherman)
S	אזן OZeN, the ear, (recently discovered organ of balance) אזן EeZaiN, to weigh or balance (Ecclesiastes 12:9) עזניה [A]ZNeeYaH, the wind-balancing bird, osprey, hawk, etc. (Leviticus 11:13)		
S	איבה AYBHaH, hatred תעב Ta'[A]hBH, to abhor		TABOO
S	ארג ARahG, to plait or weave on a loom (I Samuel 17:7) ערך [A]iReKH, to set in order, to arrange Just as weaving a web is like making a RUG ארגון IRGOON, organization, is an extension of these weaving and loom words.	S-G	ARRANGE RUG
S	אמה OoMaH, tribe, race, people (Genesis 25:16) עם [A]hM, people, nation (Exodus 15:13)		MAMA
A	גיל GeeYL, gladness, געל Ga'[A]hL, scorn		GALA GALL

S			PHONETIC
S	נבא NaBHAh, to pour forth, hence to utter words, prophecy נבע NaBH[A]h, to bubble forth, pour forth, flow (Prov. 18:4)		PHONETIC
A	שוה SHaVaH, worthwhile, equal to (Proverbs 26:4) שוא SHahVA, nothingness (Ex. 20:7) or false (Ex. 23:1)		SEWAN

BILABIALS S-B

S or A = Synonyms or Antonyms

S A	S-B = bilabial shift – interchangeable lip letters: B, F, V, W	More Shifts	Entry to see
S	אהבה AhHa[V]aH, love אוה AhVaH, desire תאב Ta'ABH, to desire תאוה Ta'AVaH, lust; (*Bhet = Vav*, ב = ו)		GIVE TABOO
A	אפלה APHayLaH, darkness בהיר BaHeeYR, shining, bright	S-L	PALL PURE
A	בעל B'[A]hL, owner פעל Poa[E]L, worker		BULLY
S	ברח BaRaK[H] is to flee (Genesis 31:22) פרח PaRaK[H] is to fly, blossom forth (Genesis 40:10), or to break out like a disease (Exodus 9:9)		FLIGHT
S	בתר BeTeR, a part, cut off (Genesis 15:10) פטר PeDTeR, to separate פרת P'RaDT, a particular פרד PaRaD, to separate בד BahD, separate	S-D M132	PART BAT
S	גב GahBH, back (Psalms 129:3); גו GahV, back (I Kings 14:9)		BACK
A	גבר Ge(V)eR, powerful adult male גור GOOR, vulnerable young of animals (Genesis 49:9)		VIRILE

S	דוב DOOBH, anguish (Leviticus 26:16) דוה DaVaH, sick, ill (Leviticus 12:2)		

S	חרב [K]HeReBH, sword, is about physical sharpness
	חרף K[H] aRaPH is to reproach with sharp words
	    to taste pungent or sharp
	    and to feel the biting sharpness of winter
			CARVE
			HARROW
			REPROACH
			SHARP
			PICRIC ACID
			HIBERNATE

2 *2* *A*	כבה KaBHaH, quenched or extinguished When thirst or fire is put out (II Samuel 21:17) כוה KeeVAH, to burn (Isaiah 43:2)		KI**BOSH**
S	נבל NaBHaL is to decay or degrade נפל NaPHahL, fail		VILE FALL
S	נפש NePHeSH, breath of life (Genesis 20) נשף NaSHaPH, to blow, breathe (Exodus 15:10). נשב NaSHaBH, to breathe or blow (Isaiah 40:7)	M132	ANIMUS
	ענב GHayNaBH, grape, berry (Genesis 40:10) ענף GHaNaF, branch, bough (Leviticus 23:40) גפן GeFeN, vine (Deuteronomy 8:8)	M132	VINE
S	צב TSahBH, is covered (covered wagon in Numbers 7:3) and a turtle (a living covered wagon). צפה TSeePaH is to cover, to overlay (with gold, Ex. 36:34).		TOP
S	קבץ QaBeTS, to gather (Deuteronomy 30:3 קפץ QaPHaTS, to draw together (Deuteronomy 15:7)		COP
S	רוח ReVa[K]H, space, (Genesis 32:17) רחב Ra[K]Ha[V], wide, broad (Isaiah 30:23).	M123 M132	ROOM
S	ספק $ayPHeQ, sufficiency שבע SaBH[A]h, plenty, abundance שפע SHePH[A]h is abundance, overflow שבע Sa[V][A]h, abundance, (Deuteronomy 33:19) שפך SHaPHahKH, poured out (Genesis 9:6) –	S-F S-G	SUFFICE
S	שרב SHaRaBH, parched ground (Isaiah 49:10) שרף SaRahPH, to burn (Genesis 11:3)		SAFFRON

שרקות **FRICATIVES**

S or A = Synonyms or Antonyms

S A	S-F = fricative shift,|interchangeable whistling letters: Soft C, S, TS	More Shifts	Entry to see
	אז AhZ, then; at that TIME עת [A]i(S), time, season As seen in the external, global evidence of Edenic data, Tahf as Sahf is a legitimate variant, not a mistake of Ashkenazi Jews.	VOWEL	ETERNAL
S A	אזר AZaR, to gird together (II Kings 1:8) אסר A$aR, to tie up (Genesis 14:20) צרר TSaRaR, to bind or wrap (Exodus 12:34) שר SoaR, sinew, muscle (wrapped around bones) שרר SaRaR, to bind, to knot שרך SaRaKH, to twist, knot של SHahL, remove or loosen, (Exodus 3:5 – Moses is told to remove his sandals)	 S-L S-L	SARI ARREST LOOSE
A	ש-ב *Bhet-Shin* sub-root appears in wet Edenic terms like דבש D'[V]ahSH (honey, honey dew, the camel's watery hump, – Proverbs 16:24) זב Zev, flowing, ooze יבש YaBHeSH, means dry באש B'aAhSH, stench and rot of stagnant, dried up liquid.	 REV	SEEP WIZEN
S A	זוב ZOOBH, to flow (Exodus 3:8) צוף TSOOPH, flow or overflow (Lamentations 3:54) שאב S(H)AhahBH, to draw liquid, SIP (Genesis 24:13) סבא $aBHAh, to drink in	 S-B	SEEP SIPHON SOP
	זנח ZaNahK[H], "stank" in the *Lexicon*; translates to "turn foul" (Isaiah 19:6) צחן TSa[K]HaN, foul, stinking (Joel 2:20).	M132	SKUNK
S	זוד ZWD, to act maliciously צדה TSaDaH, to stalk. (Exodus 21:13,14)		STEAL

S	זהר (Aramaic-Syriac), to shine. זרח ZaRa[K]H, to rise (as the sun) שחר SHa[K]HaR, to rise early; (noun) dawn/daybreak צהר TSoaHahR, skylight (Genesis 6:16) זר ZaiR border or edge, as a corona or crown of gold (Ex. 25:11).	S-G M132 S-G	RISE
	זחל ZaK[H]ahL, crawl, is for creeping reptiles. Two larger, mammals who creep up on prey when hunting are שועל SHOOGHahL, fox שחל the SHaK[H]aL, the name of the lion (Hosea 5:14). These predators are not real זוחלים (creepers); they merely crawl on their bellies to hide from the prey they stalk. But the unusual, similar locomotion warrants the designer of these creatures to have sound-alike names.	S-F del. S-G	SLUG JACKAL
	זעק Za'[A]ahQ, cry (Genesis 18:20) צעק TSa[A]hQ, cry, (Genesis 27: 34) צחק TSaK[H]aQ means to laugh (*Genesis 17:17*).		CHUCKLE
S	חמוץ K[H]aMooTS is a violent man (Isaiah 1:17) חמס K[H]aMa$, to do violence (Jeremiah 22:3)		HAMSTER
S	יצב YaTSaBH is to set, put or place (Ex. 2:4) ישב YaSHaBH, to sit, stay in place (Ex. 17:12, Genesis 18:1)		STABLE
S	יתר Ye(S)eR, exceeding (Genesis 49:3); rest, remainder, or what is "left over" יתר Yo(S)aiR, more, too much (Ecclesiastes 7:16 advises us not to be "*OVER*wise" or "the wise man to *excess*." סרח $eRa[K]H, overhanging, superfluous part – the part hanging over in *excess* (Exodus 26:12).	S-L	SURPASS
S	כזב KaZeBH, falsehood, deceit (Ezekiel 13:7) כשף KeSHePH, magic, sleight of hand (Isaiah 47:9)	S-B	FAKER
S	מזג MeZeG, mix or mingle, especially wine (Songs 7:3). מסך Ma$ahKH, to mix (Proverbs 9:2).	S-G	MIX

S	משא MaSAh, burden (II Kings 5:17) עמס [A]Ma$, to load, bare a burden (Psalms 68:20) מס Mah$, a financial burden (tax, tribute – Genesis 49:15)		MASS
S	סב $oaBH, to turn aside (Genesis 29:19) שב SHa(V), to return to a position, or to remain in place		SWERVE WAS
S	סוף $OAF and Aramaic סופא SOAFAh, the end or extremity of the earth (Daniel 4:8). סוף $OOF is the edge of a sea that is full of reeds שפה SaFaH, the lip or edge of the mouth (Isaiah 6:7); the edge of brim of a cup (I Kings 7:26); the edge of a garment or a border (Exodus 28:32); the bank of a river (Exodus 2:3); the shore of the sea (Exodus 14:30) סף $ahPH is a threshold (I Kings 14:17).		SURF SWAMP
A	סלל $aLaL, to raise up (Isaiah 62:10). צלל T(S)aLaL, to dive, plunge, sink (Exodus 15:10)		SLALOM TEAL
S	סלע $eLaGH, stone צור TSOOR, rock סקל $aQahL to stone סקל $eeKail, to clear of stones	S-L M132	SILICON RAZOR
S / A	ספן $aFaN, covered, secured (Deut. 33:21); buried (Deut. 33:19) צפון TSaPHOON, hidden, closeted away (Exodus 2:2) שפן SHaPHaN, to hide as buried treasure (Deuteronomy 33:19), and is the shy hyrax/coney of this name (Lev. 11:5) צף TSaPH, float, on top, in plain sight		STEPHEN TOP
	סור $OOR, turn aside from the straight and narrow סלל curving ramp for a hill (Numbers 20:19) שורה SHOORaH, a straight row ישר YaSHaR, straight	S-L	SWERVE SERIES SLALOM
S	סתם $aTaM, to close up (II Kings 3:25) שתם SHaTaM, to close (Numbers 24:3) עצם [A]TSaM, to shut, close (Isaiah 33:15)		STEM

293

S	עלז GHaLaZ, to exult rejoice (Psalms 28:70) עלס GHaLa$, exult in Job 20:18 עלץ GHahLaTS or [A]LaTS, exult, rejoice (Habakkuk 3:14) [Dismissing cases like these as mere "scribal variants" displays a profound ignorance of vocabulary – which is about SOUND not spelling conventions.]		EXULT ELATED
S	פזור PaZOOR, to distribute largely, to lavish (Psalm 112:) פרס PRah$ in Aramaic is a reward, prize or gift. בשרה BiSoaRaH, reward (II Samuel 4:10, Harkavy). פרס PRah$, to distribute (Harkavy), to "deal" or give out (Isaiah 58:7). Elsewhere, it means to break or spread. פרוש PaROOSH, to spread, part PaROO$ and פרז PaRaZ (Deut. 3:5) can mean decentralized פרוץ PaROOTS, unruly and dissolute	M132 S-B	PRIZE DISPERSE SPRAY
S	פסל Pa$aL is to sculpt פצל PaTSaL is to peel both are cutting away the outer surface		FALSE
A	פסח Pe$ayah[K]H, lame (Leviticus 21:8) פשע PaS[A]h, striding (Isaiah 27:4)	S-G	PACE
S	פצע PeTS[A]h, skin opening, wound (Gen. 4:23). פתח PeTaK[H], opening, doorway, passageway (Gen. 18:1)		PATIO
A	צחר TSa[K]HoaR, white (Judges 5:10) שחור SHaK[H]OAR, black		OBSCURE
S	צצצע TS[A]TSoo[A]h, carved or sculptured work (II Chronicles 3:10); later a plaything, toy source of Czech, then Yiddish *tsotchke* (knick-knack). שעשע SH[A]SHoo[A]h, delight, joy (Proverbs 8:30) extended form, to play, toy with, dandle. שש SahS, to be happy ששון SaSOAN, joy (Jeremiah 7:34)		PEGASUS
S	צרב TSaRaBH, to burn (Ezekiel 21:3) צרף TSaRaPH, to smelt (purify by burning –Isaiah 1:25) שרף S'RayPHaH, a burning (Numbers 19:6).	S-B	SAFFRON SULPHUR

S / A		More Shifts	Entry to see
S / A	שתום SHaTOOM, open; שתם SHaTaM, to unseal, שתם SHaTaM, to close (Numbers 24:3) סתם $aTahM is stopped up closed (Nehemiah 4:1).		STOMACH STEM STYMIE
S	שטר SHoaDTeR, administrative ruler, officer (Exodus 5:8) שלט SHaLahDT, to rule (Ecclesiates 5:18) שרת SHaRaiT, to minister (Numbers 1:50)	S-D S-L	SATRAP SULTAN

גרון **GUTTURALS**

S or A = Synonyms or Antonyms

S A	S-G = guttural shift – interchangeable throat letters: Hard C, G, K, Q	More Shifts	Entry to see
S	אהבה AhHa[V]aH, love אחוה A[K]HaVaH, fraternity חביב [K]HaBHeeYBH, dear		AVARICE
A	אהל OHeL, tent היכל HeYKHaL, palace		HALL
S	אחור AhK[H]OAR, rear, buttocks, back (Ezekiel 8:16) ירכה YaRKHaH, hind part, rear (Exodus 26:27)	REV	RUCKSACK
A	אחר A[K]HahR, to remain long, tarry (Genesis 32:5) מהר MaHeR, "in a hurry," soon מהר MeeHaiR, hurry or "hasten" (Genesis 18:6) מהיר MaHeeYR is quick and diligent (Proverbs 22:29) נהר NaHahR is to flow or run (as a river) הרף HeReF, a "moment" or "instant"	S-N	HURRY INERT
S	בלה BaLaH, to decay, wear out, consume (Deut. 8:4) בלע BaL[A]h, to destroy (Psalm 21:10) בלק BaLaQ, to destroy (Isaiah 24:1)	M312	ABLATION BALE

295

	חבל K[H]aBHaL, to destroy, ruin		
S	בער Ba'[E]R, to consume (see above) ברה BaRaH, to eat		BURN DEVOUR
A	בקע BeQ[A]h, indentation, valley, split גבעה GiBH[A]H, a hill, height קו QahV, a straight line	M132 S-B	CAVITY VACATE GIBBON QUEUE
S	גל GahL, wave, mound The Galil or Galilee is named for its waving hills הר HahR, hill or mountain. Combining both, Russian *gora* is a hill or mountain.	S-L	OROLOGY
S	גבל GeBHeL, plait or braid; made by folding over two strands (i.e. of dough or hair) חבל K[H]eBHeL is a string or rope כבל KeBHeL is a cable. כפל KaPHaL is to fold over		COUPLE CABLE BALL
S	גלה GaLaK[H], strip, uncover (Genesis 9:21) גלח GaLaK[H], bald, bare, shaven (Deut. 21:12) חלק K[H]aLaQ, smooth, bald, bare (hairless) (Gen. 27:11)		CALLOW GALYAK
S	גרון GaROAN is a neck (Ezekiel 16:11) or throat גרגרת GaRGeReT, windpipe, (throat in Proverbs 3:3) ערף GHoReF is the back of the neck על GHoaL, collar.	S-L	GROAN SCRUFF COLLAR
S	גרז GaRaZ, to cut off כרת KaRahT, to cut off, (Numbers 13:23). כרת KoRaiT (Leviticus 17:4) a curtailment of life. קרץ QaRahTS, to slice or cut, (nipped – Job 33:6) קצר QoaTSeR, shortness (Exodus 6:9) Elsewhere, it means the cutting down of harvesting or reaping (Genesis 8:22)	S-F M132	GRAZE CURT CASTRATE
S	גשמי GaSHMeeY, bodily, physical עצמי GHaTSMeeY, essential, of the body	S-F	COSMOS ESSENCE
S	דחה Da[K]HaH, to push (Psalms 118:13)		

	דחח Da[K]Ha[K]H, pushed forward (Jeremiah 23:12) דחף Da[K]HaF, to drive on, push forward (Esther 3:15) דחק Da[K]HaQ ,to press, oppress (Judges 2:18) דפק DaFaQ pressed upon/against (Gen. 33:13)	S-F M132	
A	הלל HaLeL, praise קלל QeeLaiL, curse, esteem lightly (Exodus 21:17) קלס QaLe$, scorn, rebuke, threaten (curse) or mock (II Kings 2:23) In later Hebrew the same Qale$ came to mean to praise or laud.	S-F S-L	HAIL
A	הר HaR, hill חור K[H]oaR, hole Swelled mass as opposed to missing mass		OROLOGY HOLLOW
S	חוג [K]HOOG, circle (Job 26:10) עוג GHOG, "to form round" (Harkavy – Ezekiel 4:12)		HOG CAKE
S	חיים K[H]aYYiM, life קים QaYaM, existing		HYGIENE
S	חמר K[H]oMeR, heap (Exodus 8:10) עמר GHaMeR, to heap together		CAMERA
S	חנה K[H]aNaH, to encamp, incline, settle down עון Ayin-Vav-Noon, to dwell, מעון MaGHOAN, dwelling; קן QahN, nest, dwelling שכן S(H)aKHahN, to settle down, abide, dwell (Gen. 9:27) כאן K'AhN is the preposition "here," and the core of מקום MaQOAM, a place.	S-N	HAUNT HEN
S	חסוי K[H]ee$OOY, shelter; כסה KHaSaH, to cover		HOUSE ENCASE
A	חפר K[H]aPHaiR, covered by shame (Psalms 71:24) חרפה K[H]eRPaH is shame, outrage כפר KaPaiR, to cover by forgiveness or expiation of sin (Exodus 32:30)	M132	COVER CULPABLE
S	חרב [K]HaReBH, heat or dryness (to dry, Genesis 8:13; waste and desolation, Deut.		RIBOFLAVIN

	28:22 and Jeremiah 33:10) ערבה GHaRaBHaH, desert (Jeremiah 2:6) ערב GHeReBH, desert (Habakkuk 1:8)		
S	חרד [K]HaRaiD, to tremble or to fear (Genesis 27:33) רעד RaGHahD, trembling from fear (Exodus 15:15) חרדה [K]HaRaDaH, terror דחל Da[K]HaL, terror (Aramaic) ערץ [A]RahTS, to dread (Deuteronomy 1:29)	M213 S-L S-D	TERROR DREAD RATTLE CARDIO
S	חצר K[H]aTSaR, to surround, enclose (Genesis 25:16) as in a courtyard עטר GHaDTaR, to surround עטרה GHaDTaRaH is a crown כתר KeTeR, 1) to surround, 2) a crown (Esther 2:17)	S-D S-D	COURT TIARA
S	חתה [K]HaTaH, to abhor קוט QOODT, to feel a loathing or disgust (Ezekiel 6:9). קץ QaiTS, to loathe or fear (Numbers 22:3, where fear of Israel is synonomous with hatred)	S-D	HATE
S	כון KOON, prepared (Ezekiel 28:13), established (Psalm 9:8) קן QaiN, a nest (Deuteronomy 22:6), is where life is prepared and established. תקן TaQeN, to repair, straighten, improve		TECHNICAL MACHINE
S	כבר K'BHahR, long ago (Eclessiastes 1:10); עבר GHaBHahR, passed by		OVER
S	כל KoL, all קהל QaHeL, to assemble or call everyone together to one college or collection (by voice or קול QOAL) Note the L-K and K-L in the metathesis pair below: לקט **LaQ**ahDT, to gather (Genesis 31:46) לקט LaQaDT, choosing by lots in Joshua 7:16. התלקט HiT**LaQai**DT, to unite קלט **Qe**LeDT, to absorb, to take in (Numbers 35:11)		CULL ELECT
A	כפיר K'PHeeYR is the young lion (predator) עפר GHoaPHeR is the young of deer, ruminant (prey)		CAPRICORN

S	כרובים K'ROOBHeeYM, cherubs on the Ark of the Covenant which face one another, with divine love in that interface (Exodus 32:9) קרובים Q'ROABHeeYM, near and dear ones (Lev. 10:3)		CRAB
S	להן LaHaiN, therefore (Ruth 1:13) לכן LaKHaiN, therefore (Genesis 2:24)		
S	לחך LAK[H]aKH, to lick (Numbers 22:4). לקק LaQaQ. to lick (I Kings 21:19)		LICK
A	מהר MaHeR, hurry Someone wants something in a HURRY, but a response might be מחר Ma[K]HahR, tomorrow (Judges 20:28); in time to come (Genesis 30:33) Putting off until *manana* (later, tomorrow) אחר A[K]HahR, to remain long, tarry (Genesis 32:5).		HURRY
S	מוג MOOG, to dissolve (Ezekiel 21:20) .. מק MahK, decay, "rottenness" or "rot" (Isaiah 5:24)		MUCK
S	מכון MaKHOAN, dwelling place (Exodus 15:17) מקום MaQOAM, place (Genesis 40:30)	S-N	ENSCONCE
S	נגח NaGa[K]H, to thrust, push, gore (Exodus 21:28) נגע NaGaGH, to strike, reach or touch (Genesis 32:32 when Jacob is injured in the thigh) נכה NooKaH, a depression		NICK (to strike, catch or hit)
S	נגר NaGaR, to flow, pour or run (II Samuel 14:14) נהר NaHaR, is a river or stream (Isaiah 6:12) נחל Na[K]HaL is a stream (Deuteronomy 2:13)	S-L	INNERT NIAGRA
A	נוח ← NOOaK[H], to rest נוע NOOaGH, motion, movement The restless wandering of Cain (Gen. 4:12)		NIGHT
S	נחמה NiK[H]aMaH, consolation (Genesis 38:12) נקמה NiQaMaH, revenge		AMITY
A	נשיקה NiSHeeYQaH, a kiss (Songs 1:2)		KISS

	נשכה NiSHeeKHaH, bite (Genesis 49:17)		
S	סגר $aGaR, to close (Genesis 7:16) סכר $aKaR, to close, stop up (Genesis 8:2)		SECURE
S A	ענג [A]NaG, a verb of being tender, ענג [O]NeG, delight and pleasure ענה [A]NaH and עני [E]eNOOY, afflict, torture ענה [E]eNaH, rape (Genesis 34:2)		HONEY ANNOYANCE
S A	פקע PaQaGH, to split open (II Kings 4:39) פקח PaQaK[H], to open (usually eyes or ears) (Gen. 3:5) פקק PaQaQ, to stop up		PICK
A	צחק TSaK[H]aQ, to laugh (Genesis 17:17) צעק TSa'GHahQ, a cry of pain (Genesis 27:34)		CHUCKLE

A	קמה QoaMaH, high point
	מוך MOOKH- diminished
	נמוך NaMOOKH, low
	Related word and its opposite:
	    קמה QaMaH, standing corn (Deuteronomy 23:26)
	    קמח QeMa[K]H, ground corn, meal (Genesis 18:6)
		REV	ACME
			
			MEEK

S	רגש RaGaSH, rage, intense feelings (Psalms 2:1) רחש Ra[K]HahSH, to move, feel (Psalms 42:2) later: emotion, meditation		RAGE
S	שגח SHaGaK[H] is to look or gaze (Isaiah 14:16), שכה SaKHaH is to see or look (seen in Semitic) שקף SHaQahF is to look (Genesis 26:8)	S-F	SEEK
S	שכן SHaKHaN, settled שען SHaGHahN, to stay, rest (Numbers 21:1)		ENSCONCE

שנים DENTALS

S or A = Synonyms or Antonyms

S A	S-D = dental shift – interchangeable tooth letters: D, T, TS	More Shifts	Entry to see
A	בית, ב *Bet* or Beth, the 2nd letter and number 2 בד BHahD, the root of בדד BaDahD, alone, and a word meaning an isolated limb		BOTH BAT

S
 	
 A
	דור DOAR, generation
	 טור DTOOR, straight row (Exodus 12:17)
	     Succesive generations are as rows
	 טור DTOOR can also mean to turn around, encircle
	     תור TOOR (go around – Numbers 13:34).
	     עטר [A]DTaR, to surround, encompass (I Sam. 23:26)
	     [A]DTaRaH, crown (Songs 3:11)
			TIER
			
			 TIARA

S	דק DahQ, crushed or milled to a fine, very small size (Exodus 16:14). טחן DTaK[H]aN is to grind or crush. (Exodus 32:20)	S-N	TALCUM

A	טבע DTaBH[A]h, to sink into liquid
	 צף TSaPH, to float above
	     In more of a *drash*, טבע can be contrasted with the
	     unsinkable תבה ark of Noah.
		S-B	DIP
			
			 TOP

S	טירה DTeeYRaH, a fortress (Songs 8:9) fortified encampment צור TSOAR is a high, rocky refuge or redoubt (Psalms 27:5) טירה DTeeYRaH is also a TURNing TURRET צואר TSaVAhR, the swiveling neck or throat (Gen. 41:42)	S-D	TOWER TURRET
A	טמא DTaMAy, religiously impure defiled (Psalms 106:39) תם TahM, whole, perfect, innocent (Genesis 25:27)		CONTAM-INATE
S A	טרף DToaRaiPH, a violent predator, to tear apart פריץ PaReeYTS, used for predatory beasts and men תפר TaPHaR , to sew together	REV M132	TROPHY PIRATE

S		Entry to see
S	מוט MOADT, tottering, stumbling (Psalms 66:9) מעד MOAD, totter (II Samuel 22:8) עמד [A]MahD, to stand firm	MOAT
S	עד [A]hD, until such time; eternity עת [A]iT, time	AT ETERNAL
S	צורה TSOORaH, shape תאר To'AhR, form (Genesis 39:6)	STYLE
S	צמיתת TSiMeeYTooT, forever (Leviticus 25:23) תמיד TahMeeYD, always or continuity (Exodus 28:29).	TIME

S	צר TSoaR, sharp flint knife (Exodus 4:25)
	 תער Ta'[A]hR, razor (Numbers 6:5)
	     Combine the above two synonym sets, keeping in
	     mind that a STYLUS cuts a STYLE or shape, and that
	     reversing *Tsadi-Resh* gets RAZOR.
		RAZOR

S	שדף SHADahf wind-blasted (Genesis 41:6) שטף SHaDTahF, torrential rain A powerful wave of wind has replaced one of water	SPATE

לשון LIQUIDS

S or A = *Synonyms or Antonyms*

S A	S-L = liquid shift – interchangeable tongue letters: L, R	More Shifts	Entry to see

S	אלה ALaH, a curse (Numbers 5:27)
	     Elsewhere it is a solemn oath
	 ארה ARaH means curse! (imperative – Numbers 22:6)
	     The infinitive of ARaH is ARahR		

S	אציל ATSeeYL, joint, (Ezekiel 13:18). ציר TSeeYR, to twist or turn like a door hinge (Prov. 26:14)		ARTHRITIS TURN
S	אצר ATSoaR, to store (Nehemiah 13:13)		STORE

	אצל ATSahL, to put aside (Numbers 11:17)	S-F	LIST STEAL
S	בלה BaLaH, to wear out (Genesis 18:12)	S-G	BALEEN
A	בלע BaL[A]h, to destroy (Psalm 21:10) or to devour בער BHee[A]iR, to consume ברא BaRAh, to create (Genesis 1:1)	M132	
A	ברר BaRaR, separate בלל BaLaL, mixed BaLaL appears in Genesis 11, when language is mixed up, while the "Pure" Language at the other end of human history, at Zephaniah 3:9, is ברורה BaROORaH		PURE BALL
A	בשל BaSHaL, full grown, ripe בסר Bo$eR, unripe	S-F M132	BOLSHEVIK

S	גמל GaMaL is to bring to an end, as in fruit ripening
	    (Isaiah 18:5); or a baby weaning (Genesis 21:8).
	גמר GaMaR, finished (Psalms 12:2)
	גמיר GiMeeYR in Aramaic is to perfect (Ezra 7:12).
	    Gammel in Danish, Norwegian and Swedish means old.
			MEGALO-MANIAC

S	גער G'[A]hR, scorn (Isaiah 17:13) געל G[A]ahL, reject, abhor		GALL
A	דלג DaLaG, to skip, leap over (Psalms 18:30) דרך DaRaKH, to tread down or firmly (Jeremiah 51:33) דרג DaRahG , steps for step-by-step gradation	S-G	DIRECTION DEGREE
S *A*	חרה K[H]aRaH, to burn קלי QeLeeY, roast, toast קר QahR, cold	S-G S-L	SCORCH ALKALI CRYOGENICS
A	אט Lih'AhDT is slow or sluggish (Isaiah 8:6) רהוט RaHOODT, quick רהט Aramaic RiHaDT, to run רץ RaTS, run	s-d	LATE RACE ROTATE

S A			Entry
S	מלט MeLeDT, translated as "smoothing over" מרט In I Kings 7:45 נמרט NiMRahDT is "polished."		MORTAR
A	נבר NaBHahR, a pure-hearted man (II Samuel: 22: 27) נבל NaBHaL, villain		PURE VILE
S	קל QahL, lightweight קלה QaLaH, lightly esteemed, disgraced קלקל QiLoaQaiL, worthless (Numbers 21:5)		ACCELER ATE CHERISH
A	יקר YaQahR, dear, expensive		
A	שפל SHaFahL means lowly שפר SHaPeR, beautiful, source of "super" and "superior"		SIMPLE SUPER

אף NASALS

S or A = Synonyms or Antonyms

S A	S-N = nasal shift – interchangeable nose letter: M, N	More Shifts	Entry to see
S	זנה ZaNaH is to go astray, to commit harlotry or adultery or to fornicate. זמה ZeeMaH is lewdness, incest.		SIN
A	מוט MOADT (1), tottering in place נדד NaDaD, wandering far (Psalms 55:9) מוט MOADT (2), stumbling (Psalms 66:9) עמד [A]MaD, standing firm	S-D	MOAT
S	נין NeeYN, a descendant or grandchild (Genesis 21:23) מן MeeN, from תמונה TiMOONaH, likeness, image (Exodus 20:4)		MINI MINE

METATHESIS

For example, an **M213** metathesis is French blanc (white)
coming from the **second, first** and **third** letters of Edenic לבן LaBHaN (white).

S or A = Synonyms or Antonyms

S / A	M = METATHESIS (root letters switch places.)	More Shifts	Entry to see
S / A	אגר AhGahR , to gather עגור AGOOR, amassed גרע GaR[A]h, to lessen, reduce, deduct (Exodus 5:8, 11)	M312	ACCRUE
A	אמין AMeeYN, believe, accept – saying YES מאן Ma'EN, refuse – saying NO	M213	AMENABLE
S	אמצה AMTSaH, strength (Zechariah 12:5) עצמה [A]TSMaH is might, power (Isaiah 40:29)	M132 VOWELS	CENTER OSTEOMA
S	אזר AZahR, to bind, gird (Jeremiah 1:17) ארז ARahZ, fimly bound, packed (Ezekiel 27:24)]	M132	RICE
A	בדק BeDeQ, breach, gap (II Kings 12:6) דבק DeBHeQ, welding, soldering together (I Kings 22:34), glue	M213	
A	בחור Ba[K]HOOR, young man גבר GeBHeR, mature man [BIG]	M213	BACHELOR
S / A	בטח BeDTaKH, certainty, assurance, insurance, promise, guarantee. עבט [A]VoaDT, a pledge Extensions meaning aFFIDavits to assure conFIDence). They give English B-Fwords like aFFIDavit, , deVOUT, FIDelity and VoTe. The common theme is trust, good faith and surety. בדא BaDAh is to invent, concoct or lie (I Kings 12:33) דבה DeeBaH, a factual report (Genesis 37:2).	M231 S-G M312 S-D	BET WED TAB
S	בקר BaQaR, cattle עפר [O]PHeR, fawn, or the young of hoofed ruminants פרה PaRaH, young cow or heifer	S-G S-B	BUCKAROO CAPRICORN

S	בשר BaSeR, to announce, relate, good tidings (II Samuel 18:20) ספר $aPeR, to tell, relate, declare (Genesis 40:8)	M213 S-B S-F	GOSPEL
	בתולה B'TOOLaH, virgin פרצה P'RooTSaH, one who is licentious פרוץ PaROOTS, immodest (Genesis 38:29) פרזה PiRaZaH are open, unwalled towns (Deut. 3:5)	M132 S-B S-F S-L	PROSTITUTE
S *A*	גרש GaRahSH to expel (Exodus 34:11); שגר SHaGahR to cast forth (Harkavy); An increase (of cattle) Exodus 13:12	M231	GRASS
S	דלק DaLahQ, to burn, kindle, להט LaHaDT, heat, flame, Let there be *licht* (light).	M312 S-G S-D	LIGHT
S	עצל GHaTSeL, lazy זחל ZaK[H]ahL, creep (as in caterpillar) זחלן ZaK[H]LaN is a SLUGGARD while the lazy עצלן GHaTSLaN, sloth, lazy person is also sluggish	M21 S-L S-G	SLUG LAZY
S	זכר ZaKHahR, male (Exodus 34:19) זרע ZeRGHah seed, semen	M132 S-G	SOW
S	חבל K[H]eBHeL, string - source of some "hair" words פרע PeRGHah, hair of head out	M312 S-G,S-B, S-L	CAPILLARY PERIWIG
S	חבש [K]HaBHaSH, to bind חשב [K]HaSHaBH, to bind, knot, weave	M132	HASP
A	חלץ [K]HaLahTS, to draw off, withdraw, to loosen (Deuteronomy 25:9) [to relieve pressure]. לחץ La[K]HahTS, pressure (Numbers 22:25)	M213	LOOSE
S	חלש K[H]aLahSH, weak , powerless (Exodus 17:13, Job 14:10) חשל K[H]aSHahL, weak, feeble (Deuteronomy 25:18)	M132	SLACK

S	חמל K[H]aMAL, to spare, have pity (Deuteronomy 13:9) מחל MaK[H]aL, to pardon, forgive. This word is post-biblical, but not borrowed. רחם RaK[H]eM, means "please have mercy" (Genesis 43:14; Exodus 34:6)	S-L	CLEMENCY MERCY
A	חמץ [K]HaMeTS, leavened bread מצה MaTSaH, unleavened bread	M312	ZYME
S	חמר K[H]aMahR, to boil מרק MaRaQ , soup, broth	M231 S-G	MURKY
A	חפוי K[H]aFOOY, covered יחף YaK[H]eF, barefoot	M231	COVER
S	חרד K[H]aRaid, shuddering in fear רעד RaGHahD, trembling	M213 S-G	RATTLE
A	חרם K[H]aReM is to fully destroy, exterminate רחם RaK[H]eM, to have mercy, compassion	M213	HARM MERCY
S	חשב [K]HaS(H)A[V], to think, calculate, design with skill (Exodus 31:4) שעף Sa'[A]PH, thought (Job 4:13).	M213 S-G S-F S-B	GUESS
	חשך [K]HoaSHeKH, darkness, obscurity שכח SHaKHa[K]H, forget (thus "blacking out.")	M312	OBSCURE
S	טרוף DTaROOPH, turning around פתל PaTaL, to twist פתלתל P'TaLToaL, twisted, perverse (Deuteronomy 32:5).	M231	DISTURB
S	כפרת KaPoReT, covering on the holy ark (Ex. 25:17) פרכת PaRoKHeT, curtain before holy of holies (Ex. 26:33)	M312	COVER
S	כבש KaBHahSH, Haman wanted to "ravish" Queen Esther (Esther 7:8) EDK's 3rd definition (rape) שכב SHaKHahBH, to lie with carnally (Genesis 19:32).	M321	KIBOSH
S	כנף K'NaPH is a wing or extremity פנה PeeNaH is a corner	M321 S-G REV	CANOPY PINNACLE

A	נגע NaG[A]h, to strike, smite or touch to cause injury (Genesis 26:29). ענג [A]NaG, to fondle tenderly (Deuteronomy 28:56)	M231	NICK NOXIOUS
S	נוזל NOAZeL is to spout or flow צנור TSeeNOAR, pipe	M213 S-F S-L	NOZZLE SNORKEL
S	נוקש NOAQaiSH, snared (Psalms 9:17) 　　　Harkavy, "seduced" (Deuteronomy 12:30) נשק NaQeSH, to kiss מוקש MoaQaiSH, a snare (Exodus 10:7)	M132 S-N	CATCH
S	סער $a'[A]hR, to storm, to rage (Jonah 1:11) רגש RaGahSH, to rage	M321	SQUALL RAGE
S	עלף [O]oLahPH, to faint (Isaiah 51:20) [] רפה RaPHaH, weak (Judges 8:3)	M312 S-G S-L	LIMP
S	פקל PaQaL to peel (onion) קלף QaLaPH, to peel or remove a shell or rind 　　　Hebrew lexicographer, Ernest David Klein, writes that these two words are "related by metathesis." He needed to see several 100 more of these, and antonyms too.	M312	CALIBER
S	פרש PeReSH, excrement (Leviticus 4:11) רפש RaFaSH, to make filthy or dirty (Ezekiel 34:18)	M213	REFUSE
S	צניף TSNeeYPH, turban (Leviticus 16:4) צפן TSaPHahN, wrapping or winding (Isaiah 22:18).	M132	STEPHEN
S	צפה TSaPHaH is to look or observe שקף SH'KaPH, to look out	M132 S-F S-G	SPY SCOPE
S	צרך TSoaReKH, need (II Chronicles 2:15) רצה RoaTSeH, desire (Psalms 147:10) רוץ ROOTS, to run… as in need	M213	ESTROGEN ROTATE
S	קשב QiSHaBH, attending by ear or listening (Exodus 32:3). שקף SHaQaPH to look out at, see (another form of observation)	M213 S-B	SCOPE

S/A		More Shifts	Entry
S	רצף ReTSeF, a burning coal (I Kings 19:6) רשף RaSHahF, to burn, glow רשף ReSHeF, flame (Songs 8:6); sparks (Job 5:7) burning plague (Deuteronomy 32:24) שרף SaRaF, burn, burn down	S-F M213	SAFFRON
S	שטר SHoaDTeR, administrative ruler, officer (Exodus 5:8) שלט SHaLahDT, to rule (Ecclesiates 5:18) שרת SHaRaiT, to minister (Numbers 1:50)	M132 S-L S-D	SATRAP SULTAN
S A	שלג SHeLeG, snow שערה S'GHaRaH, violent tempest or storm סער $aGHaR violent tempest or storm (Jonah 1:4) שעירים S'GHeeYReeYM are gentle, light rains (Deut. 32:2)	M132 S-G S-L S-F	SLEIGH SQUALL

REVERSALS

S or A = Synonyms or Antonyms

S A	← = REVERSE the (root letters of) the Edenic word	More Shifts	Entry to see
S	אור OWR, light ראה Rah'AH, to see are profoundly related. There is no sight without light.		AURA LO!
S	אות OWT, sign, mark (Genesis 9:13) תו Tahf, sign, mark (Ezekiel 9:4)		OATH
S	אל AhL, nothing, naught, (adv) Not (Genesis 22:12) לא LO, No		ILLICIT
	אם EM, mother - May or Mee, the *Mem* prefix meaning **from**, originating from the matrix		MAMA
	אף AhPH is the nose (Genesis 2:7)		OPEN

	פה *Pey*, a mouth or other OPENING (Exodus 4:11)		
s	בור BOAR, a hole, pit or grave (Exodus 21:33). ארבה ARooBaH, an opening, a chimney, window or floodgate (Genesis 7:11) [*Aleph*, *Hey*, and *Vav* are weak vowels]		BORE
s	בל BahL, heart (Aramaic of Daniel 6:15) לב LaiBH, heart (Genesis 8:21)		VOLUNTEER LOVE
	בזז BaZaZ, to steal, embezzle זבד ZEBHeD, gift, source of "sponsor"		BUZZARD SPEND
S	גיל GeeYL, gladness לעג La'[A]G, laughing at		GALA LAUGH
S	גלש GaLaSH, to slide, ski, slog (Songs 4:1) שלג SHeLeG, snow (Exodus 4:6)		GLISSADE SLEIGH SLUDGE
S	גפן GeFeN, vine נפג NeFeG, sprout, shoot (Exodus 6:21).		VINE FUNGUS
A	גרד GayRaiD, scrape, make level, דרג DaRahG, to make steps,(terracing was common in Judea)		GRADE DEGREE
S	דרום DaROAM, south רד RaiD, to go down		ROOT

S
 	
 A
	דק DahQ, thin (Genesis 41:3)
	 חד K[H]ahD, sharp, streamlined and thin
	 גד GahD, fish (the streamlined creature)
	 כד KahD, rounded, as in כד KahD, pitcher
	     כדורי KaDOOReeY, spherical, globular; based on
	     כדור KaDOOR, a ball or globe. Arabic *kadira* (thick)
		
		 S-G
			ACUTE
			
			 GADOID
			
			 CADDY

S	דשא DaSHAh, to sprout or grow grass;
	 דשא DeSHEh, "grass" or lawn (Genesis 1:11)
	     Dalet-Shin is about green herbage and verdure.
	 שדה SoDeH, field, land (Genesis 4:8)
	     Primarily indicates irrigated and cultivated land.
	     This is evident in Polish *sad* (orchard) and the
	     (reversed) פרדס PaRDeS, orchard (Songs 4:13).
		
		 S-F
			SODDEN
			 SOD
			
			 PART

S	הלך HaLahKH to go, walk (Genesis 3:8) עלה GHaLayH, ascend, go to, come to (Genesis 2:6).		WALK ALLEY
S	חוף [K]HOAPH, shore, coast פאה PEyaH side, corner (Leviticus 19:9)		
S	כיס KeeY$, pocket; כסה Ka$eH, to conceal שק SahQ, sack	S-G S-F	ENCASE SACK
S	כסה Ka$aH, to cover, conceal, encase (Leviticus 13:13). Reversing to *Samekh-Khaf* are several "cover" words, including the Edenic CASE-Word most like a *casa* (house in Spanish) סכה SooKaH, hut, tabernacle		ENCASE HOUSE SHACK
S	מאס Ma'Ah$, to find contemptable [MISANTHROPY] שנא SahNAy, despise	S-N S-F M231	XENOPHOBIA
	מוך MOOKH, to become poor עני GHaNeeY, poor	S-G S-N	MEEK ANNOYANC E
S *A*	מות MaVeT, death תם TaM, completion (both in Deuteronomy 2:16) מתח MaTa[K]H, to extend, stretch out (Isaiah 40:22)		
S	נטה NaDTaH, stretching out צנום **TSaN**OOM, shrunkeness and meagerness (Genesis 41:23)	S-D	NET THIN
S	על GHoaL, yoke, collar (Leviticus 26:13) לע LoahGH, throat (Proverbs 23:2)		COLLAR GROAN GULLET
S	ערה GHaRaH, to empty, to pour out (Genesis 24:20). ריק RaiYQ, empty, void (Genesis 37:24)	S-G	KARATE
A	עשיר [A]SHeeYR, rich man (I Kings 3:11) רש RahSH, poor man (II Samuel 12:3)		RICHES
A	פלס PeeLay$, balance, even (Psalms 78:50) סלף $eLePH, perverseness (Proverbs 11:3)	M321	BALANCE
S	צר TSaR, narrow, thin, pressed tight	S-F	STRAIT

	רזה RaZeH, lean, skinny		
S	ראש ROASH, political head, chief, primary (Exodus 6:14, Exodus 30:23, Exodus 12:2) שר SahR is a chief, leader, captain, minister or ruler ("officer" in Jeremiah 17:25)		SIR

Synonyms Conclusion

At the "BARE" entry are several synonyms with a bilabial, vowel and liquid and non-consonant:

:

1) פרוע PaROO[A]h, bareheaded (Leviticus 13:45).

2) בע Be[A]iR, "I have *cleared out* the consecrated portion" (Deuteronomy 26:13)

3) בר BaRAh, to cut down trees – "go up to the forest country and *clear* an *area*" (Joshua 17:15)

4) בר BahR, pure, clear (Psalms 24:4) [PURE] Purification and waste removal often comes from fire [BURN]

5) באר Ba'AiR, expose, explain (Deuteronomy 1:5)

6) ברור BAROOR, evident, lucid, clear
French glass is *verre*, and self-evident truth is VERITY [VERY].

7) בהיר BaHeeYR, clear, bright (Job 37:21)
While this family is BaReeY ברי (surely) exceptional, it is by no means rare.
The opposite bilabial-liquid: בלל BaLaL, mixed up [BALL]

Word families that are not extended to sound-alike synonyms are deficient.

Various BREAK words include variations of bilabial-liquid-guttural:

    ברג BeReG   screw, the corkscrew metal BREAKS through wood

    ברח BeReKH the knee, which BREAKS the length of the leg

    פלג PeLeG   a BREAK-off division, block, **brig**ade or flake

    פלח PeLeK[H] BREAKING up soil, ploughing; **paroch**ial places

פלך PaLaKH a **frac**tion, as a BROKEN-off segment of fruit

פרח PeRaK[H] the BREAKING out that **freck**les or **plag**ues might do

פרכת **PaRoKHeT** the curtain or space BREAKER; פרך PaRaKH fluke

פרע PeR[A]h BROKEN order, wild and freaky

פרק PeReQ a joint, or BREAK-off: breeches to **br**anches to a fork.

פרק PayRahQ, to remove, pluck off, flake off, BREAK away

Antonyms Conclusion

ש-ל *Shin-Lamed* is to loosen bonds, as in the command to remove or LOSE a sandal SHahL (Exodus 3:5). SHiLSHOOL is not Biblical, but we are all painfully aware of this *Shin-Lamed* loosening of the bowels. SHaLaBH is to bind, join or fit together (Exodus 26:17); SHaLaK[H] is to let go (Genesis 49:21); *Shin-Resh* appears in SHiRAh is to lose or unbind (Daniel 5:12);   SaRaH (Aramaic SiRAh) is to let loose, release (Jeremiah 15:11)

The ש-ר *Shin/Sin-Resh* sub-root is a liquid shift away (R →L) and the built-in opposite. SaRaG is to knot together (Lamentations 1:14); SaRaD, twisted, knit together (Exodus 31:10); SHaRaR, to knot or bond; SHaRSHiRaH, chain (Exodus 28:14). שרוך SiROAKH, shoe latchet (Genesis 14:23). Wrapping up this family is *Tsadi-Resh* צרר TSaRaR, to bind, wrap (Exodus 12:34). [LOSE]

The Five Books of Moses often puts sound-alike opposites in close proximity in its incomparable artistry. In Genesis 41:53 the seven years of plenty have finished - ותכלנה. In the very next verse the seven years of famine have begun - ותחלנה. *Tahf-Het-Lamed*, to begin, is a dental-guttural-liquid opposite of *Tahf-Kahf-Lamed-Hey* end, purpose, aim. Only the guttural has shifted.

SIMILAR OXYMORONIC OPPOSITES – IDENTICAL ANTONYMS

The poetical play of Biblical Hebrew does this often, using a repeating root form both similar and opposite meanings. In Genesis 6:7, the Lord says that He regrets (*Noon-Het-*

Mem, נחם Na[K]HeM) making Man. But in 6:8 He is comforted (נחם Na[K]HeM) since Noah (*Noon-Het*, as in נח Noa[K]H, respite) finds favor in His eyes.

In Chinese too, reversing the נ-ח *Noon-Het* sub-root above to H-N, *han* means 1) regret, not satisfied (X240) and 2) rest (sleeping soundly, contentment). This second *han* (X237), is the reverse of נח Noa[K]H, rest and נחת Na[K]HaT, rest, repose (Isaiah 30:15).

Contrary to theories about words evolving for semantic clarity, Edenic has several oxymoronic couples of the same letters (*no letter shifts needed*). These are examples of what the sages called דבר והיפוכו (the thing and its opposite). These most non-human, paradoxical words include:

אזרח EZRa[K[H is a citizen, native (Leviticus 16:29). An alien or stranger is a זר ZahR (Leviticus 22:13). זר *Zayin-Resh* is the core of these built-in opposites.

אפס APHai$: The פ-ס *Pey-Samekh* opposite of אפס APHai$, running out of something, (like money in Genesis 47:15), is the abundance of פסה Pee$aH , like the corn in Psalms 72:16.

ברח BaRaK[H] is to flee (Genesis 31:22). בריח BaReeYaK[H] is a fugitive. The built-in opposite of all this breaking out and escaping is בריח BaReeYa[H]K, a bar or bolt to prevent escape. The opposite of בר BahR as obstruction is seen in terms like בר BahR, open field, suburb [BARRIO] and ברור BaROOR, clear [BARE].

גרף GaRaF means both to sweep away and to gather [PURGE].

חלץ [K]HaLahTS is to gird (also Syriac). Its built-in opposite is the identical חלץ [K]HaLahTS , to draw off, withdraw, to loosen [LOOSE].

חסד [K]He$eD is grace (II Samuel 9:3). חסד [K]HaSahD is disgrace (Leviticus 20:17).

טמום DTaMOOM means stupid or senseless; טמטם DTiMDTaiM is to make stupid; נטמה NiDTMaH (Job 18:3) is to be stupid. טעם DTa'[A]hM (wise – Proverbs 26:16) is a like-sounding antonym.

מוש MOOSH can mean touch or feel [MASSAGE at "MASS"], and the opposite, to withdraw [MISS].

מלח MaLa[K]H means to rub small, to reduce to dust (Harkavy –Isaiah 51:6), but also מלח Mala[K]H is the noun and verb of salt or salting, a preservative which prevents organic material from breaking down (Exodus 30:35). [MILL] מלך MeLeKH (king) is the Go-Maker. He makes people LaiKH (go!). A מלאך Mal'AKH (angel) is an agent told to "go."

מסך Ma$ahKH is to mix (Proverbs 9:2). [MIX] Paradoxically, the same מסך Ma$ahKH means curtain, screen [MASK]; that which separates space, and prevents areas from mixing.

נחם NaK[H]ahM means both to grieve, regret and to be comforted, consoled [AMITY].

נכר NeeKahR means both to be recognized and NeeKaiR (to treat as a stranger— Genesis 42:7). [MARK]

נצח NeeTSayaK[H] means both to beat and to be beaten. [SANGRIA]

Samekh-Phey, סוף $OAF, end and הוסיף HOA$eeYF, to add [PHASE OUT], and *Samekh-Phey* spacial ending has its opposite number in, ספ $ahPH, a threshold (a beginning of space).

עד *Ayin-Dalet*, עד [A]hD is eternity (infinite) [ETERNAL] or it means until, up to a certain point (finite). Similarly, עוד [O]aWD, further, still, is the opposite of finiteness [ADD].

עולם [O]aWLaM is This World , our visible reality (Ecclesiastes 3:11) where the spiritual reality of our Creator is עלם [A]LahM, hidden (Leviticus 4:3).

עור [O]WR (our sensitive skin) is the source of AWARE, [CORIUM] [ORIENTATION]. Read slightly differently, *Ayin-Vav-Resh* also provides the opposite of awareness – blindness. [UMBRELLA].

עזב [A]ZahBH means both to leave and forsake (Genesis 39:13), and to strengthen, fortify and build up (Nehemiah 3:8).

ערבה [A]RaBHaH means both a dry desert (whence Arab) and a willow tree (that grows near water) –[ARBOR]

פנים PaNeeYM means both interior [PENETRATE] and exterior [PANE].

רב RahBH means plenty, much, many [RIFE]. רעב Ra'[A]BH is a famine, time of scarcity. [RAVENOUS]

ר-פ *Resh-Phey* words are for both healing and ill health: רפא RaPHAh is to heal or cure (Exodus 15:2). רפות RiPHOOT is health in Proverbs 3:8. רופא ROAPHAy is a doctor. תרופה T'ROOPHaH, treatment [THERAPY] is the opposite of תורפה TOORPaH (weakness [TORPID]); רפה RaPHAh is weak (Jeremiah 49:24) and רפיון RiPYOAN is weakness (Jeremiah 47:3).

שבות SH'BHOOT means both captivity and repariation. [SABBATICAL]

שד SHahD is a nurturing breast or teat (Lamentations 4:3), and the name of the deity as hidden, natural nurturer is שדי SHaDahY (Exodus 6:3). Yet, the same *Shin-Dalet* שד SHoaD means robbery and oppression (Psalms 12:6), and שד SHaiD is a destructive demon (Deuteronomy 32:17). [SHADE]

שחור SHaK[H]oaR means dark or black, and שחר SHaKHahR means light or dawn [SWARTHY].

שנה *Shin-Noon-Hey* means both to change and to repeat the same thing. [CHANGE] Conventional Hebraicists who believe that Hebrew "grew" or evolved only with semantics or human usage have long noted, and have made peace with a few oxymoronic pairs that make sense in context. Like having the identical letters of a word mean both "root" and "to uproot."

תאם Ta'AhM, couple (never alone); יתום YaTOAM, orphan (always alone) [TEAM]

But the list is longer than they know, and identically spelled words which mean something AND ITS OPPOSITE does not reflect a human coinage for unambiguous communication, but the non-human design of an intelligence subtle enough to reflect the paradoxical aspects of things.

גרם GaRaM as bone, and to crush bone

סעיף $a'e[E]F is a branch, and $ay[A]aiF is to lop of branches. [PHASE OUT]

סקל $aQahL is to stone, and $eeKail is to clear of stones

עצם [E]TSeM is a bone, and [E]eTSaiM is to break bone

ערף[O]ReF is the neck, and [A]RahF is to break the neck . [SCRUFF]

שרש SHoReSH is a root and to uproot

Pairs like these are as natural as to SKIN a rabbit or to BONE a fish. They certainly must have come from human usage. The set of oxymoronic pairs, and the hundreds of opposites which are separated by a letter shift of two, appear, instead, to be engineered – perhaps by very clever chimps or cavemen

There are many more such word families, of two-sound roots, to be found in the Word Family chapter of *The Origin of Speeches*.

Chapter Eight CONCLUSION

This chapter attempts to build bridges to science, but conventional wisdom would associate the Hebrew Bible with unscientific superstition. But anything that appears unnatural is merely that which has not yet been scientifically proven. This book begins to make the case for a historical Eden-Babel scenario for an intelligently designed language.

The Intelligent Designer in Genesis has no problem with identifying as Natural Law. There are several names for the Creator in the Hebrew Bible. They carefully fit the divine attribute for each context. The third word in Genesis, the subject of the creation verb phrase, means "The Lord of Natural Law." Edenic letters have numeric values. *Aleph+Lamed+Hey+Yod+Mem* adds up to the same number as the word for nature. An agnostic may conclude that the Intelligent Designer of the universe and of the world of words may be called Nature. Edenics, the program for thought and speech that still drums within our masterfully designed cerebrums, is all about natural law.

Ignorance of the Law of Gravity will not allow a person to float. Ignorance of Edenics is no crime against nature. But grasping some might add some gravitas. This chapter's metaphors of the chemistry and physics of Edenics are inadequate, but hopefully useful.

Of course spelling is of premier importance in studying Biblical Hebrew. But anyone not recognizing beyond spelling the significance of Sound and SENSE, MUSIC and MEANING is deaf to significant aspects of Hebrew's design. The same patterns (letter shifts, metathesis, reversals) that are allowing us in the 21st Century to document Proto-Semitic or Edenic as the primary human language program, are present within Hebrew to discover undocumented synonyms and antonyms. I end with a section of the "CUT" entry from the E-Word CD Dictionary (see edenics.org):

CUT	KahT	*Kaph-Tahf*
CUT	כת	[K-T]

ROOTS: Icelandic *kuta* (to cut with a knife) represents one of the oldest KT cut words. There's Latin *caedere* (to cut), but somehow no Indo-European alleged root. Edenic has many guttural-dental CUTTERS. גדד GaDaD is to cut off (Daniel 4:11). גזה GaZaH is to cut (there's a ד-ז *Dalet*/D-*Zayin*/Z link via Aramaic).

Both *Gimel-Dalet-Ayin* and *Koof-Tet-Ayin*, גדע GaD[A]h (Isaiah 9:9) and קטע QaDT[A] mean to cut off; חטב K[H]oDTa[V], to cut, hew (Deuteronomy 29:10); חתך K[H]aTahKH, to cut; Aramaic כת KahT is a sect, a special group cut away from others; קצב QaTSa[V] and קצף QaTSaF mean to cut off; קצה QeeTSaH, to cut off; קצע QeeTSay[A]h, to trim; קצר Qa*T*SeR, cut down, harvest (Leviticus 23:10); and חצה K[H]aT(S)aH, to halve (Exodus 21: 35). קץ QaiTS is the cut off or end. [COAST] Harkavy compares קוץ QOOTS, to cut or pluck off, קצץ QaTSaTS and קוט QOODT (Job 8:4) as "cut off" verbs. קטף QaDTaF, to pluck or crop (Deuteronomy 28:26) is another cutter. Arabic *qadda* is "he cut lengthwise." Syriac has similar Q-D cutters.

Het-Tsadi cutters include חצב [K]HaTSaBH, to hew out; חצד [K]HaTSaD, to harvest; חצה [K]HaTSaH, to divide in two, separate, partition; חצי [K]HaTSeeY, half (Exodus 24:6) and the arrow, חץ [K]HaiTS. [HASTATE] More cutters with a *Koof* include קדד QaDaD and קדח QaDa[K]H, to cut, drill; קטם QaDTaM, to cut off, lop off (in Syriac-Aramaic); and קצץ QaTSaTS, cut off (Deuteronomy 25:12). This group is all related, according to E.D. Klein, to Aramaic and Syriac קצץ QaTaTS, he cut off, decided; Arabic *qasa*, he cut, clipped; and Akkadian *qasasu*, to hew or cut off.

The guttural *Ayin* and *Tet*, עט GHaiDT, stylus, pen (Psalms 45:2) also has the sound and sense of cutting, though the cutting is finer. The built-in antonym, that which is whole and uncut is אחד EK[H]aD, one, also a guttural-dental [EACH] [ACUTE]

Chapter Eight ACTIVITIES

Find ten pairs of Hebrew words that are either synonyms or antonyms (thematically), the pairs being made up of similar sounding letters… in the same sequence or a different sequence.

Chapter Nine

Charting Word Families

Introduction

Using the techniques of last chapter, as well as those of several previous ones, we can establish a *word family* (named for its characteristic sound and sense) for a large group of words which share the same theme. That family is initially begun by like-sounding, like-meaning Edenic words with a dominant two-letter sub-root that can be isolated with the Chemistry of Edenics.

Most often the members of these extended word families are not acknowledged as being related by genetic design, despite sharing a sub-root with similar spelling. The common theme that binds them often does not fit dictionary definitions. How is it possible that any such patterns remain uncharted in the world's most studied ancient language? Because scholars value spellings, not sounds. Especially those who venerate the traditional spellings of words in the Hebrew Bible. Spellings got standardized many centuries later in languages other than Hebrew, so one might suspect that linguists would be more open to sound-based similarities.

In the perspective of the new Edenics findings, we see that words of similar music and meaning only differ because of Rashi-Grimm's letter shifts. Hebrew scholars have not been exposed to the discipline of general linguistics, and have not applied sound-based principles in Hebraic or Biblical studies. Like the general linguists, Hebraicists have largely overlooked the sound-based family patterns within Hebrew, and have certainly dismissed the possibility of an intelligently designed, original Edenic language.

It does not occur to the average Western-trained scholar that BREACH and PLOUGH are similar bilabial-liquid-guttural BReaKing terms. To the linear, compartmental mind, one is a negative verb of destroying a wall during war, while the other is a positive term for agricultural seeding.

Rabbi Samson Raphael Hirsch (1808-1888) came closest to tracing word families within Biblical Hebrew. His large achievement was largely ignored because he was too often unscientific, because Judaic education stressed legalism at the expense of letters, and, possibly, because he did not attract global attention by applying his Biblical Hebrew word families to world vocabulary.

Word families are most obviously traced by noting that words with similar meanings begin with the same two root letters. Edward Horowitz has some of this in his *How the Hebrew Language Grew* (see Chapter One), and he assumes that primitive Semitic speakers coined three-letter extension-words from two-letter stems inherited from grunting gorillas and gesturing cave men.

It is this book and chapter's goal to present the case for Intelligent Design of both the Edenic two-letter sub-roots, the three-letter roots to which they extend, and the many global two or three-letter roots and words that were spun off them.

For example, the פ-ר Peh-*Resh*/P-R word family of "breaking apart" has been noted by Horowitz and others:

פר PaRad is to divide;

פרט PaRaDT means a piece;

פרך PaRooKh is broken;

פרס PaRoo$ means spread;

פרץ PaRooTS is broken;

פרק PayRooQ is to take apart

פרר PaRooR means a crumb.

The idea that an original modern human might have been gifted with a well-designed vocabulary and grammar is dismissed as mythological. When the Neanderthal hunter came home with a side of beef, his family, lacking other words to implore him to break it into pieces for them, must have just yelled "par." Trouble is, "par" meant many other things besides breaking.

This is like the problematic reconstruction of Proto-Indo-European roots by the folks at the *American Heritage Dictionary*. If a caveman said "kel" he could mean 1) cut, 2) cover, 3) drive, 4) tilt, 5) dark, 6) hill, 7) to prick or 8) to deceive. These reconstructions do approximate K-L sub-roots of (world) word families, but it is bizarre to imagine that they were primitive words that evolved. Sure, we constantly extend vocabulary and coin new terms. But this doesn't mean that a modern human once thought and spoke without developed language. The evolutionary theory doesn't fit the enigma of human language.

It is speculated that ר-פ *Pey-Resh* or P-R "breaker" words seem to have germinated and spread forth from botanical P-R words like: פרו PiROO, be fruitful; פרג PaRaG, to germinate; פרה PaRaH, to be fertile; פרט PeReDT, a single grape, part of a bunch; פרח PaRa[K]H, to blossom, flower or break out; and פרי P'ReeY, fruit like the pear and apricot, apple, plum or berry.

F-R and other bilabial-liquid shifts from the פ-ר-ה *Pey/Phey-Resh* two-letter root are bolded to give you a small sample of the scores of English words spun off from this molecule of music and meaning. To see hundreds more, see *E-Word* entries like BREACH (with words like BROACH and PORT), BREAK (with words like FLIGHT and PLOUGH), FLAKE (with a nasalization like PLA[N]K), FLAG (with words like BLOCK, BRIGADE, FLAKE, FLAGSTONE), FRACTION (with words like DEBRIS and FRAGMENT), FREE (broken lose), FREAK (broken out from the norm), FRIABLE (with words like FRAY, FRAZZLE and PULVERIZE), FRUCTIFY (with FRAGRANCE and PLAGUES that break out), FRUIT (with FERTILE PARENTS BIRTHING) and PART (with words like COMPARTMENT and FRITTER).

The reader may sense that this bilabial-liquid family of ר-פ *Pey-Resh* "breakers" in Edenic has resulted in many thousands of similar bilabial-liquid around the world. And, yes, if one Edenic root or word took seventy forms at an initial Big Bang of neuro-linguistic diversity at Shinar (Babel), each of those seventy clans (later, language superfamilies) would have developed many new words through semantics (usage) to encapsulate new distinctions or innovations.

Word families can only be observed in their original, Edenic form. Only Edenic word families can be traced through related synonyms and built-in antonyms. These terms are used lightly, since Edenic did not have an ancestor word like *sker* that later split into SHIRT and SKIRT.

This unique intelligent design evident only in Edenic (NOT in Modern Hebrew) reflects the Physics of Edenics taken up in the last chapter. The reader will decide if these word families reflect an overactive human imagination or an early attempt to chart the majestic and universal workings of the שפתים ניב בורא BOARAy NeeYBH SFaTaYiM, (roughly) the Originator of Speeches (Isaiah 57:19).

Every Edenic word belongs to a tight, but ever-widening family. If two words share some element of meaning, they are bound to share some genes or letters in some form. From the other side, where words more clearly share sound than sense, it is up to us to find that common meaning that justifies the similar music. For example, both נשר NeSHeR, eagle and נשל NaSHaL, to fall or drop, share the נ-ש *Noon-Shin* sound, with only the two varieties of liquid (*Lamed*/L and *Resh*/R). All birds, especially eagles, are high fliers, not fallers. There ought to be something about falling in "eagleness" – but for years this eluded me.

Then, I chanced upon a nature show on TV. It seems that the eagle is the world's best sky diver. It seeks prey from great heights (with its eagle eyes) and plummets down at incredible speed. So "eagle" and "drop, fall" ARE related after all. The eagle is the plummeter, at least in the original language. Apparently, extending word families, like understanding animal names (next chapter), requires extensive knowledge of the intelligently designed Creation.

So, even in such challenging cases where the sound or sense of words is elusive, every word belongs in a family. Every human word, like every human, has only several degrees of separation, and deserves genealogical research. This small chapter in this second Edenics study cannot do more than provide a small tip of a large iceberg. In the *E-Word CD Dictionary,* some word family work is provided in most entries, especially for the reader ready to follow a thread of music and/or meaning over several cross-references.

The entries begin to trace a word family with English entry words usually given at least the immediate Edenic family of the etymon. Related foreign words, known cognates and never-considered "cognates" can be seen as "second cousins" or distant relations who share our Edenic ancestors.

This chapter allows us to fully chart a sample word family. The isolated sub-root, two-consonant sound or phoneme is stretched on a Vowel Rack of A-E-I-O-U. Not limiting us to the five vowel variations of the sub-root (only five possibilities), we fill out the word family Sound Grid with all the Letter Shifts available from at least the sub-root's first letter. Future books will chart these word families more fully, and including all letter shifts, nasalization, metathesis – using hundreds of foreign language words as reinforcement. These super charts of the next generation will provide a far deeper and wider picture of what happened to our factory-installed language program at the Tower of Babel.

THE PEY-NOON, P-N POINTER FAMILY

For now, an example of an extensive Word Family involves the פ-נ *Pey-Noon* of פנה PoaNeH (to point). Of course, we can only isolate the sub-root after noting a pattern of words with similar sense and sound, alerting us the presence of another large family. Now we take the פ-נ P-N of the POINTERS, and place it on a Vowel Rack and larger Sound Grid, where פ-נ P-N is expanded across by all the vowels, A-E-I-O-U, and then downward by its Rashi's/Grimms' Laws Letter Shifts. Because P is a Bilabial, that downward extension involves B, F, V and W as well as the original P. The N, Nasal, can only shift to an M, so we can keep it in mind – but not have to enlarge the Sound Grid.

Similarly, all 5 X 5 variables (25), could be inverted to Nasal-Bilabial, but we could also keep it in mind rather than extend the grid. "Pointing" or the theme of spatial directions is not an adjective, but will involve similar terms, synonyms and opposite meanings or antonyms. The creative reader will consider the theme of spatial directions, and not just dictionary data. Readers with foreign language skills will recognize foreign words that fit the grid. Please email your discoveries to us. (They will be acknowledged in the next edition or on our website.)

We'll take a look at the chart for פ-נ P-N, referring to each possible sound variation with a bracketed number to better refer to each audible variation of our sub-root:

פ-נ Pey-Noon (PN) Word Family – the POINTERS

BAN [1]	BEN [2]	BIN [3]	BON [4]	BUN [5]
FAN [6]	FEN [7]	FIN [8]	FON [9]	FUN [10]
PAN [11]	PEN [12]	PIN [13]	PON [14]	PUN [15]
VAN [16]	VEN [17]	VIN [18]	VON [19]	VUN [20]
WAN [21]	WEN [22]	WIN [23]	WON [24]	WUN [25]

Note how each of the twenty-five boxes in the this chart is numbered. Glancing at the chart even before we flesh it out with actual words, you may have already noticed that only a third or so seem to spell out actual words that you recognize. That's fine. As extensive as the possibilities are, we will have to limit ourselves to Edenic and English words here. Related foreign words will have to be added later. All the words that we do chart will share the sense of POINTING, (pertaining to a special space or direction) as well as echoing a specific (and numbered) sound from the chart.

The Edenic words here are all authenticated in the Bible and/or with Semitic words like Syriac *pina*, he turned. Many of those citations are in *E-Word* or *Word* entries like FAN, FIN, PANE, PENCHANT, PENETRATE, PENULTIMATE, POINT and VINE.

The lead word here, at the head of the family, is פ-נ-ה *Pey-Noon-Hey* (to turn to or from, to POINT or indicate direction. פ-נ-ה *Pey-Noon-Hey* can also be a פנה PeeNaH, a corner; a high POINT, like a summit or cornerstone (Psalms 118:22), a *pinna* in Latin (a wing or a battlement atop a wall). Other *Pey-Noon* words that most strongly establish this family's sound and sense include: פנה PaNaH, to decline or WANE; פנה PeeNaH and פני PiNahY, empty of space or time, to clear out space in a house (Genesis 24:31) or for a road (Isaiah 40:3); פנים PaNeeYM, face or surface (like a window PANE); פנים PiNeeYM, interior – as large as a BIN or as small as a *pen* (pot or vessel in Chinese); פנינה PiNeeYNaH, a pearl (that most interior of objects); לפנות LiPHNOAT, towards; and לפני LIPHNaY, before.

פ-נ-ה Pey-*Noon-Hey* is also an emotional turning to something, yearning for something. In I Kings 8:28 and Deuteronomy 31:18 the people are told not to "turn to" foreign gods and idolatrous practices. In other words, פנה PaNaH here means inclining towards something with desire. To PINE for meant "to yearn for" before it came to mean languishing away in the unfulfilled desire for something. In the **PEN**CHANT entry is Chinese *pan* (to long for).

The bilabial-nasal cognates of IE root *wen* (to desire, strive for) all fit our Pointer Family. These include: BANIAN, VENAL, VENERATE, VENERY, VENEREAL, VENISON (that which hunters point at or desire), VENOM, VENUS (the result of, not a source of VEN desire words) and WEAN (more like an antonym of no longer turning to), WIN and WONT.

Next to consider are א-פ-נ *Aleph-Pey-Noon* words, with only that weak, initial *Aleph* disguising them as פ-נ *Pey-Noon* cousins once removed. אפן OPHaN, like face or countenance, means a visible manner, mode or style. The אפן OPHaN, wheel, (Exodus 14:25) has a round surface that extends in all directions. This is why אפנים OPHNaYim, wheels, is a bicycle in Modern Hebrew. The אפנים OPHaNiM, a type of angel in Ezekiel 10:12, are not Hells' Angels doing wheelies, but are multi-faceted and omni-directional.

But, between the prefix letters of normative Hebrew grammar, and the isolated sub-roots we have just learned about, there will be several other Edenic words in the larger POINTER family here that do not begin with פ-נ *Pey-Noon*. One such standout is *Tsadi-Pey-Noon*, צפן TSaPHoN, north, the one Biblical purely directional-pointer that doesn't merely mean seaward (west), or towards the desert (south) or towards the rising sun and earlier time (east).

Since facing or turning is a verb, with noun forms that mean a face or turn, there are few antonyms here. The closest opposite concept of knowing a direction would be not knowing it. Thus, צפן TSaPHaN is hidden (Proverbs 27:16). In Genesis 41:45, in Egypt, Joseph is renamed צפנת פענח TSaPHNaTH P[A]Naya[K]H, the **FIND**ER of hidden or

VANISHED things. To find such things, one might use a lantern or פנס PANa$, used in modern Hebrew for a projector.

Gimel-Phey-Noon, גפן Ge**PHeN**, is a vine. You might think of a vine as something botanical, like a tree or grass, which doesn't belong here among spatial words of pointing and direction. But a VINE is unlike other plants. It wildly spreads out across whatever surface is available, **BEND**ING and **WEN**DING its way to the four **WIN**DS (directions), like the **WAN**DERING Jew plant.

In a brief diversion to Chinese where a similar word means many things: *wan* means WINDING, the BEND of a stream, along with a VINE, an inner cavity and late evening.

נ-פ-ח *Het-Phey-Noon*, חפן K[H]oPHaN means a hand and a hand measurement. [FIN] A FIN, too, can mean an **APP**ENDAGE or a five (as in five dollars or **FIN**GERS). Many words from **PEN**TATEUCH and **PEN**TECOSTAL to **PUN**JAB give this branch of the POINTER FAMILY its PUNCH. FINS FAN water better than fan-less **FIN**GERS FAN air, but these anatomical POINTERS connect well with the spatial ones. Research on proto-Earth language have found FN finger words to be among the planet's most ancient and universal. The Proto-Indo-European root source of FINGER and PUNCH, *penkwe* (five), is a פ-נ *Phey-Noon* derivative where the *Het* has shifted from a prefix position before the PN sub-root to a suffix position after it.

Internal letter shifting of bilabials within Edenic only allows for פ *Pey/Phey* to shift with ב *Bet/Bhet*, since there are almost no words that begin with *Vav*, to give us a V or W sound. Of the various "building" *Bet-Noon* words that came up in Chapter 7 with BONES, one of them fits in well here in this family of spatial terms. That is *Bet-Yod-Noon*, בין BaiYN, BETWEEN. Remember that *Yod* is a "weak" letter, so this *Bet-Noon* word is related to the *Pey-Noon* clan. There is a בן BeN word without the *Yod*. This means a branch. As a biological offshoot, it recalls בן BeN (son). But purely as a physical extension, it involves directions and pointing. This is why we can bring in words like גפן GeFeN, vine, [sound 7], ענבה [A]yNaBHaH, berry, grape, grain [sound 16] inverted, and ענף [A]NaF, branch, bough [sound 11]. נוף NOAF means scenery in general, but specifically the boughs of a tree. *Noon-Phey* is [sound 9] inverted, with both נוף NOAFeF and הנף HeyNeF [sound 7] meaning to wave, swing or fan.

Other relevant P-N words are also N-P inversions. Some nasal-bilabials with the sense of turning directions are נפה NaPHaH, to winnow), הניף HayNeeYPF, to wave or fan and כנף K'NaPH, wing, (but literally "like a fan"). These are documented at the FAN entry. The Latin *vannas* (a winnowing fan) belongs here, but especially as the source of FAN [6], VAN [16] and WINNOW [23].

נ-ב *Noon-Bet* is POINTY enough to be considered an extension of this nasal-bilabial family, and ניב NeYBH in Semitic is a canine tooth. The pointy tip of a pen is a NIB. Sharp words like FANG, NIBBLE and NIP belong here. A NIPPLE isn't NIPPY or sharp, but it is defined as "a projection and protuberance" that belongs with the POINTERS. A sharper cognate of **NIP**PLE is NEB, the beak of a bird or the **NIB** or "the projecting end or point of anything" (*Webster's*).

We can now review our bilabial-nasal Sound Grid to mark the many English derivatives of the פ-נ *Pey-Noon* POINTERS. We have encountered several of them above, but there are many others to align with the appropriate sounds in the chart. As needed, check the *E-word CD* or *The Word* dictionary to check the etymons or cognates of any of these words.

BAN [1]	BEN [2]	BIN [3]	BON [4]	BUN [5]
FAN [6]	FEN [7]	FIN [8]	FON [9]	FUN [10]
PAN [11]	PEN [12]	PIN [13]	PON [14]	PUN [15]
VAN [16]	VEN [17]	VIN [18]	VON [19]	VUN [20]
WAN [21]	WEN [22]	WIN [23]	WON [24]	WUN [25]

[1] BANANA (a pointed, FINGER-like fruit, if not a nasalization) [BUNTING]; BANK [BENCH]. A BANNER yet waves, and points.

[2] BEN (mountain peak, from Irish); BENCH (like a river BANK, any spatial extension for walking, sitting, etc.); BEND (to turn). BEN (inner room, from Scottish is about interior space – like PEN, and from פנימה P'NeeYMaH (toward the inside, within).

[3] BIN (container) is another inner space. [PENETRATE]

[4] BONE is a distant relative via בין BaiYN, between. Whether BOUND for or by someplace, our *Pey-Noon* family is recalled.

[5] The buck-toothed BUNNY may be a reverse of ניב NeeYBH, canine tooth – the pointy or prominent tooth..

[6] FAN, FANG. (See the FAN entry below and the teeth above).

[7] To DEFEND is to FEND off or turn away an attack. A car's FENDER should be like a FENCE. In FENCING one parries or misdirects attacks. Direction is what *Pey-Noon* is about.

[8] A FIN is a pointy APPENDAGE, but the premier human POINTER is the FINGER. FINE hair or a FINE-toothed comb makes it clear that the point of FINE is minute, non-coarse, not, as published, a derivative of Latin *finis*, a limit – although a boundary might link up with our *Pey-Noon* extremities.

[9] Perhaps תיפן TeYPHeN, turn, is relevant to the flowing FONT and FOUNTAIN. Some reference books guess that these "fon" words came from a FINGER of water; that's fine, FINGER is certainly a pointing term.

[10] FUND and FUNDAMENTAL are bottom terms via Latin *fundus*; this is the opposite of our Pointer words meaning *the top* or *apex*.

[11] פנם PaNiM is a *face*. פני PiNey, occurring twice in the second verse in Genesis, refers to the surface. This is where façade words like a window PANE or a door PANEL come from.

When a camera PANS a scene, it POINTS to a **PANORAMA** in all directions. **PAN**IC involves running in all directions. PANIC also means a grass that points in all directions, and may link up to the PAN grass term many languages use for bread. It's a panic that some dictionaries say that PANIC is from the satyr PAN. Perhaps some desperate lexicographers think that this gentle, mythical creature (who did not predate bread words) played a frighteningly loud flute that made people run away.
PAIN is one of the sharply pointed words.

[12] A PEN **PENETRATED** clay tablets long before ink was invented. A holding PEN is interior (see פנים PiNeeYM, above), while a **PEN**NANT extends outwards (like the BANNER above). A **PEN**ULTIMATE line or a **PEN**DING case dangles like a hanging **PEN**DANT. A **PEN**INSULA is an almost-island; it is a finger of land pointing away from the mainland (suggests Norman Rowe). These halfway, swing words are pointing nowhere definite. They are from PeN (lest, maybe, it DEPENDS) – which scholars link to פנה PaNaH, to point. Male animals **PEN**ETRATE their mates with a PN anatomical word – but this is a family project. Welsh *pen* means top or head. Therefore, a PENDRAGON is king (top dragon), and the **PEN**GUIN means a creature with a white head or top.

[13] A PIN is a sharper PEN, see above. The tree of pin-point pine needles is the PINE. The Edenic pine is the ברוש B'ROASH, whose needles gave us BRUSH. Nonetheless, lexicographers place Latin *pinus*, pine tree, with words meaning resin (like PINE TAR). The emotional PINE, seen above, is strangely filed with PAIN under the invented Indo-European root *k(w)ei*, to atone. Latin *pinna* and a high pinnacle came up earlier.

[14] POINT needs no comment.

[15] See PUNCTUATE, PUNCTURE and PUNISH at entries like PUGNACIOUS, PENGUIN, and FIN.

[16] A weather VANE points to the four winds (directions or compass points). VANDAL and VANGUARD are at WANDER and PANE. VANISH covers the clearing away *Pey-Noon* terms. Clearing away area for a new road road, as in Isaiah 40:3, creates an important directional pointer.

[17] VENEER is a façade (like *Pey-Noon* face); VENERATE is another turning towards with desire; VENTILATE is what FANS do, waving with WIND.

[18] A VINE runs through some of the text above.

[19, 20] (There don't seem to be any VON or VUN words *in English*.)

[21] WANE and WANDER are here. The IE root of WAND means to turn.

[22] WEND and WENT are cognates of turning.

[23, 24] WINNOW was strongly related to the *Noon-Phey* FANNING words. The WING of a bird or a building points to a side. To WIN is traced to the IE root *wen* (to desire, strive for) echoing *Pey-Noon* terms of turning towards. WON is the past of Win. It is also what Mankind will have done when they lose the secular theory that words evolved randomly from gorilla grunts and gestures.

[25] One has to go to German for a WUN word, but *Wunsch* (desire) fits the WN sense and sound above.

The large *Pey-Noon*/PN Pointer Family was good to chart for its many sound variations within the same sense. It presented the one chance we have room for in this chapter to follow those variables, but other word families, that contain more adjectives than nouns, will offer us opportunities to see like-sounding antonyms, not just synonyms. Smaller families will reflect a more focused sound and sense, as the POINTER FAMILY can be overwhelming.

A *panama* is a compass (a pointer) in Hawaiian. Expanding Edenic-English word families to the wider family of Man would require a large book.

To illustrate how one of these bilabial-nasal Pointers pans out as an entry in the *E-Word CD* (the future *Edenics Dictionary* data base), here's the FAN entry:

FAN	NaFaH	*Noon-Phey-Hey*
NAWPH-AH	נפה	**[N-F —> FN]**

ROOTS: FAN is from Latin *vannus* (winnowing device), linked to IE terms of blowing. For the Edenic origin of FAN, point the *Noon-Phey* root backwards. נוף NOAF is to move back and forth, to swing, wave or fan. NaF is the Syriac. נפה NaPHaH is a FAN; נפה NeePaH is to winnow (requiring swinging in the wind); הניף HaNeeYF is to swing, wave or FAN (Exodus 35:22). נוף NOAF means landscape or scenery (Psalms 48:3); related to Aramaic NOAFAh (bough, branch). This entry clarifies that נוף NOAF refers to flora that wave or fan in the wind. Using the N-F sub root of fanning is nature's most prolific, uplifting fan, the bird's wing or כנף K'NaF (Genesis 1:21). כנף (K')NAF (wing) literally means "like a fan."

> **BRANCHES**: Related to the breeze-making of FAN, נפח NaPHa[K]H is (to blow, swell, breathe — *Genesis 2:7*). This is more than a match for IE root *pu* (to blow, swell), which is credited with EMPHYSEMA, PHYSO-, PREPUCE and PUSTULE. The same PN (NP, VN or WN) root appears in words like PNEUMA, PNEUMONIA, VENT(ILATE), WIND and WINNOW. Greek *pnein* and the IE root *pneu* mean to breathe; Germanic root *fneu* is to sneeze.

The wind must have blown the word *pniw* (to blow) to the Klamath Indians of Oregon. All the N-P and P-N fanners and blowers point to the large plosive-nasal family of POINTERS [POINT]. The four winds are the four directions. נפש NeFeSH is breath or soul (Genesis 1:30). *Nafas* is breath and *njawa* is soul in Indonesian (where J replaces S). "Breath" in Modern Greek is *anapnoe*, and in Swahili it is *pumzi* (akin to our PN terms).

Similar to the PN Pointer Sisters, we can stretch out just the double bilabial *Bet-Bhet* on the Vowel Rack, to get many related derivative words from a small theme suggested by just two Edenic *Bet-Bhet*/B-BH words. The two words are 1) אבוב ABOOBH, a hollow pipe or tube derived from jointed reeds or knotgrass, an extension of אבה AiBHeH, reed (Job 9:26); and 2) NiBHOOBH is hollow (Exodus 27:8).

The many derivatives can be classified by three kinds of pipes.
1. Pipes one blows air out of – BAGPIPES, the FIFE, and the OBOE
2. Pipes one sucks liquid into like a straw – as a BABY IMBIBING in PAP.
3. Other pipes – like the nasalized (extra M) BAMBOO, BOMB and PUMP.

In Spanish the water-pumping fireman is a *bombero*.

We shall limit the bilabials on the Vowel Rack to just BB, FF and PP.

BAB [1]	BEB [2]	BIB [3]	BOB [4]	BUB [5]
FAF [6]	FEF [7]	FIF [8]	FOF [9]	FUF [10]
PAP [11]	PEP [12]	PIP [13]	POP [14]	PUP [15]

[1] The BABE, BABY or nasalized *bambino* (Italian) suckles pap from papilla (nipples). The nasalized BAMBOO is a hollow reed and pipe borrowed from Malay. The suckling baby as drinker is established by Spanish *bebe* (baby) and *beber* (to drink). A *bebida* is a BEVERAGE.

[3] The young BIBER (drinker) IMBIBING from his mother's BIBB (faucet) often spits up and needs to wear a BIB. BIBLE and BIBLIO- words are from the reed that gave us PAPER. Egyptian PAPYRUS is not a better etymon than אבוב ABOOBH, but it IS further away from Israel.

[4] A BOB is a sucking calf. The baby at his BOOB TUBE is considered a BOOBY (idiot). *Bobo* is a fool is Spanish. Grown fools play with BOMBS. All bombs were prepared in pipes or shells for pipes or cannons.

[8] The only relevant word in this area is FIFE, worth the row of F's since the fife is such a patriotic PIPE.

[10] Hungarian *fuvola* is a flute; a fine reed-like derivative from אבוב ABOOBH for a wind instrument.

[11] PAP is the mushy baby food drawn in through the PAPILLA (nipples). PAPYRUS is the Nile hollow reed from which came PAPER.

[15] PUMP

The פ-ח Het-Pey family of covering

חפא K[H]aPHAh, to cover (II Kings 17:9), later, a cover or case; חופה K[H]OOPaH or חפה K[H]ooPaH, canopy, a bridal canopy (Joel 2:16); חפה K[H]aPHaH is to cover or veil, as in חפוי K[H]aFOOY, covered (II Samuel 15:30); חפיפה K[H]aPHeeYPHaH, covering (post-Biblical); חפף K[H]aPHaPH is to cover, protect, shield (Deuteronomy 33:12) and חפש K[H]oaPHeSH is an "outspread covering" (Harkavy) as for horseback riding (Ezekiel 27:20). The second subroot here is seen in פשה PaSaH, to spread (Leviticus 13:5). רחף RaK[H]aPH, to hover, as a mother bird covering her young (Genesis 1:2).

Built-in פ-ח *Het-Pey* antonyms of uncovering include יחף YaK[H]eF, uncovered, barefoot (Jeremiah 2:25), חפר K[H]aPHaR, to dig up [GOPHER] and a similar uncovering is חפש K[H]aPHaSH is to dig or search for (Proverbs 2:4). חפשי K[H]aPH'SHeeY, free, exempt (Exodus 21:2) may also be understood as not covered.

The BALL FAMILY – meaning: balled up

Sub-root ב-ל *Bet-Lamed*, B-L, bilabial-liquid; See *Word* entries: BABEL, BALE, BALL, COUPLE and GARBLE

Edenic family members include: בבל BaBHeL, Babel; בול BOOL, a lump, a wax seal for a letter; בלבל BiLBooL, confusion, mixture; בליל BiLeeYL, a mixture; בלל BaLaL, mix, confuse, stir; גבול G'BHOOL, border, where different territories meet; מבול MaBOOL, deluge, mixture of Earth's dryness and water; ערבל [E]eRBHaiL, to mix, confound; תבל TeBHeL, confusion, world. For ב-ל *Bet-Lamed*/BL strands intertwined in three grades of growing strength: 1) גבל GeBHeL, plait, braid; 2) חבל K[H]eBHeL, string, rope; 3) כבל KeBHeL, cable [CABLE].

Edenic variations of this bilabial-liquid sub-root include: הפיל HiPeeYLPOOR, to cast a lot; כפול KaPHOOL, double, folded; תפור TeePHOOR, sewing , two things together.

Reversing BL will LOB such BLUBBERY words at you as LUBRICATE and LABIAL.

The CUT FAMILY – meaning to cut

Every possible guttural-dental. See entries: ACUTE, CUT, CURT, HASTATE, SAXON and SUICIDE.

Both ג-ד-ע *Gimel-Dalet-Ayin* and ק-ט-ע *Koof-Tet-Ayin*, גודע GOD[A] and קטע QaDT[A] mean to cut off; חטב K[H]oDTa[V], to cut, hew (Deuteronomy 29:10); חתך K[H]aTahKH, to cut; Aramaic KahT is a sect, a special group cut away from others; קצב QaTSa[V], to cut off; קצה QeeTSaH, to cut off, קצע QeeTSay[A]h, to trim; קצר QaTSeR, cut down, harvest (Leviticus 23:10); חצה K[H]aT(S)aH, to halve (Exodus 21:35); קץ QaiTS, is the cut off or end [COAST]; Arabic *qadda* is "he cut lengthwise." Syriac has similar QD cutters.

More ח-צ *Het-Tsadi* cutters include חצב [K]HaTSaBH, to hew out; חצד [K]HaTSaD, to harvest; חצה [K]HaTSaH, to divide in two, separate, partition; חצי [K]HaTSeeY, half (Exodus 24:6) and the arrow, חץ [K]HaiTS [HASTATE].

The GRATE FAMILY – meaning: to scrape

Guttural-Liquid-Dental – Note: A word beginning with the same two root letters usually offers an evident family member, a sibling that has likely been recorded before. But a three-letter root that ehoes an Edenic word often offers much focused sound and sense. It might be a cousin, rather than a sibling, but could be carrying meaningful genetic material. See entries CARD, CHARACTER, GRADE, and SCRATCH.

קרד QayRaD, to scrape, curry; גרד GaRaD, to scrape, scratch (Job 2:8) have a shorter form in גרר GaRaR, to scrape, plane (I Kings 7:9). This GRR etymon is a fine source for

CURRY. קרצף QaRTSaiF is to curry. The Ten Commandments are חרות K[H]aROOT (graven) into the stone tablets in Exodus 32:16. חרט K[H]eReDT is a writing style (Isaiah 8:1). חרט K[H]aRaDT is to engrave or chisel; the חטים K[H]aRDT(OOMeeYM) or "magicians" of Exodus 7:11 are masters of hieroglyphics or scraped engravings.

צ-ל Tsadi-Lamed – SIDE words.

אציל ATSeeYL is an extremity (on the side – Isaiah 41:9); אציל AhTSeeYL is the wing of a building (Ezekiel 41:8); אצל ATSahL is to put aside (Numbers 11:17); אצל AyTSeL means side or beside ((I Samuel 20:41); הציל HeeTSeeYL is "he rescued," but this can now be better understood as "he put aside…out of harm's way [STEAL]; צל TSaiL is a shadow, which falls to a side. צלע TSeL[A]h is to incline to one side [LIST]

The CROWN FAMILY – meaning: horns and other cranial gear

Guttural-Liquid-Nasal – This is unusual for having one basic Edenic etymon (קרן QeReN, horn, extension), but a wide family of English spinoffs. See entries CORNER, CORNET, CORNUCOPIA, CORONA, and UNICORN.

The largest family of English derivatives of a single Edenic word involves ע-ב-ר Ayin-*Bhet-Resh*, עבר [O]BHaR (over in time or space), as seen in entries like ABERRATION, BEAR (to carry over), FUHRER, FERRY, and OVER. As often the case, there will be many more English words involved if the Edenic cognates appears in Greek and Latin prefixes and suffixes.

Speaking of fixes, *E-Word* entries are not based on two-letter sub-roots, even if Edenic word families are often extended by means of a molecule of meaning involving only two of the three root letters. One exception was made for a word of interest to Christian readers. The first part of this entry appears below:

(CRUCI)FIX	$aFaK[H]	*Samekh-Phey-Het*
(SU)FF-ahkh	ספח	[(S)FK→ FX]

ROOTS: For the first element of *CRUCI*FIX, see CROSS" The SUF*FIX* is from Latin *figere* (to fasten, fix). ספח $aFaK[H] is to join or attach. This term is translated "cleave"in Isaiah 14:1, where the friendship of Christians and others is prophesied to be a FIXTURE of the repentant, revived Israel:

But the Lord will pardon Jacob, and will again choose Israel, and will settle them on their own soil. And strangers shall join them and shall cleave to the House of Jacob.

דבק DaBHaQ is to attach, glue or join (Genesis 2:24). קבע QoBHaGH is to fix or drive in, the verb for fastening nails (confirmed in Aramaic-Syriac). The Torah observant Jew fulfils a commandment by affixing a parchment to his doorpost. The blessing made for this act uses this ק-ב-ע *Koof-Bhet-Ayin* verb. This ב-ע *Bhet-Ayin* form of our bilabial-guttural two-letter root makes painfully clear what the FIX of CRUCI*FIX*ION can refer to driving in nails. Bilabial-guttural-guttural antonyms (driving apart, instead of pinning together) include בקע BoQ[A]h, to cleave, split (Genesis 22:3) and פק PaQ[A]h, to split [PICK].

The very large families, like the Bilabial-Liquid-Guttural BREAKER FAMILY, deserve a treatment as detailed as THE POINTER FAMILY. This will have to wait for a larger book. To make your own Sound Grid, matching English words with their Edenic etymons, begin with the BREAK entry and follow the cross references.

One of many *E-Word* entries where a family is lined up for a group photo, is the Openers at PATIO:

PATIO	PaTaH	*Pey-Tahf- Hey*
PA-TAH	פתה	**[PTH]**

ROOTS: PATIO is an open space, now traced to Latin *patere* to open; the IE root is *pet* to (spread). הפיץ HayPHeeYTS is to spread, but PATIO deserves Edenic PT words meaning "open" – and there is a large family of these. First פ-ת *Pey-Tahf* words:

פתה PaTaH is to open wide; פתח PaTa[K]H is to open or begin (Deuteronomy 15:8); פתח PeTa[K]H is an opening (Genesis 18:1) [PASSAGE]; פתוח PaTOOa[K]H means open (Genesis 7:11). When a problem is knotty or twisted, פתיל P'TeeYL, one must solve or "open" it. פתר PaTaR (Genesis 40:16). [FUSE at PUZZLE] The overly naïve, tactless and open fool or simpleton is a פתי PeTeeY [FATUITY (A)].

A פ-ד *Pey-Dalet* word of opening, release and redemption is פדה PaDaH (Leviticus 27:27). Switching to פ-ת *Pey-Tet*: פטר PaDTeR is to let open, release, free (I Kings 6:35); פטר PeDTER is the womb opener or firstborn (Exodus 13:2). Switching to פ-צ *Pey-Tsadi*: פצה PaTSaH is to open a mouth or to set free (Genesis 4:11); פצח PaTSa[K]H is to burst or open. For the "wound," where skin is opened, פצע PeTS[A]h (Exodus 21:25). [PUTSCH]

The built-in opposite of all these bilabial-dental openers are similar sounding closed things. Nature's perfect enclosure is the egg, ביצה BaYTSaH. The opposite of the open PATIO is the closed house, בית BaYiT [BOOTH]. בית BaYiT also means "within" (Genesis 6:14).

An Edenic etymon or source word can have a prolific amount of descendants in English and all other languages. A good example is דרך DeReKH, way, manner, road [DIRECTION]. Only when split into two sub-roots, can one see how DIRECTION, to DIRECT, TRACK, TRACK and TREK, are related to both dental-liquid words like TIER and liquid-guttural words like REACH.

For its huge number of derivatives, עבר [A]BHaR, over in time and space [FERRY] and [OVER] also didn't need a large family of Edenic relatives. Try counting all the English words with prefixes like FORE- and PRE-, and the suffixes and stems like –FER, FER or PH + vowel + R.

Whether that family is a large or a small one, no divine Edenic word or divinely derived human word exists without a family. (Not counting made-up words like SONAR or brand names).

Chapter Nine Conclusion

Edenic etymons often morph into English words of similar sound and sense. But some knowledge of Edenics is required before one can successfully prosecute an Edenic paternity suit based on some old and often altered linguistic DNA. The key word of this chapter was family, related to the word familiar. But much effort was required to make English words from Edenic look and sound more familiar. Too many distant cousins were twice removed, requiring more patience on the part of readers who expect the exact semantic parallels provided by travel dictionaries. No, millennia after Babel-babble, things aren't that straightforward, and the family/familiar equation is less appropriate. The Edenic word for family seems more appropriate for the expansive diversity we've seen in these word families. The Edenic family is משפחה MiSHPaK[H]aH, from the root שפח SHaPHaK[H], to pour forth. The post-Babel derivatives appear to have poured forth from their Edenic source. When poured or dispersed over a Sound Grid, even a professor might mistake cognates as unfamiliar words.

Over millennia of conversation, of usage, there has been a semantic survival of the fittest. The words we now use to mean what they mean have sometimes strayed from a familiar family that can be easily uncovered with some linguistic genealogy. With Edenic research, words can come home again. Even clean-shaven words in Western outfits can be tearfully ingathered when a large clan is assembled in the arrival hall. Even if that young word sports a pierced navel and speaks only Valley or Hip-Hop, one great-uncle will recall a particular gait or posture from the family. Another great-aunt might recognize the voice of a long-lost sibling. "Unrelated" words will spill forth to the familiar … the more things change, the more they remain the same.

Chapter Nine ACTIVITIES

1. Assemble the BETS Family with several Edenic and English words with the bilabial-dental sound and the sense of surety and trust. Go to entries like AFFIDAVIT, BET, FAITH, VETO, VOTE and WEDDING.

2. VETO and VOID are the opposite of VOTE and FAITH. They are not linked by current linguistics. Document a case that reveals these as built-in antonyms within the same family, reinforced by Edenic antonyms of similar sound and sense.

3. There is a large CANE Family that rests on only a few ק-נ *Koof-Noon* and כ-נ *Khaf-Noon* Edenic words [CANE], [KEEN]. What are the thirty-plus English words that spilled forth from this guttural-nasal family, and how can a root meaning a cylindrical post mean things as diverse as a CANAL, CANDY and CANARY?

4. The CARVER Family gives a clinic on Letter Shifts. Document seven *guttural* and/or liquid and/or bilabial shifts in both Edenic words and their English descendants by following scratching, notching, engraving and carving terms at entries like CARVE, CLEAVER, GRAVE, and HARROW.

5. The Family CIRCLE has at its hub the Edenic עגל [E]GoL (circle), sub-root ג-ל *Gimel-Lamed*, as in גלגל GaLGAL, wheel. As you round up this family in entries like CAKE, CURVE and CYCLE, give several repercussions of the versatile *Ayin* being an unvoiced *vowel* or a guttural.

6. Explain how such different sounding and meaning words as APPEAL (to fall in supplication), FAIL, LAPSE, SLIP, SPILL, SLEEP, SLOPE and SLUMP might come from the same Edenic FALL Family. See entries like FALL, and SPILL.

7. BURN and FIRE are not even cognates in our dictionaries. See BURN and the Exodus 22:5 citation in the FIRE entry to record ten other words besides BROIL, BOIL, BLAZE, BRAISE, and assorted PYRES and CONFLAGRATIONS from

the ר-ע-ב *Bet-Ayin-Resh* source of the verb and noun FIRE. Not forgetting antonyms, add a few FRIGID words from FROST and SANGFROID.

8. The large PART Family includes a few examples of *metathesis* in the expansion of the bilabial-dental-liquids and bilabial-liquid-dentals seen in entries like BURST, PART, and SPREAD. Note examples in both Edenic and English.

9. There are many examples of metathesis and letter shifts among the members of the SYMBOL Family seen in entries like SIMULATION. There are at least four different spellings for Edenic words meaning likeness, image, allegory or picture. Characteristic of even such expansive families, a two-letter sub-root emerges. Here it is a fricative-nasal sound, like מ-ש *Shin-Mem*, best seen in שם SHaiM, name, essence. Which two very common English prefixes (from the Greek, loosely translated as with) allow us to add scores of SIMILAR English words to this family?

10. Families often have an extensive relationship to one another, especially if they compete for similar turf. It seems like hundreds of bilabial-guttural or guttural-bilabial English words meaning a CAVITY or a VACUUM derive from a set of Edenic etymons that wear the same reversible jacket. Go to entries like ALCOVE, CAB, CAP, CUP, CAP, and GOBLET, then BEAKER, BUCKET and VACATE. List several of the Edenic patriarchs in both camps, the most likely classical ancestors, and the clearest English descendants.

Chapter Ten

Animal Names – The Origin of Species Names

Introduction

Some have difficulty with the concept that in Edenic a word not only signifies a particular animal, but ALSO offers the meaning behind that name. The Edenic name always presents the essential uniqueness of that creature.

In all normal world languages, animal names have no meaning – outside of the sound one makes when a certain creature is recalled. "Horse" doesn't mean anything. Perhaps it once did, as the post-apes say, "gazillions of years ago," but the meaning is long lost now. Of course we don't mean descriptive names like "anteater" or "hound" (hunter).

Here in the garden of Edenics, is a world of restored meaning. Animal names like "horse" will have a meaning (see below) – but only in Edenic. Eventually, all lost meanings will be thus restored. But, once again, in a chapter rather than a large book, only a few score animal names can be discussed.

Why are there so few Edenic animal names, and so many hundreds in English? The history of species proliferation has much to do with it, a topic touched on below.

Judging from Genesis, dividing waters, time, the continents, etc. appears to the Creator's M.O. That signature *modus operandi* of the Lord, diversity, is clearly what this study of language after the Tower of Babel is all about. In no area of the natural world are we so filled with wonder at diversity than with the spectacular species diversity in zoology.

Just as language diversity didn't begin until ten long generations after the first recorded modern humans, Adam and Eve, there is good reason to think that animal species diversity did not explode exponentially until later. Many readers, it is hoped, have begun to take the Tower of Babel more seriously by now. If Noah's Ark is, likewise, far more than an ancient myth, it would figure that only a relatively small number of proto-species of animals fit in to the ark. Just as the original Tower of Babel spun off (traditionally) seventy ur-, super- or proto-languages from the one, original Edenic (which then continued to devolve into thousands of dialects), there may have been only one pair of ur-canine, super-dogs or proto-pups aboard the ark. At very most, judging from Biblical and proto-Semitic writings, there may have been wolves, foxes and jackals. All the scores of breeds of contemporary domestic dogs probably have a combination of genes from these first wild canines. Human diversity may similarly be traced to genes implanted in Noah's three sons. By now, of course, there are dozens of human sub-races and many hundreds of dog breeds. Even today, professional and amateur geneticists are trying to breed some special new plant or animal hybrid.

Considering the scenario above, there will not be Edenic animal words for later sub-species. There will be Edenic words describing such animals, however, because humans still use the original language program with which to think and coin new names. The terriers, for example, are too new for there to be an Edenic dog word behind them. (The צ-ר-א *Aleph-Resh-Tzadi* source of Latin *terra* words may be seen at EARTH.) The entry DACHSHUND also treats a newly bred dog's name. Typically descriptive in a utilitarian sense and with combined elements, DACHSHUND means badger-hound in German. The domestic dog does get called the generic כלב KeLeBh in Exodus11:7. The KLB term, ב-ל-כ *Khaf-Lamed-Bhet*, contains the LB element found in most global canines, see the chart on pages 349. Given the wide range of these LB critters (far beyond the Near East), it does appear that Adam named the animals (Genesis 2:20) and that the Edenic terms were "remembered" in some form after Babel by the linguistically divided migrant clans who would ultimately found peoples and nations.

The Bible's wolf word, זאב Z'Ai[V], is not behind any of the world's wolf or canine words. The Edenic כלב KeLeBH is more general, a generic word with staying power, fitting the canine's remarkable ability to CLEAVE loyally to humans.

זאב Z'Ai[V], on the contrary, fits the wolf more scientifically (and less attractively). Now added to the SEEP entry, the ז-ב *Zayin-Bhet* term refers to the characteristic saliva seeping from and frothing at the mouth of wolves. Thus their big bad rep. Even the tamest of canines has this species-wide trait. It wasn't just Pavlov who's dog had overactive saliva. In warm weather all canines SEEP, drip or sweat from the tongue of an open mouth.

Whether or not the Collie is linkable to the hind parts, to colliers or miners, or to the first two root letters of כלב KeLeBH, the JACKAL (via Persian) is certainly from the שוגל SHOOGHaL. This word has been mistranslated in the Bible as "fox" by certain British translators who worked for a king named James.

It may seem like this chapter has gone to the dogs, but certain points have to be made about why the most generic animal names in English, etc. do come from Edenic, while other Edenic animal names do not seem to have survived to linguistically range through the planet, adapting to foreign environments.

All Lost Dogs Find Their Way Home to Eden

KeLeBH = Canine	כלב	Change Reverse ← Metathesis Nasal M or N	Kahf Guttural (Throat)	Lamed Liquid (Tongue)	Bhet Bilabia l (Lips)
Language	canine				
Ainu	fox	extra M, M132)	Kim	eL	oPP
Arabic	dog		Ka	L	B
Aramaic	dog		Ka	L	Ba
Avestan	wolf	vehrka ←	aK	R	heV
Bulgarian	wolf	vilk ←	K	L	iV
Catalan	wolf			LL	oP
Cherokee	dog		Qi'	Li	
Chinese	wolf	lang ←	Gn	aL	
Cornish	wolf	blyth ←	H	tyL	B
Czech	wolf	vlk ←	K	L	V
Danish	wolf			uL	Ven
English	fox (f.)	vixen ←	X		iV
Fijian	dog		Ko	Li	
Finnish	dog		Koi	Ra	
French	wolf			Lou	P

Galician				Lo	Bo
Georgian	wolf		mG	eLi	
German	fox	Fuchs ←	sHC		uF
Greek	fox	alopex M231	X	L	P
Greek	wolf	lukos ←	soK	uL	
Hungarian	fox	roka ←	aK	oR	
Hungarian	wolf	farkas ←	saK	R	aF
Icelandic	wolf			uL	Fer
I-E root *	wolf	wlkwo ←	owK	Li	W
Italian	wolf			Lu	Po
Latin	wolf			Lu	Pus
Latvian	wolf	vilks ←	sK	Li	V
Lithuanian	wolf	vilkas ←	saK	Li	V
Mandinka	dog	wulo←	O	Lu	W
Maori	dog		K	uRi	
Malagasi	dog	alika ←	aK	iLa	
Maltese	dog		K	eL	B
Modern Greek	dog		sKi'	Los	
Norwegian	wolf		U	L	F
Old High German	wolf			woL	F
Old Norse source of whelp	whelp		wHe	L	P
Old Persian	wolf	varka ←	aK	R	aV
Polish	wolf	wilk ←	Ki	L	W
Portuguese	dog		C	Lio	
Portuguese	wolf			Lo	Bo
Quechua	dog	allqu ←	uQ	LLa	
Romanian				Lu	P
Russian, Slovn., Maced.	wolf	volk ←	K	L	oV
Samoan	fox			aL	oPe
Samoan	wolf	luko ←	oK	uL	
Sanskrit	wolf	vrika ←	aK	iR	V
Scottish	dog		Co	LLie	
Serbo-	wolf	vuk ←	Ku		V

Croat					
Sinhala	dog	bahl-laah ←	Haa	LLha	B
Spanish	wolf			Lo	Bo
Swedish	wolf		G	Ra	V
Tongan	dog		Ku	Li	
Yiddish	wolf			vuL	F
Zazaki/ Iranian	wolf	verg ←	G	R	eV

This last canine word also exists in the Mazandarani and Parthian languages of Ancient Iranian. Note: CUR (mixed breed dog) is thought to be a "growl" word [GROAN], but K-R "dog" words like Balochi/Iranian *gurkh (wolf),* Estonian *koer,* Finnish *koira* (above), Kurmanji/Iranian *gur (wolf),* Nepali *kukur* (dog) and Turkish **kurt** suggest that *Kahf-Lamed* should not be ruled out as the source of K-R canines. See COLLIE above.

[* I-E = Indo-European theoretical reconstruction]
The Edenic כלב KeLeBH, generic canine, and a combination of a KL and an LB element meaning all heart, need not be recalled by many peoples. The next most popular dog names appear to be linked to Edenic words meaning tame, domestic and hunt. [HOUND at HUNT]

Those antagonistically skeptical academics are wolves with sheepskins. Sure, all this would seem like an imaginative stretch IF scores of other animal names weren't similarly treatable, and IF tens of thousands of stray, orphaned and meaningless terms were not already tracked, corralled, tagged and led back to Eden.

Deciphering animal names is fun. It challenges our knowledge of Edenics, history and, of course, zoology. Since we have a pretty good idea of which animals were native to which lands, we also have a fairly good clue whether an animal name was borrowed from another culture (which thinks in Edenic anyway) or was actually "remembered" from the dawn of time, as per our Edenic or Biblical thesis. This thesis is another good reason to concentrate on animal names. The Bible specifically states that animals were named by the first zoologist, our common ancestor, Adam.

"...And Adam called out names to for all the beasts, for the birds of the sky and all the living things of the field..." – Genesis 2:20

As you visit the menagerie of meaning in this chapter, decide yourself if animal names reflect the profundity of Edenic. If you disagree, then the concept of Edenic and the Tower of Babel scenario seems like a foolish superstition, (or an occasionally useful fiction – like proto-Indo-European roots). If the animals were NOT named by some ancient Cro-magnon ancestor using a proto-Semitic tongue that we could call Edenspeak, then why do animal names like BUZZARD, GIRAFFE, GOPHER, HORSE and SKUNK only have meanings in Biblical Hebrew terms such as בז BuZ (looter, hawk), ערף GHoReF (scruff of neck), כפר KHoPHeR (digger), הרש HoReSH (plower) and צכן TSaKHaN (stinker)?

You may have already known that the SKUNK was an Algonquian term. There is no way that these American Indians of the Northeast (where skunks live) took Hebrew lessons. But Native Americans are children of Adam, no less than the Greeks or Celtics. Either all people have Edenic-based words, or none of them do.

The Bible places a profound emphasis on the naming of every person, place or thing. What's in a name? Everything, apparently. Semites are named for the son of Noah named שם SHeM (name). The name is the essence of the thing, its שמה SHayMaH or reputation. Commentaries have much to say about the meaningful name of each unknown person in a list of begats and begots or of each unknown, one-camel town on the journey to somewhere else. Reputation – or name – is something to live for or die for to a Shemite or Semite. No less than the Creator is referred to by the Jews as השם HaShem, The Name.

The name of an animal is therefore far more than an echoic device for identification. If the Chinese call a cat something like a meow (it sounds much like it) and if we've named a bird a Chickadee (after its call) – these are sure signs that the creature was not named at Eden by our first human ancestors. No Edenic animal names are merely echoic. No Biblical animals of a sub-species are named. All primordial animal names are generic. There are words for the generic bird and for the venerable raven. The raven is in the Noah saga, and is the Creator of Eskimo creation myth. But the Bible has no name for later blackbirds, like the crow or grackle. Long after Genesis, Psalms 147:9, will refer to "the children of the raven" – or the genetic sub-species that the raven genome was programmed to engender.

Because the ranges of animals are geographically specific, native animal names are as commonly borrowed as are foreign plant or food words. One might think that some Near Eastern animal names got borrowed, so it only looks like they came from some prehistoric, early Eden. But acknowledged, recognizable borrowings are rare – like the CAMEL. But how did the camel of the Andes, the LLAMA, get a name that reverses the גמל GaMaL (camel)? And how did the remote Tupi Indians of Brazil get *sainha* (tooth) from שן SHaiN, tooth [TINE] in the naming of their toothy fish, the PIRANHA? Disbelievers of the Edenic thesis will face many more questions in this chapter.

Edenic words are used by all nations to name (usually describe) their animals. But the actual, original Edenic animal names are not always "remembered" after the neuro-linguistic trauma of Babel. Even an animal as basic as the goat can be named something other that the Edenic guttural-dental. Even that language which does use the Edenic term has no clue as to why it is profoundly appropriate. It is interesting to note which peoples do and don't use Edenic animal names. Compare the quality of Edenic names with those in English. You will probably agree that Adam was number one.

Sample EDENIC animal names: < = from or named for…

Note that several Biblical animal names echo a fitting adjective that is changed by a *letter shift*.

RAM

איל AYiL (ram – Genesis 22:13)

< איל AYiL, leader, strength, as in אל AiL, power (Genesis 31:29) or אלם AiLiM, plural of "mighty" ones, like "powers that be." The Ram alpha male of the flock is an emblem of powerful leadership.

MOUSE

אכר AKHBaR, mouse

< אכל OKHeL, devour + בר BaR, grain [BARLEY]; the mouse is the grain destroyer or eater.

LOCUST
ארבה ARBeH, locust

< רב RaBH. a multitude [RIFE]. Their swarming in the many millions brings on a רעב R'[A]BH, famine [RAVENOUS].

LION
אריה ARYeH, lion

< רוע Roo[A]h, to shout, blast a war cry; the lion is the roaring creature [ARYAN].

HARE/RABBIT
ארנב ARNaBH or ארנבת ARNeBHeT, hare or rabbit

< ארן OReN, pine, fir tree [ELM] + ניב NeeYBH, tooth [NIB] so ארנב ARNaBH is the forest nibbler.

SHE-DONKEY
אתון A(S)OAN, she-donkey

< איתן AY(S)ahN, strong, or איתן AYTahN, as in to TONE muscles [ASININE].

BUZZARD
בז BahZ, hawk, any bird of prey or especially a carrion bird.

< בוזז BOAZeZ, plunderer [BUZZARD]. This bird mostly flaps its wings, unlike the mid-air balancing hawk or osprey of the entries below.

CATTLE
בקר BaQaR, large cattle are the cattleman's or BUCKAROO's major asset

One's "stock" is examined, בקר BaQeR, with every light of morning, בקר BoaQeR , to note every pregnancy or illness. Searching בקר BaQaR in the *E-*

Word CD will get you everything from AL**BACORE** tuna to CARIBOU (an M312 metathesis). The water buffalo of the Phillipines, the CARABAO, is also an M312 of בקר BaQaR. It is a Spanish spelling of the Malay *karbau.* You'll see many cow terms from בקר BaQaR in this chapter. [BUCKAROO] [CARIBOU]

בקר BaQaR also means to cleave or split, as in Arabic *baqara,* and these larger beasts do the ground breaking or plowing. The בקר BaQaR of the Andes is a cameloid like the llama. The Andean ALPACA is just *paco* in native Peruvian. Their staple cattle is another bilabial-guttural form of בקר BaQaR, with the *Bet*/B shifted and the *Resh*/R dropped.

GOAT

גד GiDi, goat

< גדד GiDuD, troop…group…the premier herd creature [GATHER] [GOAT]

CAMEL

גמל GaMaL, camel, work animal of the Middle East

< עמל GHaMaL or עמל [A]MaL, work [AMERICA]

FISH

דג DaG, fish

< דק DaQ, thin, the streamlined creature [HADDOCK]

FLY

זבוב ZiBHooBH, fly

< shoo it away, and it makes a סבוב $iBHooBH, circle… and it will שב SHaBH, return. You may recognize the בעל B'[A]L or lord of the flies: *Belzebub.* [SWIVEL]

GIRAFFE

זמר ZaMeR, giraffe (Deuteronomy 14:5)

< זמר ZaMeR is to prune or pluck off botanical material (Leviticus 25:4) – like this creature does from tall trees.

WOLF

זאב Z'EBH, the wolf (Judges 7:25), is related to the זב ZahBH, the person with an emission dripping from his body that makes him ritually impure (Leviticus 15:25) and to the land "flowing" with milk and honey (Exodus 3:8). All canines uniquely drip saliva. The salivating, seeping wolf gave us the expression "hungry as a wolf." Yes, food stimulates the flow, but dogs sweat through their mouths. The "sip" in Mississippi is one of the global SEEPERS that one finds at the SEEP entry.

GRASSHOPPER

חגב K[H]aGaBH, grasshopper, locust (Numbers 13:33)

< חג K[H]aG, circle or cycle + גבב GaBHaBH, to gather, or together. This is "the cyclical gathering or swarming creature."

DONKEY

חמר K[H]aMoR, donkey

< 1) חמר K[H]AMooR, heavy, strict, serious in its behavior, especially as compared to the spirited horse.

< 2) The חמר K[H]aiMeR, material it lugs to a work site. The M-R of this horse-family term gives us MARE, and the M-L of MULE.

CAT

חתול K[H]aTOOL, cat is Edenic (via Aramaic), but is not a Biblical Hebrew word. The cat is named for חתל K[H]eeTooL, swaddling (Ezekiel 16:4), for the way it wraps itself up in repose.

LAMB

כבש Ke[V]eS, lamb

< כבש Ka[V]aSH (to subdue). The docile lamb doesn't have to be cowed into submission [OVIS]. The lamb is subdued, passive. The same verb can name a creature which actively subdues and captures its prey, see אכביש [A]KaBHeeYSH, spider, below.

DOG

כלב KeLeBH, dog

< כל Kol (all) + לב LeBH (heart). Unlike cats, this "all-heart" creature always shows its feelings, and CLEAVES loyally to its owner. All-heart infers courage too, or lion hearted as לבי LaBHeeY is a lion. [LOBO]

SNAKE

נחש NaK[H]aSH, snake – is source of the nasalized ANACO(N)DA. The *Shin*-to-D shift, like the animal, is not European. N-K-S reverses to the S-N-K of SNAKE. נחש NaK[H]eSH means to divine, with a HUNCH (a metathesis of *Noon-Het-Shin*) because the snake cannot see or smell, but hunts with heat detection. [SNAKE] More snake magic below.

ANT

נמלה NiMaLaH, ant (Proverbs 6:6)

< נמל NaMaL, porter…the carrying creature.

HORSE

סוס OO (horse)

< A few animals play, but the horse (especially the gamboling colt) exemplifies joyous movement. SaS is to rejoice in Deuteronomy 30:9, and ZOOZ means get moving! – imperative – (see the SUS in PEGASUS). The sense of the double-*Samekh* name is revealed when we shift fricatives from the double-*Sin*.

FOWL

עוף [O]WPH, fowl, any flying creature

< ע-ו-פ *Ayin-Vav-Phey* is to fly **up**wards. A common feature of fowl is eggs. This is why the French egg is *oeuf* and where **OVARY** came from. [AVIATE]

HAWK

עזניה [A]hZNiYaH, hawk (Leviticus 11:13) is a wide-winged bird that אזן AZeN, balances (spelled with an *Aleph*, not an *Ayin*) in the air currents.

SPIDER

עכביש [A]KaBHeeYSH, spider (Isaiah 59:5)

< the initial *Ayin* is a "weak" prefix letter, so the real root is כ-ב-ש *Kahf-Bhet-Shin* 1) to subdue – active, not passive like the כבש KeBHeS above, or 2) to imprison). For the Edenic source of this genus in English, see ARACHNID.

ASP, VIPER

עכשוב [A]KHSHOO[V], viper, asp (Psalms 140:4)

< like the *Ayin* name above, drop the *Ayin* to see the root: a variant spelling of כשוף KeeSHOOF (magic, charms). As with נחש NaK[H]aSH (snake) above, these creatures have the unique neurological ability to be hypnotized "magically" by Western snake handlers or Eastern snake charmers.

BAT

עטלף [A]DTaLeF, bat (Leviticus 11:19)

< ע-ט *Ayin-Tet*, cloaked [COAT] + ט-ל *Tet-Lamed* [TILE] The two sub-roots combined to name this creature deserve separate study.

   1) ע-ט *Ayin-Tet*: Those who translate the עיט GHaYiDT as a vulture may be right, in that these ע-ט *Ayin-Tet* creatures [COAT] and the עטלף GHaDTaLeF, bat, are uniquely wrapped or draped in their wings when in repose. In Edenics, the best approach is to combine both sub-roots, giving us both the ע-ט *Ayin-Tet* sense of a coat of hide and the ט-ל *Tet-Lamed* theme of covering up. For an alternate translation of the עיט GHaYiDT, and its Biblical citation. [KITE]

   2) ט-ל *Tet-Lamed*: The resting bat is wrapped in its טלת DTaLiT, prayer shawl wings, covered up like a hoof (טלף DTeLeF). [TILE]

SCORPION

עקרב [A]QRaBH, scorpion, any crustacean

< קרב QRaBH, engagement, battle – for cantankerous creatures like the armored helmet crab. [CRAB] French *ecrevisse* (source of the Anglicized CRAYFISH)

was given this Edenic name, fitting for a similar creature with an exoskeleton and an exposed קרב QeReBH, stomach. [CRAW]

MULE

פרד PeReD, mule

< פרוד PaROOD, se**parate** or APART [SEPARATE]

The פ-ר-ד *Pey-Resh-Dalet* root is Edenic, but this mateless, sterile and forbidden mix between horse and donkey was not named by Adam. This beast, therefore, does not appear in the Bible until II Samuel 13:29. Its Hebrew name is like the Arabic term for an odd number, *fard*, since the sterile mule is indivisible. Arabic *farad* means single. This didn't prevent the PRD mule from naming the German horse *Pferd*.

VULTURE

פרס PeRe$, vulture

< פרס PeRe$, spread, referring to its wide, spread-eagled wingspan.   The OSPREY is a buzzard or fishing eagle with a wingspan three times its height. Its name is thought to come from Latin *ost-fragga*, bone-breaking, but all predators break bones, and this animal is more likely an M231 metathesis of פ-ר-ס *Pey-Resh-Samekh*. [DISPERSE]

BUTTERFLY

פרפר PaRPaR, butterfly

< פרפוף PiRPOOR, to twitch or flutter (Job 61:12). The Tagalog *paruparo* is one of so many similar exotic butterflies netted by Edenists, that the פרפר PaRPaR belongs here – even though, as an animal name, it is not in the Bible.

TURTLE

צב TSaBH, turtle

< צב TSaBH, covered wagon… the living mobile home creature.
Biblical citations for both the *Tsadi-Bhet* animal and vehicle are at "TOP."

DEER

צבי TSiBHeeY, deer, gazelle, hart, stag – this BEAST in Deuteronomy 14:5 has been translated may things in the deer family

< צבי TSiBHeeY, beauty, glory. The reader who has mastered metathesis can see both the BEAUTY and the BEAST in this name when the *Bet/Bhet* is put in front of the *Tsadi* (TS or often ST).

SHEEP

צון TSOaN, sheep or goats, small cattle (Genesis 13:5)

< צא TSAi, go out… creatures who go out to pasture, and while the cows will come home by evening, sheep and goats are צע TS[A]h'ah or צען TS[A]oN, plural, "wander for plunder" (*Lexicon*). That is, they "wander" (Jeremiah 48:12 – KJV) for grazing and get lost without shepherding from sheepdogs or goatherds.

BIRD

צפור TSiPOAR, bird

< several characteristic צ-פ *Tsadi-Phey* traits, including: chirping, spying, floating, hiding, being covered (with feathers) and having a talon. They are spelled out below at the SPARROW entry.

APE

קוף QOAPH, ape, monkey (I Kings 10:22)

< KooF (eye of needle); the monkey is striking for its human-like head or *Kopf* (German, Yiddish)

< כפת KePHeT, head of a pillar) [CAPITAL] At this entry it will be clearer that *Koof-Phey* ק-פ is related to various "head" words and to APE. The Darwinists cannot enjoy a Biblical source for a monkey.

HEDGEHOG

קפוד QeePOAD, hedgehog and related critters (Isaiah 14:23). The same ק-פ-ד *Koof-Pey-Dalet* term means contracted in Syriac, and so it refers to those creatures who roll themselves together.

SEAGULL

שחף SHaK[H]ahF, seagull

< it circles (ק-פ *Koof-Phey*) the shore (קוף K[HOAF), to שקף SHaQaF (SCOPE out) the scene of its SCAVENGING. More on this source of SCAUP, seagull, at SCAUP and SCAVENGE.

LIZARD

שממית SHiMaMeeYT, lizard (Proverbs 30:28)

< שמם SHaMaM, poison; Aramaic SuM, poison

HE-GOAT

שעיר Sah[E]eYR, he-goat, Pan-like satyr or demon (Isaiah 13:2)

< שעיר S[A]eeYR, hairy (Genesis 27:11), and other ר-ע-ש *Sin-Ayin-Resh* terms meaning rage and horror. Esau embodies all three of these, is called and is placed in שעיר S[A]yeeYR/Sair, and is like the twin he-goat banished to Azazel. [SEROW] (a goat antelope of Tibet).

JACKAL

שועל SHOO[A]hL or שעל SHOOGHahL, jackal, wild dog, mistranslated as "fox"

< שול SHeOOL is cough; in other words, "the barking creature." [JACKAL]

ROCK-BADGER

שפן SHaPHaN, rock badger (Psalms 104:18) is extremely wary and is largely שפון SHaPHOON, hidden.

SERPENT

שרף SaRaPH, serpent

< its venom burns or שורף SOARaiPH [SERPENT]

The שרפם SeRaPHiM, angelic Seraphs, burn with spiritual fire. This is why Buddhist monks wear SAFFRON, to appear as though they were (spiritually) on fire. SERPENT has the same SRF sequence as שורף SOARaiF (to burn), while for SAFFRON one must employ a M132 metathesis.

OX

שור SHOAR, ox

< solid as a שור SHOOR (wall), this creature instinctively knows how to plough in a straight line, or a שורה ישר SHOORaH YaSHaR – sources of SHEER and SERIES [TAURUS]

TURTLEDOVE

תור TOOR, turtledove

< this pigeon-like bird TOURS but circles home to roost. For the source of the confusing "turtle" element of TURTLEDOVE, see TOUR and TURTLEDOVE for more avian circuitry.

CATERPILLER

תולע TOALGHah

< a caterpiller or thread-spinning worm, related to Biblical words for silk and scarlet. With the ת *Tahf* pronounced as a *Sahf* you can hear SILK. This insect is not merely a רמה ReeMaH, worm – "the lowly creeper" [WORM]. The ת-ו-ל-ע *Tahf-Vav-Lamed-Ayin* is about threads and suspension – תלה TaLaH is to suspend. [ATLAS] This creature's name means "the suspender." These worms dangle from tree limbs, from thin lines of stringy secretions. In Isaiah 41:14 sloppy translators call the תולע TOALGHah a "worm;" it is רמה ReeMaH that is the source of WORM. Non-poets rendered the phrase "fear not, thou worm Jacob" for the תולע TOALGHah without depicting Israel as a tiny, vulnerable insect whose existence is hanging by a thread.

WHERE DID THE ENGLISH ANIMAL NAMES COME FROM?

According to the "bow-wow theory", all words are echoic, some grunting caveman's attempt to capture the essence of a thing by its sound. Despite the godless logic of this theory named for animal sounds, there are no dog words like bow-wow, or cows named moo-moos, etc. The chickadee and the Chinese "meow" cat word, mentioned earlier, are rare exceptions.

A larger set of animal names are clearly descriptive, like the grasshopper or hippopotamus (Greek for river horse). For the Edenic source of such names, one has to look up entries for the component words, like GRASS, HOP at KIBITZ, and certain horse words, like HIPPO, at HOOF. Most of the older, more generic animal names have origins that are based on meanings, even if those meanings have been lost for millennia. Latin or Spanish speakers have forgotten why the beaver was named *castor*. In Edenic, קצור QaTSOAR means to cut down plants, or to harvest. Is there a better name for the beaver than "the harvester?"

The more we salvage long lost meaning, the more we know that the "bow-wow theory" is for the dogs. Of course, the world's oldest and most widespread etymological text is the last place that a historical linguist would look for meanings behind animal names, but Genesis 2:20 relates that "Adam called out names for all the beasts, for the birds of the sky and all the living things of the field..." Let us see if Biblical Hebrew offers any insights into animal names of unknown origin and meaning.

Examples of English Animal Names from Edenic

(This segment was based on earlier essays, and many English animal names do reflect Edenic animal names – so please pardon some repetition.)

Unlike the ANT as nature's porter (see נמלה NiMaLaH at the Edenic animals above), the English word ANT is merely a nasal shift from M-T cognates like EMMET, MAGGOT and MITE. Instead of Adam's effective description, these insects are merely named for Middle Dutch *mite* (small). These words still had to be named in Edenic, because all humans still think in Edenic. But Dutch smallness or English MOTE, ultimately from the Edenic מעט Mi[A]DT, small)and מעוט MeeGHOODT, a small amount. MITE doesn't carry the same weight as Adam's ANT as a porter name.

The carrion-eating BUZZARD is traced only as far back as Old French *busart*, a word without apparent cognate or meaning. In Edenic, בז BahZ means a hawk and בזה BeeZaH means spoils or booty (as stripped from the war dead). בזז BoZeZ, like our BUZZARD, means the plunderer or looter, while a בזיר BahZeeYR is a falconer. Here, the (secretly Edenic) name does seem worthy of Adam, even if the etymology typically offers no meaning for the animal's name. Unlike the predatory EAGLE, the BUZZARD is merely a scavenger who emBeZZles WaSte or BooTy. (These BZ, BT and W-ST words are related to our ז-ב *Bet-Zayin* family of words of plunder). The Kiowa plains Indians named this same bird a *bosen* for the same reason, even if that reason was forgotten millennia later.

And where might the name EAGLE come from? Perhaps from 1) אכל *OaKHeL*, to destroy or consume (with the eagle being one of nature's deadliest predators) and/or 2) עגל [A]GeL, circle, from the characteristic spiraling of predatory birds. The GULL may come from this same Edenic source, even though flocks of gulls fly in wide circles, not tighter spirals. גל *GaL* also means wave, and no creature rides the waves better. [CYCLE] [GYRE]

Like the tale of blind men describing an ELEPHANT, this mammoth but highly trainable giant has a many-sided EMeTology (etymology) – but all from א-ל-פ *Aleph-Lamed-Phey*. Forms of א-ל-פ *Aleph-Lamed*-Peh, אלף *Aleph*, mean more than just the primary or Alpha Hebrew letter. אלף *Aleph* also means 1) an ox (Jeremiah 11:19), any large cattle; 2) training (Proverbs 22:25) and taming animals; and 3) champion or chief (Genesis 36:43), *lp* in Ugaritic. All of these meanings combine in a powerful, well-trained, ox-like large beast that best suggests the ELEPHANT (*elephas* in Greek). Many non-Israelis learn Modern Hebrew at an אלפן *ULPaN* (training school). If you haven't taught high school, you may not like the *Aleph-Lamed-Phey* domestication/training term of animals as applied to teenagers. The French elephant is spelled just like the English, and after *elephant* in many French dictionaries comes *eleve*, student, and other training or rearing terms from א-ל-פ *Aleph-Lamed*-Peh. A reversal of ElePH may occur in the Finnish word for student: *oppilas*. [ALPHABET]

The violent robbers of the animal world include the relentless FERRET, linked to the Latin word *furis,* robber. Other etymologies try to connect the FERRET to the bilabial-liquid root of carrying seen at FERRY. The robber of Edenic is the P-R-T or FRT of רייץ *PaReeYTS* [PIRATE]. PREDATORY beasts, from a huge RAPTOR to a small REPTILE are 1) bilabial-liquid-dental terms from a 213 metathesis of the פ-ר-צ *Pey-Resh-Tsadi*

FERRET-PIRATE term or 2) from an M312 of the ט-ר-פ *Tet*-Reph-*Phey* of טרף DToRePH, prey – see the bestial tearing, ripping rapine at TROPHY.)

If you think the GIRAFFE is a strange animal, check out its weird given etymology. French *girafe* and Italian *giraffa* are said to be a corruption of Arabic *zirafah*. The trouble is that no such root exists in Semitic. The etymon or source word is meaningless is Arabic too, and a G from a Z shift should have been too strange to print. Using the emetology of Edenics instead of etymology, one could salvage *zirafah* as a metathesis of Edenic צואר [T]ZaV'AhR, throat.

While Adam or any ancient human would do well to call the GIRAFFE a "neck" creature, it is the back of the neck, not the front, or throat that captures the essence of a giraffe. The Edenic term stressing the GIRAFFE's prominent back of the neck or (S)CRUFF of the neck is ארף OReF, more correctly pronounced with a guttural as ערף GHoReF. The ע-ר-פ *Ayin-Resh-Phey* in "stiff-necked" is seen at the SCRUFF entry.

Now we've got the perfect sound and sense for GIRAFFE, since ערף GHoReF means the scruff of the neck. Like SCARF, SCRUFF is a neck word whose initial S is non-historic. (Any word with more than 3 root letters in Hebrew or any language is carrying extra baggage around the root, or involves compound roots). These CRF neck words come from Biblical Hebrew ערף GHoReF (neck) just like the CRAVat (necktie) [GIRAFFE]

There's nothing wrong with "throat," but it better fits creatures more delicate than the GIRAFFE. A related ג-ר *Gimel-Resh* term, גרן GaRoN (throat, neck) gives us other long-necked animals, like the CRANE, EGRET and HERON, along with neckwear like the GORGEOUS GORGET, the throaty GROAN of a CROONer, the extension of a building CRANE, and the GARGLING of a GOURMET GARGOYLE.

Returning to animal names and addressing the interchangeable C/G/H/K sounds above, both the Edenic ע *Ayin* and the ג *Gimel* are gutturals that have the versatility of the shifts we learned earlier. The *Ayin* can harden to make the hard C of both Latin *corvus* (raven) and French *corbeau* (raven). The *Ayin* can also soften in the Anglo-Saxon *hraefn* (raven). Can these different RAVEN words in Indo-European be understood as birds of a feather, distant cousins separated since birth at Babel but linked by a common Semitic ancestor? The Edenic raven is the ערב [O]aRai[V] (*Ayin-Resh-Bet*) [RAVEN]

Etymologists don't have to dig far to get true word origins, but Eurocentrics will not consider Semitic. The prolific digger among American rodents (and net surfers) is the GOPHER. The given guess in our dictionaries is an attribution to French *gaufre* (a honeycomb or waffle). Those who dig for a true source will consider Hebrew כפר KHoPHeR (digger).

Now a HORSE is a horse of course, and of course there is no known meaning for this term. It doesn't relate to the German horse *Pferd*, a knock-off of the Edenic פרד PHeReD (mule) or to the Latin *equs* (an audible echo of Hebrew עקב [A]Qe[V] – heel or HooF. [HOOF] The mystery unraveled when it was noticed how similar HORSE is to HEARSE. A HEARSE is a horse-drawn funeral wagon named for an elaborate plow. To plow is ש-ר-ח *Het-Resh-Shin*. Unlike their Continental forbears, the British plowed with horses instead of oxen. The horse was the plower, and plower in Edenic is חרש [K]HoReS[H]. [HORSE]

The Americans continued the awkward tradition of plowing with a horse, which needs blinders and constant attention. The divinely created plowing animal is clearly the שור SHOAR (ox), which innately knows how to plow a שור SHuRa ישר [Ya]SHaR (straight row or a SHEER SERIES). True, the name "ox" doesn't sound like the שור SHOAR, but Aramaic (also post-Babel, despite many Edenic roots) consistently corrupts the Edenic *Shin* to a T. Aramaic TOAR (ox, bull) seems to have given Latin *taurus* (bull) which later became Spanish *toro* – [TAURUS] [SHEER]

The GOAT and the KID derive from the Edenic גדי GiDeeY (young goat) and the "K[H]ad **GaD**ia," the Aramaic scapegoat of the Passover song. גדוד GiDooD is a troop, as the גדי GIDeeY is the proverbial flock animal. אגד EGeD, the large Israeli bus company, means a union or a GaTHering of individuals. A HERD or עדר [E]DeR/GHeDeR of goats (note the metathesis) are gathered by a goatherd into a גדר GeDeR, fence, sheepfold – source of GUARD and GARD[EN] (another metathesis). A

Slavic city is a GRD term. So, we could even skip to LeninGRAD, once you see that the D and R have swapped places, and know that ancient Eastern European towns were built behind the GRATE-like GRID of a גדר GeDeR or stockade.

While the Danish *ged* (goat) is closer to our GD etymon than the English terms GOAT and KID, we have to go to a related guttural-fricative term, עז [A]Ze or GHaZe (male goat) to see the Edenic origin of *koza* (the goat in Slavic, Hungarian, Turkish and Modern Greek). It's no problem that we have to reverse GZ to *Ziege* for the German goat.

Reversing the GD root will get us another animal that lives in groups, the דג DaG or fish. Unfortunately, the English word FISH, from the Latin *pisces*, fell out of step with its Edenic ancestor, with someone comparing fish to the shape of the foot. So, both the fish SOLE and the foot SOLE are from the פסס PeSuS. רגל ReGeL, is step or PACE in Hebrew or the Aramaic *PaSiSa*. The Indo-European root for fish, however, is the very דג DaG-like *dhghu*. This reconstructed root is the given source of our ICHTHY (fish) words from Greek *ikhthus* (fish). Here the dental-guttural of the prehistoric ד-ג *Dalet-Gimel* is merely reversed.

More familiar DG creatures in or out of the GADOID (a family of fish) group include the HaDDoCK. דגה DaGaH is the whale of Jonah. The DK Polynesian version of ד-ג *Dalet-Gimel* is famous because of Moby **DiCK**. The Polynesian whale name is closer to דגה DaGaH than the Russian *kit* (whale) or the English CETACEAN (whale). In these two, ד-ג *Dalet-Gimel* is reversed again. This is because the whale name in older languages like the Greek *ketos* and Latin *cetus* have also reversed the Edenic dental-guttural. But their recognizable names for these fishlike mammals reinforce the concept that the דג DaG and דגה DaGaH were named for their streamlined shape. [HADDOCK]

The COD and **CUTTLEFISH** are not as חד K[H]aD, thin or as streamlined, and were named, instead, for the Edenic bag word. כד KahD is the leather water bag of Genesis 24:15 rendered "pitcher" by King James' 17th Century Englishmen. [CADDY]

While most animal names around the world have no known cognate, meaning or origin, note the large family of terms one can relate to SPARROW once we trace it to the Edenic צפר TSiPoR, bird. Now that we can work in a language of divine order, instead of human chaos, we will have many meaningful tie-ins to צ-פ *Tsadi-Pey* birdness. These include: צף TSaPH, float, צפה TSaPHaH, to waylay, watch – source of SPY, צפה TSaPHaH, covered, as in feathers – source of TOP, צפר TSaPHaR, to rise early, to whistle, hoot or honk – source of ASPIRANT, צפצף TSiPHTSooPH, chirp, and צפורן TSiPoReN, talon. There are even more at the SPARROW entry and its cross references.

צפצף TSiPHTSooPH, chirp is cited as proof that Hebrew animals names are merely echoic or onomatopoeic. It is clear that these linguists missed the other four צ-פ *Tsadi-Pey* words. Affect a bilabial shift of that פ *Pey* to ב Bet, and we get צבור TSiBOOR, community. Groups of congregating, singing birds and flocks of worshipers would sound similar in a language of Creation. The SPARR[OW] would seem to be the only SPR bird in English, but this creature ranges globally, and it is not surprising that the Indo-European generic root for birds is *sper*.

The lack of LEOPARDS in today's Middle East doesn't mean it can't be successfully tracked by a well-armed Edenicist. Leo + pard should mean "spotted lion." The LEO part sounds like a R/L liquid shift from ארי AReeY (lion). But the Latin *leo* (lion) seems to have dropped a *labial* (f,v,b,w) seen in the lion terms of Slavic (*lyef*), Scandinavian (*lev*), German (*Lowe*), and Dutch (*leeuw*). So the Edenic big cat we hunt is the לביא La[V]eeYE, lion. [LEOPARD]

If the LEO in LEOPARD means "lion," then we would expect the PARD element to mean "spotted." Greek *pardos* (simply defined as "panther") doesn't speak to the spots of the leopard, though, and a "lion-panther" is a typically inane etymology from our clawless, clueless dictionaries.

If we catch any scent of the sound and sense of P-R-D spots, we can continue our hunt for the true meaning of PARD. We don't precisely need a P-R-D. Armed with our knowledge of letter shifts and more, we only need to get close. Some promising "spot" words are Cornish and Celtic terms like *bruit* and *brith* (speckled), along with English

BLOT and BLOT[CH]. B-R-T or B-L-T is the same *plosive*-liquid-dental sequence as the P-R-D we seek. Now, can we follow these tracks to a Biblical source for PARD? The spotted and mottled animals of Jacob's dream were *Bet-Resh-Dalet*, ברד B'RooD in Genesis 31:10. PARD turns out to be closer to our Edenic etymon than to our British clues. Arabic speakers routinely pronounce P as B, as they have no letter P. Early Hellenic (pre-Greek) speakers may have done the opposite. They came to call this לביא La[V]eeYE – ברד B'RooD or spotted lion a LEOPARD.

The Sanskrit lion name is seen in the name Singapore (the lion city). The "sing" element means lion, and the "pore" element means city (see ברה BiRaH, capital city, at BARRIO.) More typical of animal names, the Sanskrit lion is not named after an Edenic lion word, but for something characteristically leonine – in this case the lion's roar. שואג SHOAEhG means roar in Edenic. Nasalize (extra N) שואג SHOAEhG (roar) and you get SH+N-G or "sing."

For other English animal names, see entries like the following: ARCHITECT (for the designing spider or ARACHNID), ARREST (for rooster), ASP, BISON, BULLY (for bull), BRIGHT (for bear and beaver), BUCKAROO (for cow to caribou), CLAM (A), EIGHT' (for octopus), FUNGUS (for sponge), KITE (includes the *nasalized* condor), GIBBON, GNAW (for gnat), HURRY (for hare), HYOS(CYAMINE) (for hog, hyena, sow and swine – or even the Basque pig, *zerri*), JINX (for pigeon), LEECH, MILL for ML soft words like the soft-shelled invertebrates or MOLLUSKS, ORIOLE, PYTHON, SCALLOP, SERPENT, SQUIRREL, TOUCAN (includes the turkey and the TK-reversed cockatoo – from the Biblical parrot or תוכי TOOKeY) and WAIL (for owl, as the owl is the vocal אבל O(V)eL, mourner, of the animal kingdom?). There's a duck at TEAL. The ZOO entry depends on short *Zayin* words of movement, and animation is what "animals" were named for.

The FLEA is so universal, that it gets a separate chart in the introduction to the *E-Word CD Dictionary*, and had a sequence of PowerPoint slides in the early Edenics slide show and printout booklet (see *edenics.org*). The world's words for flea demonstrate letter shifts (and metathesis) in dozens of languages as it is spun off or diversified from the Edenic flea. There are many animal-related words, like BEAK, CRAW, FUR, HERD,

HOOF, HORN or TAIL to be searched for in the data base. For non-English animal names, use your growing ability to think like a prehistoric descendant of Adam. For example, hunt for EEL words in the SNAKE entry.

Animal Names Postscript

When Hebrew came back to life after millennia in hibernation, many new words, including animal names, had to be coined. In looking for a name for the non-Biblical crab, the creators of Modern Hebrew looked to the German crab or *Krebitz*. Despite the fact that crabs don't scratch, the German word is linked to a root of scratching and sawing. The academic guardians of Modern Hebrew then sought a word of similar meaning, so the scratchy Biblical Hebrew סרט $aRaDT (source of SERRATED) was used to create the Modern Hebrew crab word, סרטן $aRDTaN.

Since Biblical animals can apply for an entire species or genus, a hard-shelled creature like the עקרב [A]QRaBH (translated merely as "scorpion") was a better CRAB word to consider for both sound and sense. Even the Italian cockroach, the *scarafaggio*, is from ק-ר-ב *Koof-Resh-Bhet* – see COCKROACH, CRAW and (S)CARAB. קרב QRaBH means battle, and קרב QeReBh means innards – covering both the armored exterior and the soft underbelly of the CRAB. So, once Israelis discover that the world speaks a form of Proto-Semitic, and there is no need to reflect the false etymologies of foreign lexicography, they may get the pride and good sense to rename the CRAB something like a קרבת QaReBeT.

The OYSTER was given a similar non-Biblical name, though at least this time based on a late Arabic word, צדפה TSeeDPaH. If they were aware of Edenics, or even that the צ *Tsadi*/TS is always a Western ST, they might have chosen an appropriate Biblical pearl, the word that gave us OYSTER: אוצר OaWTSahR, treasurehouse (Deuteronomy 28:12, store, source of STORE). [OYSTER] [STORE]

In Numbers 23:22 there are the "lofty horns of the wild-ox. (JPS)" The KJV translators render the ראם R'EM as a "unicorn." Swedish *ren* gave us **REIN**DEER, a mere nasal shift from ראם R'EM. These deer with the large, magnificently curved antlers most likely had not yet retreated to arctic Scandinavia in antiquity.

Chapter Ten CONCLUSION:

Names ARE everything. Via Edenic one can hear how and why words like SIMILE, SAME, SOUND and ESSENCE share a fricative-nasal root (reversed in M-S MUSIC or N-S NOISE). Names enforce the created universe's order, not a theoretically evolved world's chaos. A study of peoples' names or geographical names – like a fuller treatment of animal names – would require a large book.

Animal names that require mastery of the more challenging previous chapters, like metathesis, have been left out. Let's look at one partial *E-Word* entry for the lowly SLUG, and you judge if the etymology warrants some sliding of root letters:

SLUG	**ZOAK[H]eL**	***Zayin-Vav-Het-Lamed***
Zoa-KHEL	זחל	**[ZKL → SLG]**

ROOTS: A SLUG is a snail-like gastropod that sluggishly slides by on its own grease. The IE root given for SLUG and SLUGGISH is *slue* ("hypothetical base of a group of distantly related Germanic derivatives with various suffixes.") Middle English *slugge*, a sluggard is the only known etymon to contribute to the lazy lexicography above.

The "crawlers in the dust" of Deuteronomy 32:24 are זחלי עפר ZoaK[H]aL(aY GHaFaR). Micah 7:27 makes clear this phrase's parallel to snakes. Aramaic זחל ZiK[H]aL is to crawl or creep. Syriac זחלא ZaK[H]Lah is a locust or any creeping thing. In Modern Hebrew זחלי ZaK[H]aLeeY is catapillar, and a זחלן ZaK[H]LaN is a SLUGGARD who moves with a SLUGGISH pace. זוחל ZOAK[H]eL is any creeping creature or reptile. The ז-ח-ל *Zayin-Het-Lamed* Edenic etymon requires an M132 metathesis, with mild shifts of the fricative and guttural.

Both Edenic and Hebrew animal names were added to the following chart by Robin Allott. Student Edenicists who have learned much about letter shifts, metathesis, reversals and nasalization will find that many of these foreign animal names are familiar (or can be made to be so):

EDENIC	1. BaQaR (cattle) 2. LeK[H]eM (meat)	KeLeBH (canine) See HUNT, KENNEL, SHAG	ASOAN she-donkey RKV = ride; [BURRO]	GaDYa (goat - Aramaic) GiDee (kid)	ReKHe[V] (mount, RKV = to ride, PRD (mule)	K[H]oPHaR to dig (pigs dig up truffles, etc.)	Ke[V]eS see OVIS TSeMeR wool	KeLeBH (canine) See above
Hebrew	בקר/לחם	כלב	אתון	גדי	רכב	חפר	כבש	כלב
ENGLISH	Cow	Dog	donkey	goat	Horse	pig	sheep	wolf
Albanian	Lope	Qën	Gomár	dhi	kalë	derr	dhën	ujk
Arabic	Baqar	Kalb	Himaar	maaCiz	faras	Khinzir	kharuuf	d'ib
Armenian	Gov	Shoon	Avanag	aidz	Tsiagerb	Khok	ochkhar	ka
Basque	Behi	Zakur	Asto	ahuntz	Zaldi	zerri	ardi	otso
Berber	Tafounast	Aydi	Aghyoul eyor	taghat	Kgmar	-	izemer	ouchchen
Bulgarian	Krava	Kutche	Magare	koza	Kon	pruse	oven	vilk
Catalan	Vaca	gos, ca	Ase	cabra	Cavall	Porc	ovella	llop
Czech	Kráva	Pes	Osel	kozel	Kůň	Prase	ovce	vlk
Danish	Ko	hund	Æsel	ged	Hest	gris	får	ulv
Dutch	Koe	hond	Ezel	geit	Paard	Varken	schaap	wolf
Egyptian	Kaut	uher	Aa	-	Sesem	Rer	-	-
Estonian	Lehm	koer	Eesel	kits	Hobune	siga	lammas	hunt
Finnish	Lehmä	koira	Aasi	vuohi	Hevonen	sika	lammas	susi
French	Vache	chien	Âne	chèvre	Cheval	porc	mouton	loup
Gaelic	Bo	Cu	-	-	Each	Muc	caora	-
Georgian	Dzrokha	dzaghli	Viri	tkha	Tskheni	Ghori	tskhwari	mgeli

	Kuh	hund	Esel	ziege	Pferd	Schwein	schaf	wolf
German	Kuh	hund	Esel	ziege	Pferd	Schwein	schaf	wolf
Gitano	-	tamboru	Grel	braquia	Graste	Baliche	jouli	yeru
Greek	Agelada	skylos	Gaidaros	katsika	Alogo	Gourouni	probaton	lukos
Hausa	Saniya	kare	Jaki	akwiya	Doki	Alade	-	dila
Hawaiian	Pipi wahine	Ilio kelev	Kekake	kao	Lio	Puaa	hipa	ilio-hae
Hebrew	PaRaH	KeLeBH	K[H]aMo [K]HaMoR	E]Z, GhGHeZ[E]	SooS, PaRaSH	K[H]aZiR	Ke[V]eS	Z'eBH
	פָּרָה	כֶּלֶב	חֲמוֹר / חֲמֹר	עֵז/עֵזִּים	סוּס/פָּרָשׁ	חֲזִיר	כֶּבֶשׂ	זְאֵב
Hindustani	ga'e	kutta	Gadha	Bakra	Ghora	su'ar	bher	gurg
Hungarian	Tehén	kutya	Szamdár	kescke	Ló	disznó	juh	farkas
Icelandic	Kyr	hundur	-	Geit	hestur	-	kind	ulfur
Irish	Bo	madra	Asal	Gabar	capall	Muc	saora	mactire
Italian	Vacca	cane	Ciuco	Capra	cavallo	Porco	pecora	lupo
Japanese	Ushi	inu	Roba	Yagi	uma	Buta	hitsuji	okami
Keo	-	dako	-	longo	jara	Wawi	dhembu	-
Konni	NaagIN	gbaaN	BunIN	biiN	duuN	Periku	yisiN	-
Korean	am-so	kae	tang-na-gwi	yom-so	mal	twae-ji	yang	i-ri
Latin	Vacca	canis	Asinus	haedus	equus	porcus	ovis	lupus
Latvian	-	suns	-	-	zirgs	Cuka	-	-
Lithuanian	Karvè	shuo	Asilas	ozhys	arklys	Kiaulè	avis	vilkas
Lozi	Komu	nja	-	puli	pizi	Kuhube	ngu	-
Malay	Lembu	anjing	Kaldai	kambing	kuda	Babi	-	serigala
Norwegian	Ku	hund	Esel	geit	hest	Gris	sau	ulv

Pahlavi	Gaw	sag	Xar	Buz	asp	Xug	mes	gurg
Paiute	Saadu'u	kootsoo	Tsagase'e	gootu	pooggoo	kauze'e	koepa	esa
Persian	Gaav	sag	?olaaq	boz	?asb	xuk	gusfand	gorg
Polish	Krowa	pies	Osiol	koza	kon	Swinia	owca	wilk
Portuguese	Vaca	cão	Burro	cabra	cavalo	porco	carneiro	lobo
Romanian	Vacã	câine	Mãgar	caprã	cal	porc	oaie	lup
Russian	Korova	sobaka	Osyol	koza	loshad	-svinya	ovtsa	volk
Samoan	Povi	maile	Asini	oti	solofanua	pua'a	mamoe	luko
SerboCroat	Krava	pas	Magarac	koza	konj	svinja	ovca	vuk
Spanish	Vaca	perro	Burro	cabra	caballo	cerdo	oveja	lobo
Setswana	Kgomo	ntša	Tonkey	pudi	pitse	kolobe	nku	phokoje
Swahili	ng'ombe	mbwa	Punda	mbuzi	farasi	nguruwe	kondoo	mwitu
Swedish	ko	-hund	åsna	get	häst	gris	får	varg
Tagalog	Baka	aso	-	kambing	kabayo	baboy	-	aso
Tamil	Pacu	naay	KaZutay	nall-aaTu	kutiray	panRi	cemmari-aaTu	oo-naay
Telegu	Avu	kukka	Gadida	meka	gurram	pandi	gorre	todelu
Turkish	Inek	köpek	Esek	keçi	at	domus	koyun	kurt
Udihe	Jaha	ina'i	-	pauza	mui	wagae	-	niengu
Venda	Kholomo	mbwa	Ndongi	mbudzi	bere	nguluvhe	nngu	-
Welsh	Buwch	ci	Asyn	gafr	-	hwch	-	blaidd
Yoruba	-	aja	-	ewure	-	elede	-	-
Zulu	Inkomazi	inja	imbongolo	imbuzi	ihashi	ingolube	imvu	

(The same chart with the Edenic etymons provided is available on request. But if you have read the previous chapters well, you should be able to figure out for yourself how these global animal names got scrambled after Babel.)

Chapter Ten ACTIVITIES

1 – 4. Edenic provides 1) גדי GiDeeY, kid of goat, 2) עז [A]iZ or GHaiZ (she-goat), 3) שעיר Si[E]eYR (he-goat) and 4) עפר [O]FeR or GHoPHeR, fawn of larger ruminants, that look like a goat.

> In the following list of goat words link the animals with their Adamic names:
> a) *chevre* (French), *capra* or **cabra** (Italian, Rumanian, Spanish, Portuguese),
> b) *koza* (Polish, Czech, Croat), *kaza* (Russian) reverse to *Ziege* for German,
> c) *geit* (Dutch, Norwegian), *get* (Swedish) and *ged* (Danish),
> d) Tibetan *Serow* (goat-antelope of East Asia)

5) In the SNAKE entry, there are a few good ways to arrive at the sound and sense of snake-ness. Edenics trains one's mind to consider multiple approaches (Semitic thinking), instead of one dictionary-style etymology (Japhetic thinking). Document the multiple contributions here, comparing it to the expansive root at SPARROW. Why is the Edenic theme of "sound is sense" more solid, not less solid, when encountering such multiplicity?

6) The largest group of animal names in the Bible is in Deuteronomy 14. The questions below will ask you to analyze and classify these animal groups. What do you make of the unusual classifications? Why might (whether beasts, fish or fowl) there be no animals that cannot be domesticated, predators, scavengers or bottom feeders among the kosher (permissible to eat) animals?

7) Many words for donkey favor ASL instead of Edenic אתון AsoaN. How can an N to L change be justified when it doesn't conform to Grimm's (or Rashi's) Laws?

8) It's not a problem that only one language likes Hebrew פרה PaRaH (cow), and prefers the more general בקר BaQaR (cattle). In fact, this is a solid way to establish BaQaR as

an Edenic term, rather than a later, Hebrew one. Find fifteen varieties of BaQaR, documenting their many letter shifts, letter drops, etc.

9) In the KENNEL, SHAG and HUNT entries you will find different Edenic sources for dog names. Getting twelve names from the animal chart, offer the meanings and reasons why these terms mean dog. Briefly describe the devolution of each term or groups of names.

10) Find an animal not documented here, in English or any language, and suggest an Edenic link based on your perception of the essence of that animal, that which differentiates it from others of its genus. (Avoid a sub-species or newly bred animal).

Chapter Eleven

Edenic and the World's Most Common Words

At the beginning of this book, Dr. Merritt Ruhlen and his 1994 book, *The Origin of Language: Tracing the Evolution of the Mother Tongue* (Wiley, NY), was hailed as a major step in modern culture's reluctant acceptance of the premise that there was one original human language. Ruhlen's primary language was far from Proto-Semitic, and the "evolution" in the title maintains the secular insistence that humans developed language.

Similarly, the best of the "long-rangers" among historical linguists who support the monogenesis of language thesis, will suppose that the devolution of that Mother Tongue into today's 5000 languages was solely natural. Edenics agrees that this devolution has been natural for the last several millennia, but that there was a supernatural "Big Bang" at the Tower of Babel that got the neurolinguistic diversity underway – for the purpose of enabling our multi-national history, and our multiplicity of perception.

The Origin of Speeches confronts these secular findings, and strives to demonstrate that, both internally and externally, Biblical Hebrew is not just a humanly-evolved language. Some chapters here focus on the internal features of Edenic (proto-Semitic best demonstrated in Biblical Hebrew). The architectonics of Edenic are compared to the exquisite, superhuman engineering evident in the natural sciences. A case is made for the idea that humans no more evolved Edenic than they did chemistry or physics. To be sure, humans helped devolve Edenic, but only after the Originator of Speech (Isaiah 57:19) initiated the Big Bang of neurolinguistic diversification at the Tower of Babel (Genesis 11:1).

Other chapters of *The Origin of Speeches* focus on the external evidence, on the etymological data of Edenics. That is, how the uniquely versatile Aleph-Bet of a relatively small vocabulary -- with only a few common linguistic shifts – can account for the vast diversity of global vocabulary.

Dr. Ruhlen and his predecessors have already done the vast work of dividing the globe into large, related language families, called "superfamilies." First, the most commonly shared (thus earliest) words help establish these superfamilies. For example, instead of many hundreds of Native American languages, there are only five major families (Eskimo-Aleut, Athabaskan, Algonquian, Uto-Aztecan and Arawakan) which make up the superfamily called Amerind. (See the groundbreaking work of the late Joseph H. Greenberg of Stanford University.) Eventually, we get the most typical, and oldest Amerind words and compare them to similar words in the other superfamilies, like Afro-Asiatic (which includes Modern Hebrew) and Eurasiatic (which includes English).

The name of the most familiar superfamily for English speakers, Eurasiatic, covers a vast amount of land and languages. Scholars like the late Joseph H. Greenberg of Stanford University were able to group dozens of languages from Europe to Japan since they all had an M-word for first person, and an N-word for negativity. The Indo-European family was already large, but now Indo-European (IE) is within a still larger superfamily. Like the IE "roots" that are theoretical reconstructions, none of the terms below from all 12 superfamilies were actually spoken in the prehistory. But these theoretical roots most resemble what was probably spoken in the millennia before written records, so that careful scrutiny must be given to these reconstructions.

Here at the end of this book, a reader should be able to note the reconstructed proto-world roots in Ruhlen's Table 10 and decide whether the Nilo-Saharan or the Australian typical sound for the sense of water, hair, etc. could come from Edenic or not. There is no better book on world vocabulary than Ruhlen's, and no better test to see whether the Edenic theory, and, by extension, Genesis itself, is fantasy or fact.

In the table below there are 13 meanings (going across) and 12 language superfamilies (going down the left). There is the temptation to refer to them as the 12 tribes of Man, with the 12 Israelite tribes as universal metaphors – but this book already has too much Genesis in it for some readers. The specialized fonts for phonetic symbols were not obtained to reproduce these composite reconstructions in the precise linguistic way, the way that John Bengston and Merritt Ruhlen laid them out in 1994. That's OK. This book is for the many children of Adam, not the few princes of academe. For our purposes, a word like "tok" could just be TK or KT or, the most technical the book gets, a *dental-*

guttural." In Edenics one is tuned to the music of meaning, not to a dialect's quirks of pronunciation or to the spelling conventions of a particular lexicographer.

The readers of *The Origin of Speeches* learned early on that concern with vowels was, at best, of little historic value. Linguists know that students of Semitic vocabulary ignore vowels, which are only of use in grammar. But for other historical linguists to do similarly dispense with vowels would be too damn Semitic. It would mean giving up on the great White Hope that Sumerian might be Aryan, and ancient enough to scrap with the specter of Scripture.

Before we scope out the 156 supermodels on the linguistic catwalk, let's identify the regions and languages of superfamilies A through L.

A) Khoisan includes the click languages in southern Africa.
B) Nilo-Saharan takes in central Africa and the Sudan.
C) Niger-Kordofanian groups together the many Bantu languages.
D) Afro-Asiatic involves Semitic tongues like Arabic, Ancient Egyptian and Hebrew.
E) Kartvelian relates several languages of the southern Caucasus.
F) Dravidian groups many dialects in southern India.
G) Eurasiatic gathers languages from Portugal to Japan/Korea, including English.
H) DenE-Caucasian infers the Turkic languages and some spoken in Russia.
I) Austric refers to tongues in India, Southeast Asia and several Pacific islands.
J) Indo-Pacific covers island peoples like the various Polynesians.
K) Australian holds a continent full of Aboriginal tongues.
L) Amerind, see above, joins the native languages from North to South America.

Language Families from Around the World

Merritt Ruhlen
The Origin of Language (p.103 –Table 10)
Wiley, NY 1994
Adapted with permission of John Wiley & Sons

Language		Who?	What?	Two	Water	One/Finger	Arm-1	Arm-2	Bend/Knee	Hair	Vagina/Vulva	Smell/Nose	Seize/Squeeze	Fly (v.)
Khosian	A	!ku	ma	/kam	k"a	konu	ku	ha	gom	u	!kwai	c'u	xom	dZWa
Nilo-Saharan	B	na	de	ball	nki	tok	kani	Boko	kutu	sum	buti	cona	kankam	par
Niger-Kordufanian	C	nani	ni	bala	engi	dike	kono	boko	bongo		Butu		kama	pere
Afro-Asiatic	D	k(w)	ma	bwVr	Ak'wa	tak	ganA		Bunqe	somm	Put	suna	Km	pyaRR
Kartvelian	E	min	ma	yor	Rts'q'a	ert	t'ot'	qe	Muql	toma	put'	Sun	sxwerp'	p'er
Dravidian	F	Yav	ya	irantu	niru	birelu	Kan	kay	Menda	puta	poccu	cuntu	kamV	par V
Eurasiatic	G	kWi	mi	pala	akwa	tik	konV	bhaghu(s)	buk(a)	punce	PutV	Sna	kamu	parV
DenE-Caucasian	H	kWi	ma	gnyis	?oxwa	tok	Kan	boq	Pjut	tsham	put'i	Sun	k'em	phur
Austric	I	o-ko-e		m-anu	?(m)bar	namaw	nto?	Xeen	bayla	buku	syam	betik	Ijun	Ngam
Indo-Pacific	J		mina	boula	okho	dik	akan	ben	buku	utu		sinna		apir
Australian	K	naani (mi/nh/a)	bula	gugu	Kuman	mala	pajing	bunku		puda	mura	Maan		Paru
Amerind	L	Kune	Mana	p'al	akwa	dik'i	kano	bo/ko	buka	Summe	butie	cuna		Ta?

The readers of *The Origin of Speeches* learned early on that concern with vowels was, at best, of little historic value. Linguists know that students of Semitic vocabulary ignore vowels, which are only of use in grammar. But for other historical linguists to do similarly dispense with vowels would be too damn Semitic. It would mean giving up on the great White Hope that Sumerian might be Aryan, and ancient enough to scrap with the specter of Scripture.

1) Four of these twelve superfamilies have a "who? " word like Edenic מי MeeY, who? (Exodus 2:14). Three have shifted nasals to N. But, in six of these, the dominant form is a K + vowel. This better fits the Edenic כ-י *Kahf-Yod*, כי KeeY (that, as, like) which can function like the pronoun WHO. In Numbers 30:3, for example, the phrase איש כי-ידר "EeYSH **KeeY** YiDor..." is rendered "*when* a man voweth a vow." This usage is nearly identical to "a man *who* voweth a vow." It is certainly close enough for the newly created national and linguistic groups leaving the Tower of Babel at Shinar (Sumer) with the newly-scrambled Edenic computing language still in their factory-installed hard-drive. (The next twelve links are sharper.)

2) The "what? " words of the table are a far more striking proof of a Mother Tongue in that nine of twelve are M words. Five are M-plus-vowel, exactly like מ-ה *Mem-Hey*, מה MaH, MeH, what? (Genesis 37:10) or just the prefix מ *Mem-*/M-. The other four extend this to MN, just as the Israelites named the manna מן MahN, "what is it?" (Exodus 16:15).

3) The planet's most popular "two" word is BL, with variations like BR (the shift of *liquids*. There are also two PLs. Similarly, the Spanish BALL shifts bilabials to *pelota* [BALL] entry in the *E-Word*. Two things, unlike just one, unadulterated thing, means that the objects can be BALLED up, mixed up or confused. This is what the the ב-ל Bet-Lamed of בבל BaBHeL (Babel) was all about. [BABBLE] To mix up is בלל BaLaL (Genesis 11: 9); a mixture of two liquids is בלל BaLOOL (Leviticus 2:5).

4) For the "water" words covering the whole Earth, the English speaker recognizes AQUA even if it is spelled *akwa*. Notice how the superfamilies for English and Hebrew have nearly identical forms of *akwa*. The Edenic for water is מים MaYiM. But by now

readers know that the dictionary's offerings are only occasionally relevant. In Edenics we discover that whatever created the natural universe created the aural energy bytes of sound and sense that we call words. The primary physical law of water is that it finds its level. "Level" in the oldest written record of useful length is ו-ק *Koof-Vav*, קו QaV ("measuring line" in II Kings 21:13). Brits don't wait in line, they QUEUE up – from this same ו-ק *Koof-Vav* etymon. The first mention of water in the Bible is Genesis 1:11. There, water is the מים מקוה (Mi)**QVeH** MaYim, the "gathering" or "pool" of water (as in to "pool together"). Apparently, the world is still nourished by this primordial pool, and by the pool of liquid letters and words bathing us since Creation.

5)   The "one/finger" words are the most familiar from write-ups on the topic of monogenesis of language or the search for the Mother Tongue. Of course, with the universal one-digit gesture for "one," the sound for "one" and "finger" should be the same. The many five or ten-based number words originating in Edenic "handful" words make this clear. [MITT] Joshua Ben's work on number words proves that the most remote and isolated peoples have always used number words that are preserved in obscure Biblical counting terms. Borrowings from traders did not spread such words. The dominant "one" term here is D or T plus K. Simply invert (a common phenomenon of Babel-Babble) Aramaic ד-ח *Het-Daled*, חד [K]HahD, or Biblical Hebrew אחד EK[H]aD or אחת AK[H]aT to get "one" (Genesis 1:5). Any guttural-dental or the reverse is a fine "one." Like **DIG**IT. Yes, we had had the source of **DIG**ITAL from Day One.

6, 7)   The concept of an arm is more complex than a finger. In the first of the two examples, the arm word embracing most of the planet is KN. ה-נ-ק *Koof-Noon-Hey*, קנה QaNeH is a branch or a limb – as an arm is to the trunk of the body. To quote from the "CANE" entry: "The Indo-European root *kanna* (a reed) is admitted to be "of Semitic origin." Babylo-Assyrian *qanu* (pipe) is cited rather than קנה QaNeH, reed, tube, stem, the "stalk" of Genesis 41:5, the "shaft" of Exodus 25:31, and the "branch" of Exodus 25:32. קנה KaNeH is also a stalk or root (Psalms 80:16).

"Arm-2" is most often KB. This "arm" is more special, and less functional, echoing an inverted, shifted פ-ג-א *Aleph-Gimel-Pey*, עגף AGahF, wing or flank. While post-Biblical, the word's antiquity as Edenic is verified by Semitic terms like Akkadian *agappu* (wing).

Also verifying this GP term as Edenic are the typically similar antonyms פ-ג *Gimel-Pey*, גף GaPH (body) and ב-ג *Gimel-Bhet*, גב GahBH (back). Both are similar opposites, in that they both are the base from which an arm or wing extends. Aramaic GaPAh does mean wing. Another "wing" is פ-נ-ק *Kahf-Noon-Phey*, כנף KaNaPH. [CANOPY]. This is a match made in heaven for Eurasiatic *konV* back in "Arm-1."

8) Four of the "bend/knee" terms are BK, while three others BNK (that last guttural taking G, K and Q). That extra N is familiar to readers by now as a common corruption called Nasalization. ברך BeRaKH is to kneel, but reversing Edenic guttural-bilabials seems the way to bend into this root of doubling over, as the knee does to the leg. ב-ב-ק *Koof-Bhet-Bhet*, קבב QaBHaBH means to be bent; קפף KaPHaPh is to bend or bow down (Micah 6:6); Syriac גפיפא GiPHeeYPHAh is convex. קפל KeeP(aiL) is to fold over (Exodus 26:9) [COUPLE], and Akkadian *kapalu* is to coil or twist. The first "bend/knee" term, *gom*, recalls the GN of GENUFLECT and the KN of KNEEL. [KNEEL]

9) The most common words for "hair" on the planet are variations of S-M or T-M. The Aleph-Bet offers the perfect letter for both S and T sounds: the צ *Tsadi* (TS). The DenE-Caucasion (H) has both T and S in its composite hair word, exactly like צ *Tsadi*. ר-מ-צ *Tsadi-Mem-Resh*, צמר TSeMeR means wool (Leviticus 13:47), or any animal hair. צמרת TSaMeReT is foliage (Ezekiel 17:3). Ethiopic wool is *damr*. The Edenic changes after Babel clearly affected the Semitic languages. In fact, after Afro-Asiatic (D) and Nilo-Saharan (B), the clearest forms of צמר TSeMeR are quite distant from the Middle East. The Eurasiatic term does not sound familiar to English speakers, but see "HAIR" in the *E-Word*. The Indo-Pacific "hair" term, *utu*, recalls the various hair words from ט-ו-ה *Het-Vav-Tet*, חוט [K]HOODT, thread. [CHAETA]

10) This is a family book, so I apologize if the names of some body parts are deemed distasteful. To Edenics, anything human is divine. Still, it's unfortunate that someone sexed up this chart. ת-פ *Pey-Tahf*, פת PoaT (Isaiah 3:17) is rendered "vulva" by Ernest Klein in his *Etymological Dictionary of the Hebrew Language*. Other relevant Edenic words here include ה-ת-פ *Pey-Tahf-Het*, פתח PeTa[K]H, opening, passage way, door

(Genesis 4:7) and ב-ת-נ Bet-Tet-Noon, בטן BeDTeN, womb (Genesis 30:2). בטן BeDTeN is metathesized to *venter* in Latin. [VENTRICLE] פתח PeTa[K]H sounds more like the Austric (I) term, *betik*, than it recalls the related English bilabial-dental word PUDENDUM. Two superfamilies have shifted from PT to BT, recalling the related ב-י-ת *Bet-Yod-Tahf.* בית BaYiT, means interiority, house and family. [BOOTH]

11) Only the Australian [K] lacks the SN sound that dominates the Earth's terms for "smell" and "nose." Anyone with a nose for Edenics has **sn**iffed out the fact that SN is a reverse NOSE, and is a mere nasal shift away from the SM of SMELL. Such is the sense and sound, the music and meaning of divinely engineered vocabulary, which is introduced in this book. Before banishing the Australian Aborigines as not from our same Adamic stock, note that their term, *mura*, is an inverted AROMA.

Let us list some of the Edenic fricative-nasal "Smell/Nose" terms, (NS, SN, MS, SM, TS-N, NZ or etc.), which were diversified or "confused" at Babel to kickstart multi-national human history:

מ-ס *Samekh-Mem,* סם $ahM is spice, and so is the addition to SM, ב-ש-מ *Bet-Sin-Mem,* בשם BoSeM. Both the plural סמים $ahM(eeYM) (sweet smelling incense) and (Boa)SeM (spice) are in Exodus 35:28. [BALSAM] We may disregard the L in BALSAM. Already in Akkadian and Syriac the SM smell word is extended to drugs and medicine.

The Hebrew dictionary's word for "nose" is, once again, not the place to find the Edenic source of nosE-like words like SNORKEL and NOZZLE. If you view the nose as a breathing tube then there is צ-נ-ו-ר *Tzadi-Noon-Vav-Resh.* צנור (T)SeeNOAR, pipe, drain (Psalms 42:8). Too often the nose is a dripper, like NOZZLE, so that one must consider נ-ו-ז-ל *Noon-Vav-Zayin-Lamed,* נוזל NOAZeL (to spout, to flow…that which pours). A relevant נ-ז *Noon-Zayin* or NZ term is נזם NeZeM, nose ring (Genesis 24:22). Aramaic has a TM variant, which allows us to link to other SN words, and which gave Post-Biblical Hebrew חטם [K]HoDTaM (nose, snout).

This book always assumes built-in, sound-alike antonyms in Edenic, and they include words like זנח ZaNa[K]H and צחן (T)Sa[K]HaN, stink. [SKUNK] To sniff out the scent or SENSE (via Latin *sentire*, to feel) of other SN distant relatives in English, like OSMIUM, OZONE, SMOLDER, SNIFF, SNORE, and SNORT, see *E-Word* entries like NOZZLE, SMELL (A), and SNORKEL.

12) In the "Seize/Squeeze" category, the dominant root for a Proto-Earth word is K-M. In Edenic, this is ק-מ *Koof-Mem*, primarily in the noun and verb קמץ QaMaTS. Both are in Leviticus 2:2, "to take a handful." E.D. Klein translates the verb as "to with the hand, to grasp." Aramaic קמט QiMaDT means "he seized." קמץ QoMeTS is a closed hand, and קמצץ QaMTSooTS is a pinch. This is why the Modern Hebrew word for a miser or penny pincher is a קמצן QaMTSaN. On the periphery of this K-M core of words are קמט QaMaDT to compress; מקח MeeQa[K]H, receiving; קנה QaNaH, to acquire; and קמוט QeeMOODT, to crease, fold. Many English hand and counting words, along with foreign terms like "hand" Tagalog (*kamay*) and Malay, Gani (*komud*) and the Chinese fist (*ch'uan*) [MITT].

13) Lastly, the world's dominant root for flying is PR. E.D. Klein translates פ-ר-ח *Pey-Resh-Het*, פרח PoRa[K]H as "to fly." Aramaic-Syriac PiRa[K]H is "it flew." Syriac PiRa[K]HTAh is a flying bird or insect. אפרח EPHRoa[K]H is a young bird (Deuteronomy 22:6) – ultimate source of English PULLET. More flying and twitching creatures at PYRALIDID (A) – especially Butterflies, like the Hebrew פרפר PaRPaR or the Tagalog *paruparo*. The more common פרח PoRa[K]H in the Bible means the spreading of airborne disease (Leviticus 13:39). The PR root extends to "breaking out" or "blooming" (Numbers 17:23). ב-ר-ח *Bet-Resh-Het* is the flying away of fleeing. [FLEET] Rearranging פ-ר-ח *Pey-Resh-Het* to ר-ח-פ *Resh-Het-Phey* gets the "hover" of Genesis 1:2. In this verse the spirit of the Creator (whose name is the mathematical equivalent of Nature) is רחף RaK[H]ePH above the surface of the deep. פרחת PaRaK[H]aT is a bird or flying creature (Ezekiel 13:20). The authorities guess that PARAKEET is a diminutive of Pierre Peter.

Some of the new Proto-Earth roots, reconstructed from many global words:

BUR, ashes, dust < S-B אפר AiPHeR, dust; עפר [A]PHahR, ashes [FRIABLE]

KATI, bone < S-G עצם GHeTSeM, bone [OSTEOMA]

K'OLO, hole < S-G, S-L חור KHOAR, hole; S-G חלל K[H]aLaL, hollow space [HOLLOW]

KUNA, woman ← נקבה NiQaiBHaH, female [NOOK]

MALIQ'A, to suck(le), nurse; breast < מלק MaLaQ, to wring [MILK]

TEKU, leg, foot ← QaiTS, extremity קץ [COAST]

MANA, to stay (in a place) אמונה firmness (Exodus 17:12), security"(Isaiah 33:6) בית נאמן BaYiT N'EMahN, an abiding house, abode (I Samuel 2:3) [REMAIN]

No longer need the world of words be considered unformed and void, with secular darkness upon the face of the deep. We are grateful to the secular linguists for the vast work that allowed *The Origin of Speeches* to be written. The book concludes with this the spirit of the Creator hovering over the depths of human thought and speech. Even if the reader worships secularism and chaos, it is hoped that this book has offered a challenging new picture of language as a divine gift.

The oldest human remains ever found with the hyoid bone for speech was found in the Carmel Caves near Haifa, Israel. Until an older such skeleton is unearthed, the scientific evidence points to Proto-Semitic as the oldest language.

Until a more complete body of contradictory evidence is produced, trumping this book and the entire body of Edenics research, it must be assumed that the language of the Bible is Earth's Mother Tongue.

Chapter Eleven CONCLUSION

Some *E-Word* entries serve particularly well to recap several of the topics covered here. The STOP entry, for example, reviews borrowings, letter shifts (L to R), Metathesis (123 to 132) and nasalization (adding an N or M). It is therefore reproduced below:

STOP		*SHaBaTShin-Bet-Taph*
S(H)ABH-AT	שבת	**S(H)-BH-T → STP]**

ROOTS: SABBATICAL is a borrowing from Hebrew שבת SHaBaT, Sabbath (Exodus 20:8). As a Hebraism it is spelled with two B's. (Here is another illustration of Hebrew SH regularly rendered as an S in English.) The Aramaic-Syriac שבת SHaBTah can also mean any feast, festival or observed stoppage. The seven-day cycle is noted in Arabic *sabt* (Sabbath) – is case there's any doubt where Latin got *septem* (seven – see "SEPTEMBER.")

As common as Sabbath terms of rest and cessation are, the dictionaries leave us with questionable etymons for RESPITE and STOP. It is enough of a secular nightmare that the weekend is from the Bible. Linguists did not want to find any further stoppages in STP or SPT words.

(RE)SPITE is a delay, postponement or rest. שבת S(H)aBHaT is to "cease" in *Genesis 8:22*; השבת (Hee)S(H)BeeYT is to "make rest" or "cease" in *Exodus 5:5*; שבת S(H)eBHeT is "tarried" in Deuteronomy 1:6. The ש-ב-ת Shin-Bet-Tahf verb appears in Genesis 8:22.

RESPITE, *respit* in Old French, is currently traced to IE *spek* (to observe) [SCOPE]. STOP is merely a 2-3 letter swap away. This common linguistic phenomenon known as metathesis was more than enough to stop etymologists who were already predisposed from preventing borrowed Biblical words from spreading foreign infection. Edenic SBT becoming SPT also requires a common shifting of bilabials.

The guardians of Indo-European trace STOP to Late Latin *stuppare* (to stop up, stuff), which is from Latin *stuppa* and Greek *stuppe* (to tow). The AHD attributes STOP to IE root *steu* (to push, knock, beat). The lexicocraphers have knocked and towed the root far from the sense of STOPPING, but at least they have tried to push it away from Semitic.

BRANCHES: An all too common word in Israeli Hebrew שביתה S(H)iBeeYTaH (strike or work STOPPAGE). The Bible was the first union document, legislating that we might periodically שב S(H)aiBH (sit! rest! and return!...to being more human and less "productive"). The opposite of all this SPT stopping is שתף S(H)aTaPH, to run flow [SPATE]. *BUST*LE (1-2 letter swap of SBT) fits better here as well, rather than linked to "busk." A BUST can also mean a decline in activity.

Just as a Sabbath day, now the weekend, is perhaps the Bible's most widely adopted institution, one would expect a wide world of forms for ש-ב-ת Shin-Bet-Taph. Some of these include: Greek *sabbaton*, Latin *sabbatum*, Italian *sabato*, Spanish-Portuguese *sabado*, Old Provincal- Catalan *dis-sapte*, Czech and Slovak *sobota* and Russian *subbota*. Saturday in Bahas Malasia is *Sabtu*.

Nasalization of שבת SHaBaT began as early as Ethiopic *sanbat*. Adding an M (not N) was done by Vulgar Greek and Latin *sambaton* and *sambatum*, Rumanian *simbata* and Hungarian *szombat* (Saturday) and *sambati-dies* (Sabbath day). The same nasilization and a "day" element disguises French *Samedi* (Saturday) which was *sambE-di* in Old French. German *Samstag* is similarly a Hebrew mischling trying to hide on the Aryan side.

The reader who has seriously gone through this book in its entirety is now qualified to come to a conclusion. There are two choices.

1) You may parrot the current academic beliefs that language is chaos, that words from different language groups can only be similar by "coincidence" or borrowing. You may reject the notion that sound is sense, and stick to the established concept that words only have meaning because humans have assigned them such.

2) You can deduce that language, from its primeval essence, is order. It was demonstrably fashioned by a superhuman intelligence, implanted within humankind, then scrambled in a psycholinguistic manner (as in The Tower of Babel scenario).

This planet's multiculturalism, apparently, was not the accidental result of distant, grunting monkey troops evolving into muttering tribes of cavemen who spoke a dozen original languages (now called language superfamilies) that continued to DE-evolve into the 6,800 dialects that we often call "languages."

Are we from a monkey-uncle, or the descendant of an Edenic creature formed "from dust of the earth" as a sentient, speaking modern human? You are allowed to respect both *The Origin of Species* and Genesis 2:7, since "dust of the earth" could refer to matter already on Earth, a slight alteration of the pre-existing simian genome. A literal belief in a dust-man fashioned *ex nihilo* better fits a believer in magic than a believer in Intelligent Design.

Because post-Edenic languages are only human, all human languages have homonyms with the same spelling and different meanings. Anyone familiar with English is excused for thinking that language is a very human mess. Is this sloppy human trait of homonyms true of Edenic?

Rabbi Major Yehoshua Steinberg formerly of Ft. Bragg, NC, reports: The root ש-ש shin-shin has three meanings: 1) the number six, 2) silk and 3) marble.

Rashi (Exodus 26:1, based on Talmud Yoma 71b) says that the silken fabric is called *shesh* because each thread is woven "six times" (with six fibers, or wound six times). This immediately puts you on notice that the Rabbis believed that the disparate meanings of Hebrew roots are somehow to be connected, and it's just a matter of finding out how. As for marble, I was baffled until I looked up the chemical makeup of marble. Marble is composed of limestone or dolomite, both derivatives of Calcite. Pure calcite is 100% calcium carbonate ($CaCO_3$) which is crystallized in hexagonal form…SIX-sided.

The reader of *The Origin of Speeches* may have gained some insights into the awesome mystery of literacy, language and existence itself. Perhaps the reader has some new respect for that ancient language of that much loved, much-loathed book called the Bible. It should be less preposterous to imagine that a Force behind language wants us to think, speak, read and write. If we were created or divinely evolved for speech, there is good reason to value communication as a special gift.

The vast patterning and purposefulness exhibited in this initial study of Edenics may have helped some readers decide that intelligent design was behind a theoretical grunting ape's transformation to a speaking human, with a hyoid bone, enlarged brain, and more.

More briefly, we are free to choose between I.D. and D.L.: Intelligent Design and Dumb Luck.

Closing Statement:

Of course there is much that is valuable and true in evolution-tinged science and linguistics. Species did adapt, and speeches (languages) did DE-evolve. But it is more logical to assume that they did so according to a well-engineered plan.

Let us listen and look at some final words. אזון EeZOON is listening (Deuteronomy 32:1). אזן OaZeN is an ear (Exodus 29:20). With the same א-ז-נ *Aleph-Zayin-Noon* there is אזן EeZaiN (to weigh or balance – Ecclesiastes 12:9). We only recently discovered that balance is profoundly linked to the inner ear. The Intelligent Designer behind natural sciences apparently has also designed this primeval vocabulary. (This is also apparent from the six-sided calcite above.)

Note: The above is quoted in ad copy for an excellent 2010 book by Prof. Haim Shore. An engineering professor friend who gives Edenics presentations remembers telling this to Shore several years ago. It was first in print in 1989. May all Edenics insights become public domain, public knowledge.

Let us make the short jump from א-ז-נ *Aleph-Zayin-Noon* to ע-ז-נ Ayin-Zayin-Noon. The osprey or hawk is the עזניה [A]ZNeeYaH (Leviticus 11:13). The term fits many spread-eagled predators who balance in the winds.

Did some bright up-and-coming ape-man really evolve all these like-sounding "balance" words, with an insider's grasp on all sciences?

391

The alternative to our last centuries' Kingdom of Chaos is to return to the idea of Intelligent Design.

The acceptance of our Edenic legacy can lead us all back to the Garden.

In January 2010 the article, "**Could Pre-Hebrew be the שפה אחת "Safa Achat" of Genesis 11:1?" by I.E. Mozeson** appeared in The *Jewish Bible Quarterly* (Jerusalem), the only English language peer-reviewed journal under Jewish auspices that is indexed or abstracted by: Internationale Zeitschriftenschau fur Bibelwissenschaft und Grenzgebiete, Old Testament Abstracts, Religious and Theological Abstracts, Index of Articles on Jewish Studies (Rambi), Index to Jewish Periodicals and Religion Index One: Periodicals Theology Digest

SELECT STATEMENTS OF SUPPORT FOR EDENICS

There is some scholarly support for monogenesis of language, the thesis that all human languages are derived from a single mother tongue. The Word *makes a strong case for Hebrew being that language.*

Dr. Alvin Schiff, Honorary president of the Educators Council of America, professor at Harvard University, Hebrew University, and several others.

...full of interesting comparisons – many of them new to me. As a professional Semitic scholar I cannot become involved ... for the harm to my doctoral students.

Dr. Cyrus Gordon, premier Semitic history and language scholar of his generation

...a challenge to linguists ...calls for a reexamination of our etymologies.

Dr. Joseph T. Shipley, author of *The Dictionary of Word Origins*

Isaac Mozeson's monumental work, The Word, *and now his current project,* The Origin of Speeches, *have admirably taken up the banner in the area of vocabulary comparisons. I highly recommend them to anyone interested in a very fascinating alternative view of history, or in tracing the origins of humanity.*

Prof. Terry Blodgett, Southern Utah University; author
Phonological Similarities in Germanic and Hebrew

Christian Authorities

Biblical Hebrew was the language of Adam (Genesis 2:23). This primary and universal language was confounded at Babel (Genesis 11:9) and will be revived in the Millennium (Zephaniah 3:9). All mankind, and especially Christians, should realize that we are speaking "confounded" Hebrew. The Origin of Speeches *is a comprehensive confirmation of these Biblical tenets.*

>   Dr. Thomas M. Strouse, Dean and Professor Emeritus, Emmanuel Baptist
>   Theological Seminary

...will undoubtedly touch off debate.. .will challenge Christians to begin studying the language of the Prophets and thus gain a better understanding of scripture.

>   David Bivin, author of Fluent Biblical and Modern Hebrew, Director of the
>   Jerusalem School for Study of the Synoptic Gospels, ands elder of the Jerusalem
>   Baptist Church

I am a physicist, not a linguist, but the clear analyses and presentation of data makes sense. The Origin of Speeches *confirms that our race once spoke a common Biblical tongue, and the young field of Edenics is on track to bring us back to that Eden-like consensus of knowing our Creator.*

>   Lambert Dolphin, Former Senior Research Physicist with the Stanford Research
>   Institute, International, Menlo Park, CA. Evangelical Bible teacher since 1962.
>   *ldolphin.org*

Jewish Authorities

...analysis of the probability that Hebrew is the basic language of mankind. ...fascinating. It will give the reader new insight into language, its origins and development.

>   Rabbi Berel Wein, *www.rabbiWein.com,* author of *Triumph of Survival*

Edenics has gone furthest in developing the concept of Hebrew as the mother of all languages.

>   Rabbi Pinchas Stolper, Exec. V.P., Union of Orthodox Congregations of America

A reminder that the midaber*[the speaker, humankind]had a common origin and a common language is crucial…the examples you cite are persuasive*
    Rabbi Doctor Moses Tendler , Yeshiva University authority on halacha and science

This is a work of immense scholarship that should be taken seriously by linguists and laypeople alike.
    Rabbi Dr. Tzvee Zahavy, Classical and Near Eastern Studies, University of Minnesota

Mozeson's book is passionate. He also has a sense of humor… it will make readers pay attention to the sound and meaning of words in ways that they have not thought about before.
    Dr. L. Besserman. Hebrew University, Judaism Fall 1992

My congratulations on your pioneering research; it is fascinating indeed.
    Dr. Moshe Dror, President of Ramat Hanegev College, Yehoram, Israel.

A sanctification of The Name is made for the sanctified language (Biblical Hebrew)
    Rabbi Matityahu Glazerson, author of *The Holy Language: Source of All Languages*

The Word *will provide many hours of intellectual enrichment to readers of every religion and tradition."*
    Rabbi Marc Tennenbaum, former Director of Interfaith Affairs of the American Jewish Congress

I surely appreciate your fantastic work and am delighted to have the opportunity to help you with Italian.
    Sheikh Prof. Abdul Hadi Palazzi, Instituto Culturale della Comunita' Islamica Italiana

When the Lord said 'Let there be light' it was in the language of the Hebrewman"
    From the song "HEBREWMAN" by Ehud Banai, Israeli singer, songwriter at *www.ehudbannai.co.il*. This hit reggae song is the official anthem of Edenics that greets visitors to *www.edenics.org*.

About the Author

Isaac Elchanan Mozeson (b. 1951 in British Columbia) grew up in Plymouth and Brookline, Mass. He taught English at universities like Yeshiva College (where he got his B.A.) and New York University, where he completed doctoral studies.

Mozeson published a monograph and anthology of poetry, reviewed books for *Kirkus Reviews, Publishers Weekly*, and others, and co-authored books on Jewish history, homelessness, Israel and urban slang.

Since various editions of *The Word* (1989), Mozeson founded Edenics, and heads a group of global researchers. Some of the volunteers, and samples of the data are at www.edenics.org. Edenics posts, word searches, and Edenics word games are at www.edenics.net.

In January 2010 Mozeson moved to Israel.

The Origin of Speeches

and other

Edenics Resources

can be ordered through our

website:

edenics.org

or

lightcatcherbooks.com

Other Edenics Resources

E-Word CD Dictionary, updated semi-anually

Edenics CD III
(text CD) – over 1,000 pages
1) E-Word CD Dictionary
2) Many Edenic essays and foreign word lists
3) Animated PowerPoint Slide Show

EDENICS PowerPoint Slide Show (French, Spanish, Hebrew)
Intoduction to Edenics DVD

We Are ALL Hebrews
1990 Lecture by Isaac Mozeson available on Audio CD
The Tower of Babel's Greatest Hits – MP3

These and an ever-changing list are available on the websites listed above

.

Transliteration Key

א	Aleph	A, or any Upper CASE VOWEL	ל	Lamed	L
ב	Bet/ Bhet	B or BH or [V]	מ, ם	Mem	M
ג	Gimel	G or J	נ, ן	Noon	N
ד	Dalet	D	ס	Samekh	$ (like "S")
ה	Hey	H	ע	Ayin	Bracketed UPPER CASE [VOWEL] or GH
ו	Vav	V,W,OO or OA	פ, ף	Pey, Phey or Fey	P, PH or F
ז	Zayin	Z	צ,ץ	Tsadi	TS (always read "ST" in European)
ח	Het	[K]H or K[H]	ק	Koof	Q
ט	Tet	DT	ר	Resh	R or WR
י	Yod	Y	ש	Shin or Sin	SH or S
כ, ך	Kahf/Khaf	K or KH	ת	Tahf, Thaf or Sahf	T,TH or (S)

Bet/Bhet, Kahf/Khaf, Pey/Phey, Shin/Sin, and Tahf/Thaf/Sahf are variants. Hebrew script uses diacritical marks, or "dots," to indicate whether, for example, the letter sounds like an aspirated B or a passive BH/V.

Five letters have **end forms**: צ-ץ פ-ף נ-ן מ-ם כ-ך

UPPER or lower Case:

1) Anything in lower case is not a ROOT LETTER but added to replace vowels and aid pronunciation.

2) CONSONANTS are capitalized, and are the integral part of Edenic roots.

3) VOWELS are in lower case, indicating they are merely added to help one pronounce the word.

EXCEPTIONS

1) Vav is a V or W as a consonant, but can serve as the OO or OA vowel sounds as in ROOT and BOAT. Such vowels from a Vav in Edenic word are in upper case.

2) A Yod will often render an "eeY" sound. If in the Hebrew, the "Y" is in upper case.

14862133R00231

Printed in Great Britain
by Amazon.co.uk, Ltd.,
Marston Gate.